THE THIRD WORLD AND PEACE

This book was prepared under the auspices of the Israeli Institute for the Study of International Affairs (IISIA)

The IISIA gratefuly acknowledges a grant from the Alfried Krupp von Bohlen and Halbach Foundation for assisting the research which resulted also in this volume and its publication.

Other Publications by the Author:

Nuclear Weapons and the Struggle for Peace, 1952.
The Korean Conflict, 1956.
The Nuremberg Trial Revisited, 1961.
Theory and Practice of International Relations, 1967.
International Cooperation and International Organizations, 1968.
Africa – From Colonial towards Sovereign Status, 1971.
The Dynamics of the International Community, 1977.
Le Tiers Monde et la Securité Internationale, 1978.
Die Ost-West und Nord–Sud Konflikte.
Sowie Einige Probleme der Friedensforschung, 1979.
Grotius, The Changing Image of the Present International Legal Order and the Political Disorder, 1980.
Violence and Peace-Building in the Middle East (Editor), 1981.

THE THIRD WORLD AND PEACE

Some aspects of the interrelationship of underdevelopment and international security.

MARION MUSHKAT
Israeli Institute for the
Study of International Affairs.

Gower

St. Martin's Press
New York

Published in 1982 in Great Britain by
Gower Publishing Company Limited,
Gower House, Croft Road, Aldershot,
Hampshire GU11 3HR, England

First published in the United States of America in 1982 by
St. Martin's Press, Inc., 175 Fifth Avenue, New York, NY 10010

Library of Congress Cataloging in Publication Data
Mushkat, Mario'n
The Third World and Peace.
Includes bibliographical references.
1. Underdeveloped areas. 2. War—Economic aspects. 3. Peace.
4. Security, International. I. Title.
HC59.7.M88 1982 337'.09172'4 AAC2 82-774
ISBN 0-312-839-8 AACR2

British Library Cataloguing in Publication Data
Mushkat, M.
The Third World and peace.
1. Underdeveloped countries — Foreign relations
I. Title
306'.2'1724 JX1395

ISBN 0-556-00559-X

Contents

Abbreviations

Periodicals

BPP	Bulletin of Peace Proposals, Oslo.
D–C	Development and Cooperation, the Journal of the German Development Association.
E–Z	Entwicklung und Zusamenarbeit.
EA	Europa Archiv of the German Institute of International Affairs, Bonn.
EP	Etudes Polemologiques, Paris.
GAR	UN General Assembly Resolutions.
GT	The German Tribune.
JPR	Journal of Peace Research, Oslo.
RTM	Revue Tiers Monde, Paris.
UNTS	United Nations Treaty Series
YRIA	Yugoslavian Review of International Affairs, Belgrade.

Books

Adelman	Adelman, I, *The Theories of Economic Growth and Development*, Stanford University Press, 1965.
Barnett	Barnett, R.J., *Roots of War*, Penguin Books, Baltimore, 1973.
Heilbronner	Heilbronner R.L., *The Worldy Philosophers*, Simon & Simon, New York, 1965.
Jouve	Jouve Edmond, *Relations Internationales du Tiers Monde*, Berger Levrault, Paris, 1976.
Kumar	Kumar M. *Violence and Non-Violence in International Relations*, Thomson Press, Delhi, 1975.
Les Socialites	*Les Socialistes et le Tiers Monde*, Berger Levrault, Paris, 1977.
SIPRI	Stockholm Institute of International Peace Reasearch.
SIPRI Yearbook	Yearbook of the International Peace Research Institute of Stockholm, published by Taylor and Francis, Ltd., London.
Tucker	Tucker W. *The Inequality of Nations*, Basic Books, New York, 1977.
Winks	Winks R.W. (ed.), ***British Imperialism,*** Gold, Glory, Holt, Reinhart Winston, New York, 1964.

Abbreviations

Periodicals

[illegible]

Books

[illegible]

Preface

The gravity of the socio-economic situation in many parts of the Third World (TW) and its growing negative impact on international security have become, beginning with the seventies, a fundamental issue of debates in various global and regional organizations and of research into peace and war, as well. After the Soviet invasion of Afghanistan in December 1979, the statesmen's and analysts' attention has shifted from the North-South to the West-East conflict. Does it mean that the former has entirely lost its importance because the previous apprehensions of the TW's threat to peace have been entirely groundless? Those who followed the discussions between the industrialized and underdeveloped countries at the UNIDO Conference in Delhi at the beginning of 1980 and studied the Report of the Brandt Commission submitted to the UN General Secretary a few days later do not share this view.

This Report does not reveal entirely new facts. Most of them were already known from the 1969 Pearson Report on "Partnership in Development" and from other documents that have been continually discussed for more than one decade in the UN, its various agencies and other forums.

For years it has been no secret that the North, which comprises a quarter of the World's population, has four-fifths of its income at its disposal and makes use of more than eighty percent of its production. This happens at the time when nearly 800 million people, a fifth of our planet's population, live in conditions of malnutrition and hunger. Every fourth child in the Third World dies before he reaches the age of five and every second child has no chance to learn to read and write. On the other hand, in wealthy countries life expectancy is more than fifty years and the majority can read and write and enjoy the benefits of our civilization.

What is new in the Brandt Report is its focus on the urgent need to combat the misery of the TW. It stresses that the present situation is fraught with a great and deadly menace to the entire world and emphasizes the great risks of its continuation. The Report stresses the necessity, on the highest level, to change at once the forms and extent of development assistance and increase it, first and foremost, at the expense of military budgets, if we wish to avoid a catastrophe.[1]

This claim is not only a matter of academic controversy about the origins of the TW's underdevelopment, the means of overcoming it and about the stages and effects of economic growth.[2] Nowadays it is a source of anxiety for those strata of public opinion which are concerned with human distress and are aware of the dangers of its massive size. It also increasingly worries national and international organizations and conferences. Their sometimes bitter debates increasingly concentrate on the ways to put an end to hunger and misery, to close the gap between less developed (LDCs) and the industrialized wealthy nations and on means to reconstruct the present international order for the achievement of this aim.

The thirty-fifth session of the UN Commission on Human Rights which concluded in Geneva on March 16, 1979 recommended, inter alia, to hold in 1980 a seminar on "the effect of the existing unjust international economic order and the obstacle that this represents for the implementation of human rights and fundamental freedoms, particularly the right to enjoy adequate standards of living."

True enough, no special seminar is necessary to study this question. Its manifold aspects have already been discussed at length by different bodies, governmental and non-governmental.

As we shall try to show below it is doubtful whether the proposed "New International Economic Order" (NIEO) will result in a proper solution of the TW problem, or merely benefit the nouveau riche oil-producers.

What seems to us really important is not to hold another discussion but to concentrate on the real causes of the deteriorating situation of the LDCs and on the implementation of recommendations—i.a. of the Brandt Commission, but of other bodies as well and usually worked out by a general consensus with regard to the aim of reducing TW misery.

We shall argue below that its causes are determined no less by various indigenous factors than by policies which, like the Soviet-Cuban interventions in Angola, Ethiopia, the Horn of Africa, Afghanistan and in other parts of the Third World, ruin all efforts to diminish the socio-economic backwardness and poverty of the LDCs.

The turmoil and distress in the LDCs have increased in result of this interference. They may become even more disturbing if the alleged Cuban and East German participation in the invasions of Zaire and their presence in the Middle East, the training of terrorists and militants of different national liberation movements by the Soviets, their renewed massive arms transfers to Southeast Asia and elsewhere, as well as their occupation of Afghanistan, will prove—as we suspect them to be—to be steps towards the domination of the Third World and therefore towards inducing the arms race and reduction of developmental budgets. No doubt, a special work is needed to corroborate and discuss at length this hypothesis and its consequences for the future of the world and for a comprehensive representation of the proper evidence.

This is not the purpose of this study. It only tries to prove that the specific issues of the Third World are not a main threat to world stability and peace as has been argued by the Brandt Commission, too. It also aims to show that the theories and political argumentation picturing the LDCs as the main cause of menace to international security actually distract attention, intentionally or unintentionally, from the real dangers.

That is why after reviewing, in the Introduction, in a general form some emerging problems of the above proposition, we shall primarily deal with the shape, evolution and the present role of the Third World (Chapter I), the doctrines relating to the interdependence of the levels and stages of economic growth and peace (Chapter II), the impact of underdevelopment on world politics and its perception in some peace studies (Chapter III), ending with a few observations and conclusions from this analysis. It is clear enough that this kind of study can only in a limited way contribute to the clarification of the assumption that the meager results or even stalemate in present development strategies adopted by and in favor of the Third World as well as many aspects of the so-called North-South Conflict are to a large extent a function of the East-West confrontation. Continual increase in military budgets and decrease in developmental budgets are actually determined by the threat of Soviet policies. Their aim seems to be, despite the formal acceptance of détente to reach world hegemony and to concentrate, for this purpose, on plans of military aggrandizement.

Below we shall deal with only some points of this contention, mainly as far as this is necessary to highlight the core of our thesis on the (relative) irrelevance of the Third World's economic situation and political tactics and strategies to world security. However, we find it useful to focus here on some illusions (partially, they have already been shattered after the recent events in Afghanistan), based on the policies of détente as well as on its supposedly identical interpretation in the Western and Soviet blocs. We also find it useful to point out some ensuing features of the present-day arms race, global in scope and increasingly dangerous in its implications not only for the LDCs but for the whole world.

Some students of international and particularly LDC politics are of the opinion that, whatever are the causes and dimension of TW militarization, we can rely on some superpower consensus to prevent an escalation of local wars. They argue that there is room for believing that the "Big" and their allies will make détente with time less one-sided and more strong; that they will finally agree on a reduction of their own arsenals and especially of weapon supplies to developing countries and will keep the East-West rivalry under control. The latter contention is also largely supported in non-aligned, particularly Yugoslavian and even in some Soviet-bloc writings.[3]

It seems to ignore that world military expenditure is currently running at more than $400 thousand million a year. A large part of this sum is used for the multiplication and perfection of nuclear arms.

Nuclear weapons, strategic and tactical, today are already equivalent in explosive power to more than one million Hiroshima bombs.

NATO and the Warsaw Treaty Organization (WTO) account for about 70% of the total of military expenditure and power, while TW military spending, accounting for the greater part of the rest, has doubled during the 1970s, increasing faster than its GNP. The Third World spends three times more on the military than it receives in oficial development aid.[4]

Indication of these numbers would suffice in order to realize why means are scarce for solving various socio-economic, educational and cultural problems which plague mankind, and especially, the LDCs.

It is enough to recall these problems in order to realize that they cannot be ignored in dealing not only with poverty, disease, population control, pollution, or human rights, endangered by the progress of the TW's militarization. They are also regarded as important in the studies on the efforts to revive détente, considering that it failed to terminate the present world war and underdevelopment systems.

The 1978 General Assembly's special disarmament session proved that most political leaders consider military adventures to be risky. However, it also showed that they are unwilling to give up their current military plans and subordinate their policies to long-range universal interests, directed, first and foremost, towards combatting underdevelopment and malnutrition and requiring real disarmament steps.

Some Soviet commentators explain the failure of the first Disarmament Conference in 46 years in which almost all nations of the world took part and the stalemate in other bodies created to discuss steps for limitation and control of nuclear and conventional weapons in that they all have been dominated by Western supposedly neo-imperialist tendencies. According to them, they have been aimed at the imposition of political and economic conditions on oil and other raw material trade and at the containment and weakening of Soviet influence and even the decomposition of its system.

Soviet and Marxist-Leninist sources quoted below prove that this view has not changed since the end of WWI and the birth of the USSR, at least as presented in theoretical studies and also in the press.

The foreign ministers of the WTO corroborated this opinion directly and indirectly in their communiqué published at the end of the Budapest meeting of May 14-15, 1979. It accuses the Western nations of unwillingness to respond constructively to Soviet proposals on reduction of armaments and armies in Europe.[5]

True enough, today, after the Soviet occupation of Afghanistan and the brutal break of the process of renewal in Poland, the Western European democracies have more reason to fear Soviet expansionism and continual military growth than vice versa, perhaps no less than their

TW clients. Different events give an additional proof to what has become an increasingly alarming comparison of military power between East and West.

The West German defense minister's White Paper on his country's security, the annual military balance prepared by the International Institute of Strategic Studies in London and other documents and statements published at the fall of 1981, all point out that the Soviet military threat is real; that it is on the increase following modernization of nuclear and conventional arms and equipment on a much greater scale and at a greater expenditure than in the West.

The Soviet command, above all, boosts its forces' attack potential, whereas NATO mainly reinforces defense capacities. The WTO forces retain even outmoded arms, whereas NATO scraps them, focusing only on modernizing its arsenals. Furthermore, experts have doubts whether US supremacy in warheads is sufficient to make the destructive potential of American ICBMs an effective deterrent against Soviet medium-range missiles. While in the strategic sector—presently suspended—SALT II has established approximate parity, the West has nothing comparable with which to counter these Soviet missiles capable of destroying any target in western Europe.[6]

Since the end of WWII and particularly since the late fifties, the time of speeding up the process of decolonization and entrance into the nuclear era and the time of growing prospects of ending the "cold war," the Western nations have not only given up their former possessions; they also gave up the thought of making use of their initial superiority in order to contain the Soviets. They have preferred to work out a peaceful *modus vivendi* with the Soviets; they have admitted that the nuclear factor will finally result in weakening Soviet aggressiveness and strengthen cooperative ties.

This facilitated détente and finally the Helsinki Pact. The assumption was that benefits of trade and scientific and cultural exchange would not only reduce Soviet expansionism and aggressiveness, but produce more perfect elaboration of rules of peaceful behavior; the latter would strengthen interbloc and global cooperation in various fields and thus enhance international security and socio-economic progress.

Consequently, many Western experts maintain that peace and security are attainable not through strength but exclusively via interdependence and cooperation, especially in Europe.[7]

This was an optimistic and to a certain extent formalistic and legalistic approach rooted in democratic traditions. It relies on mutual willingness to respect the rules of the accepted political game. It has characterized some former American administrations, the West German Ostpolitik and the position of other Western European countries and Japan, even after the Soviet conquest of Afghanistan. This approach, however, seems to completely ignore the Soviet interpretation of détente—*razriadka napriazhennosti* or "dispersal of tension"—primarily among the superpowers and their closest allies. This interpretation admits not only the continuation of ideological competition, but also the continuation of class struggle, too, in national and international dimensions; it regards such a struggle as a historically inevitable, objectively determined and irreconcilable conflict. Peaceful coexistence is regarded only as its operative form in conditions of the nuclear era and not relating to the Third World. This form, therefore, means neither a socio-political status quo, nor the abandonment of political and military interventions outside the frontiers of NATO and its closest allies, nor the abandonment of designs for military supremacy.

The latter is conceived as necessary not so much for security or other defensive ends than for steps directed towards a continual limitation of the Western sphere of influence. It is regarded as instrumental in limiting the West's access to oil and sources of other raw materials and towards change of "the correlation of forces" (*sootnoshenie sil*) in order to assure the final victory of the socialist system over the capitalist one.

There is of course a serious difference between Lenin's formulations of the international class struggle, its methods, direct and indirect aims, and those of Khrushchev and Brezhnev. The latter most probably does quite a lot in order to avoid a risky global war. He probably tries to contain militaristic tendencies of some parts of his military-technological complex and of other hawks in the Politburo and in the high command, first and foremost, of the navy and the nuclear forces. However, they are also characterized by a continuity of strategic purposes, ideological outlooks and sometimes even of tactics.

To believe this it would suffice to read V. Smolyansky, Y. Zakharov, A. Vakhramev, E. Tabarin, A. Sovietov and other leading theoreticians and commentators of the ideological Party monthly *Kommunist* or the important reviews of world politics *Mirovaya Ekonomika*, *Mezhdunarodnye otnosheniya*, and *Mexhdunarodnaya zhizn*.[8] Particularly instructive are their articles on peaceful coexistence, the role of national liberation movements and on correlation of military forces of the Communist bloc and the West.

It is enough to read all this in order to conclude that military parity and a proper defense system are not the aim of the Soviet leadership. It strives for superiority and intensifies tensions, for the time being only in the Third World in order to get the upper hand there. Hence, the conclusions of the director of the International Institute for Strategic Studies seem entirely convincing. He expects the eighties to be rather turbulent and difficult years for world security.[9] Quite probably this will be not because of a nuclear clash between the giants and their allies, but rather the result of Soviet expansion in the TW. Another cause for anxiety is the Soviet determination to establish supremacy and dominance in the name of deterrence and freedom and wellbeing for post-colonial nations.

What is going on today, not only in Ethiopia or Afghanistan but in many other parts of the TW, frequently in conditions of extreme distress, mass repressions, intertribal tensions and the military presence of Soviet bloc military and police personnel, might randomly explode the East-West rivalry into a Third World War. This might happen particularly when Soviet hawks of the post-Brezhnev era will be sure that they have the upper hand.

No matter what some LDC students say about underdevelopment and modernization—which they regard as a conflict-productive or evolutionary post-traditional stage of economic growth and social change[10]—or what they say about Western dependency or structural violence, the danger of the transformation of the TW into a theatre of Soviet domination and a springboard for world hegemony seems quite real. This danger challenges many politicians and academics more profoundly than some of them are willing to admit. This study argues that the core of the TW, that is, the TW with the exclusion of its richest components who are probably the richest on our planet,[11] has no power to wage a global war. However, at a certain moment it might be used by the Soviets as a means for this purpose. In this sense our study to some extent is about the above-mentioned challenge.

Naturally, this study is based on the critique of some contentions about the nature of the TW, about North-South, East-South and East-West relationships, discussed from different angles in various paragraphs. However, no particular effort has been made to work out fundamental propositions for solving the problem, since we hope to have the opportunity to do so in a future study, The purpose of this book is to acknowledge the danger, to understand its roots, and to point out the shortcomings of the prevailing diagnosis and of the proposed therapy.

The author rejects the assumption of the continuing polarization of the world into the aggressive West and the peace-loving Communist East and into poor peripheries and rich capitalist centers, which "structurally" or by means of war and destructive terms of trade enslave and exploit dependent nations. He equally rejects the view that the existing socialist states have shown the road which would lead the developing countries to full independence, both political and economic, and the surest way to solve all problems facing them.[12] This is an absurd statement if we consider the situation not only of different Soviet republics, but of European people's democracies which enjoyed much more freedom before their subjection by the USSR and particularly of present-day Poland. The author rejects also the supposition that all indications point to the fact that both superpowers are thinking in terms of and are actually striving to achieve a nuclear first-strike capability,[13] neither does he accept the thesis that militarism is an instrument of struggle

struggle between the giant nuclear powers for world hegemony, for neo-colonial presence, political subjection of other nations and their economic exploitation.[14]

These statements are a rather simplistic generalization, ignoring the internal factors of TW militarization, the differences in the giants' positions, the threat to world security deriving both from the possession of nuclear arms and technologies by other nations and from the efforts of the "nouveaux riches" to get these arms for themselves or their protegées.

Some authors of the above statements pass over in silence the fact that pursuing certain arms-control aims, such as restricting the transfer of conventional weapons, might adversely affect prospects for nuclear proliferation or nuclear-free zones. It can also have the effect of stimulating local production of arms in the Third World. They also ignore another important fact, namely, that the accumulation of military force for which its leaders are primarily responsible is not equivalent to accumulating power. Most frequently it leads to maintaining an order favorable to the ruling elites or to the supplier-states "haves" against the interest of the recipient "have-nots."[15] It is worthwhile to stress that the chief supplier of arms to the most conflict-saturated areas of Africa and Asia—probably with the exception of some parts of the Middle East—is the Soviet bloc.

The current world order, therefore, most profits the Kremlin.

An attempt is made in various parts of this study to emphasize this fact, but at the same time to criticize the spread of gloom and doom, bred by those who contend that a global Sovietization is unavoidable or that the prevention of a nuclear war is no longer possible. Detente even before the Soviet occupation of Afghanistan—to paraphrase Clausewitz—frequently was a continuation of the cold war by other means, but often also by the same means.[16] Its preservation obviously depends on stopping placation of the USSR because the only answer to Soviet withdrawal from detente seems in achieving a true detente. This means putting an end to unilateral Western concessions, insistence on reciprocity in the ideological, political and strategic struggle and efforts to avoid breaches in the Western front. Not only in the past but today, too, these breaches have made possible Moscow's deals with various European countries, which sabotaged the proper American steps. The efforts to bring the USSR into the process of peace-building will be fruitless for so long as its aggressive undertakings are not met with a proper reaction, for so long as Moscow is allowed to spend— frequently with the help of Western credits and technology—between two and three times more per capita on armaments than the US; and for so long as the USSR's strategy of continuing endless negotiations on arms control and disarmament issues is used to distract the world's attention from its attempts to establish military conventional and nuclear superiority.

Unilateral concessions, disunity, rhetoric protests against violations of human rights and of other commitments and tolerant attitude towards brutal interventions in the TW can only speed up the shift from uncertain detente to confrontation.

The economic problems of the TW countries are by no means unsolvable. However, they themselves must make the decisive effort to remedy their situation. But its success will be the more rapid the more effective Western assistance is and the more the brutal Soviet inter vention (direct and by proxy) in large parts of Africa, Asia and even South America[17] is restrained.

The author therefore intends to stress the need for working for more constructive solutions with regard to the miserable situation in the TW and for contibuting, in this way, too, to the containment of the Soviet attempts to use it in the struggle for world hegemony.

It seems to the author that the Western democracies still have all the cards in their hands and are therefore able to counteract the danger to world peace resulting from the Soviet offensive in the TW.

This belief cannot be sufficiently tested not only because certain relevant formulations are not based on first-hand duly verified findings and figures but also because of the fact that they are deduced from realities which are rapidly changing and getting a new meaning.

Hence, some paragraphs of this study are intentionally open to scholarly reappraisal, the more so since the author took the risk of errors in hypotheses and propositions which require further sub stantiation and reexamination.

The notes at the end of each chapter acknowledge principal sources of facts and ideas used in this study. They might, therefore, facilitate the discussion and correction of the author's analysis and the redressing of his argumentation.

Many people have helped in the preparation of this study by their encouragement, advice and critical remarks. Although the author remains solely responsible for this work, he is grateful for their assistance and hopes that the final product will at least partially repay his debts.

The author is especially grateful to the David Horowitz Institute for the Research of Developing Countries of Tel-Aviv University for its assistance in typing the manuscript.

Marion Mushkat
January, 1982

Notes

1. See I. Sommer, "Eine Welt oder Keine Welt?" *Die Zeit*, No. 8/1980, p. 1.

2. Beginning with Marx's interpretation of these problems, through non-Marxist approaches of W. G. Hoffman, W. W. Rostow, A. Gerschenkron, till the neo-liberal, dependency and neo-Marxist theories, the dispute is still far from receiving clear-cut conclusions. See, e.g., C. Keyder, Rostow, Gerschenkron "Capitalism and Proto-industrialization," in *Studies in Development*, Ankara, No. 2/1978, particularly pp. 68, 70, 71 and 78; for the first presentation of the doctrines on the stages of economic growth see G. W. Hoffmann, Stadien und Typen der Industrialisierung, Kiel, 1931, and for the consideration of "internal" and "external" forces see A. Gerschenkron, *Economic Backwardness in Historical Perspective*, Cambridge, Mass., 1962.

3. M. Dromujac, "USA—USSR: "Controlled Rivalry," *YRIA*, vol. XXX, No. 702-33, 5-320, VII. 1979, p. 49.

4. For recent data on the continual arms race see *SIPRI 1978—1980*.

5. *EA*, XXX 34, No. 13, 10. VII. 1979, p. 330

6. K. Becker, "Missile facts faced; America has a Dilemma in the Pipeline," *GT*, No. 907, 16. IX, 1979, p. 2.

7. K. W. Rothschild, "Peace and Security via Interdependence and Cooperation in Europe," *Osterreichische Zeitung fur Aussenpolitik*, vol. XIX, No. 1/1974, p. 14 and ff.

8. For the translation of statements of Lenin, Brezhnev, Smolyansky and other mentioned Soviet theoreticians and commentators and for their persuasive analysis see R. Harrison, "US-Soviet Relations in "A Quantatively New Era," (mimeographed) *Backgrounder*, No. 96, The Heritage Foundation, Washington D.C. 24. VIII. 1979, pp. 1-39. See also E. Tabarin, "Africa in a New Round of the Liberation Struggle," *Survival*, XXI, No. 4, July-August 1979, pp. 172-175.

9. Ch. Bertram, "Arms Dynamics and Arms Control," *GT* No. 34, 15. VII, 1979, p. 6.

10. For details of this latter approach see, i.a., R. Hettlage, "Modernitaet als Post-Traditionalitaet," *Die Dritte Welt*, vol. 7, No. 1. 1979, p. 38 and ff.

11. This statement is based on figures taken from *Die Zeit* (No. 12, 16. III. 1979), which reproduced them from the *Weltbankatlas*.

12. L. J. Milovanovic, "Attractive Debate of Theoreticians, *Yugoslavian Life*, vol. XXIII, No. 10-11, October-November, 1978.

13. S. Lodgaard and M. Thee, "High Military Technology, Security and Mass Control," *BPP*, No. 4/1977, p. 293.

14. M. Thee, "Militarism and Militarization in Contemporary International Relations, *BPP*, op. cit. p. 299.

15. See Mary Kaldor's contribution "Opportunities for Disarmament. A Preview of the 1978 United Nations Special Session on Disarmament," in Current Endowment for International Peace, edited by J. O.Sharp, New York, 1978 and the review of this publication by R. Haas in *Survival*, XXI, No. 4, July-August, 1979, pp. 187-8.

16. A. Fontaine in *Le Monde*, 30.X.1973.

17. W. Laqueur *The Political Psychology of Appeasement*, Transaction Books, New Brunswick—London, 1980, pp. 141, 160, 195, passim.

Introduction

Since the end of World War II, most nations have increasingly sought to maintain their security by means of a military buildup. The un restricted worldwide military preparedness was given a new impetus by the 1973 "energy crisis," when the oil producers began to invest a part of their revenues in the armament of themselves and of favored Third World clients.

The resurgent arms race has raised a number of questions: 1. has the massive military preparedness increased national and international security, and 2. have all post-World War II conflicts resulted from superior military preparedness and various economic causes?

Discussion of these questions is inextricably linked to the issue of economic strength. There is no doubt that prodigious investment by the Third World countries of capital, raw materials, and skilled labor in military preparedness has had a profound impact on their development.

But whatever the impact of militarization on economic development, the question remains whether economic development has been conducive to international security and whether internecine conflict within the Third World has been caused mainly by economic or by other factors. With regard to these issues, diametrically opposed arguments have been advanced.

One view holds that the gap between the more developed and the less developed countries is the only source of international insecurity in the present-day world; that quest for military sophistication in the Third World is the inevitable outcome of failed economic and social development. Frustration and fear of continuing inferiority are said to induce Third World leaders to lash out with political and economic vindictiveness against First World industrialized and rich Third World countries alike. This rage has been aimed primarily at the Western Bloc countries, the former colonial masters, and more recently also at the Eastern Bloc, because of USSR's interference in their affairs and its reluctance to assist them.

Internal conflicts within the Third World may result from attempts to divert the attention of restive populations from the real sources of their misery and from the inability of their leaders to improve their situation. The resort to military violence at home or abroad may also stem from envy of the "haves" and an attempt to "steal" their wealth. Third World tendencies of this sort may also conceivably represent well-conditioned reflexes against real or imagined exploitation.

Thus some believe that the narrowing of the gap between the industrialized and underdeveloped countries would make the behavior of the "have-nots" less disruptive and their economy less susceptible to exploitation. Others fear that economic development and industrialization of the Third World might intensify the competition for scarce world resources and thus initiate conflict. A third possible outcome of efforts to narrow the development gap is a more intensive utilization of existing resources and recycling of waste, as well as exploitation of thus far untapped resources and technological innovation. This prospect, of course, should dissipate threats to world peace.

Another approach raised the question as to whether the intra-Third World conflicts are the result of underdevelopment and exploit ation, and whether the realization of collective economic security would pave the road to world peace. If economic growth is the key to peace and security, then more Latin American countries suffering from underdevelopment today are threatened with endless guerrilla and counterguerrilla activities. This also applies to many African and Asian nations (Socialist Angola, Vietnam, Cambodia and Soviet-occupied Afghanistan being far from exceptions).

Even worse than the Southeast Asian condition is the deteriorating situation in Africa. The southern part of the continent is beset with problems that reach far beyond the issues of independence and majority rule in Namibia (Southwest Africa). South Africa was obliged to introduce structural changes, realizing that *apartheid* and other forms of racial segregation and discrimination were endangering the support of the Western democracies in the long run. In May, 1977, concurrent with the increased focus of world attention on Third World problems, the United States promised to exert greater pressure on Pretoria. In his Indiana University speech the former US president, Jimmy Carter stressed that the rule of law could not exist under minority governments and it may be claimed that this is the position of all Western countries.[1] To be sure, the South African government, representing a well-organized wealthy community, aware of its importance to the security of the free world, could not be expected to give up its policies entirely, which is another cause of increasing scissions on this continent.

In the first decade after World War II, when Africa had not yet recovered from the wounds of conflict, fresh strife erupted: for example, Nasserete, Egypt's involvement in and, indeed, sponsorship of Pan-Arab, Pan-Moslem, and Pan-African and Middle East confrontations. The turmoil affected such widely disparate countries as Sudan, Nigeria, Congo, Burundi, Chad, Libya, and Angola. In 1977, Africa was stricken with new conflicts between Algeria and the Polisario (the Front for the Liberation of the Western Sahara), on the one side, and till summer 1979, Mauritania and Morocco on the other; between Ethiopia and Somalia over the latter's support of the Somalian and Eritrean National Liberation Movements; continuing resurgent civil war between the Chad rebels supported by Libyan invaders and the legal but exiled government of Chad; between Egypt and Libya; between Zaire and Angola over Shabe (Katanga) and Cabinda; between Amin-ruled Uganda and Tanzania and some of Uganda's other neighbors till Idi Amin's fall in 1979; and recently between Iraq and Iran. This by no means completes the list of current African wars or foci of tension. It does not include conflicts and tensions involving Soviet and Western indirect interference, or Cuban presence in Angola and Ethiopia, as well as the continuing fighting in other parts of the continent. With evidence of Western or Soviet financial and military support of other African and Middle East clients, Africa and the Middle East seem to have become an arena for ongoing, indirect conflict between the world's two superpowers.

Some Western politicians considering the danger of this conflict explicitly expressed the need to increase development aid to Africa and remove it from international rivalry and strife. The European Community thus having in mind this proposal had authorized one billion dollars "special aid" to the "poorest countries," mainly in Africa.[2]

In view of these favorable developments many Third World leaders have become a little more optimistic over prospects of receiving effective assistance.[3] Needless to say, Western help has not only been aimed at promoting human progress and democracy in the LDC's and abating malnutrition and backwardness, but is also to a large extent a political weapon of the West. In recent years, in spite of détente—or perhaps because of its limitations and decline—continuing American-Soviet rivalry remains a quiet but powerful motive for meeting Third World needs. At the same time, superpower and interbloc rivalry continues to make the Third World not less an important source of raw materials and a potentially lucrative market, than a future contact point for political support and even alliance, above all in international organizations dominated by a Third World majority.

On the other hand, continuing intra-Third World conflicts with external involvement raise the question of whether continuing strife in Africa, Asia and Latin America will go on indefinitely,[4] and perhaps evolve into a catalyst of a new world-wide conflict. Realistic prediction in this regard necessitates a prior comprehensive evaluation of the origin, character, evolution and prospects of the Third World; furthermore, it requires not only a reappraisal of past surveys of this "alliance," but especially a reassessment of recent developments and their impact on the security-underdevelopment relationship, as well as of the proper conclusions of political theory generally and peace research particularly.

This study as we have already mentioned, is designed to deal with some important aspects of these problems. Emphasis will be on the concept of collective economic security, stressed in the UN General Assembly Resolution 2880 (XXVI) of 21 December 1971 concerning the reinforcement of international security. In this resolution, the United Nations calls for the establishment of a collective economic security system. The resolution notes the allegedly close relationship between international security, disarmament, and development. Many other resolutions of various UN agencies have made allusion to the relationship between disarmament and peacemaking, on the one hand, and the promotion of human rights and welfare on the other hand.

Discussion of such problems and the means to solve them date back to antiquity. Such concepts and their proposed solutions are rooted in the holy scriptures of all religions and they are frequently embodied in utopian outlooks and moral teachings in all ages. These concepts were quite clearly established by the prophet Isaiah more than two-and-a-half millenia ago. In modern times they were faced by the Quakers, who in 1815 established their "peace society." A few generations later they were repeated by the "Political Pope," Leo XIII. Their proposed resolution was the core of disarmament *pourparlers* during the five years preceding the First Hague Peace Conference in 1899. They are stressed in the work leading to the Declaration on Disarmament at the Second Hague Peace Conference in 1907.[5] And, of course, the dispositions of the League of Nations Covenant and the United Nations Charter, various resolutions of these and other bodies and conferences, and even agreement on some kind of conventional, nuclear experiments and armament limitation since, and recent debates on this subject and on a new international economic order all bespeak of continuing efforts to deal with these problems.

Current attempts to define and investigate these questions have resulted from the widespread exposure to world public opinion of the backwardness and malnutrition in the majority of postcolonial states while billions are wasted for military aggrandizement. The contours and enormity of socioeconomic stagnation and famine and of the parallel growth of military budgets were described by the United Nations and other international bodies. Heightened awareness of the gap between the LDC's and the developed world, the vast advantage obtained by the latter in international trade, and exploitation of the LDC's by them even through forms of assistance, and the disproportion between the means for help and those used for purposes of militarization was realized at the highest international level. These facts in turn led to the introduction of the term," Collective Economic Security." Soon the concept became an essential element of any drive to establish stability and to reduce threats of violence occasioned by the division of the world into rich and poor countries; indeed, it was perceived as the *sine qua non* of both those striving to preserve the *status quo* and those seeking to change it by military and revolutionary means in the interest of peace and progress.

The UN Secretary General defined the need for collective economic security in his Note of 19 March 1973 to the 54th Session of the UN Economic and Social Council (ECOSOC Doc. E/5263). He referred to Article 65 of the Charter and various General Assembly and UN specialized agencies resolutions, explaining the direct link between disarmament and development, which was stated, i.a., in the Preamble of the UN International Development Strategy, and in numerous UN documents relating to disarmament and development. The Secretary General asserted that the continuous efforts to promote peace by arms limitation could be crowned with success through the emergence of economic security. Arms limitation was also essential to maintain the momentum of economic and social cooperation. This was said to be equally necessary to establish more satisfactory systems of collective and individual welfare. The Secretary General, in the note mentioned, pointed out that the concept of collective economic security as a basis for political security was already envisaged by the framers of the Charter and remains valid to this day.

The Secretary General's Report on the Second Development Decade to the 54th ECOSOC session (Doc.E/5369) stated that many delegations recognized the direct connection between political and economic security and that the latter supplements the former. They furthermore professed to attribute the utmost importance to the issue of the close relationship between development and complete general disarmament asset as set forth in the Charter of Economic Rights and Duties of States. The idea of collective economic security complied with the principles of the Charter not only because of the political and economic security that it was hoped to ensure, but also because it was considered fundamental to all multilateral relations. Also, the Charter on Economic Rights and Duties was deemed necessary to enhance operation of a collective economic security system, as an instrument of political security.

The Secretary General's 29 May 1974 Report to the 57th ECOSOC Session (Doc. E/5529) pointed out four main roles of economic collective security: 1) Actions of evaluation relative to problems of population, science, and other important issues. 2) Action in emergencies. 3) Operation as a factor of equity. 4) Regulation, for instance through harmony with national policies.

The Report stressed that security was no longer an exclusively military concept. It further claimed that the economic crisis of the 1930s and the competitive politics of "pauperization of the neighbor" induced by it played an important role in precipitating World War II. It also stressed that many threats to national and individual welfare and even to the status and autonomy of nations are often of a non-military nature. Tensions and conflicts affecting political security were ascribed by the Report also to nonmilitary measures. The Charter of the Economic Rights and Duties of States (Res. 3282 (XXIX of 12 December 1974) and all later resolutions of UN agencies and conferences likewise adopted conceptions of collective economic security. Furthermore the General Assembly, contrary to the precedent set at the different special sessions, which dealt only with political problems, considered at the Sixth and Seventh special sessions the most important issues of the world economic situation, including those following the 16 October 1973 OPEC's Organization of Petroleum Exporting Countries decision to raise oil prices.[6]

The concept of collective economic security and specifically of the relation between economic development, stability and international security was elaborated not only by official international bodies and conferences,but also at scientific conventions, in important journals[7] and in the daily press.[8] Yet there is serious doubt whether the correlations established by them with regard to the impact of economic issues on military security are entirely correct and exceed politically acute and humanitarian aspects.

One is inclined to admit that international and national conflicts as well will probably continue even if the aims sought by the programs on economic security are attained. Laying the foundations of collective economic security only implies the establishment of a new and it is hoped more just international economic order, very important by itself, playing a considerable role in promoting political and military security, but far from being the most decisive factor in this field.

An attempt will be made to examine in greater detail the assumptions and motivations behind the various theories of economic determinism, especially Marxist and the wide variety of opposing theories pinpointing the priority of economic considerations in problems of peace and war. Contemporary economic experts and ideologists frequently seem to confuse the economic consequences of armed conflicts with the causes of war. For example, they are prone to ignore the fact that the recipients of abundant sophisticated armaments paid for by oil profits and aimed at the realization of religious, tribal, racial or national revendications remain unable to master military technology on their own, hence they increase the waste of resources but fail to achieve their goals. Needless to say, a conflict precipitated by the proliferation of sophisticated mass extermination weapons supplied to socially and technologically backward nations could have disasterous consequences for human survival in various areas or even on this planet as a whole.

Theoretically, it might be conceded that in spite of the danger of thermonuclear holocaust, the developed countries would not tolerate the continued freedom of military action of such economically threatening LDC's. In practice, there does not seem to be today the remotest possibility of a developed western country contemplating such an attack against this kind of threat. Certainly, it defies both fact and logic to imagine that any country on earth would mount a nuclear or even a conventional armed attack on an LDC because it is believed to be an economic threat. It is equally absurd to believe that any socially advanced industrialized country would knowingly entrust the deployment of sophisticated thermonuclear armaments to the discretion of any LDC or any other political body noted for revolutionary zeal rather than social or technological knowhow. However, the bounty of sophisticated armaments to a backward LDC may not only lead to the impairment of the LDC's real economic progress, but to the creation incidentally and in an extreme situation intentionally of an inter-superpower clash and nuclear catastrophe.

But this eventuality, too, calls for not disregarding the historians' consensus, in these speculations, that the causes of past and present major wars were basically not economic. For those who persist in denying this reality because of their Marxist approach, it may be worthwhile to consult the texts of Karl Marx himself. Indeed, Marx stressed the primacy of the material and economic factors in history, but never precluded the role of other factors. Friedrich Engels, Marx's lifelong associate, taught that it was *not* possible to explain the essence, existence and conflicts of every small state in Germany and elsewhere by economics without making oneself look ridiculous. On the contrary, he concluded that there were numerous interacting influences that give rise to one result: the historical event. Engels confessed, "Marx and I partly are to blame for the fact that the younger people sometimes lay more stress on the economic side than is due to it. I cannot exempt many of the more recent Marxists from the reproach of producing the most amazing rubbish in this regard. . . I would surely be pedantic to try to find economic causes for all this primitive nonsense."[9]

The same may be said, of course, for those who preclude economic factors altogether, that they, too, introduce further confusion rather than clarify the origins of various political tensions, diplomatic scissions and wars. Understanding the causes and origins of internal and international conflicts might be better served by research into a multiplicity of causes. In the present inquiry, the thesis that underdevelopment has markedly determined the character of the Third World, which in turn seems prone to precipitate international security problems, will be explored thoroughly. The undoubted complexity of the relationship between development and peace calls for a reassessment of the hypothesis on the exclusivity of the economic factor as the cause of armed conflicts, rooted in absolutist determinism.

All too often, study of their interdependent relationship has been relegated even by eminent experts to the role of axiomatic truth. In fact, each claim of this kind must be supported by relevant historical, empirical evidence; moreover, such verifiable evidence must be carefully weighed against other causal factors. The allegation that the search for raw materials and investment opportunities is the major or only cause of political dissention and war finds its reflection even in the writings of experts who in principle deny it.[10]

This is not to say that there is no place for postulated hypothesis in scholarly research. On the other hand, resort to many assumptions "for the sake of argument" in studies of international relations, law, political science, and history must be undertaken with the greatest caution. This applies particularly to the axioms about the economic base as the inevitable cause of political tension and war. Were the economic factor a major force in the ongoing Israeli-Arab conflict, for example, then the most rational and likely outcome would be that each side's self-interest would lead to immediate peace.

Axiomatic statements about the inevitable role of economic determinism tend to prejudice the validity of research. Powerful states in all ages have undoubtedly indulged in territorial aggrandizement in order to expand their political and economic power, but whether this role of economic might is true in all or even in particular instances can only be established by critical impartial evaluation of all relevant facts.

Many scholars of different political orientations have recently demonstrated once more: a) that war tends to be the outcome of a large number of variables interacting in extremely complex patterns; b) that traditional explanations have if anything, been seriously over-simplified; c) that it is possible, in spite of serious conceptual difficulties, to handle the complex patterns in a systematic way in order to generate and test theories; d) that, by and large, policymakers deal more or less unavoidably, at least up to the present, with grossly oversimplified "models"—as do peace activists and others; and e) that continuing investigations, however slow and painful, are unavoidable if we are to find ways of averting war in the long run.[11]

This is one more reason why some scholars caution decision-makers against commitments to a specific organizing assumption regarding the nature of a particular crisis. Such action, as not only J. Stein and R. Tanter imply, might be tantamount to irrational behavior.[12]

Some students maintain that today we do not know much more about the causes of war than Quincy Wright told us back in the 1940s (*The Study of War*, 1942) or Kenneth Walz in the 1950s (*Man, the State and the War*, 1954, 1959)[13] and—I might add—than what their predecessors told us in the inter-World War period and in earlier times.

We are therefore entirely right to admit that the correlation between socio-economic malaise and instability in international relations may be more apparent than real, although economic considerations play an essential role in putting an end to conflicts. Governmental and non-governmental international agencies and conferences have recently lavished attention on problems of food, demography, ecology, trade, investment, raw materials and natural resources as decisive factors in all programs aimed at international peace. However, the most important target of these discussions is the amelioration of human and social conditions, international security being determined mainly by other considerations. Behind these efforts is, of course, the belief that the betterment of human life through economic and social advancement will result in a more just and stable political order as well as in diminishing tensions of an international character, but this is still far from being able to prevent a military encounter between the superpowers, the main danger to mankind's survival in our time. To what extent unrest bred by underdevelopment is a danger to international peace is one of the main issues with which this inquiry will deal.

It is not the first time that these problems have been studied, even by this writer.[14] The present study is not intended to corroborate previous research, nor to formulate revised models, but rather to probe current trends of LDC's to promote economic progress and security through military preparedness and to find out to what extent, if at all, these tendencies are economically determined and can be successful. This in turn raises subsequent research questions as to whether trends towards militarization enhance or impede economic and social development and whether the failure of development efforts in the past decades has tended to create international political instability and a real danger to peace in the world. Implicit in these research problems is the further question of whether maldevelopment is always associated with political weakness, social indifference, and acquiescence with the *status quo*. An ancillary question in any research into the relationship between development and security is the extent to which the frustrations of underdevelopment induce LDC's to take part in the arms race that subsequently drives them towards military adventurism in foreign policy. And on the domestic scene, are successful economic development and growth necessarily contingent on enslavement, conquests, exploitation, and the insatiable greed of the mighty states on the international scene.

Research along the aforementioned lines necessarily entails comprehensive reassessment of the "devil theories" of imperialism advanced, among others, by John Hobson, Vladimir I. Lenin, Charles Beard and Joseph Schumpeter.[15] Evaluation of these doctrines of expansionism is especially vital to the understanding of underdevelopment today, where neoimperialism and neocolonialism is suspected. The allegations about resurgence of imperialism and colonialism may merely refer to the necessary economic and administrative control on developmental aid imposed by its patrons. On the other hand, the possibility of reimposing political control under the guise of developmental aid cannot be ruled out entirely. A reasonable criterion for the degree of neoimperialism and neocolonialism is the extent to which LDC's can evade alliance with the contending blocs that sponsor their economic development. The relevance of "devil" theories to present-day development aid to LDC's depends on whether the patrons' control measures can be shown to be economically determined.

Recently, a relationship has been proclaimed between the development-international security question and the individual human rights cause. Revival of an authentic democratic and progressive tradition has been asserted to be vital for imposing peace and deterring aggression.[16] Furtherance of the revival of democracy to promote human rights was proclaimed in Jimmy Carter's 17 March 1977 speech to the United Nations. The then American President promised on this occasion to multiply efforts to satisfy social needs as a means of advancing human rights of LDC populations; but recent Western and first and foremost European Community declarations suggest that such rhetoric is still devoid of substance.[17]

The idea has been advanced recently that the concept of economic collective security may only be useful for the effective promotion of development aid by encompassing the communist countries. Western development aid efforts must, of course, be matched by Soviet Bloc efforts and its abandonment of the notion that the USSR is absolved of obligation to the LDC's by the alleged absence of a colonial past.[18] Today, the Soviet contribution to development aid is 0.003 percent of the Soviet gross national product (GNP), while that of some Western countries, mainly for the benefit of their former colonies, approaches 0.7 percent. (Seven-tenths of one percent was the standard set by the UN Second Development Decade). Disparity between Western and Eastern contributions is thus seen to be considerable.[19] The message of the May 1977 London European summit was a challenge to COMECON (the economic organization of the Soviet Bloc) to follow the Western example in development aid. The European proclamation was said to be expressive of the desire of all states to intensify the struggle against underdevelopment. A positive Soviet response may well complicate Western designs initially, but in the long run can be expected to provide more viable economic stability and security on the world scene. Whether Soviet cooperation would really contribute to economic security and indirectly in this way to political and military security of the Soviet Bloc and stop its expansionist political designs remains doubtful.

What emerges from various studies of these and other problems mentioned above is contradictory and inconclusive. Undoubtedly, this may be accounted for partly by the different perspectives and interests of investigators. It may also be ascribed to differing conceptual frameworks of various studies and the absence of complete and up-to-date data. Some students view economic power and development as the best means of strengthening peace; others consider these same factors as the principal source of internal and international strife. The former is rooted in the classical formulations of Hugo Grotius, Emmerich Vattel, Immanuel Kant, Adam Smith, John Stuart Mill, and others. They viewed industry and free commerce as instruments of international peace.

Free trade views were opposed by those who perceived evolving nationalism from a mercantilist perspective, which justified imperialism and colonialism as a means of acquiring national economic wealth. Mercantilism early gained the support of militant expansionists in the initial stages of the industrial revolution because of its vindication and even glorification of protectionism in international trade. A present-day rebuttal of classical mercantilist theory was articulated in the conclusion reached that threats to world peace could be eliminated by bridging the development gap between the LDC's and the rest of the world. Rejectionists of mercantilist approaches argued that as a matter of self-interest the former colonial masters of the LDC's were obligated to eliminate the latter's social and economic backwardness after granting them independence.

The concept of aid to post-colonial countries as a security factor has been put forward by such diverse personalities as Charles de Gaulle, Lester Pearson, Robert MacNamara, Jimmy Carter, on the one hand, and Julius Nyerrere, Indira Ghandi, and other Third World leaders on the other.[20]

Another approach is represented by the followers of R. Dahrendorf and L. Coser,[21] who consider economic growth and development as factors of domestic and international conflict. They hold among other things that growth and development provoke repression and exploitation for the enrichment of the mighty. This line of reasoning patently reflects Socialist theories of capitalist production and imperialism. Today, they paraphrase Marx's statement that organized concentrated force is always the *accouchement* of each society.[22] As suggested above, under discussion of "devil theories," these concepts will be dealt with in greater detail below. Such an assessment should be revealing with regard to the claims that capitalism always leads to aggression and the counterclaim that aggression inevitably appears in the policies of Communist states.

Suffice it to underscore here that in their extreme form articulated by some representatives of Western schools of peace research,[23] all threats to international peace and the Third World militarization are viewed as the result of structural violence and a peripheral status imposed on the LDC's by the advanced developed countries.[24] Every catastrophe that can befall an LDC—exploitation, enslavement, starvation, repression and, of course, neo-colonialism and neoimperialism—are blamed on the Western developed countries. War is considered a routine if not a subsidiary means to acquire economic profits. In this approach, noneconomic or otherwise indigenous causes of underdevelopment, nationalism, micro-imperialism, and war either are not understood or are ignored. Recent developments favoring greater mutual security and interdependence are suspect as camouflage for imperialist conspiracies of the developed countries.

Another gaping research void is the passing in silence over the recent appearance of *nouveaux riches* in the Third World and its implications for the poorer have-nots and those involved in armed intra-Third World conflicts. The phenomena of newly rich underdeveloped countries arose in the wake of the 1973 Middle East war and the drastic price hike imposed on crude oil by producers afterwards. A byproduct of excessive profits to crude petroleum miners used for purposes of militarisation or banking business and not developmental purposes was the sequel of an emerging Fourth World consisting of the remaining impoverished LDC's. The windfall revenues have enabled the newly rich crude oil producers to bankroll the arms race of their favored allies but not to aid the true poor brothers. Crude petroleum consumers incurring heavy deficits to pay higher prices for oil may well be tempted to sell arms to aggressive-minded LDC's to compensate for negative balances of payments.

The impact of oil profits on world trade and the ongoing arms race is clear. What is not clear and therefore wide open to intensive pioneering research is the effect of arms sales on world peace and, more importantly, the impact of extensive arms production and procurement on the real economic development processes of the LDC's. What is the likelihood that arms sales and militarization sponsored by oil enriched underdeveloped countries will reawaken superpower arms competition throughout the Third World? In the absence of serious bona fide research, it is left to the speculative and not always rational imagination whether such a course of action leads to security and real development or to a new dark age of strife and chaos.

If militarization in general and particularly of LDC's ultimately portends world-wide descent into the abyss of a new global armed conflict, it is not easy to dismiss summarily the pessimistic views like those of the German philosopher and physicist C. F. von Weizsacker. These views envisage continued rapid development and perfection of military technology as inevitably leading to a thermonuclear clash. It is even more difficult to refute this hypothesis by mere appeals for disarmament.[25] The clear danger posed by the extension of the superpowers' arms race into the Third World seems to become more imminent every day. Although both the East and the West are aware of this peril, continuance of present trends may one day make it impossible to avoid a face to face confrontation and of worldwide nuclear catastrophe.

The emergence of affluent and well-armed Third World countries has emboldened some socially backward and economically primitive countries to defy the advanced developed countries. Following the successful blackmail of the oil-hungry industrial countries by means of the 1973 oil embargo, some oil producers became virtually immune to superpower pressure and restraint. Since the Soviet Union is not yet dependent on the newly affluent oil producing countries for oil, the adverse effect of the 1973 oil embargo fell mainly on the United States and its allies and on the poor socialist and less developed countries as well. The independent position of Third World nations based on the oil power has recently been reflected in the UN and other bodies' resolutions promoted by the "Group of 77" regarding, among other things, a New Economic World Order (NIEO).

Under the pressure of this Group and with Soviet support, the UN General Assembly even decided in December 1977 that the individual rights issue were no longer its principal concern. Two new priorities stressing collective and national rights were adopted. The first new priority was to combat violations of the "human rights of peoples," like apartheid, racial discrimination and colonialism. But the subsequent categories were far more striking: threat of aggression against national sovereignty, national unity and territorial integrity, as well as the refusal to recognize the fundamental rights of people to self-determination, and of every nation to exercise full sovereignty over its wealth and national resources.

The second new priority decided on by the Assembly was the realization of the NIEO, which was held to be "an essential element in the effective promotion of human rights and fundamental freedoms."

However, there is an abundance of evidence drawn from the experience of numerous developing countries which demonstrates that higher economic standards do not necessarily have a connection with improved human-rights conditions, whereas the focus in the NIEO is upon the benefits to be derived by the leading elites of the Third World states and not necessarily by their populations.

The NIEO, however useful its purpose might be, has little, if anything, to do with human rights, or international security.[26]

With their arsenals well stocked with sophisticated weapons and their armies trained and well organized, some of the Third World countries have become freed from any restraints that might otherwise have been imposed on them by their patrons, who are trying to prevent an escalation of local conflicts and the reducing of their spheres of influence which might result from this escalation.

The problem of this new position of some LDC's and whether it portends the global nuclear war will be dealt with in more detail later in thisstudy. But what we should already assert here is that since the proliferation of Third World arsenals financed by inflated oil revenues,[27] present-day wars might no longer be exported from the advanced developed "North" to the under-developed socially backward "South," but could be exported from the LDC's to the industrialized world.There is no doubt that there is a perceptible increase in indigenous Third World military adventurism since the 1973 oil embargo and a growing impact of intra-Third World conflicts on the global security situation. This is the reason why there is room for more common East and West positions vis-a-vis the South,[28] first and foremost in order to aquire greater control on dangerous developments in the Third World. However, is this possible after the Soviet invasion of Afghanistan?

Some observers still continue to assert that the inchoate East-West détente presages the growth of a North-South conflict as the salient feature of presently evolving international relations.[29] Such a trend, however, does not appear to be mirrored in reality because the South, in fact, is becoming more and not less dependent on the North, not only for developmental aid. Yet it has become almost fashionable to argue that strategic considerations are being eclipsed by economic growth issues, that questions of raw materials are becoming more explosive than ballistic missiles, and that the hazards of creating a new economic order are the main source of current world tensions.[30]

The developed countries that aborted the June 1977 North-South dialogue do not seem to share this view. The People's Republic of China (PRC) sided with the anti-Soviet poor Third World countries rather than their oil-enriched "brothers," while the Soviet Union sided with poor Ethiopia and South Yemen. The Chinese, who claimed to be a part and even a leader of the Third World persistently berated the superpowers as the world's greatest threat to human existence and peace. Culminating against real or imaginary evils of American imperialism and Soviet social imperialism, the Chinese ignored the obvious menace of the oil-financed arms influx into the Third World. Dividing the world into three camps—the superpowers, the industrialized countries, and the LDCs— only the economically and socially backward Third World was regarded as a peace-building force. Some Western students of national security affairs shared the unrealistic Chinese view hoping to achieve peace through other countries' cooperation in banishing superpower influence from the world scene.

The Chinese argument may be faulted on a number of grounds. It totally disregarded factors tending before the Afghanistan Soviet Operation to weaken East-West and not just North-South tensions and encouraging peaceful cooperation. Against the record of history and the prognostications of their own ideologies, the Chinese and some of their Western followers vainly hope for universal revolutionary change. They seem completely oblivious of the fact that issues of the North-South dialogue whose former phase ended on 2 June 1977, are continuing to be dealt with in other forums.[31]

The Chinese view also completely ignored indigenous South-South conflicts endangering peace that occasionally provoke intervention by states of the North. It is difficult if not impossible to determine today whether the US Central Intelligence Agency (CIA) promoted the Greek colonels' coup a few years ago or whether the insurgents provoked foreign intervention in their favor. The bloody and violent overthrow of the Chilean Marxist regimé with the suspected aid and abettment of the CIA might have been avoided if Chilean President Salvador Allende had been more cautious in the execution of his nationalization of domestic capital, limiting his program at least initially, to foreign enterprises. The Chilean Secretary General of the Communist Party recently observed

> It is by no means certain whether nationalizations of holdings elsewhere (e.g., in the Arab world or Northern Africa) could be accomplished if they affected domestic and not foreign enterprises.[33]

Likewise, the Chinese and some peace researchers' argument conveniently ignores the role of all forms of indigenous authoritarian ism, totalitarianism, militarism, and tyranny in the tensions and conflicts that tend to compound exploitation and enslavement in the Third World. The dictatorships and despotisms of the Third World perpetuate and extend socio-economic miseries and backwardness as well. The enslaved and exploited populations in such instances serve local tyrannical élites who claim to act "for the good of the people" or in the name of lofty but irrelevant principles; thus, ideological propaganda becomes the hand maiden of the most atrocious specimens of dictatorial government.

Most South-South tensions and conflicts seem not to be provoked by foreign intervention or economic motivations. Perceptions of tensions and conflicts frequently lie in the survival of primitive obsolete institutions such as tribalism, partriarchalism and slavery. Persistence of such institutions in the present-day world almost seem to invite neo-imperialist and neo-colonialist activities of the advanced developed countries, Western and Soviet alike. In his speech commemorating the hundredth anniversary of Rumanian independence, President Nicolae Ceausescu observed that internal conflicts of young African states only favored the interests of foreign interventionists.[34] The validity of this statement and the theory that lies behind it remain also to be confirmed or refuted by the research in the present inquiry.

Notes

1. *Le Monde*, 24 & 25 May 1977. Also, *Le Monde*, 7 & 8 Aug. 1977.

2. *Le Monde*, 5 May 1977. For the nature and magnitude of the Soviet threat to the Black Continent see, i.a., H. Bienen, "Perspectives on Soviet Intervention in Africa," *Political Science Quarterly*, Spring 1980, pp. 294—342, and on Africa as becoming a scene of a heated confrontation, also produced by the East-West rivalry see, i.a., K.L. Adelman, "African Security: Facts and Fantasy," *Comparative Strategy*, vol. 2, No. 1, 1980, pp. 974—3108.

3. The Declaration of Perez Guerrero, *Le Monde*, 3 May 1977.

4. E. Jouve, p. 17.

5. Its importance was discussed in more detail in my book (in Hebrew): *International Cooperation and International Organization*, 2d Edit. (Tel Aviv: Bronfman Publishers, 1967) p. 400.

6. Cfr. M. Salem, Vers un nouvel ordre économique international, *Journal du Droit International*, No. 4 (1975) p. 753 and ff.

7. Cf. J.S. Nye Jr., "Independence and Interdependence," *Foreign Policy*, No. 22 (Spring 1976), p. 143.

8. See f.i. P. Drouin, "Quelle securité économique mondiale?" *Le Monde*, May 5, 6 & 7, 1977.

9. See Karl Marx and Friedrich Engels, *Selected Correspondence*, (Moscow: Foreign Language Publishing House, 1953), pp. 489, 499, 500, 505.

10. Renouvin et Duroselle, pp. 86, 93, 153, 157, 168.

11. See D.P. Forsythe, "An Epidemic of Wars," *International Studies Notes of the ISA*, vol. 4, issue 3 (Fall 1977), p. 15.

12. T. C. Wiegele, *Progress in International Crisis Research*, idem. p17.

13. Forsythe,op. cit., p. 14.

14. See M. Mushkat, "The Small States and Research into Problems of International Security," *International Journal of Group Tensions*, No. 2, (1971); "The Economic, Political and Human Factors and the Reassessment of Underdevelopment," *Die Dritte Welt*, No. 3 (1973); and "Génèse et Avenir du Sous-développement," *Etudes Polemologiques*, No. 11 (1974); "Sous-Developpement en Afrique: une situation imposée par des élements exterieures?" *Africa*, vol XXX, No. 1, 1975, p. 39 and "Tiers-Monde et la Securite Internationale," *Etudes Internationales*, vol. IX, No. 4, 1978, p. 539.

15. H. Morgenthau, *Politics among Nations*, 4th Edit., (New York: Alfred A. Knopf, 1967) pp. 414—36.

16. See A. Zorgbibe, *L'occident, l'Est et le Sud, Report for the Council on Foreign Relations of New York*, Manuscript put at my disposal by the author, soon to be published by McGraw Hill.

17. Cf. P. Drouin in *Le Monde*, May 6, 1977.

18. Zorgbibe, loc. cit.

19. See P. Drouin, *Le Monde*, May 7, 1977.

20. See MacNamara's conclusions in his *Essence of Security*, (London, 1958); I. Ghandi's statement in 5 *U.N. Monthly Chronicle*, No. 21 (1960) 45. For references to President Carter's speech, see i.a. *Le Monde*, May 24 & 25, 1977.

21. L.A. Coser, *The Function of Social Conflict*, (1956); and R. Dahrendorf, Zu einer Theorie des sozialen Konfliktes, (1958); also see on this problem some conclusions of Tucker.

22. See *Le capital, Livre prémier*, (Paris:Editions La Pléiade), p. 1213.

23. See f.i. D. Senghaas, "Militarism Dynamics in the Contemporary Context of Periphery Capitalism," 1977, p. 103.

24. See f.i. J. Glatung, "Violence, Peace and Peace Research," *JPR* No. 6, 1964, p. 169.

25. See F. Barnaby, "Peace Research: The Whys and Wherefores," *265 Nature*. (Feb. 24, 1977).

26. W. Korey, "The U.N.: Swapping Individual Rights for Collective Rights," 101 *Washington Post*, No. 37 (Wed. 11 Jan. 1978), p. 23.

27. See J. Ki-Zebro in *Le Monde*, May 28, 1977.

28. Zorgbibe, loc. cit.

29. Cf. M. Virally, "Vers un droit international du développement," XI *Annuaire Francais du Droit International*, (1965), p. 3 ff.

30. Cf. P. Windsor, "The Savior from the Sea," *Foreign Policy*, No. 22 (Spring 1976), p. 171 ff.

31. G. Hoffman, "Brandt Commission Aims to Break Deadlock," GT No. 820 (Jan. 1, 1978), p. 6.

32. *Le Nouvel Observateur*, No. 640 (Feb. 144—320, 1977), p. 75.

33. Cf. A. Emmanuel, "Le societé's internationales et le développement inegal," XXVII *Revue International Sciences Sociales*, No. 4 (1976), p. 840.

34. *Le Monde*, 11 May 1977.

Chapter 1
The Third World—What is It?

1. Emergence and Evolution of the Third World

The international system shaped in the aftermath of World War II, particularly in the Cold War, was characterized by a division of the world into two camps opposed by political and economic viewpoints, ideologies and systems of government. One of them, led by the United States, was made up of countries with democratic, multi-party governments. Most of these countries, which include Japan, were located in the Atlantic and Pacific areas. The heartland of this bloc, however, was Western Europe and North America. The political and social institutions of these countries developed out of the bourgeois revolutions of the 18th and 19th centuries. Their social and political institutions were conceived as agencies for the promotion of individual human rights and equality before the law. The defeat of the fascist Tripartite Axis Powers in World War II and the subsequent onset of the Cold War, inspired their extension of institutions to promote individual human liberty.

At the same time, the victorious Allies concentrated on economic recovery, including such matters as higher living standards, technological development and expansion of production. While economic and technological improvement, quantitatively and qualitatively, was mainly based on individual initiative, public sectors of national economies played significant roles in the resultant expansion of social services. Collectively, that part of the world striving for postwar recovery and development mainly through private enterprise under democratic institutions became known as the "Western Bloc." Because of its achievements in technology, in science, in economics, in social welfare, in culture and in industry, the Western Bloc also became known as the bloc of industrialized nations, the world of "developed" countries, or simply the First World. Due to the emphasis on individual rights and and democratically elected representative government, this American-led bloc is also known as the Free World. In view of its military power, its dominant and vital role in the world economy and the continued dominating influence of the United States and former European colonial powers in territories outside of their frontiers even after decolonization—this bloc has been called by its opponent the "imperialist" or capitalist camp.

The Second World, headed by the Soviet Union, is made up of countries that are characterized by one-party authoritarian governments and planned economies run by public agencies. Both political and economic institutions are based on this model. Loyalty to the USSR is imposed by force on individuals, domestic nationality groups and formally sovereign states belonging to this bloc. The ideology supporting the necessity for such dependence may be classified as Socialist and totalitarian, since only the collective proletariat and its party are regarded as having any organic reality and as ruling the countries in the interest of the masses. Because of explicit Soviet Communist Party pretensions to that effect, based on the writings of Karl Marx and V. I. Lenin, the Soviet-led coalition is known as the "Socialist Bloc." In order to expedite economic and social development, private initiative has been almost entirely replaced by party and bureaucratic central planning in the authoritarian régimes. In spite of a growing pragmatism which here and there has produced more liberty in trade, as well as cooperation with capitalist countries in other fields and the adoption of aspirations of peaceful coexistence with them, this camp remained theoretically faithful to the idea of overthrowing bourgeois regimes in the Marxist-Leninist-Stalinist revolutionary tradition which, in practice, strives to promote worldwide Soviet hegemony. The Soviet-dominated alignment is called by its partisans the "socialist" or "anti-imperalist" camp, in spite of many clearly imperialistic undertakings by it over the years.

The process of decolonization that reached a high plateau at the end of the 1950s gave birth to a Third World in the contemporary international system.

In the beginning, the "Third World" group consisted mainly of new states that had been removed from colonial dependency since approximately 1956. The term most probably was coined by the Frenchman, Albert Sauvy. He used it in the Foreword of a work edited by G. Balandier that dealt mainly with underdevelopment.[1]

The relation of the term to the famous saying of Abbé Sieyès in 1789 with regard to the "third state" is clear. He defined it then as nothing and everything because it could develop into something in the future public order.[2] Although the group is still comprised to a large extent of postcolonial states located in the southern hemisphere, Asia, Africa and America, it no longer has any geographical, cultural or specific political connotations.

Poor European countries such as Greece, Portugal and Turkey have difficulties in joining Third World because they belong to NATO and are thus considered as pro-imperialist, capitalist nations. However, countries like once pro-Chinese Albania, non-aligned Socialist Yugoslavia or Rumania and Cuba formally belonging to the Soviet orbit, are sometimes considered Third World countries because of their economic situation. The potential superpower China and other non-European nations that have never been under colonial rule are also ascribed Third World status along with countries whose independence has been recently proclaimed and whose national image is not yet finally shaped.

If the diversity of location, government, time of emergence and the near completion of the present decolonization cycle is taken into account, it seems obvious that Third World status is more easily defined by reference to the economic situation of these countries than in terms of their political alignment and geographical location, ideological orientation or governmental structures.

The economic terms of reference explain not only the enlargement of Third World ranks, but also the inclusion of states that may never have been under colonial status but which aspire to rid themselves of underdevelopment. Such Third World countries clearly lag far behind First and Second World countries in their economic growth and viability.

Even Italy, far from being "rich," had, according to some 1977 statistics, a gross national product equal to that of all members of the Organization of African Unity combined, France twice as great and the German Federal Republic three times as great as that of all African countries.[3] Underdevelopment as the basic common feature of all "Third World" countries does not mean that these societies are by any means homogeneous and undivided into rich and poor states and classes, into exploiters and exploited. Furthermore, their rich people are relatively richer, and the poor are relatively poorer in these countries.[4] Another specific characteristic of the Third World is that the bulk of the population suffers from malnutrition and a high death rate. Populations of Third World countries are mainly employed in agriculture at a very primitive level, while industrial capital equipment and production tend to be extremely limited and illiteracy extremely high. Such economic poverty and backwardness in the Third World varies very little from country to country, regardless of wealth or deficiencies in natural resources.

Even Third World countries with abundant natural resources suffered until recent times from backwardness and stagnation as well as economic and political dependence, a situation which is in a process of metamorphosis following the radical change in terms of raw material supplies, particularly of oil prices.

It thus seems correct to conclude that economic underdevelopment is the most salient characteristic of all Third World countries. Third World countries actively participating in various international organizations and conferences on underdevelopment, as well as others seeking special treatment to expedite economic development, support demands to change the *ancien regime* in the world economy. They press for abolition of international trade and commercial practices based on principles of profit and unlimited free competition that leads to domination of one country by another.

Adoption of economic-developmental criterion for definition of the Third World seem to facilitate understanding of why colonialism or the length of time since the establishment of political sovereignty or the beginning of decolonization no longer play a role in establishing Third World solidarity. Such criteria for definition of the Third World may explain further why economic development and underdevelopment determined chiefly by the processes of capital accumulation, investment, productivity, labor skills and sometimes exploitation of foreign territory, may be present regardless of the dependent or sovereign status of a country or the extent of its financial power.

It may also be worth noting in this connection that even temporary monopolistic or quasimonopolistic control of raw materials—mainly oil—resulted in an unprecedented historical divorce of military power from economics.[5] The times when states at the top of the hierarchy of military power controlled world affairs belong to the past. Conventional wisdom regarding the role of territorial expansion has already been complicated and diminished by the industrial revolution. Nuclear weapons as well as nuclear power as an alternative source of military might and of energy generally has proven to be astronomically expensive and risky. The constructive use of nuclear power seems to be restricted for the time being to a limited number of extraordinary circumstances. The complimentary relationship between control of energy and the strength of arms has been drastically reduced, because the impact of releasing nuclear weapons can neither be controlled nor accurately predicted.

This in no way implies that military power has become obsolete. Yet weaponry remains in its ultimate form more an instrument of deterrence than a means of mass destruction. Applications of nuclear weaponry in the latter sense appears to be undergoing a process of erosion in the democratic countries because of public opinion. Widespread public fear has been expressed in the West both with respect to the political and economic consequences of using nuclear power and the risk of war escalating from the use even of conventional sophisticated weapons.

The United States remains the most powerful state in all fields, but without hegemonic capacity, as is proven by the American reaction to the seizure of the US Embassy in Teheran.

Power is really the possibility to assert interest effectively, or more simply to make others do what one wants them to. From this point of view, American power nowadays is diminishing, and not only because of the existence of another, though less mighty nuclear leviathan. The USSR is an economically disadvantaged country. It is technologically deficient. It has half the gross national product of the US. It does not produce either the industrial goods or the civilian technology that the rest of the world wants, so they are obliged to rely for supply on the Americans and their allies. The Union is bureaucratically sclerotic. Its government and alliances are incessantly threatened by societies, which are like a boiling volcano, following the suppression of national freedoms and human rights. However, because of its nuclear armament it can oppose the United States and its alliances. Even less productive countries than the Soviet Union, and far from being nuclear, are able to act similarly with a growing degree of success, frequently as a result of the deepening economic interdependence of all nations, which confronts all of them with the risk of suffering more, the more others suffer and revolt, and depressing their chances of prosperity and no longer merely their prospects of tranquility.

The impact of undeveloped oil-producing countries appears to be rising, in spite of their relatively weak military postures and the fact that their oil-power will not last indefinitely because of the gradual depletion of the material basis for the exercise of this means of influence and might, and the intensified search of oil-consumers for alternative sources of energy.

On one hand financial accumulation in the Third World is not necessarily an index of real economic growth and thus of the political and of military vulnerability of industrialized economies. Frequently, it is only a sign that importation of raw materials by the latter is cheaper and more beneficial than full exploitation of their own domestic resources. On the other hand, financial might, such as that of the oil producers, does not necessarily increase the prospect of industrialization, though it does permit for the time being expansion of financial and political influence. Even the acquisition in consequence of the new sources of income of sophisticated technology and knowhow does not guarantee automatic entry into the club of strong military and industrialized nations, which are still strong enough to preclude the use of this technology in any way dangerous to them.

Only development rooted in real capital accumulation and other factors of production remain catalysts of economic and social transformation. However, true economic development occurs not only through augmented production and enrichment of some states, but also by a decreasing preoccupation with painful matters of human and social health,[6] in this way, too, paving the way to both political influence and military strength.

In the past, Portugal was a great world power. It returned to the path of development only a few years ago after discarding its obsolete socio-economic political structure, and dissolving its former colonial overseas empire.

Spain entered a new era of industrialization quite recently, as did Brazil, which had been independent for over a century but whose economy was hampered by chronic authoritarian government. The present superpower, the United States, threw off colonial subordination in the 18th century, but only succeeded to world-power status after 100 years of independence. The U.S.A.'s archrival, the Soviet Union, only developed within the territories of the former Tsarist Russian Empire at the end of World War II after more than two generations of accumulation and investment through forced labor, a ruthless system of repression of individuals and groups, and foreign aid. Its power lies primarily in the military domain.

Basically two systems of national government can be discerned in the sovereign states that make up the international political community today. The first is the authoritarian type of government, including both the so-called Socialist and non-Socialist forms of dictatorship. The second is the democratic form of government, which extol the individual's freedom of choice and inborn rights, respect for the rule of law and equality under it, and unobstructed spontaneous cultural development. The international system itself is only to some extent democratic insofar as sovereign states are free to determine their own vital national interests, but unfortunately also free to take action in terms of such interests as they see fit, and to assume responsibility for all acts of state, only when they fear retaliation or are obliged to do so. Within such a framework of domestic and international government, it seems reasonable and practical from the socio-economic point of view to divide the international system into the three distinct "worlds" of the present inquiry.

A few years ago this conceptual division of the world was questioned by the Albanian Communist Party in its analysis of the Chinese Communist approach. It accordingly adopted the Stalinist concept of two absolutely opposed world camps: the revolutionary one on the one hand composed of Socialist countries allied with "progressive" movements in the rest of the world, unalterably opposed by the "imperialist" one consisting of the Western democracies in alliance with reactionary and treacherous socialist elements everywhere.[7]

Needless to say, the Soviets are consigned in the Chinese-Albanian consensus to the enemy reactionary camp under the heading of "Social imperialists"; the Chinese and their former Albanian supporters correctly noted similarities of Soviet and American policies and points of convergence between the Western and Eastern blocs. Such policy parallels and convergences were represented by struggles for economic growth, to a certain extent also for peaceful coexistence, above all of the super-powers, for greater access to the world's raw materials and markets, for military supremacy, and for other political and economic benefits. However, even some convincing Chinese points which recognized not only this convergence but also the peculiarity of the Third World and of the Albanian thesis on the division of the world in two camps, were grossly undermined by dogmatism of their presentation.

Moreover, it is necessary to take into account in any analysis of the world arena, that struggles of nations and classes for more freedom also continue within the Soviet sphere of influence and that some anti-détente anti-Third World and even racist tendencies persist in the West, mostly sustained by continued fear of Soviet aggression and the worsening economic situation resulting from the rise of oil prices, growing inflation, unemployment and the issue of migrant workers.

However, tensions in the Soviet bloc and ideological propaganda inspiring the mentioned fear in the First World seem less significant in the shape of the international situation than superpower competition, to a larger extent determined by new forms of Soviet aspirations, sometimes, no doubt, reflecting imperialistic tendencies. By and large, beginning in 1975, the impact of the inter-bloc competition on Third World policies and of ideological issues began to decline somewhat, while local concerns strengthened. In Latin America and elsewhere in the Third World, good relations with all kinds of investors consequently became an important preoccupation of public affairs.[8] This is reminiscent of the radical shift away from ultra-revolutionary zeal of the Soviets only a few years after the October Revolution, when they urgently sought developmental aid from the capitalist countries which they tried previously to revolutionize and whose imminent overthrow was ordained by Party dogma. A similar tactical shift to pragmatism occured in post-Maoist China because of Peking's urgent needs for military expansion and modernization and for allies against Soviet threats.

What this illustrates is the interaction and interconnection of political and economic problems with respect to the three distinct "worlds" composed of groups of national states, so different in many respects. Countries of the Third World differ from those of the other two chiefly in the socio-economic conditions of their recently acquired independence.

The decolonization process, which helped to bring about the sovereignty of underdeveloped dependencies, replaced political and institutional forms of colonial subordination with economic and cultural ties.[9] Such limited decolonization was but a first step to complete independence, which includes economic and cultural independence as well.

Historically, the beginning of the decolonization process is tied to the achievements of the Philadelphia Congress of 1774. The representatives of the 13 North American British colonies opened the way to the political independence of what subsequently became the United States. Under the impact of the French Revolution and Napoleon's victories in Spain and elsewhere, the decolonization process expanded, especially in Latin America, sowing seeds of independence in other dependent territories as well. The Monroe Doctrine enunciated by the American President in 1823 contributed to the failure of the Holy Alliance to reconstruct European rule in Latin America, and at the same time expedited US expansionism.

The beginning of anticolonial solidarity for the liberation of nonwhites was linked with the 1893 Congress of Columbia, which was held at the same time as the world exhibition in Chicago. Representatives of all religions participated, including Christians, Jews, Buddhists, African Churches and others. For the first time in history, the Congress called for the end of European rule overseas. The Congress also asserted that it was the duty of European powers to help nations on other continents to put an end to their misery. Stressing the importance of preserving peace in this way, the appeal of the Congress gained momentum. Ultimately, it played a great role in shaping actions taken at the end of World War II to speed the decay of colonialism and subsequently the emergence of the Third World. The appeal had already been supported before World War I in the conventions of the Socialist Internationals, and by peace and anti-racist movements. It became much stronger in the period between the world wars, of course, and especially after World War II. As early as 1928, the Congress of Representatives of All Religions in Brussels discussed demands to end colonialism and to speed up development; but only after the establishment of the United Nations could such demands be implemented under that organization's Charter.

The call for European assistance to former colonies and the need to organize for this purpose came about at a 1964 meeting in New Delhi when 25 representatives of people liberated from colonial rule, as well as observers from Arab countries and the Hebrew University in Jerusalem came together. The main speaker was Jawaharal Nehru, who asked that everything necessary to be done to close ranks of those who were divided in the past. He also stressed that unity was vitally essential to solve immense social problems and to assure development. Nehru also pointed out the necessity for peaceful cooperation between all nations and non-alignment of colonial and post-colonial peoples with the Western and Soviet blocs, a point he had stressed in previous years.

Cooperation in this area began in consultations which were initiated in the first days of the United Nations by the Egyptian Representative, Dr. M. Fawzi, and the Indian Representative, B. Rao. Both of them gained a large following—the first among the Arab delegations and the second among the Asians. This allowed them to speak on behalf of their respective continents and regions so as to elicit a positive response from their fellow African and Asian delegates. These consultations became a larger and more systematic forum in 1950, when the Cold War sharpened and the danger of escalation of the Korean War into a great power conflict seemed probable. The post-colonial states, which a few years later shaped the Third World, thought that they had to do everything possible to avoid a clash between the superpowers that might endanger their newly formed independence. Action along these lines was begun and became stronger following the different conferences of Asian and African peoples. The 1954 Colombo Conference of India, Indonesia, Burma, Ceylon and Pakistan discussed the possibility of hastening the end of the war in Southeast Asia and the methods necessary for increasing cooperation between Asians and Africans.

In December 1954, during a gathering in Burma, Nehru proposed acceptance of five principles of peaceful coexistence for all postcolonial countries. These principles became a starting point of the 29 April 1954 agreement between India and China relating to Tibet and trade. The parties committed themselves to (a) mutual respect for their territorial integrity and sovereignty; (b) non-interference in each other's domestic affairs; (c) mutual nonaggression; (d) equality of rights for common benefit; and (e) peaceful coexistence. Acceptance of the aforementioned principles facilitated the Peoples Republic of China's (PRC) ultimate adherence to the Third World. The Chinese were particularly interested in this prospect because of their fear of the American and Soviet alliances, especially those extending to Asia and the Pacific.

The New Delhi Conference in the beginning of April 1955 was a demonstration of the fears of all post-colonial Asian and African countries which contributed to their growing solidarity and to the convening of the Bandung Conference on 25 April. The Five Principles of Coexistence formulated by Nehru were reiterated in the 10 Principles for a peace policy, for national freedom, and for nonalignment. During the conference, anticolonial sentiments voiced were extremely strong, but not in connection with anti-Western demonstrations. On the one hand, the Soviet Union and Asian Soviet Republics of the USSR and Israel on the other were prevented from participation so as to satisfy both anti-Soviet delegations and the Arabs. Consequently, the principle of nonalignment became the moving force and catalyst of the Third World. Nonalignment became especially important following the Franco-Algerian War, the 1956 Egyptian nationalization of the Suez Canal, and the subsequent Anglo-French invasion of Egypt.

However, closer cooperation of the Third World countries, could not be achieved because of political and other differences. The Arabs, for example, especially Egypt, asked that priority be given to anti-Israeli measures. They ignored the position of the Africans interested in collaboration with industrialized countries and with Israel as well, in order to facilitate economic developments. While Gamal Abdel Nasser claimed leadership on the African continent generally, the Arabs actually were opposed to Pan-Africanism, which was quite strong not only in Ghana during the time of Kwame Nkruma, but in other countries as well. By reason of geography alone, Pan-Africanism patently conflicted with Pan-Arabism. Other Third World frictions arose because of conflicts between Nkruma and Achmed Sukarno of Indonesia. In the mid-1960s, the PRC also strove to create its own regional or even worldwide alliances only with "progressive" revolutionary regimes as opposed to associations with "reactionaries." As a result, some one-time British and French colonies in Africa that were interested in cooperation with their former European metropolies became victims of subversion. This precluded convening of a second Bandung Conference whose advocates and sponsors only managed to hold a nongovernmental meeting in Cairo in 1956.

The PRC at this time was obliged to give up a part of its influence, especially after Moscow's commitment to build the Aswan Dam, to supply arms to Egypt and other Arab countries, and otherwise to support them in their struggles against Israel. This development seriously weakened nonalignment policy, in spite of the fact that at the July 1956 Brioni meeting, Nehru, Nasser and Tito reaffirmed the need for "positive neutralism," as nonalignment came to be called. By 1960, twenty new African states had joined the United Nations, and they were less interested in nonalignment than in developmental assistance.

The 1960 Congo civil war, Ben Bella's removal by the new Algerian President Hourani Boumediénne in 1962, and the Chinese attack on India showed Third World solidarity to be a fiction. Some of the countries were fighting each other and looked for support from the great powers. On the other hand, withdrawal of Soviet nuclear bases from Cuba confirmed that it was more important for Moscow to improve relations with the United States than to remain faithful to Third World commitments, even with regard to its countries of socialist orientation.

The Soviet posture at the time foreshadowed détente-a tendency which became stronger with the signing of the 20 June 1963 Agreement establishing direct communications between the United States and the Soviet Union, the 5 August 1963 limited Nuclear Test Ban Treaty, and the 3 September 1971 arrangement that finally led to the four-power agreement on the status of Berlin.

The Organization for African Unity established in 1963 and other African international agencies and conferences were faced with very acute internal problems.[10] The solution of these problems was much more important to those countries than taking a clear stand regarding the superpowers. Their involvement in decolonization problems and containing racism in Africa increased; moreover, they became engrossed in civil wars in the Congo and Nigeria as well. They were especially absorbed in the task of trying to obtain greater development aid and in improving their own deplorable domestic situations, these problems and not nonalignment determined their political cooperation and organizations.[11]

In Asia too, attention was concentrated on problems other than nonalignment, such as those relating to the Vietnam War and its consequences when it ended in 1975, and to the 1971 Indian-Pakistan War that gave rise to an independent Bangladesh and brought India closer to the USSR. Other concerns resulted from India's acquisition of a nuclear capacity, Indira Ghandi's coup establishing emergency dictatorship, the end of her premiership and a more pro-western tendency in the politics of this country, even when she returned to power in 1980. All these became matters of greater importance in Third World policies as did Soviet intervention in Angola in 1975 and in Afghanistan in 1980. These and other events in Africa and Asia and the role of Cuba as host of the nonalignment summit in 1979 and as its formal leader since then, resulted in ending the image of the Third World as a nonaligned and monolithic bloc. Following the 1973 energy crisis, the poorest of the Third World countries striving for development and modernization were harmed by rising oil prices in addition to their other painful problems. However, political differentiation itself did not prevent forms of common action and closer cooperation. Tendencies sown at Bandung became stronger with the growing wealth of the oil producing countries and their impact on policies of the different world blocs. Expanded influence of the oil producers in fact raised the hope of even greater solidarity and mutual aid. Above all, it served to press the First World to give more effective assistance. This, of course, facilitated Third World enlargement and unity for handling certain problems common to all less developed countries, rich and poor alike.

The first steps toward enlargement of Third World ranks were tied to the 1966 Three Continental Conference in Havana. Although organized on a nongovernmental basis, there proved to be extensive common interests not only among the various Asian, African and South American organizations and movements but governments as well. The majority of the Latin Americans were as shocked by the recent American intervention in San Domingo as they were to be much later in 1975 by the bloody violent overthrow of Marxist President Salvador Allende in Chile. The conferences gravely noted other signs of weakness and danger to the underdeveloped countries following the intervention of the superpowers in their internal affairs.

Regarding the PRC, the country claiming leadership of the Third World but obliged to give it up to the Soviet satellite Cuba, it had already become clear earlier that its path of development was unattractive to other less developed countries. It was also apparent that China was too weak to help increase Third World pressures on the First and Second Worlds. Since it was too big to be accepted as a member of the group of 77,[12] the fairly important role played by it in 1964-65 had actually since then contracted. China remained in fact outside any broad group and still quite insignificant in the international arena, despite the normalization of the Sino-American relations since 1977. This put an end to the illusions of those Third World countries which relied on this potential superpower.

In any case, with China and without her, with diplomatic and rhetoric Soviet support and without it, the Third World was for many years evidently unable to exert efficient pressure on the industrialized countries of any type. On occasion it became apparent that the First and Second

Worlds even began to disregard Third World interests as they became increasingly absorbed by their own immediate problems or their mutual relationships.

The First and Second Worlds continued support of the Third World but on a restricted basis. Not only leninist Cuba was, as already mentioned, supported by the Soviet Union only to a limited degree. The same was true with respect to Soviet and PRC support of North Vietnam, as well as American backing of South Vietnam and other Southeast Asian countries, and the Soviet backing of the Vietnamese invasion in Cambodia.

Many of these countries were abandoned before the Soviet occupation of Afghanistan, when the Soviets and Americans decided to turn from passive peaceful coexistence to more active cooperation under the banner of détente. The Peoples' Republic of China also preferred closer ties with the US in order not to remain isolated in the event of a clash with the USSR. All these developments increased the awareness of Third World countries that it might be worthwhile to deal less with political global problems and more with economic issues that would facilitate Third World solidarity and thus support from all quarters. Third World countries became increasingly aware of the prospects gaining support from all quarters for the essentially human aspects of decolonization, antiracism and economic underdevelopment.

To deal with some of these humanitarian issues successfully, it was necessary to concentrate on problems that could be resolved in different international agencies with the support of both Socialist and some Western countries as well. The first steps toward action in this direction were undertaken following Nehru's 1961 proposal that resulted in the 1965 proclamation of an International Cooperation Year and the First Development Decade scheduled to begin the following year. Different United Nations General Assembly resolutions on decolonization, sovereignty over natural resources, principles of international cooperation, promotion of progress and economic development, and preparation of a second and third development decade proved in spite of failures and disappointments to be to some extent effective. The same was true of the General Assembly's creation of committees, commissions and special agencies to deal with various aspects of developmental aid. Political issues, on the other hand, proved to be decisive. Debate on world food and demographic problems relating to industrial development, as well as training and research which were undertaken by old and new UN specialized agencies contributed to easing political tensions. Détente in this regard tended to improve the climate for concentration on important social and economic problems, first and foremost of the Third World. Also, it produced a wider understanding of Third World needs especially because the less developed countries gained majorities in most international organizations; thus it became impossible to ignore their claims. The preponderance of Third World participation in these bodies brought their issues to the top of international conference agendas.

In the 1950s, common interest of the postcolonial states in weakening the Cold War was facilitated by closing Third World ranks through nonalignment. On the other hand, Third World solidarity was vitiated by political discord, internal conflict, and gravitation to opposing blocs. As impotence and loss of influence began to increase from these causes, attention reverted to concentration on nonalignment. The new united front in the beginning reflected the common needs and interests of all poor nations, which were mainly agricultural and industrially underdeveloped. Most of them were concentrated in the Southern Hemisphere. The countries from which they sought assistance and trade were for the most part the rich industrialized nations of the Northern Hemisphere with predominantly white populations.

However, geographical and racial divisions soon lost their importance as controversies arose regarding standards of living and prosperity. Such issues were not affected by the location or origin of the population, but rather by their social and economic structures. This was one more reason why the Third World could enlarge its ranks to encompass both aligned and nonaligned underdeveloped countries of Asia, Africa and Latin America, and even some European and Socialist nations as well. Identification of the Third World countries sometimes based on proletarian or plebian solidarity actually stemmed less from Mao Tse-Tung's terminology than from economic realities.

Poverty, social and economic backwardness, and the need to combat these conditions became the common cause of a large group of nations. They pressed for solution of their problems through a wide variety of governmental and non-governmental international agencies. The latter were called on to deal with issues of disease, hunger, overpopulation, underdevelopment and a host of other social and economic issues. This was the result of the Third World demands for social change and betterment that frequently were not remote, at least theoretically, from Marxist principles of class struggle.

The aforementioned issues were discussed in the United Nations and its specialized agencies and conferences, especially in the United Nations Conference on Trade and Development (UNCTAD). These debates were a starting point for changing the image of the Third World into an association of developing countries. This terminology was used not only to avoid offense to underdeveloped countries, but also to facilitate enlargement of Third World ranks so as to encompass nations at different levels of development; thus, they sought to take into consideration the economic needs of all economically and, above all, industrially less developed countries.

The first UNCTAD meeting was held in Geneva in the spring of 1964. It aimed to continue and strengthen efforts for social and economic improvement also through increased trade, establishment of tariffs favorable to Third World products, and agreement to stop falling raw material prices.

In order to promote the realization of this program, the Group of 77 was established, which included African, Asian and South American countries. At the end of 1977 this group numbered 116 countries, an absolute majority both in the United Nations and in other parliamentary bodies of international organizations and conferences. The Group of 77 remains as always heterogeneous because of its members' differences in level of development, in social and economic structure, in political orientation, and, of course, in population and territorial expanse. All of them, including the newly wealthy oil producers, on the one hand, and poor countries without valuable natural resources, on the other, share common interests, and they close ranks with respect to their claims for assistance from the First and Second Worlds.

In 1968, the second UNCTAD Conference provided an excellent opportunity to demonstrate Third World solidarity after having reached a consensus at a 1967 meeting of the enlarged Group of 77 in Algiers. The charter adopted in Algiers attacked the paucity of assistance from industrialized countries. It sought an increase of up to three percent of the military budgets of the industrialized countries and formulated demands regarding Third World countries' customs tariffs and other trade privileges to improve their position in world markets. The Algiers Charter strongly criticized the prevailing trade conditions and development aid abuses that were becoming instruments of exploitation and pillage; it asked for modification of the conditions of economic cooperation so as to favor developing countries.

However, measures taken at the second UNCTAD Conference were of little help to the less developed countries because of the deepening financial crisis and shocks to the world monetary system that prevented the industrialized countries from putting larger sums at the disposal of the Third World. Consequently, awareness grew in the Third World that it could not rely on the good will of their industrialized donors. Now the Third World countries became aware that they had to redouble pressure on their First and Second World benefactors but to rely more on themselves, first and foremost with regard to political issues. This view became quite evident at the 1970 Lusaka Non-alignment Conference, which concentrated particularly on different aspects of the anticolonialist struggle, of racism and apartheid, and on support of all liberation movements.

During internal discussions of the Group of 77 on preparations for the third UNCTAD Conference in Santiago a year later, attacks against the West and imperialism became even stronger because of growing Third World dissatisfaction with both existing bilateral and multilateral assistance programs.

Not only were results of such aid programs ineffective, but they served to enhance stalemates, indebtedness and dependency of Third World countries on the industrialized ones. Finally, the latter agreed, that they would have to reconsider their positions so as to make their aid more effective. However, piecemeal efforts with respect to different commodities and between different exporters and importers could not contribute much to improvement.

A new consultative body was established by the International Monetary Fund with half of its representation given to the Third World. The new body passed resolutions on the use of special drawing rights, which were mainly for development purposes, but resolutions alone would not improve Third World conditions exacerbated by mounting debts at a rate of 14 percent annually.[13] The total public debt of the Third World countries increased from $51 billion to $119 billion from 1967 to 1973, even more than 15 percent yearly, compared with their annual GNP growth of 5.9 percent.[14]

No steps were taken, however, to put the new proposals for solving the debt issue into effect. Lenders were asked to negotiate with each debtor individually regarding all terms of trade problems. It was decided that these new arrangements would be undertaken through the General Agreement on Tariffs and Trade (GATT) in 1973. The Santiago Conference disclosed not only the selfishness of the industrialized countries, but that of the rich developing countries as well, since they used their oil profits from the Organization of Petroleum Exporting Countries (OPEC) exclusively for their own purposes.

Nevertheless, the poor countries of the Third World decided to continue their alliances with their rich "brothers" on the assumption that they would become more generous and effective in their help. They really had no choice and rightly believed that only by Third World solidarity was it possible to exert sufficient pressure on the First World and perhaps also to influence the Second World in their favor. These Third World tendencies became pronounced during the 1973 Nonaligned Algiers Summit Conference that dealt mainly with means of curtailing dependence on industrialized countries. The same issue highlighted debates at the summer 1976 Colombo Summit Conference despite Yugoslav pressure to stress nonalignment. Finally, the fourth UNCTAD Conference held a few weeks later in Nairobi pressed for continuation of Third World solidarity in spite of proliferating stratification of these countries that followed the emergence of rich oil-producing countries under the aegis of the "underdeveloped" bloc. Yet only through their solidarity and concerted action could Third World countries expect to make progress and to secure effective aid.

It may be worth stressing that in Nairobi the Third World countries openly decided to criticize the Second World for the first time.[15] In doing so, they emphasized the fact that aid from Communist countries in 1975 was diminished by $ 300 million and hardly reached 0.16 percent of their national incomes, while the German Federal Republic (West Germany) alone gave 0.4 percent and some other Western countries 0.7 percent. The unaffluent Third World countries failed to attack the rich oil-producing countries at Nairobi even though the Arab countries until 1974 received much more money from the United Nations than they gave. The oil producers actually concentries, theie assistance on "fraternal" countries, mostly in the form of military aid; above all, they supported Egypt, Syria and Jordan while refusing proper compensation to poor African countries to cover drastic oil price increases.

In 1975, the total assistance of oil-producing countries to less prosperous "brothers" diminished compared with 1974, as did their balance of payments generally. Correspondingly deficits of debtor states increased, rising from $ 11.3 billion in 1973 to $43 billion in 1975.[16]

It is worth noting that when OPEC raised crude petroleum prices in 1973, prices of many other raw materials plunged downward. This drastically reduced export earnings of non-oil producing countries, above all, those in the Third World. The Arab leaders asked their customers to accept the hardship as the beginning of a new economic order that would bring them future benefits.[17] Even the countries most strongly affected by these oil price measures (the socalled "MSACs") acquainted so as not to impair their solidarity with their rich "brothers." This was not pure irrationality, since it bolstered their hopes for better treatment; moreover, it was indicative of their awareness of true common interests, at least for the time being. They assumed that it ultimately would prevent making them a scapegoat of an eventual alliance of all rich countries regardless of race or level of development.[18]

Common interests have lately come to the fore in discussions at international conferences on demographical and food problems. To a certain extent, common interests were also ventilated at the Diplomatic Conference on the Development of International Humanitarian Law and at the Conference of New Sea Law. The importance of a united Third World became particularly apparent during the two 1974 UN General Assembly special sessions, which produced among other thing resolutions on the New International Economic Order and the Charter on Economic Rights and Duties of States.

Actually the production of these documents was more a formality than a substantive accomplishment. In addition, it contributed to a harmful confrontation in the North-South relationship. Nevertheless, tension began to be reduced during the following UN General Assembly session and with the opening of the North-South dialogue on December 16, 1975. This indicated that all parties were willing to come to an understanding, although pressure on the West continued and had a great success at UNCTAD IV in the spring of 1976. Again, this appeared as a formality for the time being. Tangible progress began with the realization that it would not be easy to pressure the West into action by one-sided resolutions. However, the Third World became aware, that it might be worthwhile to cooperate with the West both in order to pressure the East, and also in order to strengthen its readiness to compromise and to formulate concrete, more realistic and effective aid programs than in the past, as had already occurred, for instance, with the West German developmental aid program.[19]

The changed attitudes of all parties may be attributed to many causes. One of them is the belief of Third World countries that what OPEC could do with oil also could be done by other Third World producers of raw materials. Intra-Third World solidarity was all the more essential because OPEC's power was not expected to be diminished soon.

It is apparent today that new energy sources will not be put into full operation before the next decade or even later, and neither Alaskan nor North Sea oil is the remedy for tomorrow.

However, the Third World, in its hopes of using the oil weapon and other raw materials in its favor, has not taken into consideration many important factors. It is worthwhile to note that the world's resources and to some extent, oil, too, are far from being at the command of the developing countries. Actually, they are controlled by the great powers. The Western malaise with regard to oil supply, accounts not in a small degree for the passivity with which it has reacted to the LDC's challenge in the belief, after all, justified, that the challenge is not as menacing as it is frequently described: first of all, because raw materials do not represent an imnipotent lever; secondly, because the developed countries still keep most of the economic trump cards, not to mention the military one. If petroleum was effectively utilized as an economic weapon, this would provoke a military reprisal if it proved too successful.[20]

On the other hand, the fact of nuclear weapons limits the possibility of industrialized nations using force; rather, preference is given to peaceful interbloc competition, including steps for further gratification of even the poorest countries. The latter, being so numerous, carry considerable weight in international organizations. This also has to be taken into account in considering influence in various parts of the globe.

This is the reason for the growing awareness that Third World countries require supplementation of their sovereignty with economic substance on the basis of more genuine partnership. Western global approaches make no sense in the Third World. The problem of fighting economic disparities was the main theme of the North-South dialogue, suspended rather than finally interrupted and no less difficult than the debate on other important world issues. Not only are the East-West disarmament negotiations relevant to human survival frozen for the time being, but they are sometimes even counterproductive. The great powers continue to build up their arsenals. They escalate both military expenditures and the proliferation of weapons and the same holds true for nuclear technology. These vertical and horizontal dimensions of the arms race did not, however, end hopes of reviving some elements of détente even after the Soviet occupation of Afghanistan and thus did not eliminate the prospects of finding a solution likely to promote beginnings in arms reduction and control and the increase in development assistance.

Misery and frustration in the Third World today are to a great extent attributable to the results of the arms race but also to the greed of oil producers, who have hiked prices radically, frequently without proper economic justification and without considering the conse quences for themselves and their partners. Since there are no solutions to the perils of the arms race other than voluntary agreement to revive and strengthen détente and promote disarmament, there is likewise no solution to painful conditions in extensive parts of the Third World, other than the use of armaments money for developmental purposes and radical changes in the terms of trade, developmental aid and in the ways of using it by the recipients. Nor are there any alternatives to the abuses of the oil producers other than drastic reform of the present economic and monetary systems and more extensive search for new energy sources.

Third World solidarity is considered by the majority of this bloc as a *conditio sine qua non* for the realization of the first aims of economic and political advancement in this way and of Soviet and, even more so, Western supplementation of the required aid. It also serves as an instrument of pressure for the progress of the latter purposes. Therefore, solidarity continues in spite of internal and external, and frequently deepening, contradictions, whereby humiliation and injury are endured by Third World countries as the result of the enrichment of others. Solidarity even gains momentum due to the unprecedented achievements of OPEC. Its success, as already mentioned, raises the confidence of poor partners that they, too, ultimately will be favored. The poor Third World countries realize that it is because of them that many resolutions are passed by the United Nations and other international organizations and conferences, changing the image and role of the Third World on the international scene, and that this cannot be ignored too long. As late as 1973, renowned experts in the West who noted the weakness and transient prospects for growth in the Third World despaired of the bloc's ability to become an important factor in the world arena.[21]

The views of the Communists were not much different. During a roundtable of Socialist and Communist representatives in April 1975 in Belgrade, the Yugoslavs claimed that there was no basis for the existence of a Third World bloc distinguishable from the capitalist and Socialist blocs. They argued that cooperation among the less developed countries is determined only by the decision to eliminate backwardness, whereby each country tries to solve its own problems in its own way. The Yugoslavs claimed that the only important link among such countries is nonalignment. However, the Polish delegate dissented with the observation that there was no reason to deny the particularity of the Third World while maintaining special ties with Socialist countries like Yugoslavia and Rumania, as well as with other Marxist countries. (The latter reference to Marxist states was probably intended to include the PRCs). The Soviet delegate confined himself to pinpointing the rôle of the Third World as a partner in the struggle for peaceful coexistence.[22]

While the Soviet view was the outcome of perceiving the Third World as a partner in the front against "imperialist warmongers," the Yugoslav definition was reminiscent of the illusions of neutralism. Both views were dissipated quickly by the reality of a militarily nuclear bipolar but politically multipolar world. The stress of the genuine representatives of the developing countries was always on economic problems and on the task of closing the gap between themselves and the industrialized nations.

Members of OPEC held many trumps for reaching these aims. Using the criterion of only per capita national income, some OPEC members already had surpassed the most highly developed nations. However, their entrance into the arms race determined above all by South-South conflicts and OPEC arms suppliers' lust for petrodollars may hinder their effective progress. In principle, they are also interested in rebuilding the international economic order. OPEC with its Arab majority is aware of the West European and even American pressure on Israel, of the admission of the Palestine Liberation Organization (PLO) to observer status in the United Nations, and of various anti-Israeli resolutions that only could be passed through joint Third World action. Third World solidarity was no less necessary for the isolation of Israel than for the 1974 ousting of the South African delegation from the UN General Assembly. The wealthier and poorer Third World countries alike therefore were bound to maintain their solidarity and to give priority to economic issues, the main cement that binds politically diversified ranks.

Ironically, the aforementioned Yugoslav and Soviet denials of the Third World's specific features of disunity and unity disregarded its economic underdevelopment basis; the latter brought together pro- and anti-Soviet countries like Iran, Saudi Arabia, Pakistan, Indonesia and the majority of African and Latin American states, but some pro-Chinese countries and the formally nonaligned countries like Egypt and India as well. The Soviet views on the Third World role in the struggle for peace, against the West or true nonalignment were more expression of wishful thinking than of reality.

It is unnecessary to stress that the common economic basis and the unity of ranks in the efforts of Third World countries to improve their economic situation and to impose for this purpose commitments on the First and Second Worlds bore fruit.

Consider the efforts finally resulting in the program of the New Economic World Order, the Charter of Economic Rights and Duties of States, and UNCTAD IV's postulates! Consider the 28 February 1975 replacement of the Yaoundé Convention by the more beneficial (for the least developed countries) Lomé Convention of the European Community with 46 developing countries from all continents and its recent reelaboration and extension. Consider the changes that occurred in the Third World's favor in the World Bank, in the International Monetary Fund, in the GATT, and in other international economic agencies and in the UN itself following the Brandt Report of 1980. It seems therefore quite correct today to view the Third World above all as an instrument for reconstructing the international division of labor and shaping anew the international economic system. The prevalent thesis is that the Third World still consists as a loose cooperative framework of politically diversified states, that are above all the postcolonial, economically backward and underdeveloped, but all of which are vitally interested in bringing an end to their impoverishment and to their lingering vestiges of colonialism and imperialism.

It may be noted in passing that many analysts of imperialism have seriously complicated the understanding of the functioning mechanism in the Third World. They have contributed to an almost complete disregard of indigenous causes of underdevelopment and of the intra-Third World (South-South) conflicts, which were also important hindrances to progress. The negative impact of such enitrely internal factors is no longer denied by either radical researchers[23] or Communist writers.[24] By and large, they are essential to a correct perception of the primarily economic essence of the Third World "brotherhood" and of the North-South Conflict. The protracted character of the latter is also a consequence of the West's diminishing interest in territorial expansion and of its extensive concentrations on wealth modernization, on technology, on efficient administration, on production services, and the aggrandizement of power in this way.[25] This is generating some forms of indifference toward the fate of the developing countries and favoring intra-First World trade. In 1973 the exchange value within the West was 76.9 percent and their exchange with the Third World only 18.6 percent.[26]

While a lot was done to facilitate the political decolonization process, only little has been undertaken for the sake of promoting socio-economic progress in the Third World; recently more is done in this direction but still to the extent that it is conducted by dependence on oil or other vital commodities, supplied by less developed countries. Dependence on Third World oil, even temporarily, explains partly the halfheartedness of Western aid to the Third World, but considerations of humanitarianism, of global strategy, and of interest in stability on the world arena seem to be today a more compelling reason for the West to reconcile itself to the essential postulates of the Third World. The Soviet assumption is that it would pay to act as an ally of the Third

World because of its rôle as a reserve of anti-imperialist forces.[27] For this purpose, they thought it sufficient to provide diplomatic support and arms. The groundlessness of the Soviet assumption becomes more than obvious not only from the political divergence between many Third World countries and the Eastern bloc, but the clash of economic interests as well, the Soviets being exporters of raw materials and looking for credits and supplies from the West. On the other hand their role as arms suppliers is to a large extent similar to that of the West, a fact which is very important to the Chinese perception of their politics.

According to the Chinese concept, the First World consisted of the two superpowers, the Second World of all other Socialist or capitalist industrialized countries and the Third World of all developing countries regardless of their political structure.

Today the Third World and in particular the postcolonial states realize that their progress depends on the help of the Western democracies and not of the Soviet Union or the PRC and their respective allies, which themselves look to the West and Japan for knowhow. Therefore, they do not locate the USSR in the First World, since credits from the Socialist countries are quite limited and hard cash repayment terms are even demanded for arms sales. Exports to the Socialist Bloc frequently are not beneficial because of the inconvertibility of currency, and imports from there because of relatively high prices and because of the poor quality of merchandise. More often than not, Socialist countries are considered competitors because of the low wages that allegedly permit them to underprice goods exported to the West. These same commodities constitute an essential part of Third World export trade as well.

Most of the Third World pursues extremely nationalistic policies and, like the Socialist countries, conducts trade through government channels and operates almost Soviet-style centralized economic planning and production. This makes their great admiration of Eastern European developmental models understandable. It nevertheless appears that it is not enough to see in the Soviet Bloc a useful partner, despite the importance of its political support, particularly in international organizations.

As long as the industrial West threatened military intervention against the dangers of a petroleum export embargo or an exhorbitant politically inspired price hike, Soviet backing was considered particularly vital to the Third World countries. Once these threats passed, Third World countries felt themselves strong enough to exclude the Soviets from the North-South dialogue.[28] Moreover, many Arabs abandoned the Soviets, even on Middle East issues, while the conquest of Afghanistan produced anti-Soviet feelings not only in the Muslim countries. The foregoing suggests possibilities of the Third World becoming a significant, independent and a rather pro-Western coalition in the present-day economic and political constellation if the Brandt

Report is put into operation.

These possibilities are the more real, the more unity is preserved in the Third World ranks, also in view of the power emerging from "group activities." The "group power" was most frequently ignored in the past analysis of Third World problems whicn not to a small extent were also caused by the split produced by Soviet subversion.

It should be stressed that wealth, particularly in modern times, as illustrated by the case of West Germany and Japan, is not necessarily an indicator of power. More than that, the powerful, if we consider the various failures of American and Soviet policies, are not always effective.[29] The contrary is also true; the small, underdeveloped sparsely populated countries are not always helpless and ineffective in the international arena. However, many of them are aware that in order to avoid erosion of their ever-growing role, it is not sufficient to rely on revolutionary zeal (Iran, Libya), or on their numbers and unity. Consequently, the majority do much to acquire economic strength through the impact of their numbers at international conferences. True enough, they use the still changeable circumstances of their political might determined by their numbers and by financial growth of a small part of them that are rich in natural resources in order to speed development of their military establishments rather than to close the gap between them and the industrialized nations. What follows is the consolidation of the politically divergent ranks into a voting bloc in international organizations. It will be easier to understand this process if the ideological foundations of the Third World are considered.

2. Ideological Characteristics of the Third World

The manner of conceiving historical developments and the basis and functions of political systems are some of the various meanings ascribed to ideology. For the purpose of the present study, ideology is defined as an expression of views aimed at influencing the activities of governments in both domestic and external affairs.[30] Specific ideologies are determined by the socio-economic conditions existing in different countries, in the international situation, and in ideas developed from their own and extraneous experience. Justice, equality, freedom, political and economic independence, modernization, industrialization, notions of plebeian (or proletarian) and bourgeois nations, socialism, revolution, and other conceptions are frequently used today in the Third World. They are invoked less in consideration of local needs and interests than as ideas developed outside of the Third World based on foreign experience and thought. These foreign ideas and traditions are applied and adapted to their own circumstances and struggles for modernization; moreover, they are invoked for the purpose of influencing world politics in self-serving ways.

Yet common tendencies do not exclude particularism. Therefore, if the African Continent alone is considered with its mosaic of tribes, races, nations, religions, languages, socio-economic structures, and political orientations, to discern Guinean or Tanzanian or other forms of African Socialism is justified.[31]

One differs from the other and from apparently similar forms of Socialism in Asia or Latin America. Common features are frequently the result of identical positions and experience under the rule of white colonialists, of racial discrimination and exploitation and of suffering in wars of liberation; moreover, they tend to reflect the difficulties involved in shedding the heritage of obsolete tribal and patriarchal structures and values and in struggling against underdevelopment. The importance of anti-colonialism and anti-imperialism is stressed above all, in the first stages of shaping a Third World ideology.

The Cold War added yet another element in the formulation: nonalignment. It has been noted above that nonalignment was devised as part of the effort to avoid involvement in superpower rivalries and to avoid perils of a third global war. Such involvement was considered a certain path to restored colonial subjugation of newly independent states. Actually, nonalignment was more an instrument to demonsrate and reaffirm newly acquired independence and national identity by convening pompous conferences. These forums appeared to succeed as worldwide gatherings and to give their initiators reputations of sorts as champions of world peace. The conferences concentrated on speeding up decolonization, ending racial discrimination, and opposing war; for these were issues that at least were not opposed openly by any country. Apparent success was made even easier by the expedient of bypassing the difficult problems of mutual cooperation and economic reform. Any confrontation within the Third World or between it and the First and Second Worlds was avoided by merely raising questions of peace, racial equality and decolonization. However, in order to avoid intra-Third World conflict and to oppose the other worlds, issues were debated in global bloc terms of "we" and "they."[32] This was soon to become the standard terms of reference in all discussions of Third World problems, especially at international conferences.

True enough, what contributed to the cementing of the nonaligned and Third World front and, to a certain extent, is still binding its partners, has been not only high-sounding rhetoric and the ambition of leaders manipulating the masses. Today it is necessary to take into account the absence of political freedom in most of these countries and their leaders' common interest in avoiding demands from outside, demands concerned with human rights issues and various democratic reforms which, according to the West, are a condition of a more effective struggle for socio-economic progress.

Yugoslavia, of course, has been anxious to stress that the framework of nonalignment is powerful because of the nonaligned countries' interest in some kind of collective action and organization in order to oppose Soviet pressures. All the other participants tried to picture their conferences as an evidence of a dangerous revolt against the West and, with the help of this groundless argumentation resembling poor phantasy, tried to get, *inter alia*, military supplies, not infrequently used for the oppression of the population.

There is no essential difference between Western and East European perceptions of the Third World's actual and potential very limited influence in the international arena.[33]

Third World meetings began with preponderant stress on the declaratory and ceremonial, so important for reasons of evading confrontation with the former lords, especially as all post-colonial countries were very eager to preserve their traditional links with their former metropolises so as to receive their aid and advice. Being weak and thriving in a "brotherly" but rather hostile environment, they dreaded a total severance from their former sovereigns that would be an inevitable consequence of adopting a genuine nonalignment position. They faced the threat of neighbors covetous of their territory who frequently instigated subversion, open military intervention, and aggression. They had to rely on the help and protection of their former colonialist rulers who would be alienated or offended by a realization of a true nonalignment. In practice, direct or indirect alignment with one of the superpowers under the banner of nonalignment occasionally served as blackmail or an excuse for refusing alignment with an opponent. The independent former colony could thus maintain complete freedom of action in making the decision to eschew or join an alliance while extracting the maximum benefits from all concerned.

Although the principal antagonists on the world scene, the United States and the Soviet Union, feared mutual confrontation more than anything else, they could not bring themselves to trust one another and thereby establish an effective détente that could create a margin of pressures tolerable to the less developed countries. After the 1972 proclamation of Soviet-American "détente" hopes to prevent a clash between the giants grew and Third World countries experienced a measure of relief, however, the former's pressures on Third World countries nevertheless remained, frequently at an intolerable level. Another factor contributing to ongoing tension was the increase of local and internal conflicts in the ranks of the "nonaligned." In the past they resulted in the Sino-Indian and Indo-Pakistani wars, the Egyptian intervention in Yemen, the South Sudanese insurrection, the Nigerian and Congo civil wars, numerous border conflicts in Africa, and other bloody South-South collisions; beginning in 1977, conflict encompassed Zaire, Angola, Ethiopia, Somalia, Algeria, Morocco, Mauritania, and various Asian countries, in the form of ethnic and inter-state conflicts like the war between Iraq and Iran or between Vietnam and Cambodia.

An apparent cause of the decline of nonalignment proclamations was the death of Nehru and other Third World leaders for whom alignment was more an instrument of personal than of national politics. Nehru once stated that there were four big powers in the world, namely, the United States, the Soviet Union, the People's Republic of China, and India.[34] This conception of global balance of power was promoted on a worldwide scale by the putative authors of nonalignment, who portrayed themselves as saviours of human survival and freedom and architects of peace and détente. Actually, they were never really very influential and, of course, not strong enough to promote such goals successfully. Peaceful coexistence, which eventually evolved into US-Soviet détente, was brought about by its authors' realization of the dangers posed by conflicting interests and arms races of the superpowers.

R. L. Rothstein's past and recent discussions of nonalignment—including consideration of Chinese, Indian, African and other sources—do not leave much room for doubt about the flabby role played by nonalignment (propounded first and foremost by its Yugoslav architects and believers) in the rise of Third World political activities and ideologies. It seems, however, that he under-estimated its contribution not only to a frame of mind, but also to strengthening Third World unity. In spite of its many contradictions, it was never a fiction; without it, the transformation of the Third World into a kind of "brotherhood" would have been at best difficult, if not impossible. Today, that "brotherhood" is waging a sort of class war against the industrialized countries.[36] The essence, final goals and perspectives of this war are admittedly still nebulous, but it is difficult to imagine that the gains from existing solidarity will not ultimately be shared, mainly by the most affluent "brothers."[37] It is difficult to imagine that the eventual victory of the struggle will enrich all partners equally with its bountry, or will become an authentic contribution to the elimination of poverty and misery of even the most deprived.

To cite A. Mazrui, as an expression of the desire for equal dignity,[38] non-alignment was long ago converted into a tool for promoting economic equalization. As long as it began on the basis of common emotions and its continuation could be justified by similar common goals, the struggle could not be stopped for many years to come.

Bandung, like the preceding conferences in New Delhi in 1949, in Bogor (the Philippines) in 1950, and afterwards again in New Delhi in 1975[39] characterized nonalignment in its ceremonial, symbolic and personal aspects. Through stress on peculiarity and solidarity, a louder response to the specific situation of the Third World was created. With Tito's departure, the early characteristics will most probably be relegated to the status of an historical reminiscence. Later features already had started to dwindle at the 1964 first UNCTAD Conference, when the Third World was transformed into a kind of confederation of less developed countries. This image and reality of the majority of them is unfortunately bound to last for many years, but it is not likely to end the "brotherhood."

Only when the Fourth World of the poorest rids itself of illusions about prospects of aid and support from rich allies that already openly align themselves with the First or Second World can the "international class struggle" fall on the shoulders of authentic "plebian" peoples. The myth of former unity will then begin to fade; however, it will quite possibly continue to play a certain restricted role similar to that of nonalignment today.

In discussing the ideological features of the Third World, it seems important to concentrate on its perception as a factor of strength and as a basis to its requests for developmental aid. Its operation, as well as its inertia and exploitation, also may become apparent in this way. Belief in the necessity for and power of solidarity grew in spite of all contradictions, disappointments, and intensified suffering produced by oil price increases imposed on the MSACs. Above all, in the wake of OPEC's success it was assumed to be the proper pattern for countries with raw materials for all members of the "brotherhood" to benefit. This belief was strengthened with the approaching end of classical colonialism, of racial discrimination, and with the decline of non-alignment, all of which lost their effectiveness in sustaining solidarity.

It seems a mistake, on the other hand, to view OPEC's impact only as a function of oil's importance to modern industry and the opportunity to use it as a makeweight in economics and politics. It should rather be viewed as part and parcel of the malaise of the world economy and its political superstructure.

The majority of the establishment and of the academic community both in the East and West attribute underdevelopment to lack of skill, of technology and capitalist maturity, or to colonialism. The remedy is tied either to external inputs or to radical changes in the global political economic structure. Some liberal statesmen and scholars rely on mere Socialist reforms in particular countries. Extremists conceive reform only through world revolution.

Views have been mentioned above pinpointing the exogenous causes of Third World misery. In some modern theories of international relations, there is also a tendency to limit analysis of these causes and internal ones as well to the consequences of the behavior of nation-states with respect to their territorial, socio-political, and conflict-producing problems; priority is frequently given to implications of transnational elements and developments.[40] These kind of orientations result above all from the growth of global problems needing global solutions and of matters decided by the superpowers. The proper decisions are sometimes echoed even in international legal concepts and arrangements.[41]

Conceptualization, however, suffers from oversimplification both when it follows Marxist-Leninist concepts and uncritically relies only on socio-political models of dependence-domination relationships or is based exclusively on transnational trends and beliefs. In such instances little if any effort is made to differentiate occurrences within various policies and to find out how this frames the socio-economic infrastructure and ties in with the outside world.

P. A. Baran and P. M. Sweezy present the first paradigm.[42] They are silent on the matter of Soviet imperialism in general, but particularly in the Third World. They neither consider the peaceful trends in the West, where growing interest thrives in intra-First world trade, technical and administrative viability, scientific progress, and industrial and labor productivity; moreover it burgeons absolutely independent of the fear of nuclear war. Nor did the writers mentioned and their followers try to discover the roots of the West's tendencies to meet evident Third World needs in matters of decolonization and its readiness to reconstruct the terms of international trade in an emerging ambience of post-industrialism.

The School of Dependency, particularly that in Latin America, is much more up to date and less dogmatic, but still one-sided in spite of extensive resort to statistics. By and large, many of this school's representatives minimize the indigenous factors and heritage of socio-economic backwardness and deprivation[43] depicting it mainly as the result of "international feudalism."[44] Radically developing some old reasonable theses of international stratification[45] and impregnating them with Marxist conclusions about international class struggle, they played a very important role in paving the way for the Scandinavian and later West German schools of peace and development research. The latter, with all their originality and sometimes brilliant but frequently nebulous or insufficiently substantiated formulation, failed to move beyond confirmation of the former's conclusions. Further attention will be given later to various concepts of their exponents, above all, to J. Gatung, H. Hveem and D. Senghaas[46]; at this point, it is sufficient to emphasize that all of them view the socio-economic evil as determined by a relationship of subordination and domination on a global scale.

In the eyes of H. R. Targ this constitutes a step forward, at least methodologically, compared with the analysis of the world community as a collection of individual nation states: a decentralized, atomistic, symmetrical and culturally, politically, and ideologically pluralistic world order. According to Targ, it expresses a more comprehensive and valid outlook of today's international scene that is described as holistic, centralized, stratified and technocratic.[47]

Although a compact global system may indeed be very desirable for many reasons and in any case an unavoidable *de facto* development in the future, the Third World states for the time being are sovereign-orientated and militaristic. As their freedom of action increases, the impact of their presence in world politics at least through their voting bloc and oil riches is quite obvious. However, the global international system of our day, especially in matters of war and peace, is still dependent above all on the wills of the superpowers. By and large, approaches lauded by H. R. Targ are concentrated largely on socio-economic issues. This harks back to the old concepts of imperialism, and these approaches ignore expansionism of states with vastly different ideologies and political organization. To pinpoint only Western imperialism today, to remain silent on the fate of the Baltic states, the Peoples Democracies, the 1956, 1968 and 1979 Soviet aggressions against Hungary, Czechoslovakia and Afghanistan, respectively, the PRC conquest of Tibet, proclaimed Chinese irredentism regarding Mongolia, the Vietnamese-Chinese war, various manifest Arab and African imperialist designs, and the intimidation of the 1981 Polish camp of reforms, does not square with the historical record.[48]

Attention should be concentrated on the painful realities of Third World countries and on their discussion in international conferences rather than on the foregoing schools and their conceptions. It seems clear that the growing economic misery of the Third World is to a large extent the result of international trade and foreign investment terms. Continued raw material price decreases, industrial commodity price increases and high profits of loans and investments cannot be denied as prominent causes of declining Third World living standards and curtailment of development projects.

The following statistics of the 1950s and 1960s still are cited frequently to illustrate growing economic deterioration. The price of a jeep in 1954 was equivalent to 14 sacks of coffee and the following year many sacks more.[49] Similar rises were noted in regard to other industrial goods and they increased the awareness that without concentration on these problems and solidarity in fighting them, no improvement could be expected. Multinational corporations and Western trade unions concerned only with profits and wages were therefore more and more strongly blamed for the continued economic deterioration in the Third World. The deepening gap between the Third World and the industrialized countries was also ascribed to the crisis in the world monetary system and the ensuing inflation. It was claimed that the West thereby conspired to impoverish the developing countries and to promote neo-imperialism and neo-colonialism; it was furthermore asserted that Western aid programs were instruments of exploitation and pillage.[50]

In another context, an attempt will be made to analyze the liberal and radical concepts on the causes of underdevelopment. Here it is emphasized that argumentation of both concepts strengthened the feelings that in order to preclude further catastrophic deterioration, existing international division of labor and income distribution can no longer be tolerated.

The analysis of the Latin American situation (particularly by A. G. Frank) and of other regions as well (e.g., by A. Emmanuel and S. Amin), focusing on Africa had a growing impact on changing attitudes not only of researchers. Frank argued that First World aid projects were a link with neo-imperialism; operated by local bourgeoisie in their own interest and the interests of their foreign associates.[51]

Emmanuel used to demonstrate one of his assumptions by the illustration that the same work done in the United States today is paid 30 times more than in the Third World and similar to existential minima given to slaves 4,000 years ago. In all cases, the effort and physical movements were not much different.[52] If this argument is taken into account, and also the fact that the Third World masses grew poorer following payment for Soviet arms, it will not be difficult to understand the cause of extrapolating Marxist terminology, particularly on the class struggle, to the interrelationship between "prolaterian" and "bourgeois" nations; nor will it be difficult to understand the call to unity in order to fight "international feudalism" and the "structural violence" in the present world economic system.

Raoul Prebish, the first General Secretary of UNCTAD, pointed out as far back as 1964, that the sum total received by South America in the years 1956-1961 was $9.6 billion. However, the industrialized nations received in the same period $13.4 billion from South America in addition to $10.1 billion through capital reduction resulting from trade terms.[53] Similar developments have occurred in Asia and Africa.

The proper statistics helped to promote the solidarity of the Third World countries and their mobilization for imposing a program of radical change on the industrial nations by force, if necessary. However, not only military weakness but socio-political differentiation of the Third World leadership precluded a call for world revolution, or in Chinese Communist terminology, a war of the poor nations against the rich ones. The substance of nonalignment gradually eroded with corresponding progress in decolonization and the falling into disuse of anti-colonialism, both of which lost their former relevance. With the oil producers' enrichment and persistence of some of their aggressive designs and with the advent of political and economic conflict between some of them and the Soviet bloc, anti-imperialism could no longer be a basis for a joint program; therefore, the only reasonable ideological foundation of the Third World became the program to rebuild the international economic order.

The "alliance" started through efforts for self-affirmation, the struggle to put an end to colonial dependence, to gain influence in the international arena by opposing new world war tendencies while favoring peaceful coexistence, and by the hope for more aid to combat backwardness. This was the catalyst of nonalignment. Political stratification because of Third World conflicts and the search for military and economic aid from any source reduced the importance of the "bloc." All this and other things gave prevalence to Third World ideology concerning the struggle for improving the economic situation through radical change in the world market. This main new thesis of the Third World has prospects of being understood also in terms of meaningful supplementation by important elements of the West and it has the potential of facilitating an offensive for larger support of the Soviet Bloc as well. True, even in 1977, Western Aid did not grow and actually diminished a bit[54] while the Soviet contribution continued to be ridiculously minimal.[55] The Arab oil producers also have not contributed seriously as yet to the improvement of the poor countries' situation.[56]

As already mentioned above, the struggle to promote so-called economic decolonization is not the only cementing factor in the Third World, but the *raison d'etre* of its political action and to some extent of its militarization and of its prospects for improving the situation at least on a step-by-step basis in the short run. Most likely, improvement will come about almost exclusively through cooperation with the West.

The question remains therefore of how to reconcile Third World nationalism with Western global outlooks on economics and technology . How can an end be brought to the continuing lack of economic viability of Third World countries while sustaining their continued opposition toward security of foreign investments? Curtailment of economic backwardness is the main purpose of the New International Economic Order (NIEO); other points related to the means of achieving their goal are an alteration of raw material dispositions, a better industrial international division of labor, reduction of debts, and obtaining more development finances. The realization of this program raises numerous contradictions because 1) of emphasis on absolute sovereign rights in regard to foreign investors and self-reliance, on the one hand, and greater foreign dependence entailed by importation of capital needs on the other; 2) of the neo-mercantilist approach based on state planning and operation of development projects; 3) of the tendency to strengthen all government activities, while looking for foreign investments dependent on private deals and protection of alien property; 4) because of the need for labor-intensive industries on one hand and the will to avoid replacement of "banana" republics by unviable "pajama" republics on the other; 5) because of the reliance on a common Third World front, with its "collective autonomy" and autarchic tendencies and the need of global relations and widespread international cooperation on the other. Some experts are of the opinion that increased cooperation and a proper integration of the Third World in the process of the world division of labor is the only mean to speed up the elimination of the contradictions mentioned and the working out of an effective and more just solution of the painful problems of the developing countries.

Others consider all efforts in this direction as favoring the interests of the industrialized nations and aiming to perpetuate their domination. They prefer, like D. Senghaas, a complete disassociation of the Third World from the capitalistic market as the best method for the preparation of a subsequent "rearrangement" with their former metropolises.[57] However, this view disregards the fact, that such a "disassociation" actually exists and is extremely detrimental to the less developed countries, who struggle to put an end to it and to place their relationship with the rest of the world on a closer and more favorable basis.

In 1976, exports of the industrialized countries to each other amounted to 459 thousand million dollars. Exports to Third World Countries were 148, and to Communist countries only 36. Thus industrialized countries tend to become "richer" mainly as a result of their mutual ties, particularly since they were able to import from the less developed countries only to the value of 183 billion dollars and from the Communist countries a mere 28 billion. At the same time, intra-Third World Trade was 55, while Third World Trade with the Eastern bloc and China was only 10. Intra-Communist trade was 52, while Communist trade with the Third World totalled no more than 15.[58]

What is more, there are no prospects of diversifying the trade of the LDC's through "disassociation" and promoting their development in this way. Such "disassociation" would tend to perpetuate the present situation, because of the extremely limited absorption possibilities of goods already available for exports inside the Third World and even more limited possibilities for vital imports from this source. To a certain extent the same is still characterizing the communist market. This is one of the reasons for the lack of essential changes in world trade in the past twenty years.

The share in world exports in 1960 and 1976 of the developing countries with their population of 2000 million did not much exceed 20% while that of the industrialized nations with their population of only 750 million was nearly 72%. Moreover, while in 1975, the total of 585 billion of exports of Western countries comprised 77% industrial goods, 12% food and 11% raw materials, that of 85 billion of the Communist bloc and China 63% industrial goods, 11% food and 26% raw materials, while the 215 billion of the LDC's comprised only 17% of industrial goods, 12% of food and 71% of raw materials.[59]

A breakthrough and end of the rivalry between the Second and Third World both seeking technology and knowhow in the West may be therefore expected only through better coordination, association and effective integration and, of course, in conditions of peace and of limitation at least, if not complete, cessation of the armament race. It should also be added that the "disassociation" theory supplements the doctrines of "structural violence" and "peripheric capitalism"; it does not take into account the stratification in the Third World, the shape of the Fourth one; it ignores the ever closer ties between the oil-producers and the high industrialized oil-consumers and the eventually catastrophic results of an absolute self-reliance policy of the poorest countries, their survival almost exclusively depending on external, mainly western aid. The assistance they gained till now from the rich "brothers" was sometimes, as already mentioned, almost minimal, not much larger than that from the Communists. Hence suspicions multiply that selfish, above all prosperous kith and kin but also those of them who are divided by personal ambitions, ethnic or other controversies frequently indulge in imperialist and subversive ventures (e.g., Libya vis-a-vis Chad before her conquest in 1981, Libya vis-a-vis Egypt, Algeria vis-a-vis Mauritania (till 1970) and Morocco, Iraq vis-a-vis Iran, Somalia with regard to Ethiopia, Angola in her relations with Zaire) and snatch for themselves a better place in world markets; and, of course, also preferences in international trade, other privileges and growing influence in the community of nations. All this as a result of advantages based on oil and the outcome of the still solidary front in international organizations and conferences.

All this prevents viewing the NIEO, its ideology, and the extreme self-reliance and disassociation blueprints as something novel and salutory, especially since the advocates of NIEO are also attempting to realize this end through a new international military order (NIMO). At the same time, the present outlines of NIEO cannot rid itself of old features that find an expression in the tendency to improve roles, particularly of previously exploited participants that have become now affluent. Hence, ambiguities remain: intermixture of the new and old, continuation and change, and the possibility of shaping more than one or two economic orders concurrently.

The latter occurrence may become dominant for a long time to come because the poor countries have no means to force their rich "brothers" to aid them on a strictly altruistic basis. It is well known that the common Marxist-Leninist outlook was useless to the poor participants of the Council for Mutual Economic Aid (CEMA or COMECON), where prices and trade terms are much harsher than in the capitalist market and frequently lead to revolts against Moscow.[60]

The ideologically, politically and economically multifarious Third World cannot provide to its poor members better results than those granted to the poor participating in the economic agencies of Socialist countries, mainly in COMECON. Through joint action, however, it is likely to succeed in extracting substantial concessions from the First World (and perhaps in time from the Second World as well). The former will be very careful not to make a final break in the dialogue which has been formally interrupted for the time being. This interruption can be considered merely as the end of the beginning, as the first step in a complicated negotiation-process and an arduous journey to a more peaceful and also more prosperous future for all nations and in conditions of more equality. The interrupted Conference on International Economic Cooperation (the CIEC) did, after all, pave the way for a better understanding of the need for continual dialogue. It also helped to understand the need for common efforts to find solutions, at least for the most painful Third World problems which hinder the achievement not only of a more certain tranquility but also the realization of prospects of greater prosperity for the word as a whole.

In fact, a new stage of the dialogue, this time under W. Brandt's chairmanship already began at the North-South Commission at Schloss Gymnich on December 9, 1977. It resulted in the working out of the above-mentioned report which has more prospects for realization than ever before in the new international situation after the recent events in Iran, Afghanistan, Nicaragua, San Salvador and Poland.

As regards the Second World, it will not abandon hope to capitalize on the anti-imperialist reservoir. It will continue to strive for the reduction of "warmonger" influence and to multiply various forms of intervention, for the sake of its obviously imperialistic ends.

But whatever motivates the contributions of the First and Second Worlds, the most important fact is that in spite of all troubles, the continuing socio-economic malaise and the fact that development does not always result in social progress, continual change for the better is becoming an essential characteristic of numerous Third World nations, most frequently as a result of their own efforts.[61]

The poor have after all financed almost 90 percent of their development investments in the last decade out of their meager income.

Nearly half of them grew by an average of four percent per capita during the last 10 years. Some experts maintain that the problems of soaring birth rates, declining food production, increasing indebtedness, growing income maldistribution, pathological urban growth, and other painful problems of large parts of the world can be ameliorated on a "minimum need" basis with self-financing programs, such as that promoted by James Grant of the Overseas Development Council; this program focuses on elimination of absolute poverty by the mid 80s. This kind of program is welcomed by many Third World speakers who are pushing for opportunity equality rather than income equality. They fear that effective Western aid because of internal difficulties may be abandoned leaving the poorest and troublesome countries to stew in their own juice; thus, an implication of latter-day Ricardian pessimist thought appears to be rather well-founded and not overruled in practice,[62] if some form of self-reliance is not quickly realized and development assistance not increased and made more effective.

A more detailed analysis of the NIEO suggests that its main objectives are well within the means of the West to bring about. People of the Western establishment and some of the opposition and academia as well, are therefore more and more inclined to perceive the solution of problems in terms of compromise.[63] The majority dismisses the exclusivity of alternatives tied to the egalitarian or nonegalitarian nationalisms or to the same two kinds of globalism. It is believed that NIEO is too pragmatic a concept to split Third World ranks or preclude joint negotiations with the First World; nor does it seem likely that NIEO will be compelled to relinquish continuing pressure on the Second World.

The New Integrated Commodity Program of UNCTAD based on NIEO includes: 1) agreements to organize and stabilize about 20 major commodities; 2) provisions for adequate financing of the foregoing scheme; 3) organization of better market information and access for Third World countries; 4) broadening compensation schemes like those adopted by the Lomé e Convention; and 5) rapid building of the producers country's share in raw materials processing and manufacturer. According to experts, this package is no utopian prescription[64] and an essential part of it has already gone into operation under the limited results of the North-South Dialogue.

It seems that all parties are prepared to continue the debate and concurrently to work diligently on the most pressing Third World problems by an ongoing step-by-step *modus operandi.* Consequent reformation of the world economy may continue to strengthen Third World present—merely inspired by economic needs—ideology to the extent of making it dominant in its ranks also in the coming years. However, such ideological orientation may be really effective if practical reform also begins with a divorce from the theory of continuing exploitation; it was the starting point in the successful struggle for human dignity and independence of colonial territories, but cannot contribute to the solution of new, complicated economic issues. The theory of exploitation has provided a rational basis for the demand for solidarity that in the beginning was almost wholly emotional;[65] but it cannot be substituted for concepts necessary not only in order to understand the clarified situations, but to change it for the better by self help and proper cooperation with the rest of the world.

3. The Third World Function in the International System

Definitions of the Third World have been dealt with above taking into consideration also its role in the present international system. The official Yugoslav view continues to focus in this regard on nonalignment. However, the majority of statesmen and students of the Third World emphasize the impact of social, cultural and economic aspects. Economic aspects are stressed strongly by the Soviets as vital to the struggle against imperialism, while the Chinese Communists have in mind the imperialism of the USSR as well.

Some Western experts are also of the opinion that growing Soviet interest in knowhow, technology, food, and credits from the capitalist countries will lead to convergence. This is attributed to similar results of the industrial process and of greater cooperation betwen the First and Second Worlds favored by détente. Some students, however, consider that because such convergence may not necessarily benefit the Third World, détente—even if reconstructed—is ever likely to aggravate its relationships with all industrialized countries, regardless of the forms of their government.

As regards detente, doubtless it is not a recipe for harmonious condominium of the superpowers, but rather a framework for competitive diplomacy. But while reducing the danger of global war, it could favor more attention to the needs of the Third World as well as strengthen pressure for solution of its most painful problems. On the other hand, it may augment in some circumstances the possibilities of East-West conflict because an unscrupulous power like the USSR could be tempted to intervene in chronic local South-South encounters and provoke the hostile reaction of its superpower rival.[66] Such First and Second World confrontations could well terminate any consideration of Third World needs; furthermore, such superpower hostility would most likely even impose harsh political and economic conditions on the Third World clients of the rival. However, stronger political and economic cooperation of the superpowers based on common interests could also produce negative results for the Third World. This is precisely what happened at the Sea Law and other Conferences when the joint Soviet-American vote torpedoed Third World proposals for "democratization" of the United Nations and other international organizations by curtailment of Security Council and other similar bodies' powers. Moreover, the USSR is still one of the greatest exporters of crude petroleum, natural gas and other raw materials, as already mentioned, directly competing in world markets with Third World commodities.[67]

It has already been mentioned in another context that the Socialist countries are encountering increasing indebtedness. Some authors attempt to explain it by these countries' efforts to make the West contribute to modernization of the Second World, which is similar but more successful than Tsar Aleksander III's Finance Minister, Count Sergei Witte's scheme, to industrialize 19th century Imperial Russia. (In his day, Count Witte solicited Western loans sufficient to repay outstanding debts and to keep the Empire's economy flourishing in order to prevent loss of investment and the shape of a Russian-German Alliance).[68] However, the growing indebtedness of the Third

World today is mainly due to drastic rises in oil prices with the probable result of curtailing new credits because an important part of disposable funds is eaten up by the Socialist countries, particularly by Poland after her 1980 summer.

The recent Albanian denial of the concept of "three worlds" corresponds to the view of many Third World leaders who continue to see it as divided into poor and rich or exploiter and exploited nations. Needless to say, this viewpoint has been sharply criticized by Soviet General Secretary Leonid Brezhnev because it allegedly put the Socialists and capitalists in the same category.[69] Nevertheless, the validity of the Albanian viewpoint applied to the USSR was given credence by the role of the Soviet Bloc in international trade and monetary markets, as well as by the exhorbitantly ruinous high prices charged to the poorest countries by Moscow for crude oil and other raw materials. Soviet military and diplomatic support is given in many cases only when there appears to be an intrinsic certainty of enlarging Soviet influence; however, this does not seem to be sufficient cause for an open clash of interests between the Second and Third Worlds. It is true, however, that the Third World presses on the Soviet Bloc, a pressure which has been growing since the 1976 Manilla UNCTAD Conference and which in the long run will probably not claim only development aid but also abandon aggressive politics like those with regard to Afghanistan.

The evolution of Third World ideology and its concentration on change in world economy and politics evaluated above is very important for the understanding of both Second and Third World relationship and of the Third World function in the international system generally, as well as of their perceptions by politicians and students alike. Although pretending to analyze the international relations of the Third World, Edmund Jouve actually succeeded to present merely the latter question; but his examination nonetheless is very useful for the present inquiry and will be followed critically.

Jouve among others deals with the views of F. Luchaire,[70] R. Aron,[71] and M. Duverger,[72] according to whom the less developed countries from the viewpoint of their political orientations belonged to existing rival blocs, at least in the sixties. However, he disregarded the fact that this did not change their quasi-unity and solidarity to any large extent.[73] The fact that some of the countries are or were pro-Western, others pro-Soviet, or pro-Chinese, has by and large no influence on the distinct role played by the Third World as a whole on the international scene. It finds increasing expression not only in a united pressure-front for more aid from the West, but in a real growing fight against Soviet imperialism as well. Jouve is certainly aware of this position.[74]

What is more, the Third World role continues in spite of the contradictions in its ranks that exist not only between the oil- and non-oil producers, but among its other participants and inside of all of them.

Typical South-South relationships are affected by a bewildering variety of different socio-economic and political outlooks and interests, national and tribal clashes, and conflicting claims and counterclaims. Similarly, the unity of the First and Second Worlds persist notwithstanding controversies between Europeans, Japan, and the United States or between the Kremlin and its heavily exploited but politically subordinate "allies."[75]

It is quite probable that Third World role and solidarity even in the short run will become stronger for reasons already specified above and despite growing dissatisfaction and frustration in important Third World operational and establishment quarters. Dissatisfaction is mounting not only among the poorest nations but others as well. They realize that at present continuing unity in the struggle of the Third World may benefit only part of the "brotherhood," mostly the Third World "holy alliances" in Africa and elsewhere.[76] By and large, many rich developing countries opposed granting special status to their poor "brothers," even in such matters as aid given them by industrialized countries. They did not hesitate to manifest lack of solidarity with them in other cases as well. Professor R. Kovar took this into account in his emphatic support of G. Lacharriére and others as to the need to differentiate in any analysis of Third World ranks by conceiving them as structures of categories and subcategories.[77]

Together with the rich Third World countries, various kinds of dictatorship (even of very poor nations) frequently act to make the new economic World Order a source of benefit only to the present rulers of these countries rather than to large parts of their population.[78] Jouve seems to disregard this; rather, he idealized the Third World in opposition to the view on the other side of the spectrum conceiving them exclusively in dark and pejorative terms.[79]

It seems that Jouve also shares T. Mende's reluctance to use the term "developing nations," labeled by the latter as "polite fictions."[80] However, these terms reflect not only realities but are tied to the very roots of political, economic, and ideological North-South frictions as well. As already stressed in another context, they are frequently the result of forms of cooperation and deepening interdependence of the First and Third Worlds. Interdependence generally means a situation of reciprocal effects, of even mutual dependence. Its sources are physical (e.g., the spread of ocean pollution or depletion of the earth's protective zone shield) and socially functional as well. The former impose the necessity for cooperative, mutually beneficial undertaking while the latter can take the form of penalizing the weaker party. On the other hand, dependence can easily become a source of conflict and, conversely, a source of useful cooperation.[81]

There are no illusions in Third World capitals but that assistance and various forms of cooperation with the West were effected in terms of US interests in commercial benefits and the Third World countries' interest in profits from sales of raw materials.[82] This also explains why approximately $75 billion out of the $150 billion, which the least-developed countries owed in 1976, has been borrowed from private banks on a strictly profit guarantee bases;[83] moreover, multilateral aid was also granted to a large extent within the framework of the international capitalistic monetary and trade systems.[84] The Third World is aware, too, that the "old" world economic order began to accept new "rules of the game" because of its United Front's pressures on the West.[85] This is one more reason for the new tendencies in the North-South relationship. They are divided about the priority of true cooperation, over one-sided gains and its realization within the framework of growing interdependence in postive terms. Because the West can afford to curtail its privileges, it is also willing to give up some of its strategic aims and to strengthen its involvement in humanitarian matters.

On the other hand, the less developed countries have no other choice than a compromise but only because of their military weakness. Somehow, they fumble along with a large measure of political dignity coupled for the time being with minimal prospects of useful aid from the Second World, which is itself seeking supplies and credits from the First World.

However, the rationale of previously noted tendencies is still ignored or denied by the followers of the center-periphery concept or representatives of different economic schools like C. Bettelheim, who only sees the Third World as the victim of exploitation by Western imperialism and who interprets the term "underdevelopment" chiefly as a manifestation of bourgeois ideology. This makes his stress on the problem of domination understandable[86] but the problem is, however, much more complicated; the latter fact makes solution of Third World present-day issues dependent not only on bringing an end to all forms of foreign subordination. Some features of these views concerning center-periphery theory has already been discussed above in greater detail. It should become apparent that they fail to take into account that during the early seventies, for instance, 80 percent of Western mineral investment went to the United States, Canada, Australia, and South Africa and that there was a disinvestment in the Third World.[87] In 1973, Western countries exchanged among themselves 76.9 percent of their trade and only 18.6 percent with the Third World,[88] and statistics showing that the situation remained unchanged also in 1976 and later have already been quoted. First World nations do not promote their enrichment by exploitation of the Third World any longer but mainly through trade between highly industrialized partners. This transpires because of the superiority of developed states' technology, communications, wealth and management, which in turn provides a greater need for importation of a wide variety and number of commodities extracted in a sophisticated manner and also the wherewithal to pay for them.

Clearly, use of the term "Third World" does not reveal its diversity, disunity, and conflicts. However, contrary to Debray's and Jouve's views, this does not prevent it from being any less of an historical, sociological, and political fact than the First and Second World. The First and Second Worlds also are distinguished by national, religious, social, economic, clan, and other subgroup conflicts. To be sure, Debray and Jouve admit some forms of Third World association but see it as determined by the existence of a common enemy, the Western imperialists. However, both of them ignore not only the recent evolution of the West's growing interest in peace, in human rights, and in solving Third World problems; nor do they mention that the Third World, too, has an increasingly urgent reason to maintain and to strengthen cooperation with the West.

While Debray[89] is silent about the consequences of Soviet imperialism against the Third World, he and Jouve failed to see the nonsense of describing the West only in terms of a class enemy in relation to the developing nations as a whole. In their own words, the Third World is actually an amalgam of countries, differentiated by their social structures and political orientations, only some of them being supported by the West, while others are blamed because pro-Soviet, pro-Chinese and/or governed by the worst type of dictatorship known in history. No less confusing is Debray's and Jouve's frequent perception of the Third World as an association of states, similar in their situation to movements, undeveloped regions, and even immigrant workers in the First World.[90]

Certainly, such workers are recruited by the West Europeans in Turkey, Spain, Italy, Portugal, and even in Yugoslavia and Romania, countries that belong to NATO, the Warsaw Pact, or are formally nonaligned. On the other hand, Third World countries of Africa, Oceania, Asia, or Latin America are with the exception of Palestinians and Indians in Britain or North Africans in France, conspicuously absent from the list of worker emigrant countries. Consequently all important studies of the Third World take into consideration nations of these areas only and characterize them on the basis of one or more indicators, including the GNP, demographic, geographical or other data, social and political structures, but not characteristics analogical with those determining the contrasts between various stratas, minorities or provinces in the industrialized nations.

None of these indicators taken separately or artificially combined help to understand the specifics and formation of the Third World either within its domestic confines or on the international scene. It is too complex a social, economic, political and cultural mosaic to correlate a multitude of signs of internal disunity and conflict so as to permit its precise description and evaluation with the aid of traditional yardsticks or taking into consideration the experiences of Europe, the United States or even the Socialist bloc. It is worth noting, that as regards defense policies based on the doctrine of popular resistance against any aggressor and opposition to superpowers interference in internal affairs, there is much more in common between the capitalist permanently neutral Austria and Switzerland, de facto neutral Sweden and Finland, nonaligned Yugoslavia, Rumania, belonging to the Warsaw Treaty organization and Norway, a NATO member, than between the different Third World countries, who are actually aligned with one or the other superpower.

This is one more reason why efforts to characterize the Third World through an ideological approach, particularly if focused on security policies and nonalignment, failed no less than the sociological outlook, which gave priority to the analysis of underdevelopment attributed to exogenous causes only, and to demands for its elimination by any means.[91] The psychological approaches stress the frustration produced by racial, other forms of personal humiliation and the feelings resulting from the imposition of foreign rule and civilization.[92] The political approach, pinpoints the impact of imperialism and neocolonialism, as well as economic exploitation, concentrated merely on problems of subordination and underdevelopment. By and large all have contributed to a certain degree to understanding Third World issues and their relationship to the world community.[93] It thus becomes clear that a proper and comprehensive exploration requires invocation of not only all of the aforementioned disciplines and approaches but others as well. One of the areas of inquiry that is quite important to proper understanding of the ongoing process of change in image, realities and function of the Third World in the present international economic and political system is the metamorphosis of the legal foundations.

4. The International Legal Conceptualization of Third World Postulates

It is frequently assumed that given the massive failures of the First Development Decade and the poor prospects of the second one, modernization theorists of the fifties and sixties can no longer be taken seriously. This is one more reason for their turning away from "liberal" optimism toward radical and usually neo-Marxist, pessimism.[94] Unable to foresee the consequences of the "energy crisis," it was concluded by them that the developing world is becoming irrelevant to the future of industrialized nations. They did not foresee that the weight of the Third World would one day counterbalance even the influence of the superpowers in the United Nations and in other international organizations and conferences[95], that they would gain a "collective veto" over decisions in the UN General Assembly[96] and other international forums and that they would strongly influence the evolution of the contemporary law of nations, giving birth to an international law of development.[97]

True, this law is still most frequently based on recommendations, but in fact it is no less influential than other parts of the law of nations, including those of unambiguous mandatory character. It is quite easy to take notice of the growing impact of the Third World on the international community and its legal foundations and particularly on the growth of the international law of development even without considering the results of the oil "revolution." The latter only intensified the erosion of many pessimistic conclusions and surmises on the irrelevance of the Third World. It is true, the Third World does not yet enjoy a prescriptive right to development aid, based on an unambiguous conventional obligation. But international law is not just a matter of treaties; it can also entail a prescriptive right established by common law precedent, and could well do so in the development aid sector, in consideration of long standing practice and legal conviction, confirmed by numerous resolutions of different international organizations and grants of all Western countries. Moreover, the Third World may possibly take hope from such a source of international law as "the general principles of law recognized by civilized nations." Not only B. V. A. Röling has advanced a new most intriguing line of argument in this matter. Collective responsibility for the social and economic wellbeing of members of a community is a generally acknowledged principle within individual countries. Hence the principle of collective responsibility of the international community for the wellbeing of its members is no longer an act of grace but an obligation incumbent on all states by the terms of international legal tenets as well. Hence also the extension of the ban on using force embodied in the UN Charter to the prohibition of using economic force in order to impose privileged terms of trade both by the industrialized nations and the oil producers, the latter chiefly injuring the poorest nations in a really dreadful way depriving them of any prospect of progress.[98]

The international law of development and decolonization[99] reflects therefore not only immense achievements of the Third World but its new contradictions and problems as well.[100]

D. E. Apter's thesis that the central political problem in the management of development reveals itself in the interplay of norms, structures and behavior and, let us add also, recommendations of international organizations seems very convincing. This definition should be supported with the external aspects of the proper structures as well; moreover, it should be stressed that it is also a matter of international dispositions and of behavior based on them; it also leads successively to a radical metamorphosis of the world economic order.

Yet the latter fact also justifies revision of Apter's other assumptions, namely, that the greater the degree of modernization in a system, the greater is the tendency toward *embourgeoisement.*This means development from "fused" classbound forces into "differentiated" groups expressing competitive interests while the greater degree of industrialization, the greater is the tendency toward radicalization.[101]

This seems to be an insufficiently founded generalization. It ignores the results of the common struggle of all developing countries and their international "class struggle," which are profitable to all of them and to all their strata and strengthen their solidarity.[102] This is so because the gains must be attributed to a large extent to external factors, to the industrialized countries above all; but it also disregards the fact that in the poor nations contradictory interests arise between the masses as a whole and the ruling élite and its servants; nor does it take into account that the enrichment of certain Third World countries—first and foremost of the oil producers—still has little to do with modernization and industrialization. Although natural wealth facilitates industrialization more than social progress and modernization, and even makes it possible to combat any form of radicalization through coercion, it does finally raise the living standards of all parts of the population.

As mentioned previously, the process of *embourgeoisement* on an international scale is likely some day to split the presently united ranks and lead to a coalition between rich Third and First World countries, as well as between some poor Third World or rich but radical (Libya) or Marxist-oriented—and Second World nations or China; moreover this new stratification may freeze or even sharpen the present East-West conflict and intensify inherent dangers in the ensuing arms race. However, conditions for a break between the Third World and the poor of the Fourth World are still far from ripe. On the contrary, the realization of their common grievances already are recorded in various (and sometimes very important) conventions that reinforce solidarity. In order to understand further the course already covered by the Third World as a whole, appropriate documents and their substance must be considered at least briefly.[103]

It is generally known that World War II was fought, among other things, under the banner of equality and freedom for all nations. The founders of the United Nations in 1945 aspired not only to promote peace but also to seek other lofty principles, especially equality and justice; however, they did not consider that colored people were already ripe for independence.[104] The UN Charter proclaimed the right of self-determination, but actually was concerned only with the economic, social, educational and humanitarian advancement of colonial peoples as well as the political "progress" of the trusteeship territories established in former mandates that had not yet become independent.

It took 15 more years of debate and struggle to make a step forward towards delegalization of the colonial system. This was done through the formulation of the 1960 Declaration on the Granting of Independence to Colonial Countries and Peoples.[105] This text, as well as the 1965 Resolution on Non-Intervention,[106] various resolutions on Morocco, Tunisia, Algeria, Southwest Africa, the former Portuguese colonies and other dependent territories,[107] were actually recommendations that failed to put a formal end to the Charter's norms sanctioning the legitimacy of colonial rule. Nor was this done by the 1966 Covenants on Human Rights,[108] the 1970 Declaration on Principles of International Law Concerning Friendly Relations and Cooperation Among States,[109] the 1970 Declaration on the Strengthening of International security,[110] and other documents dealing with dependent territories. Still, international practice reflected in these, and other documents on the subject of dependencies, the tendency to outlaw colonial domination. Especially pertinent were the General Assembly's recommendations that Specialized Agencies and other international institutions extend aid to peoples fighting for liberation from colonial oppression.[111]

Other important documents that described the evolution regarding dependencies and post colonial states dealt with problems of sovereignty over natural resources, developmental assistance commitments, representation of liberation movements in international agencies, reaffirmation and development of international law applicable to armed conflicts for national liberation and last but not least with the rebuilding of the world economic order.

The 1960 Anti-Colonial Declaration prescribes complete independence, freedom and sovereignty and the right of self-determination for all territories and peoples under foreign rule. The Declaration and all supplementary documents leave no doubt that the right of self-determination does not sanction a right of secession and fragmentation of all existing states; yet, they express the belief of the great majority of United Nations members that neither Article 1(7) of the Charter dealing with the prohibition against intervention in matters essentially within the domestic jurisdiction of states and constitutional issues generally can impede colonial peoples' rights of self-determination and effective UN authority for this purpose.[112] Self-determination did not become a general principle of international law until recently; however, it is already a clearly binding one regarding colonial peoples.[113]

Already by 1977, most remaining dependencies reached the status of politically sovereign states. The colonial system will end soon[114] and colonial empires with the exception of the USSR will become extinct. This is no small achievement by the Third World in less than a decade, in definite legal terms, as are—also under the pressure of the LDCs—various dispositions concerning peaceful coexistence although they frequently reflect declaratory maneouvers rather than real codificatory tenets.[115] Concrete commitments on anti-racism and the right of self-determination were formalized in international documents. Many of them deal with the suppression of racial discrimination and apartheid, e.g., the 1965 Convention on the Elimination of All Forms of Racial Discrimination, the 1958 International Labor Organization (ILO) Convention Concerning Discrimination With Respect to Employment and Occupation,[116] the 1960 UNESCO Convention Against Discrimination in Education,[117] and the 1973 Convention on the Suppression and Punishment of the Crime of Apartheid.[118] Recent agreements are concerned with problems of social welfare and progress, development, and reconstruction of the world economic order. Beginning with General Assembly Resolution 1803 (XVIII) in 1962 on Permanent Sovereignty Over Natural Resources, the 1969 Declaration on Social Progress and Development,[119] and numerous resolutions concerning the three Development Decades (1961-1970, 1971-1980, and 1981-1990), socio-economic and particularly developmental problems became the dominant theme of most United Nations and other international agencies enactments, being the main subject of the 1980 special UN General Assembly session.

Formulation in principle of the obligation to act in favor of the Third World was already embodied in the UN Charter. Its preamble stresses the duty to employ the international machinery for the promotion of the economic and social advancement of all peoples. Numerous articles show the way for appropriate action. The General Assembly and the Economic and Social Council that operate through various committees and commissions recommend action to be taken by the Specialized Agencies.

An entire Chapter (IX) of the Charter was devoted to matters of international economic and social cooperation. Article 55 defines the creation of conditions for stability and well-being as essential for peaceful and friendly relations of all nations. All corresponding dispositions have already been considered for more than a decade as an expression of a pledge of all United Nations members to take both joint and separate action paralleling UN undertakings favoring developing nations. Development assistance is considered as an important means for the achievement of this goal. Beginning in 1965 (proclaimed as a year of international cooperation) aid was granted on an annual basis.

Resolutions were passed that sought to reduce economic maldevelopment and to combat hunger and illiteracy and other social ills. These resolutions dealt with universal problems because many nations and hundreds of millions of people were involved. This fact alone explains the possibility of their impact on issues relating to stability domestically and in these states' international relations. The efforts to solve the proper problems are also growing because international instruments are used for this purpose. The relevant resolutions are usually the result of comprehensive discussions frequently exceeding the political and purely economic aspects of the problem. Technical aid given by the United Nations family stresses humanitarian concerns and corresponds with the general purposes and principles established by the Charter. Training, guidance, productivity advice; improvement of food, health, and literacy; raising standards of living generally, and all other gratuitous contributions and functions of ECOSOC fall with UN competence and are implemented at the request of the membership (Article 66).

It is enough to recall this fact to show how developmental services of the United Nations and its Specialized Agencies have a clear and legal basis, notwithstanding lack of explicit Charter authorization. The framers of the Charter did not take this problem expressly into account. By and large, the problem became acute following decolonization. It may be regarded as determined by the continually emerging requirements of international life, a notion referred to by the World Court only a few years afer creation of the United Nations.[120]

It may be worth noting that technical assistance in the form of transfer of knowledge, experience and know-how from the industrialized nations is viewed as an important purpose of the United Nations. Such intangible "technical assistance" paralleled the first humanitarian operations and grew successively beginning in 1948-1949. Different resolutions referring to the purposes and principles of the organization or based on the interpretation of specific Charter provisions included assistance programs and their financing and management.

In the beginning, the prevailing opinion was that it was sufficient to use the principal organs of the United Nations and their subsidiaries for this purpose. In time, the Specialized Agencies (e.g., the FAO, the ILO or the World Bank) became a very important tool; thereafter, new institutions evolved from international conferences, among them, the UNCTAD, UNIDO, UNITAR, UNCDF and various special bodies of regional organizations. Local operational teams also were used for this purpose. Beginning with the end of the sixties approximately 85 percent of the UN family funds were already devoted to assisting developing countries. Of the 20,000 people then working directly or indirectly for the United Nations, 17,000 were engaged in assistance operations[121] and since then the proper numbers are continually increasing.

This was indispensable, because all aid activities have been continually expanding, constituting a rather sudden development in contrast with the United Nations' initially limited involvement in international economic and technical cooperation. Their weight did not begin to be felt until 15 years after the establishment of the world organization. They entered the dynamic stage in 1965, the International Cooperation Year.[122] On the basis of a resolution proclaiming the twenty-fifth anniversary of the United Nations, a committee was formed to prepare and coordinate programs. It considerably influenced the increase of activities in developing countries; it completed the 1966 UN Development Program (UNDP) and prepared the first UN Guidelines for the Development Decade. The goal was to increase national income by a minimum of five percent annually between 1961 and 1970. This was designed to exceed the estimated population increase of 3.5 percent any year.

Initially, international aid to developing countries was based on decisions and activities of general and regional organizations. Soon, however, bilateral agreements arose between the organization and the countries concerned or between donor and recipient countries. Development Decade projects were based on short- and long-term loans from public and private sources, on grants of money, equipment, foodstuffs, and technical assistance, and called for increased activity in executing aid and in improving instruction, training, supervision, and reporting; therefore, the aid machinery, too, had to expand.

Yet all UN family assistance has been slight in the past and has not risen appreciably since. Funds were raised through voluntary contributions by member countries. Originally, the money was channelled through the UN Expanded Program of Technical Assistance Funds and the UN Special Fund. This function was later filled by the UN Development Program, as well as by the share of the UN Specialized Agencies Budget devoted to technical assistance. These activities never increased in proportion to developmental needs. In 1960, all such UN family aid did not exceed 10 percent of the aid given directly through bilateral agreements between countries, including long-term loans, fund grants, and supplies.

The contributions of international institutions have remained marginal until the present, the total contribution of the UN Development Program being in 1977 only $317 million. Between 1955 and 1959, ninety percent of the aid given the Third World was based on bilateral agreements; 20 percent was attributable to decisions of regional or specialized political organizations (e.g., the Common Market, the Organization of African States, the Colombo Plan); six percent came from the World Bank; and only two percent came from the rest of the UN family.[123] Nevertheless, the latter aid was of primary importance due to its independent character, its non-partisan orientation, its emphasis on technical and educational activities and above all its genesis of the formulation of Third World claims and increasing pressure on the First and Second Worlds.[124] Such Third World claims and pressures grew because of the failure to produce better results on the basis of the recommendations of the Pearson Report and the Jackson Study;[125] the United Nations thus failed to close the gap between rich and poor peoples. The gap grew in spite of UN efforts and the emergence of the international law of development was very important to prevent at once further deterioration of Third World countries' situations and more or less to mobilize public opinion for action in their favor. The growth of Third World demands also stressed the role of their legal foundations. These foundations facilitated organizational undertakings and resulted in improvement of different tools for this end; but first and foremost they made the people realize how serious the matter really was. And they also promoted solidarity of course, in order to exert pressure for change.

The Resolution of 19 November 1965 established a Governing Council of the UN Development Program. This unified body replaced the Special Fund Administrative Council and Technical Assistance Board. In place of these two, a single advisory board was created: The Interagency Consultative Board of the UN Development Program. These organizational reforms did not contribute a great deal to improvement of the situation. When it became clear that the first Development Decade would be a failure, the struggle of the Third World focused on the definition of goals and their legal determination, which had in fact been laid down in the 1962 General Assembly Resolution on Permanent Sovereignty Over Natural Resources and in other resolutions.

These resolutions and the Declaration on Social Progress and Development are frequently considered the basis of a special Law of Development.[126] One of the Third World postulates almost since the beginning has been the confirmation of the right to development not only on a basis of equality before the law in terms of political sovereignty, but in terms of socio-economic and cultural development as well. The Law of Development was the result of a bitter struggle for the promotion of the latter.[127]

Although frequently based on non-binding recommendations, the Law of Development grew in importance with the creation of instruments for their realization and for reports on its progress.[128] Some students, defining this Law as an offspring of internaional economic law, dealt with it beginning in the 1960s, or even earlier, following the growth of economic and social problems considered by international bodies and elaborated upon through various arrangements and techniques.[129] It owes its new form and content to the consequences of gradual socio-economic and cultural decolonization, which became quite acute in the wake of political decolonization and, more recently, by the call to build a new world-wide economic system.[130] Yet some experts deny the autonomous character of both international economic law and the Law of Development.[131] This seems to be a reaction to tendencies to supplement the universally recognized sources of international law with recommendations of different inter-governmental and even non-govern-mental organizations. By and large, a more profound recent analysis of the process of international law norm-creation confirms that there is no room for considering as international law what current opinion, even of substantial majorities in international bodies, hold it to be; likewise, votes opposed only by a small minority do not constitute evidence of a judicial consensus.[132]

Undoubtedly, however, some resolutions have no less legal force than conventional instruments. This is the case when they are the product of expressed unanimity of all parties concerned and not the result of some parties trying to impose their will on the others. Such resolutions become legally binding especially when they are followed up by the control and implementation measures.[133] By and large, parts of the Law of Development already today are codified in both bilateral and multilateral arrangements. Many law-declaring resolutions of international agencies and conferences have become statutory law because they are based on state practice considered as binding. International law is not a sum of legal norms exclusively employed in the enforcement and sanctioning of peaceful coexistence; it also has the purpose of contributing to the right of nations' economic development.

Many principles of the Law of Development, of course, can be viewed as a part of universal public international law acknowledged as legally binding by all sovereign states of the world. Emergence of the Law of Development partly resulted from changes in some of the traditional norms and the establishment of new ones hitherto unknown to the European-centered international law. This "old" international law, which was based on the principle of equality of states, often had the effect of sanctioning inequality in practice by acknowledging various forms of dependency. This had the effect of legalizing colonialism and other forms of dominance.[134] Traditional public international law also frequently sanctioned or was otherwise partial to states with anti-democratic governments by transforming the right of self-deter-mination of nations into a sacrosanct authority to deprive domestic minorities of rights and protection.[135] It mainly dealt with sovereign states' rights and status in the international commumity rather than human rights and the international legal status of the individual and his different groups, ethnic, tribal and the like. Until human rights and minority protection goals are realized in the Third World, satisfaction of collective socio-economic rights of the various mentioned social groups remain dependent on limiting the gap between the LDC's and the developed countries and on containing backwardness.

Mankind in fact has always been in the process of development. Municipal and international law alike has always reflected change issuing usually, but not exclusively, from the will of rulers of various community levels. The dynamics of development, however, underwent radical change at the end of the last century. Europe and America at that time took gigantic steps forward in the industrial revolution. The results of the European and American industrial revolution failed to reach other continents, indeed, it was even precluded in the wake of their political and economic subordination to the colonial empires. Failure of the industrial revolution to reach other parts of the world was, of course, attributable to indigenous causes as well. Even Marx and some of his followers, particularly Leon Trotsky, paid much attention to such indigenous problems in their considerations of colonial peoples, whom they did not hesitate to call barbarous and whose European masters and exploiters they did not fail frequently to praise for breaking patterns of archaic life.[136]

The GNP of today's industrialized nations rose more than sixfold during the 1870-1920 period compared with a growth of 2.5 between 1800 and 1900.[137] However it was not only the exploitation of colonies which to some extent contributed to this growth. Obsolete production forms and social standards, which meanwhile continued in the present Third World in recent times, resulted in persistent backwardness and stagnation, and also deepened in consequence of discriminatory trade practices.[138] Traditional international law acknowledged not only domination of the stronger, but its political and economic results as well. It also remained entirely indifferent to the result of differences between various parts of the world in terms of economic growth and social betterment. There is no doubt, however, that the improvement of conditions of life and of economic development must be measured not only by profits and other purely economic yardsticks, but by the human condition as well.[139] The Law of Development should be viewed as a reaction to the old measurement standards. It resulted from Third World pressures for remedies to underdevelopment and social backwardness; colonial powers were warned that failure of enactment would hamper international security, a view shared by many important western leaders and penetrating the Second World as well.[140]

The Law of Development was therefore also designed to reduce international tensions, inter alia, by building what is called economic collective security as a basis for political and military security; hence the principles of non-reciprocity and preferential treatment of the least developed countries. Further decisions were taken on more effective technology transfers, special credit conditions, reform of the General Agreement on Tariffs and Trade (GATT) Organization, the creation of such developmental aid agencies as UNIDO and UNITAR, promotion of development loans through the World Bank and the International Monetary Fund (IMF), and the creation by the UN of commissions for Africa, Latin America and other parts of the world, concerned with the needs and interests of the LDCs.

The Law of Development was consequently supplemented by modifications of many further rules and principles of the "old" public international law and international commercial law. Such amendments were the outcome of a UN General Assembly special commission created 17 December 1966 to consider modern international trade needs in general; however, the commission actually directed its efforts to a large extent to satisfy trade requirements of the Third World.[141]

Special attention is given by the International Development Law to problems of permanent sovereignty over natural resources. This is interpreted as nullification of all limitations imposed by previous colonial masters and later by multinational corporations as well. The ultimate goal in either case is the firm establishment of Third World property rights over their natural riches.[142] This is a problem naturally tied to the politics of nationalization, which is frequently regulated exclusively according to local law. The latter takes into consideration not only invested capital or real value accrued by it, but so-called excessive profits as well.[143] Among other new principles postulated by the International Development Law, are, fair raw material sale guarantees, special financial and organizational machinery for price stabilization and what is called by Professor C.A. Colliard, "principle conditions and aims," shaped to speed up economic decolonization. Along with fundamenal principles of international law, such as sovereignty, the Third World little by little not only dissipates on the basis of the said conditions and aims the Third World heritage of political subordination but also development inequities created by both exogenous and indigenous factors.[144]

Regulation of the most important raw material issues had already been elaborated in the 24 March 1948 Havana Charter, which was never ratified, even by its sponsors. This Charter's principles, however, were recommended by ECOSOC as a guideline to all United Nations members; accordingly, new international trade regulations were to be drafted also pursuant to Havana Charter dispositions proclaimed by western nations.[145] However, the basic documents having impact on the present-day Law of Development are the previously mentioned UN regulations on permanent sovereignty over natural resources (1803/XVIII of 14 Dec. 1962), on the program of the First Development Decade (1710/XX of 19 Dec. 1965), and, most importantly, the Declaration on the New International Economic Order (NIEO) (Res. 3201), the program for its realization (Res. 3202 of 1 May 1974), the Charter of Economic Rights and Duties of States (Res. 3281/XXIX of 12 Dec. 1974) and the documents relating to the Third UN Development Decade (Res. 31/182 of 21 Dec. 1976).

Some feel that the latter documents introduced a new concept of equity in recent international relations so as to eliminate any basis for charges of discriminatory policies in many parts of the world formerly under colonial rule. Equity in this connection is viewed as a basis for compensation for losses incurred in the colonialist past by countries presently independent. Price stabilization and trade preferences are seen among the many possible remedies for damages inflicted on previously dependent peoples. The sum total of these remedies amount to collective economic security, which is also considered the best means to shape the creative autonomy of Third World countries as regards the disposition of their natural resources that in turn determine in part the ultimate amount of their indemnification.[146] It is unnecessary to emphasize that realization of the aforementioned postulates will depend on proper compromise between the parties concerned, on their cooperation and consensus. Without such understanding, Third World countries will be unable to acquire needed credits from the First World, so vital for the promotion of development in the poorest of them.

It was on the initiative of the West that a special mechanism was created on 13 June 1974 for the adjustment of the most distorted Third World economies, 30 of whom already had received more than a billion dollars in the first period of operation.[147] Even the partial achievement of the North-South Dialogue and the efforts to continue it are the result of an agreement with the West, while other more effective steps proposed to ease the Third World situation were restricted by confrontations over conflicting interests. It soon became clear that the hopes of the least developed countries to throw off their miseries did not depend on war, remote world revolution, or resort to violence; nor did realization of these hopes depend either on radical UN resolutions reflecting the views only of the least developed countries or on non-binding instruments enacted by various international organizations and conferences.[148] Such measures, however desirable, were impractical and unattainable, even in the opinion of their proponents such as Ch. Chaumont.[149] They seemed quite realistic only if new forms of cooperation postulated by the South were taken into account and also accepted by the West because of its political and economic interests in responding to Third World problems. They have already found some expression in recent decisions following the North-South Dialogue and some bilateral and multilateral agreements. All of them, of course, are essential parts of present-day international law, comprising the essentials of the Law of Development directed to ease, if not solve immediately, the complicated problems of the Third World.

The study of contemporary international relations, particularly of the Third World, does not confirm the hopes placed in confrontations, tensions, and armed struggles,[150] that only tend to intensify the miseries and backwardness of the LDC's. Fruitless controversies and open disagreements inside the Third World and with the West tend to confirm that true remedies can be found first and foremost by cooperative means.

Certain opponents of this view hold that initial success was never the product of compromise. They maintain further that success was never the result of clarification of legal principles such as embodied in the Law of Development. In their opinion, progress resulted from the consequences of struggle, pressures and recently of the so-called energy crisis. Hesitations of the industrialized nations in dealing with the hostile OPEC policy contributed to the belief of many Third World leaders that the time was ripe for a united struggle against the West in order to force a closing of the gap between the First and Third worlds. This attitude of Third World leaders was reinforced by the weakness of the International Energy Agency established by the West to deal with the situation; actually the industrialized nations seemed to be inclined to accept the requests of the oil producers, while those really affected by the hikes of the oil price were the poorest of the LDC's. Beginning in 1974 there could no longer be any doubt that the new plutocratic elite of the Third World had betrayed the interests of its poorest members. Yet neither OPEC dictation in the aftermath of the 1973 Middle East October War nor the aquiescence of the West and the illusions of the Third World poor, hoping to see more help from the oil producers—although all of this had an impact on the situation with the rise of oil price—were of basic importance for the change in the world economy following OPEC's success. The latter was created as a reaction to the dramatic fall of oil prices decided upon by the international oil companies in 1959 and 1960. This decision intensified the common interest of oil exporters and inclined them to take collective action to force changed relationships on foreign oil shippers and consumers. The opportunity to act was facilitated by the convergence of political interests and economic needs.[151]

Since the 1972 OECD study commission findings[152], an oil price hike had been expected but not on a drastic scale. This explains why so little, if at all, has been done to limit excessive consumption and to accelerate the exploration of new oil fields and the search for substitutes for oil. Soon it became clear, that the western consumers were unable or unwilling to resist, that any military reaction was untimely, that oil conglomerates share the profits with the producers and that petro-dollars flow to the West for investment, military and other expenditures and that the West was, in spite of the troubles of inflation, managing to live and to cooperate with OPEC. True, the latter's freedom to decide to whom, where and for what price their product should be sold, what nationalized, who should refine and ship, grew. Actually, OPEC became at least for the time being immune. So the need for confrontation disappeared, while the legitimate complaints continued to come from the real victims, the poorest of the Third World. They now received less from the *anciens riches* and are more dependent on a selective generosity from the *nouveaux riches*.

According to UNCTAD experts, the total commitment of all oil-producing countries (including the non-Islamic and non-Arab) in 1974 reached the sum of $4.6 billion.It was approximately the same in 1975 and not too much more in 1977 and later. To be more precise, OPEC also placed $3.2 billion at the disposal of the International Monetary Fund (IMF), with $1.5 billion of this sum earmarked for the least developed countries at seven percent interest paid to OPEC by the IMF. It should be emphasized that there was a significant difference between the pledges and the sums actually given by OPEC, that the preponderance of Arab aid is given to Arab countries (particularly to the states of confrontation with Israel) and that most of the aid is for military purposes. Only a very small portion of the Arab aid is provided for the poor non-Moslem countries; nor was it particularly helpful to the poor Moslem countries until the establishment of the Islamic Bank of Development in 1974. Other Arab institutions participating in aid programs are Arab banks operating in the Gulf emirates, including the Development Fund of Kuwait since 1961 and the Arab Bank of Economic Development of

Africa opened a few years later.

However, until now, these institutions have disregarded the unanimous advice of renowned experts, who have consistently maintained that effective development was contingent on cheap oil for the Third World have-nots. Some have voiced the opinion regretfully that Arab reluctance to help the latter courts disaster for the poorest of the underdeveloped countries. At a recent Cairo social science symposium, Professor W.A. Freund predicted that a "final solution" would be imposed by the oil magnates on the poor of the Third World similar to that imposed by the Nazis on the Jews in World War II.[153] If such genocidal predictions have even the remotest possibility of future realization, it seems imperative not to disregard prospects either of intra-Third World reconciliation and growth of oil-producers assistance grants for the sake of reinforcing the common struggle for a New Economic International Order and other relevant programs and the prevention of a split of the Third World, or a bitter struggle of the Fourth World against the rich "brothers."

Most Arab plutocrats make the maximum effort to emulate the First World. They are aware that collaboration of the poor is needed for different purposes in international forums and in resolving issues in their immediate environment, such as the problem of Palestinians; above all, they are interested in preventing radicalization of the area and in easing the situation of the poorest without paying too much themselves, their proper claims being addressed mainly to western countries, though recently but still to a lesser extent to the Soviet Bloc as well. In spite of the latter's support of "counter-imperialist" policies, it proceeds in the manner of classical imperialism to search for political and economic spheres of influence both in the neighboring and Third World countries, above all, in those countries inclined to accept the "non-capitalistic" road to development and a pro-Soviet orientation[154]; but preference is given in aid even to these countries to military rather than developmental ends.

While the total Communist economic commitment to Third World countries for 1954-1974 exceeded $18 billion,[155] this strategy failed to strengthen Soviet influence or prevent its decline in different parts of the Third World to a large extent because the Soviet contribution to easing painful Third World problems remained minimal.[156] When they show begrudging and penny-pinching interest in development budgets of the Third World, the Soviets and Arab plutocrats have been willing to contribute effectively to military and sometimes clearly aggressive designs. The rich Arab countries prefer beneficial self-serving investments in the West and dictate harsh terms for quite limited loans.

They did not hesitate, however, to support legal and political documents relating to the new economic world order and other programs as a means of wresting sacrifices from the West. To be sure, they continue some activities that could in time produce a more compact coalition with the First World, but these activities are likely also to support the continuation of misery and stagnation in the poor countries of the Third World.

For the time being, solidarity of the have-nots with their rich "brothers" continues, as does their common voting bloc at international conferences in conjunction with the Soviets. As regards support granted by some of the industrialized nations to various aspects of the program on NIEO proposals, it is also to a certain extent a continuation of the line fashioned years ago. Thus the 1 May 1974 Declaration proclaiming the NIEO continued elaboration of various principles already set forth in the 1964 Declaration on Economic and Social Progress, in the Second Development Decade resolutions and the like,formally at least accepted by both the West and the East.

This suggests that various recommendations of the UN General Assembly and other international bodies concerned with Third World problems are not free from hypocrisy but also not entirely removed from a realistic approach likely to lead to a consensus. Sometimes they are elaborated and pressed for without any possibility of their iminent realization but many principles of the Law of Development based on common Third World postulates and with western support as well, continue to play a growing role in facilitating the process of social and political change that was also given impetus by their legal formulation and the entry into force of proper international legal dispositions. The number of North-South conferences was particularly impressive in 1981. True, the Cancun summit conference failed in elaborating an emergency programme and new binding norms. Now the "ball" is again at the United Nations, called on to start "global negotiations." Notwithstanding, the "spirit of Cancun" was recognized by the spokesman of the Group of 77 as a step forward, giving a real political impulse to the work on ever more effective policies for the benefit of the Third World poorest.[157]

Notes

1. An early analysis of the problem is to be found in the book: C. Balandier *et al. Le Tiers Monde, sous-développement et développment* (P.U.F., Paris, 1956) and see also L. Wolf-Philipps, "Why the Third World?" *The Third World Quarterly*, I, No. 1, 1979, p. 105.

2. Jouve, p. 13, see also Les socialistes" pp. 15-17, ew, 33-34.

3. J. Ki-Zerbo in *Le Monde*, 29 and 30, V. 1977.

4. Y. Lacoste, *Geographie du sous-développment*, (Paris, P.U.F. 1976), 3iéme Edit. pp. 73-74.

5. H. Morgenthau, "The New Diplomacy of Movement" in "Encounter" (Aug. 1974) and see the conclusions drawn in J.S. Nye Jr. "Independence and Interdependence," 22 *Foreign Affairs*, (Spring 1976) pp. 133, 143-5.

6. Cfr. W.P. Bundy, Elements of Power, *Foreign Affairs* (October 1977) p. 8; R. Legvold, The Nature of Power, *ibid* pp. 50 and 52; R. Dahrendorf, International Power, *ibid* p. 72; J.C. Campbell, Oil Power in the M.E., *ibid*, p. 110 and see also "Les Socialistes" p. 114.

7. *Le Monde*, 10 and 11, VII. 1977.

8. The Global Political Assessment, April 1976-October 1976 (The Research Institute on International Change, Columbia University) p. 31.

9. *Cf.* with the conclusions in R. Garaudy, *Pour un dialogue des civilisations* (Paris; Edit. Denoèl, 1977) and the review of this book by H. Bourges in Le Monde, 1.IV. 1977.

10. For details on the political framework of the Third World, see i.a. D. Schroeder, *Die Konferenzen der dritten* Welt (Hamburg, Hamburg University Press, 1968) pp. 1-24 and A.W. Sing and Tran van Dinh (eds.), From Bandung to Colombo, Conferences of the Non-Aligned Countries, 1955-1975, (N.Y. Third Press Reviews of Books Co. 1976), passim. For the proper documentation see O. Jankowitch and K.P. Savant, "The Third World without superpowers," *Collected Documents of the non-aligned countries*, Vol I, Oceana Publications, N.Y., 1978.

11. For an explanation of the organization of the Third World, see i.a. O. Guillard, "Organization politique du troisieme Monde," 57 *RTM* (1974) p. 88. The problem is also described in greater detail in my book in Hebrew on *Africa's Path to Independence* (Tel Aviv: Bronfman Publishers, 1971) pp. 83-114.

12. The so-called Group of 77 is one of the non-aligned countries' informal organizations consisting today of more than 120 members of the General Assembly, which had signed the Declaration adopted by the 1964 Conference held in Algiers.

13. The Debt Problem, *B.P.P.* No. 1 (1974) p. 18.

14. Les Socialistes, p. 58.

15. For a more detailed analysis of the evolution of the Third World's position in the period before UNCTAD IV and its aftermath, see M. Nitsch, "Zur Ordnungspolitischen Diskussion uber die Neue WeltWirtschaftsordnung, Stiftung Wissenschaft unde Politik, Ebenhausen 1976; for the pressures on the socialist bloc during the UNCTAD IV, see i.a. W. Hoffmann, "Der Baer an der Hintertuer," Die Zeit Nr. 23 (1976) SS. 25, 26.

16. See M. J. Williams, "The Aid Program of the OPEC Countries," 2, *Foreign Affairs*, (1976) 311, 321, "Le Fonds Monetaire arabe se donne pour l'immediat des

objectifs limites," *Le Monde*, 25. IV.1977; and "Les pays arabes jugent excessives les demandes africaines d'aide financiere," *Le Monde*, 6-7.III.1977.

17. The U.S. and the Third World (Washington: Govt. Print Office, Dept. of State Pub. 8863, July 1976) p. 45.

18. On doubts as to the possibility of maintaining this alliance, see Jouve, *op. cit.*, p. 140; cfr. also J. Amuzegar, A. Requiem on the North-South Conference, *Foreign Affairs* (October, 1971) p. 151.

19. See "Aid as an International Partnership,"*GT* (Nr. 71) 1975, 3, covering the new Bonn aid program, reflecting this direction. For a recent corroboration of this program see "17 Thesen zur Politik der Zusammenarbeit" *E+Z*, 7.8.79, p.4.

20. R.W. Arad, U.B. Arad, R. McCulloch, J. Pinera and A.L. Hollick, *Sharing Global Resources*, McGraw Hill Book Company, New York, 1980, pp. 54, 64 and 101-102.

21. J.K. Galbright, "Plain Lessons of a Bad Decade," *Foreign Policy* (No. 1) 1970, 37; Also see the conclusions in A. Buchan, "Power and Civilization in the 1970s," New York, 1973 and for an opposite attitude see: M. Mushkat, The Voice and Problems of Africa at the United Nations, XXV and XXVI, Africa (Rome, No. 4, 1970 and No. 1, 1971) pp. 386-412 and 29-58.

22. "International Round Table in Yugoslavia," Yugoslav Life (No. 5) 1975, 408.

23. M. Thee, "North South Relations," *BPP* (No. 4, 1974) 354.

24. J. Bognar, *The Future and Role of the Developing Countries in the World Economy* (Budapest: Hungarian Academy of Science, 1969) p. 26.

25. Cf. G. Abbot, "Size, Viability, Nationalism and Political Development," *International Journal* (Nr. 1, 1968) 221 and the conclusions of A. Robinson (Ed.) *The Economic Consequences of the Size of Nations* (New York and London: Macmillan, 1960) p. 56.

26. Jouve, p.58.

27. For details of this position in its recent elaboration, see L. Krizsan, *Lenin's Conception of Alliance and Emergence of the Third World* (Budapest: Hungarian Academy of Science, 1973) p. 26.

28. Nitsch, *op. cit*, pp. 34-35.

29. For this attitude see i.a. K. Knorr, *The Power of Nations: The Political Economy of International Relations* (Princeton; Princeton Univ. Press, 1975), passim, and on "Group Power" see i.a. Bundy, *op. cit.*, p. 18.

30. Cf. G. Caire, "Ideologies du développement et dévéloppement de l'idéologie" et G. Labica, "Pour une approche critique de l'idéologie," *RTM* (No. 57, 1974) 5-6 and 45.

31. I have tried to elaborate this problem in more detail in my essay "Figures du Socialisme Africain," *Mondes en Devéloppement* (Paris, 1975) pp. 59-86.

32. Cf. F.A. Sayegh (Ed.), *The Dynamics of Neutralism in the Arab World: A Symposium* (Chandler, San Francisco, 1964) p. 9.

33 See Laquer, op. cit., pp. 194 and 196-197 and comp. with J. Stefanowicz, *Stary, Nowy Swiat*, PAX, Warsawa, 1978, pp. 112 and 139.

34. Quoted in the *Far Eastern Economic Review* (No. 3, 1974) 35.

35. See L. Mates, *Nonalignment Theory and Current Policy*, (New York: Oceana Publ. Inc., 1972), passim, but particularly pp. 328-365.

36. R.L. Rothstein, "Foreign Policy and Development: From Non-Alignment

to International Class War:, *International Affairs*, 4 (1976) p. 598 and ff. Also consult Rothstein's *Alliances and Small Powers* (New York: Columbia Univ. Press, 1968), passim.

37. On the disunity of the Third World countries even during the Sea Conference see i.a. Y. Robeyrol, "La mer d'Empoigne," *Le Monde* 20.V.1977.

38. A.A. Mazuri *Towards a Pax Africana: a study of ideology and ambition*, (Chicago: University of Chicago Press, 1961) p. 142.

39. For a more detailed discussion of the developments through these conferences, see P.F. Smets, *De Bandung a Moshi* (Bruxelles, 1964) and M. Mushkat, Problems of Political and Organizational Unity in Africa, in J.C. Rolland (Ed.) "Africa, The Heritage and the Challenge," (Fawcett Publications: Greenwich, 1974), pp. 401-415.

40. See H.R. Targ, "Colonial Dominane and Dependence: Post-Industrialism and International Relations Theory," *International Studies Quarterly*, 3, 1976, pp. 461 and ff.

41. I tried to shed new light on this assumption elsewhere. See M. Mushkat, "Global Versus Sovereign-Orientated Approaches in Contemporary International Law," XVI, *International Problems*, (Fall, 1977, Nos. (102-31), p. 28 and ff.

42. P.A. Baran and P.M. Sweezy, "Notes on the Theory of Imperialism" in K.T. Fann and D.C. Hodges (Eds), *Readings in U.S. Imperialism* (Boston; Porter-Sargent, 1971), passim.

43. See A.G. Frank, "On the Mechanisms of Imperialsim: the Case of Brazil" in Fann and Hodges, *op. cit.*, pp. 237-79; E. Caleano, "Latin America in the Theory of Imperialism," Fann and Hodges, *op. cit.* pp. 205-55; and R.M. Marini, Dialectique de la Dépendence (Paris: Mapero, 1973), passim; and T. Dos Santos, "The Structure of Dependence," Fann and Hodges, *op. cit.* pp. 225-37.

44. Cf. S. Schwartzmann, "International Development and International Feudalism: The Latin American Case," *IPRA Studies in Peace Research* (Van Gorcum, Assen, 1966) pp. 52-77. For a criticism of the dichotomic approach to the international system, supposedly divided into powerful, developed and dominated, developing nations, see, i.a., I. Sachs, "Developpement, Utopie. Projet de societe," XIX *RTM*, No. 25, 1978 p.648.

45. See i.a. G. Lagos, *International Stratification and Underdeveloped Countries* (The University of North Carolina Press, 1963), passim.

46. J. Galtung, A. "Structural Theory of Imperialism," *JPR* 2 (1971) pp. 71-119, H. Hvem, "Global Dominance System," *JPR* 4 (1973) pp. 329-40; and D. Senghas "Conflict Formation in Contemporary International Society." *JPR* 3 (1973), 163-84.

47. Targ *op. cit.*, p. 473.

48. Cf. W.W. Ernst, "Friedliche Koexistenz aus spezifisch-ideologischer Sicht," *Wiener Blätter zur Friedenforschung*, 7-8, (1975-1976) p. 57.

49. Cf. K. Seitz, "Die Dritte Welt" in *EA* Nr. 7 (1975), 214.

50. For details of this position, see P.J. Jalée, *Le pillage du Tiers Monde Paris* (Maspero, 1975); E. Bosserup and I. Sachs, *Aide extérieure aux Pays Indépendents* (Mouton, 1971); T. Mende, *De l'aide à la Recolonisation; Les lecons de l'Echec*, (Le Seuil, 1972) and T. Hater, *Aid as Imperialism* (Boston: Pelican Books, 1971).

51. For details on this attitude see: A.G. Frank, *Lumpen-Bourgeosie et Lumpen-Développement* (Maspero, 1971) p. 135.

52. A Emmanuel, *Unequal Exchange* (London, 1972) p. 264.

53. *Proceedings of the UN Conference on Trade and Development* (New York United Nations Pub. Vol. II, 1969) p. 9.

54. In 1977, it was on the average 0.33% of the GNP, while a year earlier it was 0.364743 and in the years 1965-1967 it was 0.42443, never achieving the 0.70% pledged. See M. Boyer, "L'effort des pays riches en faveur des nations sous-developés a de nouveau baissé l'an dernier," *Le Monde* 30.VI.1977.

55. Of 0.03%, see P. Drouin in *Le Monde* 7.V.1977.

56. The debts of the poor countries doubled since the beginning of the rise of oil prices from 110 billion in 1973 to more than 200 billion in 1976. According to a recent UNCTAD study published in May 1977, the total debt of the non-oil Third World countries reached the total of $240 billion by the end of 1976. See Le Monde 17.18.VII. 1977. On the still limited Arab-Black cooperation in spite of operating a special bank for development since 1973 for that purpose, a fund created by the Arab League in 1974, a special Arab fund for Africa also opened in 1974, on the augmentation of bilateral aid mainly by Saudi Arabia, and the elaboration of the Charter of Afro-Arab cooperation still fictious, see Le monde 5.III. 1977 and Cf. R. Delcour, "Le fonds monétaire arabe se donne pour l'immédiat des objectifs limités," *Le Monde* 23.IV.1977.

57. D. Senghas, Weltwirtschaftsordung und Entwicklungspolitik. Pladoyer fur Dissoziation, (Frankfurt, Suhrkampf, 1977), and see his: Strukturelle Abhangigkeit und Unternetwicklung, Wirtschaftsdienst (II-1975), p. 108 and for a critic of this attitude see i.a. D.W. von Amerongen, Volle Integration der Entwicklungslander in die Weltwirtschaft, E+Z (7.8.77), p. 7.

58. *GT* (817, 11. XII. 1977) p. 5.

59. EZ (7.8.1977) pp. 6 and 8.

60. Nitsch, *op. cit.*, pp. 6, 10 and ff.

61. J. Amuzegar, *op. cit.* pp. 155-159 and see "Ein neuer Nord-Süd *Die Zeit* (50,2,XII.77); For greater stress also on the negative results of development see i.a. S. Huntington, The Change to Change, 3 *Comparative Politics* (1971) pp. 283-332 and L. Binder et al. *Crisis Sequences in Political Development* (N.Y. Princeton Un. Press, 1971) passim. On the Second World's military undertakings in the Third World. particularly in Africa see i.a. I. Greig, *The Communist Challenge to Africa* (Foreign Affairs Publishing Co. London 1977) part. pp. 165 and ff.

62. See J. Power in the "*International Herald Tribune*" 4.III.1977.

63. "Les Socialistes" pp. 147-77. For a comprehensive analysis of the NIEO see, i.a. K.P.Sauvant and H. Hasenpflug (Ed.), *The New International Economic Order, Confrontation or cooperation between North, and South?* F.A. Praeger and Campus Verlag, Frankfurt, 1977.

64. Nitsch, *op. cit.*, pp. 43 and ff.

65. Cf. R.H. Green "Petroleum Prices," XXX *International Journan* 3 (1975), 398-99.

66. Cf. Windsor, *op. cit.*, pp. 171-72.

67. Cf. A. Besanson, *Court traité de Sovietologie* (Paris: Libraire Hachette, 1970) p.76.

68. Cf. Ch. Zorgbibe, *loc cit.*

69. Jouve, p. 241.

70. F. Luchaire, *Cours de droit international de devéloppement* (Paris: Les

Cours de Droit, 1970) p. 47.

71. R. Aron, *Dix-huit lecons sur la société industrielle* (Paris: Gallimard, 1962) p. 52.

72. M. Duverger, *Introduction a la politique* (Paris: Gallimard 1964) p. 354.

73. Jouve, p. 14.

74. Ibid, p. 239-40.

75. Cf. L. Focsaneanu in "*La crise de l'Europe et le droit international*" (Colloque de Caen de la Societé Francaise Pour le Droit International, Sufflot, 1976) p. 112.

76. See Zorgbibe, *loc. cit.*

77. See "Pays en joie de developpement et transformation de droit international" *Colloque d'Aix-en-Provence* (Société Française pour le Droit International Paris 1973) pp. 41 ff., 288, 309 and see G. De Lacharriere, "Identification et statuts des pays 'moins devéloppés'," (Annuaire français de Droit International, Paris, 1971) pp. 46 and ff.

78. See Ki-Zerbo in *Le Monde* 29-30.V.1977.

79. See f.i. J. Shofman, "Hacongres Hayehudi Haolami ve 'haolam hashlishi," (21 *Gesher*, Hebrew Review, August 1975) 83, p. 46-52.

80. Mende, *op. cit.*, p. 8.

81. Cf. J.S. Nye Jr., *op. cit.*, p. 132.

82. Cf. Ph. Decraene, *Le Monde* 25-26.V.1974.

83. See "Global Political Assessment," *op. cit.*, p. 113.

84. Les socialistes p. 103.

85. *Ibid*, p.119.

86. See particularly Chap. III of C. Bettelheim's, *Planification et croissance accelerée*, (Paris, Mapero, 1964).

87. See "Global Political Assessment," *op. cit.*, p. 12.

88. See "Les socialistes" op. cit., p. 58.

89. R. Debray, *La critique des armes* (Paris: Seuil, 1974), p. 83.

90. For this concept see also R. Dumont, *L'Utopie ou la mort!* (Paris, Seuil, 1973) p. 154.

91. See J. Duvignand, *Introduction a la sociologie*, Paris, (Gallimard, 1966), p. 132.

92. M. Mushkat, Die oekonomischen; politischen und menschlichen Faktoren der Unterentwicklung, *Politische Studien*, 216, vi-vii/1974, passim.

93. See Y. Lacoste, *Les pays sous-développés*, (Paris: PUF, 1976) p. 17.

94. Cf. Jouve, pp. 16, 22, 27-29.

95. For a good illustration of this fact, see the varous essays in E. de Kaat and G. Williams (Eds.) *Sociology and Development* (London: Tavistock Publications, 1974), passim.

96. N.D. Palmer, "The Afro-Asian in the United Nations," in F.B. Gross (Ed.), *United States and the United Nations* (1964, Un. of Oklahoma Press) pp. 125-69.

97. J.S. Stoessinger, *The Might of Nations* (1969, N.Y. Random House, 3rd ed.) pp. 103-4.

98. For the relevant documents, see, i.a., *The International Law of Development: Basic Documents*, comp. and ed. by A.P. Mutharika, 4 vols., MacMillan, 1978; as for the TW's impact on international law, see, i.a., R.C. Hingorani, *International Law: Afro-Asian Viewpoints*, MacMillan, 1979.

99. G. Feuer, "Les Principes Fondamentaux dans le Droit International du Dévelopment" in "Pays en voie de développement et transformation du Droit International" (Pedone, Paris 1974), B.V.A. Rölling, International Law and the Maintenance of Peace, *Netherlands Yearbook of International Law* (IV, 1973), pp. 54-64; I. von Münch, Must we lend a helping hand? *The German Tribune* (14, 1977) pp. 5-8; see also A. Agrawal's review of the Workshop on Alternative Energy Sources, WAES Report: Energy Global Prospects 1985-2000, *Die Zeit* (30, 15 VII 1977) p. 43.

100. D.E. Apter, Political Change: *Collected Essays*, (London, Frann CAD, 1973) p. VIII.

101. Ibid, p. 27.

102. Rothstein, *op. cit.*, p. 598 and ff.

103. Cf. E.J. Sady, *The United Nations and the Dependent Peoples* (Washington, 1956) p. 24.

104. G.A.R. 1514 (XV) and for the background and evolution of this problem see also i.a. M. Mushkat, The Process of Decolonization: International Legal Aspects, II, *University of Baltimore Law Review* (1972) No. 1, pp. 16-34.

105. .G.A.R. 2131 (XX).

106. G.A.R. 612 (VII).

107. G.A.R. 2200(A (XXI).

108. G.A.R. 2625 (XXV).

109. G.A.R. 2734 (XXV).

110. G.A.R. 2311 (XXII).

111. Cf. R. Higgins, *The Development of International Law Through the Political Organs of the United Nations* (London: 1963) p. 103 and S. Kaur, "Self Determination in International Law *(I.J.I.L.)* 4 (1970) pp. 487, 499, 502.

112. S. Prakash Sinha, "Has Self-Determination Become a Principle of International Law Today?" *I.J.I.L.* (Nr. 3-4(1974) 332 and ff.

113. As to the proper UN decisions, see, i.a. ONU *Chronique*, vol. XVII, No 1(1980, pp. 49, 51 and 54, particularly the UNGA Res. 34/94 of 13.xii.79 calling for the Total Eradication of Colonialism and the 1980 resolution on "Small Territories."

114. For the first formulation of the Five Principles of Peaceful Co-existence, see J.A.S. Grenville, *The Major International Treaties 1914—1973* (London: Methuen, 1974) p. 434.

115. See these documents i.a. in *Human Rights—A Compilation of International Instruments* (New York, U.N.) 1973.

116. Idem.

117. G.A.R. 3068 (XXVIII).

118. Human Rights, *op. cit.*, pp. 20, 97.

119. The Corfu Channel Case, ICJ Reports (1949) 124.

120. R. Coomarastramy, "U.N. Technical Assitance in the Development Decade," *Annual Review of UN Affairs* (1962863), 36.

121. For details on this development see i.a. M. Mushkat, Mainfold aid through the UN family, *Intereconomics* 93 (Hamburg, 1968), pp. 275-278, M. Mushkat, Africa's Impact On the Legal Order of Today's World Community, XXVIII-3, *Africa* (Rome, 1973) pp. 357-368.

122. At the 1967 Pledging Conference for the UN Development Program, 111 nations pledged $182.6 million for 1968. This included a pledge of $26.8 million for technical assistance and approximately $50.6 million for the Special Fund. See *U.N.*

Monthly Chronicle 10 (1967) 42-3. See also "The Capital Development Needs of the Ten Developed Countries," *Report of the Secretary General* (New York: U.N. Feb. 8, 1962) p. 62.

123. See "Les Socialistes et le Tiers Monde" *op. cit.*, p. 85.

124. For a brief analysis of the Pearson Report, see *Inter economics* 113 (1964); Jackson's Report was published as "A Study on the Capacity of the United Nations" in 1969.

125. "Les Resolutions dans la Formation du Droit International du Developement" *Etudes et Travaux de l'Institut de Hautes Etudes Inter nationales* (Geneve: 1971) pp. 25, 84 and passim.

126. "Les Socialistes et le Tiers Monde", *op. cit.*, p. 132.

127. Feuer G.,"Les Principes Fondamentaux dans le Droit International du Development," *Dossier de l'Institut des Sciences Juridques du Developement* (Nanterre: Univ. de Paris X, 1974) pp. 4,5.

128. See the elaboration of this problem i.a. in W. Friedmann, *The Changing Structure of International Law* (London: 1964) and M. Mushkat "The Needs of Developing Countries and the Shifting View of International Law," *Verfassung und Recht in Ubersee* (Hamburg: vol. IV no. 1, 1971) pp. 1-8.

129. See the views of G. Feuer and A.C. Colliard in "Pays en voie de development et la formation de droit international". Colloque d'Aix-en Provence, SFDI (Paris: Pedone 1973) pp. 188 and 195, see also M. Mushkat "Les Pays en voie du development et quelques problémes du droit des gens" in *Miscellanea G. van der Meersch* (Bruxelles: Bruylant 1972).

130. See f.i.p. Weil in "Aspects du droit international economique," SFDI, *Colloque d'Orleans* (Pedone, Paris 1972) p. 31 and ff.

131. Haemmarli A.B. "International Norm-Creation for a Divided Society: A Reappraisal of some Perennial Problems," *Orbis* (vol. 20, no. 2, 1976) pp. 316-7, 327, 330 and 341.

132. See B. Bollecker-Stern in "La Crise de l'Energie et le Droit International", SFDI, *Colloque de Caen* (Paris: Soufflot, 1976) pp. 110 and M. Mushkat "Principles Underlying the Development Assistance Machinery of the UN Family", *Verfassung und Recht im Ubersee* (Hamburg: No. 2, 1972) pp. 175-76.

133. See Colloque d'Aix-en-Provence, loc. cit., and M. Mushkat, The Process of African Decolonization, 6, *The Indian Journal of International Law* (Oct, 1966, No. 4) pp. 483-495.

134. Catogeropoulos—Stratis in "Colloque d'Aix-en-Provence", *op cit.*, p. 302.

135. Jouve, *op. cit.*, pp. 81 and 82 and M. Mushkat "Modern African Nationalism," *IPRA Studies in Peace Research* (Vol. V. Oslo: 1973) pp. 239-52.

136. Colloque d'Aix-en-Provence, *op. cit.*, p. 20.

137. Comp. Forschungspolitik in Bartelt et al. "*Das Parlament* (Vol. 27, 3.VII. 1976) p. 34.

138. Les Socialistes p. 112.

139. Jouve p. 293.

140. Colloque d'Aix-en-Provence, *op. cit.*, p. 99.

141. Combacau J. in Colloque de Caen *op cit.*, pp. 18-20.

142. Les Socialistes p. 132.

143. Colloque de Caen, *op. cit.*, pp. 284-93.

144. Ibid., pp. 77-8.
145. Salem M., *op. cit.*, pp. 759 and ff.
146. Colloque de Caen, *op. cit.*, p. 228.
147. *In Recueil des Cours* (Vol. I, Sijthoff, The Hague, 1970).
148. Virally M. in Colloque d'Aix-en-Provence, *op cit.*, pp. 307-11.
149. Jouve p. 52.
150. Bollecker-Stern B. in Colloque de Caen, *op. cit.*, pp. 41-2 and 55.
151. *Ibid.*, p. 225, the study "*Perspectives energétiques jusqu'en 1975*" was prepared by A. Bilot.
152. Rustow D.A. and Mugno J.F., *OPEC, Success and Failure* (N.Y. University Press, 1976) pp. 23, 28-9,52, 55, 95 and 120-1.
153. Freund W.S. "Endlösung für Entwicklungsländer eine Makabre Anti These," *Die Dritte Welt* (no. 3-4, 1974) p. 245.
154. Lowenthal R., "Soviet Counterimperialism," *Problems of Communism* (vol. XXV, no. 6, 1976) p. 53.
155. Duncan W. R., "The Communist Powers and the Third World," *Problems of Communism* (Vol. XXV, No. 6, 1976) p. 84.
156. Lowenthal R., *op. cit.*, p. 63.
157. Cf. J. Madeley and A. Skriver's observations in D&C, no. 6 (Nov-Dec) 1981.

Chapter 2

Development and Peace:

Some Aspects of Their Interdependence as Seen by Various Economists and Political Scientists

1 From the Classics to the Study of Imperialism

Economists tend to view development as a process of transformation of the rate of growth per capita income. The range observed extends from small or negative to one of significant self-sustained increase, which has a permanent long run impact. However, even those adopting this definition are aware that it is unsatisfactory and that socio-cultural indicators should also be considered.[1]

Some contemporary experts are of the opinion that development is essentially less an economic and more a social and political process.[2] It is frequently characterized by a transition from one social structure to another as a result of their interaction. The better understanding of these processes consequently depends on studying how governments use time and power to facilitate formation of new structures and their proper operations;[3] and on the study of how political and other movements and organizations act for the same purpose.

According to F. Perroux, development is rooted in a combination of social as well as psychological factors; they also induce undertakings for the cumulative and durable growth of the real product.[4] According to him, underdevelopment results chiefly from the non-operation and non-articulation of these factors and is a consequence of low payments and investments indispensable to a satisfaction of basic human needs. In modern times on a global scale, this usually happens due to domination of the leading economies over other less dynamic national economies. This remains an important moving force up to the present moment.[5] In truth, the predominant mechanism of the existing world order favor the efforts of the stronger to maintain and expand the impact of this superiority by means of having priviliges at the expense of the weaker economies.[6]

Some of these points were already evident in the writings of classical philosophers and economists, whose influence on political science at the present time should not be belittled; for they also paid much attention to the impact of peace and war on development. It is worth remembering that Marx conceived his teachings as rooted also in classical economics. Some modern peace and development researchers regard themselves as followers of his doctrine; others do not, but many regret that neither classical nor Marxist economists are sufficiently taken into account in present-day analyses of development problems relating to peace and war. Even when considered, their views are frequently distorted.[7]

It seems to us useful to recall here some of the relevant predispositions, certainly to fathom their impact on studies of imperialism, and how they are corroborated in modern writings.

Richard Cobden, referring in 1835 to Britain's wars, particularly with Russia, stressed above all the heavy burdens they had imposed on people.[8] John Stuart Mill, the great economist of the past century, emphatically called for employment of mankind's energies for the struggle for prosperity rather than for ruinous conflicts.[9] Both of these writers are frequently quoted among the first so strongly to highlight competition and free trade as factors inducing economic development and peaceful cooperation. They also favored an international division of labor leading to the establishment of a world market. They argued that its universal benefits were impossible in situations of war, which tended to preclude the necessary mobility of capital, labor, and investments and, moreoever, tended at the same time to lower standards of living.[10]

These writers, their predecessors, particularly Adam Smith (whose "Inquiry into the Nature and Causes of the Wealth of Nations" was first published in 1776 and who is considered to be the "father" of modern economic thought and science) and many of their followers recognized that free trade contributes to raising the world output and consequently to its cumulative wealth. According to Adam Smith, this is a function of the differentiation of labor on a global scale, which becomes limited as a result of war and colonial conquests, which do not contribute to the welfare of empires.[11]

The approach of another renowned representative of classical economics, David Ricardo, differs essentially from the optimist concepts of Adam Smith. He drew rather pessimistic conclusions from the analysis of the "natural forces" which Adam Smith described as designed to bring forth harmony and peace. Ricardo even shared Thomas Robert Malthus' theory of the role of wars, epidemics, and and other plagues in the "natural" depopulation by attrition that could only be avoided by such "positive" human applications as birth control and conservation.[12] He also pointed out that evil proceeds from bad government, want of education and above all, from the uncertainty of prosperity[13] that inevitably was curtailed or terminated by war, as well as by human errors of misconception and miscalculations which were theoretically preventable.

However, most of the classical economists opposed this view and the postulates of mercantilism (e.g., J. Child, W. Petty, A. Young) because mercantilists were against free trade and recommended territorial colonization and closed trade between metropolises and overseas dependencies as the ideal means of commercial and market expansion. They also critized the neo-mercantilists (e.g., J. Terry, excluding Joseph Chamberlain, who adopted the anticolonialist position of finance capital at the beginning of the industrial revolution). Their criticism is not diminished for understanding of various interrelationship theories on development or rather economic growth and political expansionism in its present-day form known as "imperialism."[14] Imperialism, which did not have always a pejorative meaning, also sometimes was represented by religious missionaries and the so-called "civilizing" ministrations undertaken by the British and others beginning in the mid-19th century with regard to "backward" non-European peoples. The missionary and "civilizing" zeal realized mostly in Africa and Asia in more recent times had copious precedents in expansionism of Antiquity and the mediaeval world.

Today "imperialism" is mainly an epithet used by its rivals to castigate the West for past and current colonialist, racist, aggressive, or exploitative policies of some Western countries and their allies without regard to their present orientations. It is rarely used to characterize Soviet expansionism and exploitation within and beyond Moscow's Eastern European satellite sphere of influence. Imperialism in this sense is seldom if ever heard with respect to the foreign policies of medium and small powers, conspicuously among them some post-colonial states. The term imperialism derives most probably from *Imperium Romanum*, but it is virtually impossible today to determine exactly the origin. Undoubtedly, its widespread use was introduced in the seventies of the past century, first into political vocabulary of English and later of other languages. The term "neo-imperialism" today refers first and foremost to the diverse forms of the external trade policies of the great European capitalist powers and the United states.

Popularization of the word "imperialism" seems to be mainly due to two men: The Liberal English economist and journalist, John A. Hobson, author of *Imperialism: A Study*, published in 1902, and the Russian Bolshevik leader, Vladimir Iliych Lenin, whose *Imperialism: The Highest Stage of Capitalism*, which, to a large extent based on Hobson's premises, was published in 1916. Both concentrated on an economic interpretation of the process, the latter's concept being in addition based on Marx's analysis of the capitalist system. The economic determinism intrinsic to their theories sufficiently justifies examination of their concepts of imperialism in terms of the conceptions of "classical" economists, who are also important for the highlighting of the non-economic aspects of imperialism as well. (Such non-economic motives include political, psychological, strategic, and cultural impulses that since the beginning of history have also inspired imperialism, meaning empire-building or the policy thereof).

Some doubt whether even qualified historians capable of assessing the causes and effects of imperialism with great precision can discern its real operation in the policies of national governments. If the vast literature on the various aspects of the subject and available data are taken into consideration and applied to past or current national policies, preconceptions of the futility of evaluating imperialism in the real world become invalid, especially if all the major theories are taken into account.[15]

Those who interpret imperialism in terms of single determinants—economic interests, lust for power and various other non-economic considerations—and those who condemn or praise it for various self-serving reasons only risk perversion of realistic knowledge. Some believe that imperialistic "enslavement" might be prevented or that a random measure of social change will merge from the abolition of imperialism. There are those who confine themselves to the cold examination of facts that contradict the findings of others for the sole purpose of debunking "expert" opinion. It is also possible to divide all social theorists, including imperialism specialists, into three categories: the structuralists, the dialecticians, and the evolutionists. The first concentrate on static forms and patterns, the second on interaction of macrostrata such as classes and nations, the third on the world viewed essentially as a disequilibrium system of innumerable interpenetrating social forms interacting under conditions of constant change. Each of them is actually a cross section of an evolutionary process at a certain time or over a continuum of time that determines subsequent developments. The result, however, frequently is deterioration because of the failure of efforts to improve social conditions immediately. The critical perusal below of different points of view on the problem of inquiry, makes the writer to a large extent, a subscriber to the evolutionary approach espoused by Professor Kenneth E. Boulding, and which views the social ills as a product of evolution.[16]

2. Economic Interpretation of Politics and Contemporary Realities

Monopolists were already condemned by Adam Smith, who regarded them as conspirators against the smooth working of international markets.[17] The opinion that they are also hindering a smooth division of labor on a world-wide scale essential to peaceful cooperation of all nations may be therefore regarded as rooted in his teachings. This point was strongly emphasized in Hobson's study, since he may be reckoned among the first who so clearly stressed the negative role of big business in its search for profitable markets and its alleged pressures for the use of force for this purpose.

The most potent drive towards enslavement of peoples overseas was, in Hobson's opinion, the excess of capitalist production over domestic demand. Although colonial possessions ultimately became a burden to the mother countries ,they were profitable to certain powerful vested interests in each of them. The influence of these interests has been used by Hobson and others to explain imperialist adventurism. This point corresponds to Ricardo's gloomy findings on the contradictory interests of various social strata,[18] but Hobson was rather optimistic. According to Hobson, the multifold phenomena of imperialism were not inevitable. He proposed social reform as a remedy for ending the maldistribution of wealth so that absorption of commodities and services within the producing country might be facilitated,[19] and, it might be added, in order to promote a peacefully ordered exchange of goods among nations.

Moderate Socialist leaders like Karl Kautsky were inclined to accept this view. They regarded military imperialism still as a device and believed that the economic concentrations could also lead to rationalization and peace compatible with antimilitarism of the giant financial and industrial capitalists. Kautsky's concept of "ultra imperialism" was also an alternative to Lenin's vision or nightmare of an inevitable imperialist war as the harbinger of Socialist revolution.

True enough, prominent businessmen in the past that Adam Smith and his followers had in mind and those who made their fortunes much later, like Andrew Carnegie and Henry Ford, were commercial pacifists. They maintained that the salvation of mankind lies in trade expansion. This tendency, elaborated in more detail below, is currently evident again in the actions of the giant transnational conglomerates. Their managers are aware how little national security can be bought in the nuclear era through military power, how unpredictable is the payoff of war, how war tends to serve the interests of ruling Soviet elites and their security and bureaucratic apparatuses.[20] Charles A. Beard's "devil theory" of imperialism based on the role of some American bankers in the interwar years between 1919 and 1939 did not contemplate this possibility; rather, he maintained that the perpetrators of war and their motives cannot be precisely determined. Actually, the leading persons who decide on steps leading to armed conflicts and who facilitate the slide towards the abyss can be ascertained. Beard had in mind the politicians consciously or unknowingly acting under the influence of bankers, other vested interests, and classes who supposedly could profit from war.[21]

The Orthodox Marxists Rudolf Hilferding, Rosa Luxemburg, Nikolai Bukharin and, of course, Lenin, adopted a determinist point of view. They based their conclusions, however, not only on Marx' conceptions of politics as a reflection of economic forces[22] nor did they limit themselves to merely considering the war-producing tendencies stressed earlier by Hobson and later by Beard. They concentrated on structural changes of capitalism, changes which, according to them, take place through concentration breeding unavoidably armed and self-destructive wars.

This abstract Marxist conclusion drawn from Hobson's proposition was laid down in Hilferding's *Finanzkapital* published in 1910.[23] He emphasized the growth of monopolistic tendencies and the role of finance capital in competition for markets, raw materials, and opportunities for profits in all parts of the world; finance capital thus lost liberalism, which was replaced by militarism. Kautsky, as mentioned above, described the developing international situation in other terms, namely by stressing the tendency of finance capital to encourage pacific expansion. This thesis was angrily rejected by the orthodox Marxists, among them Lenin and his followers, who supplemented Hilferding's theory not only with updating statistics, but also by dialectical examination. In 1913, Rosa Luxemburg added to Hilferding's considerations conclusions from the Marxist paradigm on enlarged reproduction; this, in Luxemburg's opinion, makes perpetual growth impossible and economic crisis unavoidable. In the absence of any means except war to evade these consequences, she wrote, surplus in a capitalist society can only be absorbed by the military.[24]

Lenin adopted all these propositions, putting the stress on another Marxist hypothesis, namely, pauperization of the masses. He maintained that such pauperization in capitalist countries diminished economic growth by depriving prospective consumers of purchasing power. Without this, he pointed out, both markets and opportunities for capital investment were diminished. Lenin claimed that capitalists compensated for shrinking domestic economies by irresistably seeking economic expansion overseas with the use of force; when foreign investment opportunities and markets are saturated and dominated by the strongest, further expansion efforts leads to conflict among capitalist rivals; when such fierce competition becomes manifested in the form of armed violence, as "imperialist war" is said to exist.

According to Lenin, unequal internal economic development in capitalist countries with respect to various parts of the economy not only intensifies rivalry, but also makes possible emergence of the weak who have overcome their prior inferiority and have put themselves in the ranks of capitalist leaders (e.g., the United States and Germany at the end of the 19th century); thereafter, Lenin asserts, the newly dominant super-capitalists continue the game of "imperialist war."

According to Lenin, imperialism is the "highest" and final "stage" of capitalist development precipitating the dying out of the system.[25] Today, more than 60 years after he issued the death certificate of capitalism, it not only continues to thrive, but has dynamically developed with veritably uninterrupted growth in spite of difficulties and passing crises of different kinds. It succeeded in consolidating and to some extent integrating its ranks. Stalin's prediction, shortly before his death, of another inter-imperialistic war seems today almost ridiculous. The system was apparently strong enough to give up its political power over its dominions overseas and to acquiesce in Soviet territorial gains after World War II. It clearly favors not only political, but also economic decolonization. It demonstrates that it is more and more interested in peace. It is even willing to help all its ideological and political rivals, including those who proclaimed themselves to be its gravediggers and inheritors, to get rid of technological and economic backwardness; moreoever this it would hand to them as a price of their acquiescence and participation in peaceful competition. This seems to be done not out of fear of war *per se* or disbelief in its supremacy, but because of socio-economic self-interests and fear of nuclear self-immolation, a clearly non-economic, political and human consideration.

True enough, the Western nations regard peace as an indispensable condition of their continued progress and increase of might. Peace is not only justified by subjective considerations, but also objectively rooted in the mechanisms of the current (post) industrial revolution with all its technological, scientific and administrative implications.

Still, as shall be seen, both Marxist-Leninist and non-Marxist economic interpretations of history and their corollaries of the inevitability of imperialism leading to war—continue to be seen by some economists as the only valid, albeit frequently different form. Some later variants are based less on the operation of capitalism than on the concept of the alleged war conspiracy of evil capitalists for purpose of selfish private gain.

The latter, labelled by Charles A. Beard as the "Devil Theory" of imperialism was very popular in the aftermath of World War I. Pacifists, Communists, and others indignantly blamed World War I and subsequent conflicts on greedy profiteers and "munitioneers," who must be held accountable for all ills, sufferings, and losses incurred by mankind thereafter. This to a large extent was the position of the US Senate Nye Committee, which from 1934 to 1936 investigated, in retrospect, the alleged reasons for American entry into World War I.[26] Arguments like the one directed against "Wall Street" warmongers was raised against the Krupps in Germany and other European arms dealers. After World War II the same arguments were made—and belied—in the post-war war crimes trials against German industrialists (Krupp, Flick, I. G. Farben *et al.*) in Nuremberg. Preventive measures against alleged industrial warmongering and economic-plunder were supposedly undertaken by industrial "deconcentration" and "decartelization" policies of the Allied occupation regimes in Germany and Japan.

They were also reinforced by the concepts of the crime against peace and of economic aggression, elaborated in various international documents.[27]

The above-mentioned agruments do not take into account the fact that German industrialists did not "make" Hitler, that they joined him only after his party had become a leading political force; that it is quite possible that Hitler would have come to power even if the Nazis had not received a single pfenig from the bankers and industrialists. They also ignore the fact that the Fascist and Communist states operated and continue to operate quite independently of or even against the interests of, in the first case, the capitalist, and in the second case, the supposedly proletarian ruling class.[28]

Needless to stress here the the repeatedly proven thesis that all aforementioned economic interpretations of violent Axis imperialism in World War II, like those of the Nye Committee condemning profiteers and "munitioneers," fail completely to explain the causes of the majority of wars in history waged for an infinite multitude of reasons.

The critical reappraisal of such economic determinist theories by H. J. Morgenthau, for instance, pays attention to the ancient, medieval and modern wars to prove the primacy of politics over economics in different armed conflicts.[29] As already mentioned, past and particularly present opposition of many leading businessmen to war and their recent corresponding reliance on peaceful cooperation for expansion and profits[30] becomes increasingly evident. Big business is becoming evermore sceptical of the ability of the military to protect its interests, increasingly fearful of the destructiveness of war, and more and more in dread of becoming dependent on the monosonistic market represented by belligerent national governments. Big business influences are continually reinforced in this position by priorities given by some ruling elites to technological and economic perfection over territorial aggrandizement,[31] and by tendencies toward larger transnational commercial transactions independent of the types of government of trading partners, as recently demonstrated by the efforts to save Communist Poland, shocked by the strikes of 1980-1981. Thus, the risks and dangers of military and territorial expansion are seen to far outweigh any commercial advantage. This is one more reason why the bulk of armed forces deployed in combat after World War II was mainly operated by the USSR, in the Soviet Bloc. Contingents of the armed forces of both superpowers were sometimes used indirectly, and rarely directly; however, outside of their respective spheres of influence, principally in the Third World, whose armies have been most frequently engaged in bloody internal conflicts unrelated to economic claims and expectations.

The dangerous post-World War II East-West confrontations over Berlin, the Greek civil war, Korea, and the Vietnam war were doubtless routed in non-economic considerations. New Western military interventions seem rather unlikely after the disastrous Vietnam experience and the failure of the American rescue operation in Iran. The only superpower that continues to be still militarily active beyond its acknowledged sphere of influence is the USSR, which today threatens the stability mainly in Asia and Africa.

Theories based on economic determinism, like Socialist theories of imperialism and military intervention designs and so-called "mistake" theories about the security elites of both camps do not make sense today. Nobody considers them any more either in regard to Soviet military adventures, or to intra-Third World scissions, or to predicted but unfulfilled Marxist-Leninist prognostications about self-destructive "imperialist wars" that "inevitably" toll the death knell of capitalism. These theories have never been valid with regard to conflicts provoked by such non-economic reasons as the quest for glory, honor, prestige, nor by fear of attack or extermination;[32] the latter prevails in present superpower and the Middle East wars.

It seems needless to mention that economic theories never applied to understanding of the tribal, racial and ideological and random causes, which played an important role in past dynastic, ethnic, religious and "national liberation wars" everywhere; however, they continue predominantly to influence present Soviet and Third World policies in contradiction to the need to work for peaceful coexistence enunciated formally by government first.

These policies are less frequently motivated by valid security reasons and by attempts to distrupt the existing interbloc power relations than by the will to protect "fraternal" regimes already dominated by Communists or Communist-oriented governments; they are aimed at the enlargement of the Soviet sphere of influence, especially in political vacuums. In the case of internecine Third World political strife, tension and war are most often a result of entirely irrational intertribal circumstances. By and large, the reasoning of the economist theorists on matters of war and peace, particularly as regards the allegedly inevitable self-destruction of capitalism by imperialist war is often at wide variance with the established historical record and known habits of individual and social behavior.

The latter point was already dealt with in greater detail by Joseph Schumpeter in 1918, that is, soon after the publication of Lenin's main study on imperialism. Joseph Schumpeter put forward a psychological and sociological counter-interpretation of the economic theories on imperialism, developing the idea of "atavism" in society. According to him, capitalism is by nature anti-imperialistic. Its aggressive elements are alien elements, carried into its realm from the outside. They are presently supported by non-capitalist factors, which survived from earlier ages, when warriors played important roles in concrete social situations. These aggressive elements were thus viewed as stemming from past and not from present relations of economic production.[33]

Using the Marxist method of class struggle in forms later refined by neo-Marxists (e.g., Dobb, Baran, Sweezy, Magdoff, O'Connor, and Perlo), Schumpeter came to the conclusion that wars and imperialism contradict the "inner logic" of capitalist structure. The capitalists, he claimed, seek to win over the state for themselves. Serving the interests of the state, they often acted in favor of interests that were actually foreign to the bourgeosie.[34] This led to the conclusion that Marx' doctrine of the state as the executive of the capitalists is entirely wrong, since the capitalists are first and foremost moneymakers and not patriots or any other kind of nationalists. The same is said to be characteristic of today's multinational capitalism as it was of its predecessors all of them realizing that war did not pay, frequently supported or organized political pressure groups against armament, professional armies, and war diplomacy. Taking into account capitalists' aversion for war and the preponderance of non-economic conflicts, Schumpeter concluded that imperialism is irrational; and that it contradicted the utilitarian foundations, the individualistic philosophies, and other humanistic tendencies of capitalism. By and large, most of capitalism's authentic leaders opposed discrimination, enslavement.

This is also a result of the fact that capitalism is associated with pluralism and democracy, and that democracies, with rare exceptions, always favor pacifism. They even find it difficult to understand those who do not share this predisposition. Frequently they are so naive that they wonder how can anyone be so unreasonable as to regard war as an instrument for the solution of conflicts.[35] This view is intensively exploited by the Soviets in their expansionist ambitions and attempts to establish military superiority.

Considering the consequences of the atomic age, but ignoring some, quite probably not only Soviet, concepts of the "first atomic blow," M. Merle came to the conclusion that all armed conflicts are essentially irrational and that the only rational behavior in this respect was the one of the superpowers determined to avoid a suicidal war of thermonuclear annihilation.[36]

It is worth noting that Schumpeter did not always concentrate on the historical elements in shaping his theory of imperialism and how it distorted early capitalist forms. Under the influence of K. Renner, the leading Austrian Marxist of the time, he became interested in mainly pinpointing its socially destructive features. Highlighting, on the one hand, the adverse impact of the socio-cultural *milieu* of the economy and, on the other, the irrational motivation of most aggressive international wars, he consequently enriched the argumentation used today by many peace and development researchers. The latter conceive the South-South conflicts as predominantly rooted in tribal, religious, racial, ethnic, national and other indigenous antagonisms leading to war more frequently without interference by the capitalist West or the Communist East.

Schumpeter's writings are also important for a better understanding of some of the present-day tendencies in the West. The West in its recent stage of development—but not necessarily the "highest" (which in any case cannot be determined yet as "postindustrial"[37] but rather as a "postimperial" stage) is claimed by Schumpeter to revive the classics interest in peace. Today, the neo-capitalist—and its offspring, the social-democratic—worlds strive to settle all international disputes exclusively by non-belligerent means. At the same time, they are trying to fulfil anew the rôle stressed by Marx of speeding up the decomposition of the outdated socio-economic structures, to facilitate the access of less developed countries to technological knowhow, and of contributing to the modernization of all territories and regions, within and outside its frontiers. The Marxist-oriented expert on Third World problems, Professor Arghiri Emmanuel, underrates this rôle of the most industrialized countries; hence he is reviving his teacher's contention hat these countries also show the way to a better future for the less developed. The difference between them is said to be determined by the time necessary for transition from one stage of growth to a higher one. He also criticizes the overall negation of the rôle in strengthening the trend of universal economic modernization in all parts of the world and its internationalization. This rôle is said to be similar to that of Great Britain in India in the times of Marx.[38]

The same point is also saliently made in R.J. Barnet's writings. Quoting K. Kautsky and his interpretation by George Lichtheim,[39] he too seems to believe in the rationalization of the world economy by giant cartels, which finally have opted for peace in opposition to war that slows down the accumulation of capital and profits. Barnet points out the potentialities of the multinational corporations as a structure, likely not only to eliminate both economic feudalism and waste, but dangerous political and military rivalries as well.

Barnet doubtlessly is right in charging national security managers with the responsibility for war diplomacy along with the political, economic, and military bureaucracies and public opinion manipulators in the West and East alike; indeed, all of them are mainly interested in accumulating un-economic intangibles such as "influence" and "power." He also seems to be right when he distinguishes between war and imperialism; thus, he regards the latter in its broadest sense as domination of the weak by the strong independently of territorial expansion and the economic system from which it proceeds, which is claimed to be determined by the human condition and existing standards of development.

Barnet stressed that no tension or decisions for war are determined exclusively by economic factors. Ascribing them to any single cause is being often ludicrous. He nonetheless sees the truly essential roots of war only in manifestation of bureaucratic coalitions. True, he ignores the fact that some of them are influenced by economic interests. He therefore contradicts his own contention that bureaucracies do not exist in the air and do not respond only to their own inner logic and to their own laws; rather, they are an expression of the socio-economic and political organization of society and its dominant forces.[40]

The First World is changing and continues to change its essence and image in the above-mentioned direction fitting the post-colonial and the hopefully approaching post-imperial era. So are the Second and the Third Worlds changing, comprising, however, still strong war-productive elements in a process of interpenetration and interaction comprising also growing factors favorable to peace-building.

It is worth noting, that the First World gives now unprecedented weight to the human rights issue. This is evident also from the 1977-78 Belgrade and the 1980-81 Madrid Conferences for the appraisal of the Helsinki commitments. This issue receives today more attention by the international community than many other problems. True, the First World has now at its disposal an entirely different economic-technological infrastructure and military might that also favors the growth of interest in both, in human rights and in peace. This seems almost axiomatic because global wars in the present state of military technology quite possibly could result in the extinction of life on earth. Foreign welfare aid by national capitalists is obviously self-serving. Although such aid occasionally is indirect, it more frequently is direct and purposefully inclined to the needs of recipients and the end of all forms of colonization. By and large, colonialism ultimately became a source of embarrassment rather than prestige and profits. Thus, decolonization today is strengthened not only by a growth of sense of responsibility, altruism and justice. Its promotion was a result of the unsupportable economic and administrative burden imposed by colonialism on metropolises as the strategic and economic value of colonial dependencies correspondingly diminished. By the end of World War II, the traditional European colonial powers were no longer able or willing to continue their leading rôle in international affairs. The leadership rôle devolved on the Americans and Soviets.[41] They play this rôle in specific conditions of the nuclear era, trying to prevent a clash between them but intensifying their dangerous rivalry for influence in the Third World, particularly in the Middle East, Asia and Africa.

American and Western willingness generally to participate more actively in the efforts to successfully narrow the gap between the industrialized and non-industrialized and Socialist states determined by the will to prevent an escalation of rivalry is becoming also under the Reagan Administration more and more evident. So are Western efforts to speed up Third World industrialization and to improve the standards of living, skills, and productivity of their populations. The First World's purported drive for the internationalization of human rights, particularly by the American Carter Administration with its stress on morality, has launched a crusade for the abolition of racial discrimination and racist régimes claimed to be vestiges of the colonial past; but the human rights issue has been employed also as an American pressure tactic designed to bring about the settlement of local disputes in Africa and the Middle East on the Administration terms.

All this, of course, may denote the emergence of a new and subtle form of peaceful superpower neo-imperialist and neo-colonialist penetration in response to Soviet imperialism; apparently this conforms with the vagueries of the postcolonial international system that overtly demand "pacific settlement" and "peaceful coexistence." True, for the time being it is aimed to prevent first and foremost a thermonuclear war mainly between the superpowers.

Capitalist producers need more markets to absorb their burgeoning productions. New markets are substantially available in the Second and Third Worlds. As the Second and Third Worlds develop, new markets are thereby opened to absorb proliferating goods and services from the capitalist world of production; the capitalist system, however, needs solvent clients and is not willing to suffer from the growing indebtedness of the Socialist[42] and Third World countries.[43] Capitalist investment in Socialist and Third World countries may not yield profits in the short run—indeed, quite the opposite! In the long run, developmental capitalist investments may not only head off wars and revolutionary outbursts but also may promote profitable markets for capitalist products. Such proved to be the case of the installation free of charge of an electrical grid in Sonora Province, Mexico, where none previously existed, by the Westinghouse Corporation two decades ago. Nobody, after all, seriously expects the capitalist system to invest for other than profit motives and other non-altruistic reasons!

This gives rise to the so-called "double rationality" theory as it was labelled by Merle. Motivation according to this theory is supplied by internal politics, whereby governments demanding sacrifices of their subjects, who are not willing to give up their privileges, are only reluctantly tolerated by their constituencies. Under this scenario, the business community ruefully acquiesces in temporary profit losses for the sake of greater security and tranquility, important both for the promotion of human and national rights, and trade and its rewards, as well, although the latter may be realized in the long run only.[44] Obviously, this does not mean that there is room for an unreserved glorification of all forms of free enterprise or grounds for viewing old fashioned capitalistic models always as the best or only way to deal with painful social problems at home or abroad. The more so since they frequently ignore various cultural values so important in the process of development.

Merrill Jackson seems to be absolutely right in stressing that development depends merely on continually improving cultural values and the better consideration of personal experience and of human needs and their satisfaction potential, which has nothing to do with capitalist ideologies. True enough, there may be many roads to development; some of them result, as was convincingly pointed out in J. Chonchol's propositions, from the specifics of the cultural, sometimes still pre- or anti-capitalist traditions, orientations and situations of the various countries that are shaped within each society.[45] This does not mean that self-reliance will always be helpful,[46] or that nothing is worth studying in capitalist or socialist systems.

Although capitalism encompasses many instructive experiences, it would be wise to remember that it is based not only on egalitarian ideals and democratic traditions. It is also built on human exploitation. Hundreds of thousands of workers, including men and women and children in the 7 to 14 age bracket, paid with their health and lives for capital accumulation in the West in the early period of the industrial revolution.

Suffice to reread the famous reports of Villermé on the situation in 19th century France[47] and those of other observers, who described the squalor of life in Lancashire and other English industrial centers of developing industrial production in England. Even more tragic was the situation pictured in 1828 by the Lion magazine[48] and later analyzed by Marx and Engels and decried even by writers enthused over the existing system. It is also necessary to understand that the progress of industrial growth in the 19th century astronomically increased the terrible sufferings, injustices and contributed in different ways to the bloodshed of World War I,[49] and World War II and the later wars. But even today in times of peace and relative prosperity in the West more than 15 million people—and among them a growing number of young men and women—are unemployed. Almost like their rivals in the Communist and the Third World, they frequently live in an increasing indigence, whereas only about 10 million in the countries of the European Economic Community (EEC.) still are crippled by poverty.[50]

Although capitalism has to cope with tremendous problems of unemployment, inflation, maldistribution, unpredictable and uneven economic cycles and technological managerial complexities, it still manages to thrive and to generate impressive incomes. In turn, through savings, they lead to undreamed of and unprecedented annual production levels. Moreover, capitalist flexibility and its inherent profit motive could provide sufficient incentive for successful resolutions of difficulties occasioned by the "energy crisis," ecological threats, poverty and a host of other socio-economic problems, their prompt solution being hampered by the growing security expenses.

The arms race continues to spiral because certain militaristic and messianic representatives of Communism still preach, contrary to their co-existential principles, the sacrosant duty to protect the fruits of their revolution against the aggressive designs of the imperialists and to put an end to the bourgeois system of degradation.[51] It has provoked—as it has been recently demonstrated by the occupation of Afghanistan and the efforts to exploit the Iranian and South Yemenite revolutions—the expansionist policies of the Soviet Bloc on all continents and its strenuous efforts to achieve military supremacy.

The coercive and bloodthirsty Stalinist manner of industrialization and militarization and the similar methods of many Third World ruling elites to promote modernization and national integration often convey the impression that these governments do not govern in the interests of humans, but rather in the name of an abstract, dehumanized ideology of development. They seem to confirm an old Marxist thesis that violence remains everywhere and is always the most important economic factor that in turn determines the transition of socio-economic structures, the obsolescence of old, and the birth of new systems. Yet, nothing justifies either the gloomy conclusions of Marx, Hilferding, Luxemburg and Lenin, particularly the ones foretelling the approaching collapse of what is now called the First World or doomsday prophesies for the whole world.

Development issues were described only a few years ago in extremely dark colors as supposedly insoluable problems revolving in a vicious circle. Some economists and others indeed exaggerated the gloomy prospects of development by concentrating on paradoxes and shortcomings. These critics nevertheless conceded that the poverty of many people was attributable to their low productivity, which is caused by the scarcity of investment capital; moreover, unwillingness to invest, results from investors' impressions of unpromising markets and the non-availability of other factors of production.[52]

Today, a growing number of Western experts on Third World and particularly Africa's problems are of the opinion that the NIEO (the proposed New International Economic Order already mentioned above) comprises elements also of a quite realistically conceived program. They are also convinced that the debate on its implementation will sooner or later lead to a compromise beneficial to all parties[53] contrary to the radical prognosis that the program will completely fail or even aggravate the situation.[54] Not only renowned economists like Perroux who were inclined to subscribe to sceptical conclusions, stressed the silent revolution in economic thought demonstrated by the abandonment of market concepts.

Perroux does not accept the thesis that it was only the energy crisis that gave new impetus to efforts to improve the Third World situation. He stressed the greater rôle of the poor in the world politics and their impact on the superpowers by means of public opinion mass media. He pinpointed the human dimension of the problem and praised the Tinbergen Report prepared for the Club of Rome that postulated remedies not merely based on a new international division of labor.[55]

It is worth noting that not only futurologists like Herman Kahn, but also leading figures of the Club of Rome such as Aurelio Pescei (who for many years was fascinated by the alarming Massachusetts Institute of Technology model of the "Limits of Growth" elaborated by Dennis Meadows and his team), and even the economists of the Vassily Leontieff school are less pessimistic nowadays about the future of the world economy.[56]

Conclusions of the Bariloche group rejected the MIT model entirely. They conceded that, after all, the fate of man does not depend on insurmountable physical barriers, but rather on social and political factors that man must modify. Far from being doomed to crowd itself out of existence, to smother itself in pollution, or exhaust the planet's capacity to feed it, they and recently the International Institute of Comparative Social Research in Berlin, headed by Prof. K. W. Deutsch, assert that mankind is still in a position to choose a future free from these threats.[57] This conclusion, strenghtened by the Brandt Commission and by other bodies[58] and its possibility to initiate an objective action for this proposal[59] is far from utopian because of the achievements of the First World, and its potential capabilities. Already today, the West serves not only as a supplier of food to the Second and Third Worlds but also of technology and produced wealth; for these are vital to the living standards of non-First World populations and the prospects of further development of their industry and agriculture.

True, the capitalist system is neither ideal nor idealistic. To many, it still symbolizes only the past injustices and exploitation. Also, the most negative impact on Third World countries of capitalism is still regarded as the result of neo-colonialism; of course, nobody can claim that all that was done in the classical colonial era was good.

Besides roads, harbors, operation of mines, the beginnings of a local non-competitive industry and educational systems, sanitary improvements and other modernizing undertakings originally initiated mainly in interests of the foreign colonial rulers, there also existed some very bad things. The worst resulted from the agricultural mono-culturization, deepening exploitation and economic dependence, and through it from the dismissal of participation in politics. Worse than this cause of alienation, however, was the frustration and real social and human traumatization described by Franz Fanon, Albert Memmi and other writers and analysts of racial discrimination and degradation under colonial rule.[60]

However, the claim that the industrialized countries established in their colonies, regimes of unrestricted economic exploitation that did not contribute to their development and created what has been sometimes described as the ultimate of poverty[61] is far off of the mark and incorrect.

More precise is the thesis that Western imperialism has frequently resulted in the conversion of "predeveloped" societies into underdeveloped ones by exploitation of manpower and resources.[62] The argument is that it neglected the need to build a proper infrastructure and to train the people in modern technology, science, administration and other fields. The colonial rulers fully realized that education and training of indigenous subject peoples was the shortest road to independence. Marcel Merle, however, should be credited for recalling Marx's findings on the investments of the various metropolises in their colonies which not infrequently greatly exceeded income derived from them.[63] Even earlier Robinson and Gallagher had shown that the British colonies in Africa never turned out to be particularly profitable either as trading partners or major absorbers of capital. Writers of different orientations reached like conclusions, proving that the metropolises' wealth was predominantly attributable to their own domestic natural resources, work and inventions. Realization that the dependent and semidependent territories had become burdens from political, economic, and human viewpoints came very late. Even later grew the awareness that the best way to enrichment is the promotion of productivity, of scientific and technological development and the continuous expansion of commercial relations among the industrialized countries themselves.

This was a very important reason advanced for speeding up the process of decolonization, as well as for the birth of the so-called neocolonialism. The postcolonial states encompassed by the mechanisms of the world market lacked proper infrastructures or enough qualified people to govern their countries, to develop their economies, and to play the supply-and-demand game in international trade. Whereas old fashioned imperialism comprised elements characteristic of incipient stages of capitalistic growth whereby conquest was undertaken essentially for non-economic reasons of prestige and security, investments in subject territories defrayed the expense of their administrations. Neo-imperialism and neo-colonialism was entirely a different matter resulting in the ever growing impoverishment and subjection of former colonies under the aegis of economic and technical domination and nominal political independence. All foreign trade—exports, imports, technology transfers, developmental aid, research activities, commodity and credit exchanges, commercial services—were merely undertaken for the sake of profits and political interests of the West.[64] The frustration caused by the discriminatory practices of classical direct and indirect colonial rule was finally supplemented by frustration deriving from the feeling of economic enslavement and brutal exploitation. As many experts pointed out, it was also due to the fact that the rich countries are in fact not dependent on the core of the Third World.

This led not only to the Third World's offensive to reconstruct the international economy, but also played an important rôle in changing industrialized countries' policies. In this way, both the termination of neocolonialism and the promotion of post-imperialist capitalism was speeded up. The First World is now strong enough to challenge the new global problems of a socio-economic character without resorting to force or the degradation or subjugation of other peoples. True enough, the system still conveys an impression of unsurmountable contradictions; however, students of mass unemployment and other economic malfunctions predict prospects of recovery requiring radical, difficult economic and social but possible transformations.[65] By and large, the system is actually undergoing continual change under the impact of the social-democratic partners in the government and of the trade-unions and the press as well. Some changes are directed at reducing economic or even political, but not structural, divergencies that are fundamental to so-called Socialistic societies. This has been already reflected in growing awareness that social investment should not be neglected and that governmental agencies must play a more active role in planning and initiating a socio-economic reconstruction: and as already mentioned, freedom and peace-building initiatives should be taken as well.

It is known already that the neo-Keynesian model of a growing economy combined features of Marxist and Schumpeter approaches. They derived, among others, from R. F. Harod, E. D. Domar, Joan Robinson, J. K. Galbraith and many others. Emphasis was put on the thesis that the clue to the long-run dynamic behavior may be found in care for human needs, technical progress and uninterrupted innovation.[66]

Promotion of this dynamism and various social reforms that are undertaken for the sake of strengthening the foundations of the welfare states finally resulted in similar activities of a transnational character. The Third World leadership is aware of this process and the almost unlimited capacities of the First World. It therefore resolved not to waste time on trying to solve its problems in discussions with the Second World, which is doomed to rely on imports and knowhow from the West and has nothing to offer except arms and military technology. The Third World has decided to exclude the Second World from the North-South dialogue and continues to conceive it as a direct dialogue between the Third and First world only. True, the dialogue has recently stopped with rather limited results, but the decision has been taken to continue negotiations in the future. It took place in the expanding atmosphere of mutual understanding in which the need for cooperation and discussion in other forums was realized as well. This in no way means that Third World orientations or even alliance with the Soviets will not continue or not become even stronger, but this would be a matter of political rather than economic convenience for the purpose of maintaining voting blocs in international organizations; moreover, it would be a springboard for "anti-imperialist" propaganda, which is more declaratory than substantive.

The Third World's reorientation towards the West, which has recently produced the brutal Soviet invasion of Afghanistan, quite probably undertaken as a preventive *fait accompli* measure, doubtlessly is a result also of the First World's diminished opposition to the program of a new economic world order and its abandonment of the legitimacy of using force for economic and political purposes as a matter of principle (as it has been demonstrated to the extreme by the American reaction to the seizure of the US Embassy in Teheran). Reorientation in this connection is also attributable to the imperatives of the nuclear era, to new moral values derived therefrom, and to consequent adoption of principles of mutually beneficial cooperation supplemented by the strengthened measures of deterrence after the Soviet aggression upon Afghanistan.

All this and even the West's appeal to aid the Third World more effectively seems to justify reconsideration of the existing theories of capitalist evolution and social democratic performance. Likewise justified seems the reconsideration of the relationship with the forces struggling to reform the present international economic system and to the objective factors changing the image and functions of various social domestic and global structures. How do the foregoing tendencies effect greater convergence and better cooperation under conditions of growing political uncertainty and insecurity? That is the question!

In terms of historical perspective, it may seem that criticism of imperialism by the Liberal Hobson was more justified than the one elaborated by Lenin. Hobson, who unlike Lenin, followed in line with the tradition of the classical economists, was far more devastating in his condemnation of capitalist imperialism than Marx; the latter merely claimed that capitalism would destroy itself, but Hobson warned that any imperialism (since 1917 of Soviet type too) would destroy the world. Later, the Hobsonian thesis on imperialism was integrated into the orthodox Marxist canon, mainly by Lenin. Hobson condemned the greed of the monopolies that he claimed led to violent aggression. However, he did not fail to endorse and praise the universality and other constructive features of capitalism favoring free trade and also through it, promotion of a dynamic development. He believed in the possibility of remedying economic ills by treating economics as a humanistic rather than a scholastic science. His cherished idea was to save the country from a bloody civil war and the malady of international wars.[67]

As for Lenin, it can no longer be doubted that he was responsible for the creation of an economically unproductive, centrally governed system that eradicated individual initiative and human rights, that in turn was also to blame for Stalin's crimes. True, Leninism succeeded in becoming militarilly very mighty even though it is inefficient in agricultural and industrial production for the civilian population.

Marx focused on the internal class struggle in bourgeois societies and predicted its imminent revolutionary success in the most advanced industrialized countries: those who believe being faithful to his legacy make efforts to better the system rather in an evolutionary way, they try to reduce injustice and misery by peaceful means both in the national and international arenas.

Although overwhelmingly devoted to strengthening the Bolshevik Russian State, Lenin in his theoretical speculations concentrated on capitalism and its role in the worldwide class struggle. He believed in the future world revolution of all oppressed peoples against a few dominant industrially developed countries.

Today as in Lenin's time, the idea was divorced from reality and even more so in the 1980s. At the XXVth All-Union Congress of the Soviet Communist Party, Chairman Leonid Brezhnev emphasized the need for cooperation among all nations that was differentiated only as regards the intensity of ties between Socialist allies and the "liberated" nations vis-a-vis the capitalist countries; the same tone characterized his report at the XXVI Party Congress in February 1981, a period of further economic deterioration in Russia and in other parts of the Soviet Bloc, which was particularly painful in Poland. Some forms of the growing Eurocommunism are more sincere and even more courageous in their adaptation of Marxism-Leninism to the new conditions of present times which dictate giving priority to peace and development over ideas and methods of revolutionary violence.

Only the People's Republic of China continues on the level of theory and recently even in a lower tone, to ascribe to the Third World the role of the main anti-imperialist vanguard.[68]

Notwithstanding the adherence to the sustaining ideological orientation of the Chinese Communist Party (CCP), China is moving on a course of pragmatism in foreign and domestic policy. Those who declared that only they uphold the banner of Marxism today are anxious to prevent a clash with their greatest political and ideological rival, the USSR, without imperiling peaceful coexistence globally. What is more, they try ever more intensively, to promote their own development in cooperation with all states without any regard for their ideological preferences, their governmental structures, or their degree of economic development.

This position tends to imply that the main concern of all peoples at present is survival and development; that in the process of elaborating instruments for achieving these goals, all countries regardless of the political or social structures, their ideological outlooks, or stages of economic development will be—let us hope—obliged sooner or later to strive in the spirit of classical teachings to bring about national freedom, the elimination of social and economic misery, and to put an end to the scourge of war. Soviet adventurism justifies serious doubts regarding this optimist conclusion,since the USSR never relinquished its deterministic approach to economic and political matters.

3. Economic Determinism, War and the Ambiguity of Imperialism

Many recent studies relating to different aspects of interrelationship between development and international security are influenced by Walter W. Rostow's concepts of the principal stages of economic growth. Development in this concept involves conditions favoring continuous growth and elaboration of the economy from one stage to the other as in the late 18th and 19th century England, France and the United States on the road to economic maturity and mass consumption.

According to Rostow, all wars which occurred in the last 300 years were actually byproducts of the different stages of development. Colonial conquests are claimed by him to be determined by the import and export interests of the metropolises. The indigenous economic growth of the dependent territories, on the other hand, was said to be produced by their wars of liberation, the first substantial example being the United States beginning in the 1770s. Later local wars and subsequent wars fought by Bismarck, Napoleon. Tzarist Russia, Germany and Japan, including wars for colonial conquest, were explained as products of nationalism and aggressive tendencies inherent in it. In the same category were classified the recent wars of Egypt and India in the 1960s and 1970s. A few of this type of war were occasionally fought in order to speed up the process of national integration or to promote modernization. Global wars, including the Cold War, are regarded by Rostow as merely a product of various powers' tendencies to achieve hegemony or at least to increase their worldwide power.

The different stages of economic growth and their transition to higher levels were not regarded in this scheme as always and automatically leading to wars or determined by their outcomes. Rostow was of the opinion that war is only one alternative posed by development. He noted that decisions for war and peace are only made after consideration of both the internal and international situations.[69] Rostow of course, was aware that in the last decades many highly industrially developed nations have preferred to build welfare states and in other ways to concentrate more on issues relating to the standards of living of their own populations than on external affairs.

Rostow explained the Cold War by a combination of Russian traditions, internal needs created by the process of modernization, and by the impact of Communist ideology. He was silent, however, on the American contributions to the Cold War and on some aspects of the American-Soviet relations that brought about the present dimension of the East-West conflict. This problem will be elaborated in greater detail below.

Emphasis is made here on the point that Rostow also foresaw the possibility of détente becoming more certain. According to his calculations, it depended on the weakening of those factors which gave birth to the Soviet Cold War policy initiatives following Moscow's developmental achievements and increasing dangers of the nuclear arms race as well as the growth of Western economic and military might. Rostow believed, however, that American power and technology would save the world and that the spread of technology would end violence.

This, of course, is an oversimplified presentation of Rostow's views that seems justified because of his inclination to generalize.[70] They do not answer, among other things, the question of causes of Third World wars nor the causes which are non-economic and therefore irrational. Some very acute conflicts in the Second World, due to new forms of exploitation and national and human degradation that flourish behind the shield of ideological motivations and slogans of fraternity, have not been satisfactorily explained by Rostow, if at all; nor the changing forms of cooperation and rivalry in the First World, which has to cope with a wide range of new political, economic, and military problems (the reintegration of Western Europe, or the proposals for a strong unified Western reaction to the Soviet aggression against Afghanistan, for example, are sometimes opposed by determined elements of nationalistic, regional, ethnic, linguistic, but also political, economic, and other interests).

Still, Rostow's concept may be of a great value in exploring conflicts in different historical periods and regions, as well as in the study of various problems relating to present international security. This seems particularly true to problems relating to superpowers' convergent and divergent tendencies and various sub-relationships within their respective spheres of influence. This concept contributed to pinpoint the role of economic factors in the process of colonization and decolonization and in various conflicts, as well as in national movements and hegemonial tendencies. On the other hand, this concept is of little help both in the study of South-South antagonisms and continuing North-South tensions and in the study of the dangerous Soviet expansion in the Third World and the East-West arms race; moreover, it is not especially helpful to study conflicts inspired by the enrichment of the oil-producers, some of whom have begun to use their petrodollars to arm themselves and their clients. This is likely to favor development of intra-Third World imperialism and to escalate purely local controversies that are usually devoid of economic significance. Little meaning could also be found in the priority given by the United States to the Soviet Union over the

European powers in the aftermath of World War II and in the times of the Anglo-French intervention during 1956 in Egypt.

Today, the economically weakening impact of the exhausting Soviet war effort from 1941 to 1945 cannot be doubted. A. Voznesiensky and other leading Soviet planners were murdered by Stalin because they refused to believe in the possibility of quickly rebuilding postwar Soviet Russia and in prompt production of nuclear arms. Not only Stalin's bluffs about the Soviet might, especially at Yalta and Potsdam, secured American support for increasing Soviet influence in Eastern and central Europe, including Germany. This support had little to do with economics but mainly with American disbelief or misconceptions about the French and British efforts to rebuild their empires and the peaceful Soviet aims in East and Central Europe and elsewhere; hence the tendency of giving priority at a certain moment to the concept of an American-Soviet directorate over cooperation with Britain and France.

However, the bitter experience of the Cold War led to the American decision to rebuild Europe and make it a politically and economically viable ally through the Marshall Plan. Neither the European Economic Community (EEC) created under it nor NATO prevented the rebirth of some aspects of the former position in 1956, following the American desire to act as an agent of anti-colonialism and gain the sympathy of the emerging Third World. Some elements of disharmony and competing or conflicting interest persist today within the Western Bloc which hamper its solidarity vis-a-vis the Eastern Bloc. It is sufficient to recall the visits of the former French President to Warsaw and the German Chancellor to Moscow after the Soviet occupation of Afghanistan and the Franco-German reservations about the 1981 American policy with regard to the USSR or the West European resolution not to follow the American measures with regard to Poland and the USSR in 1981-82, to see how fragile that solidarity still is. Another evidence of this was the West's merely partial boycott of the Moscow Olympics. The approaching superpower military parity may well reflect slackness in the Western alliance rather than the consequence of conflicting economic interests.

Neither Rostow nor Edwin Staley,[71] whose research to a certain extent supplements the work of the former, answer questions raised by policies of the aforesaid kind. However, Staley's stress on regional and global cultural and environmental factors is very important for the understanding of the great changes occurring during the last decades in the different parts of the world. In the West they were claimed to have been characterized by the weakening of nationalism and militarism and by the growth of values tied to individual freedom and other human rights. The latter are disregarded in the one-party authoritarian Soviet system, which uses the language but not the substance of human rights and liberty. In the post-colonial states, however, undisguised authoritarianism and militarism are the prevailing marks. Such situations can hardly favor peace.

Both Staley and Rostow correlate the interconnections between economic strength and political-military power with ensuing foreign affairs dilemmas. They made the correlation clear under circumstances when various governments decide on war and peace after consideration of conditions in their own countries vis-a-vis the world arena. However correct their conclusions may be, they fail to explain the causes of conflicts not rooted in economic factors. As mentioned above, non-economically provoked wars continue in different parts of the world and particularly characterize Middle East conflicts. These conflicts, not less than Soviet expansionism, frustrate the most diligent efforts to establish arms control, disarmament, and other arrangements essential to various forms of pacific cooperation in an environment free of the chronic threat of war. Furthermore, conflicts anywhere, tend to escalate or provoke confrontation between the superpowers.

It goes without saying that as long as war persists there are no serious prospects of solving the developmental and other socio-economic problems of the Third World. This includes problems arising out of colonialism and imperialism and the birth of new nationalisms. Nationalism, which frequently is of ethnic origin, is no longer directed against the white rulers, but against the former liberators.[72]

In this context, it may be worth noting that the term "nation" presupposes a feeling of identity on the part of inhabitants of the whole territory that is not necessarily or wholly voluntary. It is a self-contained group of human beings whose identity and compliance with established group values and identities may be coerced or freely given. Nationalism therefore reflects the will and power to establish, sustain, or preserve a "national" body politic whose membership coincides with that of a nation and, more particularly, with the sovereign nation-state. In many new, mostly postcolonial states, it is precisely the absence of this nationalism that provokes political, economic or cultural tensions, which, if carried to the *ultima ratio*, end in armed strife and violence.

A new state is, in fact, the one which has recently acquired power to exercise an independent political control over its own affairs. Most frequently, its immediate goal is to shape its nationhood. As already mentioned, nationhood means the achievement of a full and overriding commitment to the state on the part of all its citizens above the demands of other loyalties or contrary demands. Such circumstances still remain a rare phenomenon in newly established sovereign states. These states represent actually amalgams of various tribal, religious, ethnic and linguistic or other groups. Governing elites both reflect values of their subjects and engage in the search for changing or even novel national identity for their subjects; accordingly, they build and integrate a common socio-economic, cultural and political structure for all. On the international plane, they attempt to establish, both in fact and theory, the sovereignty of the nation with respect to other such national entities.[73] As already pointed out, the majority of the Third World conflicts seem to reflect "growing pains" in the process of national integration and modernization, whereas the claims for bettering the Third World countries' economic situation unite all of them in a common front against the industrially developed nations.

Pierre Jallée thinks that the term "Third World" is sometimes a rather confusing mystification. He asserts that it would be appropriate only if the Third World was an association of states with similar levels of development that harmoniously cooperated and influenced each other rather than the opposite. As things stand now, he points out, contradictory interests actually are becoming stronger and stronger. The poorer Third World components, he asserted, are even trying to shape their own bloc, the Fourth World.

True enough, the concept of developing or underdeveloped nations has always been unsatisfactory and sometimes even misleading not only because of large socio-economic differences and dividing political orientations, but also because of subjective judgments whenever the term is applied beyond a strictly economic analysis. It seems entirely justified, however, when used to characterize the sum total of mainly post-colonial less developed states, which press for a privileged treatment by the industrialized nations and for the reconstruction of the world economic system for this end.[74] In this form, they represent a factor of growing importance in world politics today. Although many of them have no mutual contacts and some of them have less influence on their Third World "brothers," some have substantial influence on different industrialized states and even the superpowers. In this regard, one need only to mention the impact of some oil producers that frequently fail to coordinate positions with close neighbours and even are obliged to finance hostile movements and governments in order to avoid clashes with them.[75]

It has been stressed that the theories of war as a byproduct of different stages of development did not consider at all the conflicts caused by other than economic reasons. Most of their authors elaborated them before Third World countries became sovereign and before the recent phase of decolonization made it possible to reveal the intra-Third World causes of the majority of conflicts fermenting within. The difficulty in applying these theories to explain such conflicts lies in their mechanical concept of the relationship between war and economics. It can frequently become no less misleading than the mechanical studies on the cause of underdevelopment, as was recently strongly emphasized by the Latin American expert on this issue, Theotonio Dos Santos.[76]

The same should be said about the various concepts of imperialism. Some of them are classified as Orthodox Marxist. Frequently, however, they adopt an exclusive and radical economic approach and vacilitate between determinism and voluntarism. Their disciples explain the shape of imperialism and its expansionist policies breeding as an inevitable phase in the development of capitalism. According to them, the road to peace is determined by its collapse or definite defeat.

This is after all their common view, despite some differences in reasoning. It was reflected in the already quoted above conclusions of Rosa Luxemburg and Nikolai Bukharin,[77] corroborated later in an original way by Lenin, and adopted by his adherents.[78] All of them stress the capitalists' search for profits and the mechanism emerging for this purpose in the international economy, leading to colonial conquests and inter-capitalist rivalries and wars, which at a certain stage grow into global wars doomed to weaken and to deliver a deadly shock to the whole system. Consequently, on the eve of World War I and after its outbreak, they called for transforming it from a war between nations into a proletarian class war against capitalists to achieve peace through the defeat of capitalism.

On the basis of his imperialist theory and personal leadership, Lenin successfully led the Bolsheviks to victory in the "Great October Revolution," but the Leninist success in the economically and socially backward empire of the deposed Russian Tsars fell far short of overthrowing the worldwide capitalist order. The Leninist Dictatorship of the Proletariat set up after a period of civil and international war only succeeded in enhancing suffering, poverty, executions, persecutions and famine. Elsewhere, capitalism rebounded, overcame its losses incurred by war and revolution, and ultimately far surpassed its previous productivity with the help of scientific and technological innovation.

After World War II, capitalism entered a new era of further prosperity, economic expansion and realization of human freedom to a large extent as a consequence of the role of the labour movement and favorable conditions of peace. Even orthodox dogmatic Marxist students who take this into account find it reasonable to concede that it would be absurd to speak about the approaching collapse of the bourgeois system and at the same time to ignore emergent Soviet imperialism, which realistically reflects Soviet nationalism rather than Marxist-Leninist theory.[79] Some of these writers were formerly among the critics of Schumpeter and maintained that the expansion of American power and influence had little to do with elimination of atavistic features and the imminent end of pre-capitalist or other social patterns inherited from the past.

At the same time, those who, like Kautsky, viewed imperialism only as a superstructure of the aggressive big capitalists were strongly criticized, mainly for their assumption that imperialism is not the exclusive option of capitalism at a certain stage of its development, but rather a chain process of continual "natural change"; moreover, the imperialist process is said to breed tendencies to dominate as well as to integrate the world economy and is likely to achieve this aim by other means than global war.[80] This critique was based on the thesis that imperialism is the highest stage of capitalism, a stage also of its forthcoming decline and end. When writers who took this viewpoint were compelled to admit that capitalism is capable of further growth, they added that such capitalist expansion was possible only on the condition of maintaining areas of underdevelopment, enslavement and other forms of domination and exploitation. The empiricists among them, however, have not ignored present-day realities in which neo-capitalism gave preference to peaceful cooperation over domination, to economic profits over territorial expansion and political prestige, to political followed by economic decolonization over exploitation; nor do they forget that capitalism influenced by social-democratic and neo-liberal outlooks has acquiesced in the reconstruction of the world economic system, which means their concurrence, that the gap between the industrialized countries with their essential advantages and the underdeveloped nations must be eliminated.

Only the dogmatists continued to ignore these essential changes and prefer to cling to theories based on generalizations sometimes entirely detached from new realities. They continue to focus on the idea of an unavoidable degeneration of the Western democracies under all conditions and on the role of voluntarism in accelerating their agony. These writers ignore the fact that nowadays there is no revolutionary situation in the world and that power does not always force a choice between concentration on internal problems and waging war that gives preference to the latter.

It might be assumed today that there already is no ground for this kind of dilemma because small local military encounters are likely to escalate on a global scale. Consequently, there are not only reasons of humanitarian principle, pacifism, or military weakness for recent First World tendencies to strengthen peace, but clear economic and political reasons and a new perception of power as well. These tendencies already have influenced changes in the Western development aid programs and patterns of trade with the Third World. Particular reference is made here to the declaration of the German Government[81] but also to projects of other not less "imperialistic" governments as well. These kind of projects more favorable to the Third World were presented in the UN and other international bodies; they were the center of concern of the American Administration in 1977 and of the discussions following the North-South dialogue.

These discussions were, in fact, continued by the Brandt Commission and other international bodies. To no small extent they reflect tendencies rooted in the "take off" theories of Rostow, particularly as corroborated by S. Kuznets. However, they are also rooted in various self-reliance and other approaches, like those reflected in the Bariloche model, in some reform proposals of the Club of Rome and numerous UN recommendations.

Above all, however, they prove the change in Western attitude towards the TW. The 1980 Special Session of the UN General Assembly entirely devoted to developmental problems, shows how, in spite of still existing important differences in views, the West is willing to contribute more effectively to the solution of the main problems that plague the LDCs. The above-mentioned UN Session dealt with issues of energy, trade, raw materials, development and the world monetary and financial systems. This time the ensuing negotiations on a global scale, particularly at the UN Paris Conference on the LDCs' situation, held in September, at the summit meetings on August 27-28, and at Caucun in Mexico in October 1981, bore little better fruit than similar discussions in the past.

True enough, the average growth of the TW is rather impressive. In the last decade it was by 5.5 per cent, hence higher than that of the industrialized countries. This has been possible also due to the new forms of cooperation and assistance of the West.

However, further progress will doubtless take place, above all thanks to internal structural and other reforms in the LDCs themselves and will not only be a consequence of increased external inputs.[82]

It is true that the West will be asked to make further efforts to better the situation in the TW and to give up its protectionist tendencies and other restrictions on the trade with the TW. This was stressed by the German "Committee of Sages,"[83] which comprises important critical remarks about the Brandt report; but this report, too, proves the changing image of Western involvement in the TW. It becomes less and less selfish. The marks ascribed to classical imperialism are disappearing and the West is increasingly willing to act not only for economic, but for humanitarian and world security reasons as well.

The renowned Italian Marxist, Basso, concluded already in 1971 that the term "imperialism" was sometimes misused nowadays to refer to integrative tendencies in the world economy, to the internationalization of production resulting from unprecedented scientific and technological progress, and to various activities of multinational corporations. Another renowned Marxist expert in Third World problems, A. Emmanuel, went so far as to emphasize positive features in the activities of multinational corporations, stressing their attempts to remedy potentially dangerous economic situations, and comprising those who completely deny the multinationals positive role, and blaming them only as imperialistic, war instigating agents.[84] As for Basso, he even thought that it would be a grave mistake to characterize contemporary capitalism as reaching its higher stage of development and final existence. Since conditions have changed, Basso maintained that it is impossible to uphold the unmodified conclusions of the classical Marxist interpreters of imperialism and its alleged role in intra-capitalist wars that always lead to revolution and deepening permanent crisis of the bourgeoisie portending their imminent demise.

The situation is much more complicated today than it was in the past; moreover, absolutely new issues have arisen. It is imperative to re-examine the former situation and to study the present-day situation both for better understanding and for elaboration of a new strategy to fight negative features as well. Available knowledge proves, according to Basso, that illusions should not be fostered by imagining that there exists only one center of dominance and exploitation and that the peoples of the Third World as a whole are able and willing to put an end to capitalist methods, flourishing within its borders.[85] Hence the need to study not only the metamorphosis of the First, but of the imperialistic and sub-imperialistic trends, features and roles also in the Third and Second world as well.

No less useful seems reappraisal of writings concerned with First World imperialism and of problems of power in the nuclear era.

Political scientists have only recently started paying attention to the elusiveness of power in modern times indicating that its main ingredient is neither military might[86] nor industrial potential. The more so as the latter can be paralysed by stopping the availability of oil and other vital raw materials. The quest for different compensations and concessions are required when the use of force is difficult if not impossible as it became so evident in the American reaction to the case of the hostages in the US Embassy in Teheran and to the Soviet occupation of Afghanistan. S. Strange and F.S. Northledge seem quite right when they point out that power usually means the capability of making one's will felt in the decision-making process of others.[87] Doubtlessly, nuclear stalemate results in the superpowers' "impotence of force" with respect to military action in the service of politics.[88] Such impotence (notwithstanding potential) plays an increasing rôle in establishing a nation's path toward peace or war.

The economic, technological, scientific and military potential of the West is so large today that even its financial and other difficulties and political blunders cannot anymore justify the assumption that it is nearing its end or supposedly has a growing tendency to attempt the salvage of ruined economy by resort to violent force. On the contrary, its expanding potential strengthens the West's capability to make its will felt in the decisions of the East and South, to insist on solutions that take into account the interests of other worlds as well as its own; and to promote first and foremost the reinforcement of cooperation for peace favoring not only the further growth of the West; but as indispensable for the eradication of socio-economic ills in all parts of the world and today even for the survival of humanity.

These considerations suffice not only to pinpoint deficiencies of the thesis that wars are usually a by-product of the different stages of economic growth and development in general, but to show the ambiguity and often, indeed, the absurdity of using the term aggressive "imperialism" in this connection.

It seems that they also show the reasonableness of the evolutionary approach that views war, peace, stagnation, underdevelopment, growth, imperialism and other social phenomena as elements in a continuous chain reaction of change that not always accords with the dialectical formula: thesis, antithesis, synthesis. Sometimes, the chain reaction is negative, other times positive or predictable and avoidable and still other times eluding human control or predictability.

For a better understanding of this condition, it may be useful to recall the argumentation not yet mentioned, but which is frequently raised against the concepts of Hobson, Lenin and Schumpeter. Here it is necessary to consider different forms and goals that lend themselves to ambiguous interpretations of the term imperialism.

First of all, it must be stressed that Lenin, who was trying to oppose imperialism in the formative stages of capitalist development, recalled why their masters were against war, particularly against colonial conquests. He wrote: "Between 1840 and 1860 when free competition in England was at its height, the leading bourgeois politicians opposed colonial policy and believed that the complete liberation of the colonies from England was an inevitable and desirable thing. In 1852, Benjamin Disraeli, a statesman generally favoring imperialism, declared: "The colonies are milestones around our necks."[89] Bismark could therefore conclude in 1876 that "all the advantages claimed for the mother country (from the colonies) are for the most part illusions. England is abandoning its colonial policy; she finds it too costly."[90]

Many years later, G. Clark in his re-examination of the question of whether "colonies pay," found the answer in an emphatic "No"; however, A.K. Cairncross was of the contrary opinion that in a way they did.[91]

True, some colonies paid neither in 1852 nor in 1865, when a Committee of the British House of Commons recommended the abandonment of the majority of them in Africa, nor later; however, some of them were rewarding.[92] The latter was the reason for the birth of neo-colonialism, that is of new forms of dependence imposed by conditions of trade and aid that fosters their continuing exploitation after they had already achieved political sovereignty.

Yet in order to have a better understanding of the old and the new imperialism, including Soviet imperialism, whose dangers only recently have begun to be understood by the Third World,[93] it seems less necessary to consider questions of profits. Greater concentration should be focused on the variety of dominated areas and their goals in different historical periods up to the present. In doing so, the relevancy of normative criteria may be realized and consequently good or bad values ascribed to different classes and their subsequent imperialist undertakings; moreover, this proves also the importance of viewing them as historical facts determined by the will, purpose, and actions of those initiating and shaping imperialist policies, be they capitalist or socialist orientated.

It appears that their undertakings were less a trend of economic behavior than impulses of domination, or, to use the terminology preferred by the Chinese in regard to Soviets, of hegemonism.

That is why the British continued to develop and enlarge their colonies long after they ceased to pay and why Bismark and others followed them regardless of economic cost. This presumably was the cause of heavy Soviet investments in what they had frequently regarded as "treacherous" zones of influence and of American expenses like those lost in Vietnam. The Americans continued to invest in Vietnam even after they realized that withdrawal from this country would not necessarily mean a change in power relations favoring the Soviets.

No quotation from Lenin can help to understand this kind of politics or the recrudescence of forces similar to those which opposed past wars. Today, opposition to war is growing stronger than in the past, mainly because of the fear of thermonuclear weapons and the horrendous consequences. This says volumes about the interest of capitalism in peace in the late stages of its development. The German Socialist terminology for Western imperialism is "late-capitalism" ("Spät-Kapitalismus") and the German term is much more accurate but it points out Western "imperialism" only passing over in silence other expansionist and aggressive actions by various types of government whether Socialist or capitalist, authoritarian or democratic.

Professor Hans Morgenthau, examining inducements to imperialism, mentioned the attitude of victorious nations towards defeated enemies. In this regard, he pointed out, reactions of the latter to the victors and the desire of strong states to fill the power vacuums and to crush actual, potential and even illusory weak rivals. As an example of imperialist policy goals, he cited among others the expansionist impulses of powers widely separated in time: ancient Rome and Hitler's plan of establishing a world empire, Napoleon's vision of French hegemony and North American "manifest destiny" in the 19th century for the purpose of building continental empires, compulsive tendencies of Bismarck and the early Bolshevik state under Lenin to achieve local preponderance. Some of these forms were only a prelude to others, as, for instance, the precedent of Prussian-German policy that led to

Hitlerism. The USSR's recent world expansion was also preceded by its efforts to establish "security" zones on the former frontiers.

Needless to say, Morgenthau's list being far from exhaustive is nevertheless instructive. What, however, seems most important in his analysis is not the issue of goals; imperialism is defined by Morgenthau as a state's expansionism intended to effect a more or less permanent change of the balance of power in its favor—but not always, with the use of military means. Sometimes it is easier to achieve this aim by various forms of cultural and/or economic activities. This method is not regarded as an end in itself, but rather as a measure of changing power relations and expressing aspirations for dominance and subjugation.[94] Taking into consideration this balance-of-power approach, some experts thus vehemently criticize the various propositions of Lenin and Hobson as inconsonant with the established facts of political and economic history.

The British historian D. K. Fieldhouse pointed out that Hobson was fully aware that the obvious driving force behind British expansion since 1870 was predominantly the explorers, engineers, missionaries, and other pressure groups and not the people concerned with business profits; moreover, he attributed to Hobson the opinion on the industrialists as clearly anti-imperialist.

Attributing imperialism to inherent weakness of the capitalist system and arguing contrary to fact that its powerful captains directed behind the scenes policies of conquest in order to find outlets for surplus capital, Hobson and later Lenin used inadequate statistics. They also based their analysis on spurious reasoning and objectionable ideas of revolutionary violence. They and their followers made frequently ludicrous and false statements of fact. To take a random example, Fiji, New Guinea, or Upper Burma, were claimed to have been annexed by Great Britain in order to protect investments or to open fields for future investment.

They entirely ignored the fact that capital went not to Fiji or New Guinea but to countries like the United States, Canada, or Australia. This, according to Professor R. Nurkse, became a means whereby a vigorous process of economic growth came to be transmitted *from the center to the outlying areas of the world.*[95] Consequently, as the result of the applied developed skills, inspired initiative, high productivity, hard labor, instilled values of ambition and personal initiative of the settlers and self-discipline, necessary for the foregoing-links of co-operation, beneficial both to the center and the periphery were established. These values paved the way to real interdependence already envisaged at the turn of the 15th and 16th centuries, particularly by Francisco Suarez.[96]

From the earliest days of European expansion, clear distinction between economic and other motives for expansionism was blurred and many colonies were rather the product of political and military rivalries than of a desire for economic wealth.

Most of the classics from Adam Smith to John Stuart Mill examined realities in terms of national economy. They were concerned with domestic commercial growth, investments, and trade that were profitable in peacetime. The bulk of British capital sent overseas went not for colonial exploitation but rather for the development of Western Europe, North America, Australia, New Zealand and South Africa, where the investors relied on creativity of their cultural peers as a guarantee of repayment and fair income. Liberalism was inspired by the mostly British economic classics that distinguished between economic and political relations so as to represent themselves as the very antithesis of mercantilism, which almost by definition was characterized by stress on aggressive overseas expansionism for the sake of economic profit.

True, the liberals were also interested in enrichment. On the other hand, while the Calvinists claimed that poverty and exploitation were "predestined" by God and the Darwinists later maintained that they were the outcome of the unavoidable struggle for survival, the liberals attributed these personal misfortunes to inherent faults of the wretched for which charity (the development aid of the 19th century) was prescribed as the remedy.

The liberals condemned both the theory and practice of what a few generations later was termed by the Marxist scholar Maurice Dobb as a "privileged investment," which exacted profits with the backing of government authority and power in connection with both domestic and foreign private investment. Very frequently, they acted with the apparent realization that territorial acquisition is one of many and often uncertain indices of successful expansionism; by and large the chief hallmark of expansionism is patterns of domination over other peoples mostly by means of scientific skill and discovery, as well as by productive technological and commercial enterprise.

It may be presumed that the exchange of goods and services itself is also a kind of exploitation realized through a degree of coercion when trade terms are imposed arbitrarily on purchasers and consumers. Exploitation by threatened or actual coercion today is rare in commerce although the process itself is a normal part of general social interaction. The mercantilists perceived such tactics in entirely different terms, as an instrument for achieving growth, profits and glory. Their followers tried even as late as the end of the 19th century to match the glory of their international partners and rivals by counter-balancing aggrandisement by foreign territorial acquisition and by domination over non-European peoples. Because the maintenance of empire was a prestigious burden for the patrons of numerous "hewers of wood and drawers of water" it did not necessarily add to the wealth and power of the mercantilist expansionists and colonialists.[97]

Mercantilist practices undertaken by all major European states were as concerned with national power as with economic advantage. As Adam Smith already pointed out they tended to subordinate opulence to the needs of real or fictitious greatness and security. Consequently, from the first overseas European conquests until the era of decolonization, colonies were regarded mainly as assets in the struggle for power and status while ignoring the burdensome cost of their administration.

The core of Marxist criticism of imperialist ventures comes not from Marx but from Lenin. This is not only because Marx died in 1883 before modern expansionism in Europe, in the Western hemisphere and elsewhere had reached its zenith. It mainly resulted from the fact that Lenin was more concerned with pragmatic questions involving capitalism's anticipated political defeat, at least in certain "sick" areas, than with studying the origins, meaning and remedies benefitting his proletarian and peasant constituencies.[98] He did not perceive the possibility of expansion and enslavement by the future "Socialist" states. Above all, he failed to see that there is an unbreakable link between the concentration of power, irrespective of the systems and the urge to control, dominate and ultimately to exploit other nations;[99] frequently, these imperialist impulses are minimized, justified or "explained" by ideological rationalizations. What was the result of putting Leninist conclusions into operation and the price of the October Revolution's success is today well known. The price was paid by the people formerly exploited and repressed by Tsarism with no less suffering than subsequently experienced under Stalin's tyranny. The price exacted from those who embraced by it later in Europe and Asia is also well known. The enslaved subjects of the Kremlin's empire still live far below Western European standards of living, although economic conditions have improved and Soviet society relatively liberalized under the leadership of Nikita Kruschev and Leonid Brezhnev. Secretary General of the Spanish Communist Party, Santjago Carillo did not hesitate to talk quite frankly about the high price of the Kremlin bureaucracy as the sole beneficiary of the revolution.[100] He was not exceptional. Increasing criticism also comes from the ranks of other Western Communists, from loyal members of the Council for Mutual Economic Aid, and from the Warsaw Treaty Organization; thus it seems clear that criticism displeasing to the Kremlin comes also from others than opponents and dissidents.

Marx taught that revolution was unavoidable, but only useful if the circumstances are ripe and there is no way to save the unsupportable and decaying regime. In historical perspective, Marx and Lenin were at least equals in their manipulation of the human material who executed and carried out their revolutionary theories and who were the real instruments of the proletarian and peasant toilers who brought the Soviet Union into existence. Today, the USSR that was forged directly under Lenin's guidance is one of two existing superpowers equal to or possibly surpassing its chief rival—in different fields—militarily. As a practical matter, it may safely be presumed that Marx would not have called for the violent, forceful overthrow of imperialism, even in Russia's concrete circumstances at the end of World War I. Such eschewal on revolutionary violence would have been mandated almost solely by pragmatic, immediate tactical considerations of political struggle with little, if any, regard for humanitarian considerations.

Hannah Arendt argued that violence in itself was neither beastly nor irrational. Its use in public life was characterized as an index of the failure of political power.[101] She may be partly right beyond the situation in Tsarist Russia about which she wrote. However, violent outbursts inspired by racial, religious, cultural and other animosities sometimes are unrelated to political and economic mishaps by definition, such motivation is the antithesis of rational thought and behavior. Irrationality was the incentive for genocide or other horrible atrocities of Hitler's Germany. All allowances being made, imperialist and revolutionary violence in Burundi had nothing to do either with adventurist explorers or missionaries, whose contribution to the shape of modern empires cannot be underestimated, or with the traders who wavered between mercantilism and the doctrines and practices of liberalism.

Georges Sorel could well have been right in maintaining that violence has a function to perform in society. His contention to some extent was linked to Marxist assessments of the role of violence in accelerating the birth of new socio-economic structures which is likely, however, to be counterproductive if used in situations not yet ripe for revolutionary change. Violence of this sort occurred, among others, in the Soviet Republics of Bavaria and Hungary in the aftermath of World War I and in Indonesia, Sudan and Chile in recent times; today, the lessons of these episodes are carefully studied by Euro-communists, radical Third World leaders, and by the Soviets as well.

Facts calling for a reappraisal of Leninist theory and practice among other things prove that it is meaningless to draw a historical parallel between *fin de siècle* capitalist imperialism and that of the present. The latter is put into operation by politically divergent and ideologically contradictory systems, frequently called socialist, but characterized by politics of imperialism, war and structural violence.

By and large the scramble in Africa and other continents rarely developed into expansionist wars. To be true, also present multifarious forms of expansion and imperialist inclinations that will probably continue as long as there are states characterized by inequality of potentials, do not always breed war. Studying the features of corporate power which influenced past expansionist policy makers, the conclusion seems inevitable that these imperialists were never bloodthirsty, but profit-hungry. For them, peace was the best circumstance for making money. It may be worthwhile in terms of unfounded attributions of warmongering to these imperialists to recall Max Weber's "theorem" that conflict is inherent in society and cannot be eliminated; also to be recalled in this regard is its corollary that evolutionary reforms and peace are merely changes in the form of confrontations in various settings of antagonism by which their limits, ways of realization and goals, are defined. This interpretation which also became popular with many of Weber's Third World adherents, could easily be applied to financial capital which continues opposition to armed conflicts; moreover, it regards the metamorphosis of armed conflict into peacefully competitive forms as vital to the human rights issue, to improving living standards and even to the survival of mankind. Also, it is vital to maintain and continually to increase competition's benefits. What is important, however, to the aim of the present inquiry, and which takes into account lessons from history and psychology, is the contention that violence can be controlled and directed into channels desirable to economic and political leaders, to security managers and to movements and parties of all orientations.

Hence, the importance of proving in due course why and where wars and other forms of violence cannot be successful is a task that sometimes overwhelms the one whose aim is to show where and why non-violence, reform, mutual concession and especially the negotiated consensus on conflict resolution can succeed. The former approach most likely could never be a step further towards non-antagonistic national societies and an entirely non-belligerent world-system; for such aspirations would remain a utopian dream. Yet, utopian goals could serve as guidelines to enable all parties to evade ultimate disaster of the nuclear era and to control the even more dangerous use of force.[102]

If, the assumption is accepted that past imperialism was a product of irreconcilable conflicts of interest for the benefit of the stronger, today the world is beset with intensifying conflicts of indefinite duration determined by the growth of inequalities.[103] This does not mean however, that the assumed image of a future international community inevitably plagued by destructive conflict must be accepted. All active members of the community become increasingly aware that war and other forms of violence often are destructive and self-defeating and therefore ought to be prevented.[104] At the same time, objective factors, too, tend to indicate an unequivocal choice of cooperation.

There are numerous examples of the voluntary dismemberment of empires since World War II, but relatively few before (such an inchoate trend was evident after World War I). In any event, post-World War II decolonization trends may lose their significance in view of different nonbelligerent superpower forms of imperialism that have evolved because the most powerful weapon of superpower expansionism, the military option, has become too risky for practical use. Concurrently, the value of economic threats seems also to be in process of depreciation.[105]

Only a decade ago, serious observers were of the opinion that superpower detente would result in a new Third World area for both North-South and world conflict.[106] Robert W. Tucker is of the opinion that today also the Third World's desire for development could breed more conflict than consensus, given all the divergencies on methods and goals and all the uncertainties about the limits of growth.

True, there also exists an undoubted connection between abuses of wealth and economic inequalities and suffering and loss, on the one hand, and the spirit which frequently leads to armed confrontation, on the other. The desire for improving conditions of life or for enrichment may ultimately end in bloody strife. This does not mean, however, that poverty-stricken nations are therefore likely to wage war in order to force others to satisfy their economic claims. Actually, only wealth and some degree of power enable nations to fight. Even if the LDC's were effectively assisted by their rich "brothers" in the quest for sensible realistic development goals, they still would run the risk, of having to confront very strong domestic and foreign opponents. The belief that they are able to meet such challenges is, however, regarded by many experts as a piece of romantic nonsense because their avenues of disrupting the powerful are few and the costs of the disruption heavy.

What is termed the conflict between the "haves" and "have nots" may be interpreted as an expression of rivalry of the "haves" for influence in the Third World. This was so in the inter-world war period and in earlier times and continues today.[107] This is one reason more why the North-South conflict will not be the war of the future and why the LDC's confrontations are merely of intra-Third World character;[108] moreover, even if they are supported by powerful external factors, they are engendered by the indigenous, principally irrational motivations.

The aforementioned dispute between the mercantilists and the liberals proves that the old-fashion imperialism was also no less uneconomic and irrational in nature, goals, and methods than the present one and that its Leninist analysis was far from accurate. Hence, the need, arises for a continual reappraisal of Lenin's theory and for the total attention to the historical and economic background and consequences of imperialism in its first stage. To a large extent, this has already been done on the basis of a brief scrutiny of facts and findings of D. K. Fieldhouse and M. Blaug, et al.[109] They convincingly highlighted the faults of Leninist conclusions.

What is still necessary is to elaborate further the various aspects of imperialism in its process of evolution, which were stressed by E. Halevy, A. P. Thornton, W. E. Houghton and other investigators with regard to past expansionist policies. Many of them proved that imperialist practices frequently grew from human, personal and educational motivations, racial attitudes, love of adventure, and diplomatic considerations. It was found that imperialist policies were sometimes evoked by the pressures of civil service interests and reinforced by the sensation-seeking press, as was the case of American imperialism of the Spanish-American war era. In different periods imperialism also resulted from the colonial powers' search for security, from their desire to curtail and end intertribal rivalries threatening their interests and from their will to get prestige and prevent aggrandizement and dominance of others.[110]

Consideration of these factors still seems to be relevant to any inquiry into the new trends of present-day imperialistic policies, particularly those concerning the direction of capital flow and interest in peaceful cooperation, the consequences of the growth of multi-nationals; moreover the impact of the latter on the situation in the Third World and on the interrelationship between the First and the Second Worlds is steadily increasing and transcends national interests and other contingencies.

With regard to all of these issues, it may be worthwhile to pay special attention to the assessments of Fieldhouse and Blaug relating to the fact that backward countries have never been attractive to private capital, that British foreign investments (as already mentioned) went mainly to developed countries and the Americans later followed their lead. They also explained why savings of underdeveloped countries were either hoarded instead of invested or exported to the advanced capitalist world. They stressed the role, among other things, of the new rate of returns that actually blocked the emergence of local capitalists in underdeveloped countries. Discussing different cases of expansion, the same authors proved that most of them usually resulted from the priority given to political over economic considerations.[110]

The renowned Marxist expert in underdevelopment, A. Emmanuel, has recently enriched the critical reexamination of the Leninist theory of imperialism not only, as already mentioned, by highlighting the important role of multinational corporations in modernizing Third World countries, but also by picturing the local high bourgeoisie as the greatest enemy of their socio-economic progress.[111]

Needless to say, Lenin and his orthodox followers ignored not only the Marxist assumptions in this question, but also some relevant historical facts such as the benefits which different colonies have received from their foreign rulers, for example, India. This was emphasized in a very interesting kind of balance sheet of imperialism drawn up by the leading Asian historian K. M.

Pannikar.[112] The critical reconsideration of the Leninist theory does not mean that the opposite opinion that entirely disregards the economic aspects is necessarily more accurate; for at least in some instances economic determinism has been established as a valid motive.

It is enough to read the critical note on Schumpeter's *Imperialism* by Murray Green in order to understand that this essay based exclusively on a psychological and sociological approach is inadequate and misleading.[113] True enough, Schumpeter's definition of imperialism excludes in the history or prehistory of expansion all instances of conquests for the purpose of acquiring fertile lands, slaves, markets, raw materials and other wealth. Most economically motivated expansion, however, was realized by other than military means and had nothing to do with remnants of a warrior class structure or other "atavistic" factors. Its occurrence has not contradicted essential features of capitalism and its admittedly mainly irrational foundations. Nothing can be added to the already mentioned black marks of the system, whereas denying them is not less an unhistoric abstraction than the idealization of "Socialist" governments or the denial of their imperialist tendencies.

The latter observations seem to be justified by the efforts made throughout this study pointing out why one form of contemporary imperialism, the so-called latest stage of capitalist development, is changing its character and giving preference to peaceful options. They also explain why another contemporary economic institution, the Socialist system, is—in spite of all the fears of a global war—striving to continually reinforce expansive policies, determined mainly by ideological and non-economic factors.

It seems therefore that the realization of the danger of a global escalation may become a powerful factor in preventing it and this quite independently of the economic situation in the Third World, of the fundamental political contradictions between the First and the Second Worlds and of the impact of the dominant ideology on the latter one. The evolution of theories of development strengthens the above conclusions.

The need to consider the impact of continuing socio-economic changes on the capitalist system, which to a large extent nullifies past theories on the nature of imperialism and its allegedly aggressive designs, was already strongly emphasized by J. Strachey on the eve of the present stage of the industrial and technological revolution.[114] He did not regard all Hobson's or Lenin's conclusions entirely void and also thought that at the end of the 19th and the beginning of the 20th century, when the living standards were very low and the internal Western European markets extremely limited and exhausted, the accumulation of power induced the search for further profits through conquests or other forms of dominance over weak, underdeveloped, colonial countries. Strachey admitted that this expansion already could be prevented then, by limiting the inequality in the division of income and by other social reforms and that the liberals intended, but failed, to make these reforms. This was the main reason why conditions were not created for investing profits in the national economy and the capitalist looked for export possibilities and conquests.

Imperialistic politics in their classical meaning were not, according to Strachey, an economic necessity even before World War I. Of course, they are not such today, when the power of trade unions, Socialist and Liberal parties is on the rise, as well as progressive tax, social security and welfare systems in operation in the majority of capitalist countries. Hobson's conclusions on under-consumption and Lenin's on pauperization, according to Strachey, are no more valid because the rationale of colonial expansion by conquest and other wars has been disappearing from capitalist politics. The possibility of preventing imperialist aggressive tendencies seems to him, like Hobson, quite real. It is determined by the use of capital and its profits to develop the national economy and to take care of the needs of the large strata of the population. Even the Conservative Party has never abolished the reforms of the Laborites or radically changed their own programs relating to internal and external affairs. The Conservatives continued them not only out of consideration for developmental or security needs, but also because of the attitude of capitalist constituencies.

The latter, like their predecessors, so frequently quoted by Marx,[115] believed too, that peace is essential to make fuller use of industrial superiority, particularly in the age of gigantic technological progress and the nuclear arms. This does not mean that it was, or is so, under all circumstances and that uneven economic growth above all, is not likely to become a factor of tensions. Again it was Marx,[116] who contributed much more than Rostow and others to present knowledge on "commercial," colonial and other economic wars.

Already more than a decade ago, Gunnar Myrdal corroborating some Marxist conclusions, analyzed the peace and war productive influence on economic growth and other aspects of these tendencies related to economic development and conflict.[117] He did so when other students of peace focused only on violent methods used by imperialists for attaining supremacy.

Myrdal saw two parallel processes in contemporary national and international economy: The first is produced by the spread effect defined as the expansion of economic and technological achievement moving from the industrial countries toward the LDCs and reducing the gap between them; the second results from the backward effect that enlarges the gap between various countries and regions because of (a) the inability of the underdeveloped countries to compete with the industrialized ones and (b) the unattractiveness of the latter to skilled labor and capital fleeing from the former. The gap also deepens because of the consequences of the population explosion, lack of an adequate technological infrastructure, low educational standards, low professional training standards and low standards of health institutions. This is cummulative to the administrative inefficiency and the unproductivity of labor.

Myrdal considered the backward effect to be stronger than the spread effect. By and large he believed that the progress of developing countries is spontaneous; therefore it is difficult to plan how to narrow the gap between the LDCs and the industrial ones because people suffering from undernourishment and other socio-economic ills, mainly react emotionally under strong religious, tribal, and other prejudicial influences. It should also be added that bitterness, bred by the feeling of injustice and discrimination, makes rational attitudes veritably impossible in external matters as well. Instead, these people favor conflict and resort to violence with its escalation potentialities merely on a local scale. Myrdal's contribution to the exploration of these problems mainly lies in emphasizing the predominant role of indigenous factors both as regards backwardness and recession in the developing countries and also elements leading to complications in foreign affairs.

At the same time, he has shed more light on the role of exogenous factors in both creating and deepening the disparities between the less developed and industrialized countries. He has also pinpointed the capability of the latter to reduce them, to remedy the world economy and to strengthen international security. Myrdal contends that the need to use this capability and to refrain from the use of force also is growing because today weak states are far less fearful of superpowers' threats. Resort to arms is precluded because of mutual rivalry and the impact of nuclear arsenals.

Myrdal's views essentially differ from the theories on structural violence and peripheric capitalism. His conclusions entirely contradict any dichotomic approach by conceiving the world either in terms of an exploiting center and a victimized dependency or otherwise. He rejects generalizations and rather prefers a dialectical analysis of realities, based, however, on an evolutionist approach. He considers all their negative and positive byproducts and tries to elaborate concrete solutions for a successive improvement of the situation in the Third World. Such an aim must be seen as unattainable if the focus is only on an unreconcilable contradiction between a single pole of destructive dominance and a ruthlessly subjugated periphery,[118] whose backwardness and misery are conceived exclusively as an inevitable result of the capitalism's development.[119] This aim must remain an utopian dream if capitalism's regenerating role which precipitates the decomposition of ages-old forms of despotism and stagnatory, undignified, and vegetative ways of life, is almost entirely passed over in silence.

Marx's views on this rôle have been mentioned already. Since those who at present tend to minimize or ignore it in analyses of development and peace issues often regard themselves as Marxists, it may be worthwhile to remember Marx's descriptions of England. He pictured it as "actuated by the vilest interests" and "stupid in the manner of enforcing them" and also as the "Unconscious tool of history" in bringing about a real revolution. He stressed its function in nearing the end of the "barbarian egotism," the "distinctions of caste and by slavery," and the subjugation of "man to external circumstances instead of elevating (him) to be (their) sovereign." England, he noted, acted as the moving force in dissolving the parasitic units of ancient organization and "laying the material foundations of Western Society."

What has been said in this context about England, can be repeated with regard to the First World of our times and to a large extent with regard to the multinationals as well. Emmanuel's opinion on this matter has already been quoted. They, too, have "to create the material basis of the new world: on the one hand, the universal intercourse founded upon the mutual dependency of mankind and the means of that intercourse; on the other hand, the development of the productive powers of man and the transformation of material production into a scientific domination of agencies."[120]

Modern development and peace research still pays little attention to these aspects of the problem. Yet some development and peace researchers dealing with these phenomena prove the unsatisfactory value of the dichotomic approach. That is why they stress the shape of trichotomic and other more complicated relationships of dominance as well as of cooperation. These are sometimes a consequence of being in power, but at the same time being dependent or governed by others. Often characterized as subimperialist frameworks,[121] (i.e. as another product of the continual change within the national communities and their mutual ties), they grow stronger with the departure from old forms of life and production. They are dissolved and finally replaced by new ones, although they also keep some traditional features, even in the long run. This also proves the benefit of abandoning dichotomic outlooks, as was shown in a quite original way in S. Takayanga's writings. He dealt with at least three kinds of interrelationship between various groups and countries. One of them leads to cooperation on the basis of equality or near-equality, which existed in the primitive societies and is growing today in the West, particularly in the European Community. Another is a result of the imposition of dominance of the strong over the weak by conquests and today of hegemonial tendencies embodied in some forms of Soviet, American and Chinese policies. The third one is, according to Takayanga a reaction to the former and is sometimes characterized by violent attitudes of people in post-colonial states,[122] and recently by diplomatic and economic pressures as well.[123] True, violent reaction also characterizes the attitude of workers and other large social strata in the People's Democracies as a result of conditions imposed by the USSR. Consequently fraternal governments press the Kremlin to help, to reduce the harsh terms of Soviet loans and supplies and, to try (as inter alia in the case of Romania and recently of Poland) to achieve more economic and political independence. However, the most recent form of economic and political confrontation in the relationship between various groups of states is a result of the struggles for reconstructing the world economic order. This struggle is led by The Third World against the First and Second World countries in an atmosphere of a growing willingness on the part of the West to compromise,[124] while the Communists continue to argue that they should not be blamed and asked to pay for the consequences of colonialism, a problem which does not seem to concern them at all.

The fact that reaction to hegemonial behaviour is a source of violence and revolt both in the Third World and in the Socialist bloc, does not diminish the rationale of Takayangi's propositions. They maintain their validity, although there exists (as established by the findings of E. Fossum, D. J. Morrison, and others)[125] an indubitable correlation between maldevelopment and strictly internal uprisings and military coups. By and large, the aforementioned authors pay no attention to the question why the clashes and militarization occur neither within or on the borders of countries not yet affected by the process of modernization. They also disregard the fact that violent encounters frequently begin as tribal and religious antagonisms or are provoked by agents of foreign interests; nor do they observe that violent conflicts in this part of the globe are likely to gain momentum because of arms deliveries and financial support from some Arab oil producers, who are interested in preserving the status quo or changing it by strengthening their ties with the First or Second World. The struggle formerly led by a united front of less developed countries may thus become the concern, as already mentioned above, only of the emerging Fourth World of the poorest.

It may be preferable in any study on Third World conflicts of limited and global dimensions to follow researchers who divorce themselves from the mainly narrow dichotomic North-South conflict supposedly dominating the present world scene. In such studies, it would be useful to consider all centers and subcenters of political influence and confrontation and as many indigenous, exogenous, economic, cultural and other factors as possible. All of these factors are frequently intertwined with one another and continually change the scope and aims of existing and newly formed groups of states.

B. Hoselitz's studies[126] appeared when the cold war was still a prevalent characteristic of present-day international relations and decolonization was in its beginning, that is, when the situation more favored bipolar outlooks. He succeeded, however, to override them and, by concretization of the issues and differentiation of their roots and images, to open larger horizons in the research on the development's impact on foreign policies.

Hoselitz differentiated between expansionist and internal models of growth. The first one, characterized by such countries as the United States and Canada, during a long period was able to multiply its land and natural resources by construction in unsettled areas and by federating with new administrative units on the basis of equality and mutually profitable co-operation. The second model related to countries like Holland and Sweden. Economic growth has been achieved by them because of intensive exploitation of local resources.

Hoselitz also described the shape of sovereign and dependent models of growth. The first takes place in countries with relatively little interest in exports and foreign loans and shows strong autarchic tendencies. The countries of the contrary model are dependent on foreign imports and vitally dependent on exports. This was the case with the USA, Canada, Australia and other formerly dependent territories and today with all post-colonial states. The satellite or dependent model results in political dependence and facilitates foreign intervention. The sovereign model characterized nations which today have become dominant in the international arena. He also differentiated between models of authentic growth (characteristic of the liberal system based on private initiative) and those of countries with central planning and state intervention in all fields of life.

No model was conceived by him in an abstract purely autonomous way. Nor did he ignore their interplay with regard to internal and external affairs. Hoselitz's concepts are therefore of great use in the study of present trends towards interdependence of all nations. Interdependence is known to grow despite countries differences in size and population, political systems, cultural traditions, or ideological orientation. It will become even stronger when the politicians of all countries fully realize that a new global war may be suicidal for all.

Those who base themselves mainly on center-periphery criteria often pretend to be faithful to Marx. Actually, Hoselitz has contributed with his multifarious models much more to the understanding of the process of interdependence. This process has recently become dominant in the international community, but it was foretold more than 320 years ago by Suarez and more than 120 years ago by Marx.[127]

The industrial states will most probably depend for many years on the producers of oil and some other raw materials, but the process of interdependence will strenghten their reluctance to use force in the unending struggle to obtain these commodities. It will also reduce the national and world dimension of class struggle, in contradiction to Marx's prognosis; this may be all the more likely because the relaxation of the North-South tensions and remedy of the situation in the Third World does not require the redistribution of the "cake," but rather an effort to make it bigger.[128] The latter contention is also ignored by the theoreticians of peripheric capitalism,[129] although they conceive the problem in economic terms. As for the role of the non-economic factors with regard to this problem, it may be worthwhile to remember some of the still valid findings of L.F. Richardson and Quincy Wright.[130]

Richardson, analyzing the causes of wars in the years before 1820 and later before 1949, established that at least 30 percent of them did not have any direct economic justification at all and that the latter played a greater role in smaller than in larger wars, while the settlement of conflicts between developed and underdeveloped nations was usually achieved by diplomacy. Obviously, Richardson's cataclysmic approach, which regards wars as a natural phenomenon almost entirely independent of man's will, raises serious questions. Still, the findings of Richardson, Wright and others should not be entirely disregarded. Their conclusions, as applied in regard to the North-South conflict that had become critical merely because of claims of national freedom and opposition to racial discrimination and only lately against economic disparities, should not be totally ignored either.

Violence was employed in the Third World for many years to eliminate foreign rule imposed for the often unnecessary economic and military needs of metropolises and regardless of the productivity of their military industries. It has already been mentioned that it was more frequently imposed for the purpose of prestige, motivated by compulsions for power and mastery, for religious missionary success, for quasi-strategic reasons and for diplomatic and other non-economic considerations.[131]

As regards civil wars, including those which escalated into international conflicts, most of them beginning with the Reformation were inspired by political and ideological motivations much stronger than economic interests. This fact also induces some modern peace researchers to pay more and more attention to human rights issues and generally to political structures as a source of conflict and peace. R. Shiratori[132] can be ranked among those who express the tendency of updating to a certain extent the Kantian assumption of the role of despotism in breeding conflicts and of democracy in promoting co-operation under conditions of peace.

Shiratori concentrated on the competing values in each society and on the choice of aggressive policies of governments using all means at their disposal to achieve their aims and securing their constituencies support. The importance of "civil maturity" measured by Shiratori is determined by a combination of the following:

a) personal autonomy by granting to the citizen the possibility of active participation in public life and guaranteeing respect for his rights;

b) economic wealth based on a rich material culture on a great deal of equality, and on the prevention of centralizing wealth;

c) freedom of the individual including freedom of the speech and religion, tolerance and the right of dissent;

d) human solidarity by strengthening communal integration, communication and understanding among individuals and various groups and reinforcing peace orientated activities. Studying findings from 130 countries, Shiratori thus established that "civil maturity" is higher in countries of tolerance and democracy accordingly peace and development policies are favored in countries such as Great Britain, Sweden, Switzerland and Austria where society gives consideration to human needs and priority to standards of living.

In the Socialist Bloc and in some democratic countries where stress is on high productivity, such as in the USA, France and Japan, the "civil maturity" is low or tends to shrink. This is likely to reinforce lack of tolerance in external and internal affairs, to put it simply, there is a track leading towards socio-economic improvement and favoring peaceful cooperation, that results from the political system and there is a contrary path determined by the authoritarian nature of government. Clearly the passage from one system to another and adoption of the respective peaceful and belligerent policies is expounded in this concept as determined not only by economic, but by social and cultural factors as well.

Today the awareness of the danger to the survival of mankind if global war breaks out, a war which can likely grow from a local conflict, is another purely non-economic factor of the greatest importance in the struggle for both development and peace.

Once "civil maturity" affects the ruling groups and governments, it will presumably facilitate the solution of economic and other problems, particularly important to the Third world, including those germinating from domestic misery, from industrial backwardness and from overcoming the ensuing difficulties in international trade and inequality in the world economy.

4. Is the Negative Impact of Development Issues on International Security Unavoidable?

The conditions strengthening awareness of a need and possibility of more effective abatement of underdevelopment and its consequences for humanitarian and other reasons involving the dreaded devastation of a nuclear war has been frequently pointed out above. Many of the concepts quoted are based on the assumption that the various models of development, more or less reflecting realities, breed tendencies of expansion and conquest; therefore sooner or later they are likely to produce reaction against a regime of exploitation, above all foreign ones.

It also has already been mentioned how the existing forms of development assistance far from satisfy the requirements of the Third World and how frustrations from such want of satisfaction leads to confrontations with the First and recently also with the Second Worlds. Yet it is worthwhile to deal in more detail with the basic problem: does development always inherently lead to national and international destabilization of society, or does it create a situation which can be held under control with its negative aspects contained? One is inclined to agree with the latter assumption[133] because it seems that today, governments for various reasons have ceased to fight for territories[134] and because in the past conquests were neither a divine nor "natural" imperative, nor an unaviodable political act.

S. H. Eisenstadt,[135] C. E. Black,[136] S. Huntington[137] and many others who influenced or followed them have assumed that modernization is a decomposing factor of existing orders and that it creates conflicts. This approach has already been mentioned, although very briefly, in the introductory remarks. The origins of the thesis on underdevelopment as a war-productive factor was pointed out too. Clark's findings prove very strongly that there is no room for generalization in this matter.

Research experts at Cornell University dealing with various Latin American, African and Asian countries including Israel indicate that urbanization, industrialization, expanding transport, communications and other undertakings of modernization are not always relevant to social revolution. The opposite opinion is often reinforced by idealization of the old life forms and styles and the desire to perpetuate them. Various internal eruptions of domestic armed violence such as mutinies and civil war, are determined by a variety of social factors that most frequently have nothing to do with the process of modernization.[138] The same conclusion, as will be later elaborated in more detail, can be drawn from the Soviet analyses of international wars, that has taken into account their economic aspect, or even from their classification in Soviet-orientated literature.[139]

Studies of G. Almond, G. B. Powell, H. Wriginns, A. O. Hirschman and others show that social stability depends on the government's skill and ability to keep order, to establish a sound fiscal system, to prevent economic maldistribution, to be sensitive to public opinion and to foster widespread popular belief and confidence in authority by its respectable and responsible leaders. Government ineptitude in the administration of the state rather than problems of modernization and development is one of the main reasons for social unrest. The efficiency of the American and Soviet administration in spite of differences in methods and goals has contributed substantially to growth in the respective countries. On the other hand, maladministrattion in Latin America, Asia and Africa has reinforced backwardness and stagnation.[140]

These findings also confirm the dominant role of internal factors in the process of underdevelopment and tensions produced by it, but acknowledgement of the fact surely does not mean that the impact of external factors should be underestimated. Internal factors are strong in various concrete situations. Today, external factors are more important than ever because of the rivalry of the two superpowers that compete for the spheres of influence in all parts of the world and because of their role as arms suppliers and their economic mastery and might. This makes it possible to contribute more effectively to improvement of the situation of the poor members of the international community.

It is not necessary to stress that all industrialized countries today at least bear moral responsibility for situations in many developing countries. Some of these developing countries were under Western colonial rule for hundreds of years; this is a fact of indubitable relevance also to the USSR as a successor of Tsarist Russia whose colonial expansion moved through successive contiguous territories as already detailed by Hobson[141] among others. Moreover, it is recalled that Hobson was an important source of Lenin's inspiration for his famous work on imperialism.

Presently, however, Western countries declare their willingness to undertake the reduction of disparities between them and the less developed countries, by means also of risky or unprofitable investments conceived as enlightened self-interest in the long run and the challenge to work for a better and more peaceful future of mankind,[142] for its survival and the preservation of our civilization. In the era of the growing interdependence of all nations, these undertakings comprise a variety of fields and activities that actually tend to create new forms of dependence beneficial to all parties and which are successfully reducing the links of subjugation,.discrimination and exploitation.

The progress of less developed countries has been and will continue to be for many years, dependent not only on opportunities for obtaining capital, knowhow, training personnel, advice, various economic services and manufacture from the industrialized nations, but also on markets for their own products. This cannot, however, be achieved by severing ties with the West. The Soviet Bloc is also vitally interested in strengthening its ties with the developing countries, but the problem is how to change the nature of these ties, to continually improve and use them in a mutually constructive way and to benefit the weakest of them from the very beginning. Whereas it is regarded as incorrect to view the growth and might of the First World as solely attributable to victimizing present Third World countries, it seems no less fallacious to insist that the remedy to backwardness is inevitably contingent on Third World confrontation with the West. It may be reasonably conceded that self-reliance is an appropriate method and only to some extent for such a gigantic country as China; but as a matter of fact, its leaders continue to be aware that in practice it is unwise to follow theoretical principles too literally. They have worked hard to assuage foreign enmity by securing allies or at least foreign neutrality in the PRC's ongoing confrontation with the Soviet Union. They do everything possible to enlarge their commercial ties, furthermore they have never denied the role of foreign aid in accelerating development and in the effort to increase military power.[143] In this, they have been consistent both in times of "cultural revolution" and domestic tranquility, as well as in times of both international conflict and international calm.

If the mobilization of the Third World for changing the present economic world order, is to remain other than a diplomatic game directed ultimately towards equality for its rich members, and in disregard of ameliorating the hunger and backwardness of the Third World's poorest,[144] a global strategy based on proper contributions of all "worlds" is indispensable. Moreover, the First World appeal to the Soviet Bloc in this matter should not be regarded as merely tactical; for its effective cooperation is really as necessary as the efforts of the less developed countries themselves. They should first of all make important changes sine qua non for a proper use of foreign aid. The problem becomes more and more urgent, this is not only because nearly one billion people earn no more than 75 dollars a year, suffer from hunger and have no prospects of improving their situation without a measure of properly administered international assistance.[145] The deplorable situation of the poorest countries that concurrently are most effected by the energy crisis is not caused by divine predestination but could have been prevented. It can still be changed today, since the ability to change is well within the scope of human capacities to do something about it.

As the leading Pakistani economist and a senior official of the World Bank, Mahbud-Ul-Haq has stressed, referring to statistics mentioned by the Bank's Head, R. McNamara, the poor have financed almost 90 percent of their development investment in the last decade out of their meager income.

This has been done to good effect despite all the difficulties. Nearly half of the developing countries have grown by an average of four percent per capita each year during the last 10 years. It is the industrialized world itself which—because also of its prohibitive regulations with regard to the mobility of labor—makes a major obstacle to the Third World's attempt to pull itself out of poverty. However, there already exist the partial operation of realistic and useful plans, like James Grant's scheme, of eliminating malnutrition and grinding poverty by the mid 1980s.[146]

These plans as well as the numbers and opinions quoted above also stress the primacy of the indigenous origins of misery and conflicts. They emphasize the importance of the internal means to remedy them, but do not underestimate the exogenous factors, which are only the basis for refuting theories which focus on the disasterous situation in the Third World, exclusively resulting from its peripheric role in world capitalism as if only imposed on it. Many of the above mentioned opinions do not ignore even the need for changing radically the present North-South relationship for bringing all discriminative forms of dependency to an end and for elaborating and putting into operation an effective, globally conceived plan, for this purpose.[147]

Professor Kenneth Boulding's definition of conflicts refers to situations in which opposed parties are divided by so many contradictory views that compromise becomes virtually impossible.[148] Taking into account this definition, serious doubt emerges whether the so called North-South conflict is a case in point today, particularly if concilliatory mood that has prevailed even after the interruption of the 1977 Paris Dialogue is considered. This and the decline of the Third World ideological issues and solidarity may also result from the present situation which by and large is uncomfortable for all parties; moreover its negative aspects are also more and more felt in the Eastern Bloc so that all parties strive for a compromise and desire co-operative schemes. Needless to reiterate that the energy crisis has shaken the poor Third World countries more than the West. It has increased inflation and caused other monetary troubles, as well as temporary but structural economic crises, while the oil producers face difficulties in maintaining solidarity of ranks. Meanwhile the pressures of the poorest upon all are growing. All are, therefore, searching for constructive solutions. This reflects a tendency towards mutual understanding. The new situation is entirely different from the one characterized by tensions which prevailed during the 1975 UN General Assembly and other international meetings of that time.

At the end of the North-South dialogue, the industrialized nations have finally agreed to underwrite a "Common Fund" to finance stocks for commodities exported by poor countries and thus help to control wild fluctuations in price. During the periods of poor demand, the buffer stock supervisors would buy from commodity producers to buttress prices; in periods of great demand, they would sell, lowering prices. The Group of Eight (the USA, Japan, Australia, Canada, the Common Market, Sweden, Switzerland and Spain) have also accepted the plan for creating a one billion pool to aid LDCs that are suffering from steadily mounting bills for imported oil. It has also pledged to increase its financial aid commitments to international agencies. True, the LDCs greatest demands still are not satisfied; thus, for instance, the question of a moratorium on outstanding LDCs debts to Western countries still remains unsolved, as well as that of pegging commodity prices to Western inflation rates. However, the USA in turn, has not got what it has ardently sought: the continuing formal dialogue on oil. So there is room for bargaining, for bringing positions closer together and for negotiating new agreements and interim solutions. These solutions should be taken on step by step basis, and only then can they lead to a certain measure of progress. Progress of course, can not be easily achieved. Its realization may be complicated if one or all parties return to radical and intransigent positions and if the Soviets continue to behave as outsiders and aggressors looking for political vacuums and weaknesses to exploit instead of constructive economic assistance to the less developed countries.

Still there is room for some optimism, the more so since recent steps of the West favoring the Third World are actually a link in the West's continuing activities. These activities were particularly evident already with the changes decided upon in January 1975 by the International Monetary Fund, which asked for the enlargement of credits to the Third World (although it also demanded the enlargement of rights and duties of the oil-producers as well). These activities were also evident in the results of the 28th February, 1975, Lomé convention. The latter comprises some elements of a new model in the European Community relationship with 46 African, Caribbean and Pacific States. The radical criticism of this relationship is to a large extent a result of a dogmatic approach that denies any change for better in Western politics.[149]

There is still far from a consensus in all matters. However, the opinion that all parties will have to give up something before being able to reconstruct fundamentally the present economic world order—an opinion already expressed a few years ago[150]—for some time has reflected an already irreversible ongoing process. Since the Third World does not expect more help, at least in the near future, from the Soviet Bloc, it has to rely on the West. The Third World believes that economic decolonization and reconstruction will come with the end of political colonialism; therefore it still remains rather neutral in regard to the West's call to the Second World to co-operate in combatting underdevelopment in all its various forms and aspects. This also is one of the reasons why both the establishments of all kinds of orientation as well as different and sometimes quite radical quarters of the Third World, seem to be reluctant to adopt an emotional posture which postulates that violence and world revolution are the only means for putting an end to the Third World's misery.[151] Reliance on such hypothesis,[152] to a large extent, also disregards the fact that the Third World's ruling elites actually ignore the vital needs of their masses more even as happens with other nations or various social groups. Today, the Third World spokesmen are not revolutionaries, but pragmatic politicans, or worse frequently small caliber dictators and demagogues. Socialism as proclaimed by them is usually in all its manifestations nothing more than an expression of modernization programs and of very limited socio-economic and cultural reforms.[153]

Even in the countries where there are strong Soviet tendencies, their policies are based in principle on the experience of the West; however, they sometimes ignored the fact that the West, too, has known times of distress; and that if it has succeeded in curing most of its ills, it was less by conquests and exploitation outside its realm and more by hard labor and intellectual skill.

Therefore, it is worthwhile to pinpoint again that Third World leaders have adopted the liberal and optimistic approach not only as an appropriate one for the explanation of their present underdevelopment, but also as useful for improving the methods to end it. They prefer to see their maldevelopment, rather as a product of a long historical process to no small measure aggravated by their own faults, or a process which could be prevented or at least ameliorated and which currently is susceptible to a radical change. This probably cannot be achieved rapidly and certainly not at once; however, essential steps towards this goal seem to them attainable today and not necessarily in a too distant future.

Their efforts to achieve this aim, their growing pressure on the First World for more aid in this connection, and their first attacks against the Second World to secure its constructive assistance—all proves that Third World leaders do not regard their struggle as a vain exercise.

Since progress, at least towards successfully improving the situation of the poorest countries, does not require too heavy a burden on the Western economy, signs of good will as well as readiness to give up privileges and to use more effective means to stop the malaise of underdevelopment, hunger, retrogradation or stagnation in these countries are multiplying in the West.

The aims of improving the situation and reforming the world economic order no longer meet serious opposition. The continuing differences of views are determined rather by the questions: Who has to pay the entire price and under what conditions? What should be the timetable, and the extent of reforms? What has to be done in order that the scheme might encompass all the potential donors and how can the proper use of the means put at the disposal of the recipients be assured? To what extent should recipients be required to promote democracy, human rights and peace as well as employing developmental aid in a mutually advantageous manner?

These kinds of differences (some are rather of a technical character) is slowly overcome. They point to the West's reorientation and to the fact that it develops a non-imperialistic and peaceful policy because of the understanding of its economic supremacy, military might and technological growth and the impact of the nuclear era's consequences.

Opinions denying this evolution seem to be out of touch with reality. They contribute neither to a better understanding of the origins of the present situation in the Third World's areas of under-development nor to the Third World's struggle for changing this situation. The emergent constellation of worldwide political and economic affairs might, in spite of residual dangers to peace, at the same time strengthen all factors affecting the prospects for peace and the amelioration of the hungry and angry nations.

True, the dominant forms of international economic co-operation particularly with the beginning of the "new imperialism" at the end of the 19th Century and at the ends of the two world wars, have been marked by signs of what has been called imperialistic dominance, exploitation,[154] and spoliation.[155] However, it is clear that the process which was formally inaugurated at Bandung, could not be limited to a certain area and to the termination of foreign rule there.[156] It is obvious that it would rather lead towards decolonization on a global scale and towards enlarging all its aspects in time including economic ones.

It has been often said that this process' present stage indicates that the stakes in the so-called North-South conflict no more refer only to wealth, but also to political power. Today, power in the international arena becomes almost as important a goal as wealth, for the leaders of the South.[157] This is so because economic decolonization or, more precisely, the economic inferiority of the Third World compared with the other two worlds is still far from coming to an end; therefore, power is regarded by the Third World leaders as instrumental in narrowing if not entirely closing the gap between the "worlds." However, no illusions are harbored at least in serious quarters of the Third World, as to the possibility of playing a decisive role in problems of war and peace on a global scale.

As has already been pointed out, the Third World role remains today and will probably continue to be mainly dependent on the two superpowers. Only superpower antagonism may in the opinion of the Chinese and others lead to a clash because of the arms race.[158]

However, this pessimistic prognosis should not be taken as inevitable and as reflecting a sacrosanct truth. Essential changes in the West and a certain measure of deideologization of the USSR and the growing burden of armaments could result in limitation and reduction of the arsenals and in the dangerous arms trade. True, negotiations after the aggression against Afghanistan are stalemated but this may lead to reassessment of the issues and help to refute the pessimistic oulooks and to strengthen the work for reconstructing the world economy and peace as well.

Each step in this direction leads towards the realization of the latter goal, the attainment of which not only would diminish Third World divisions but interpower tensions as well. Should political realities of the coming years confirm the necessity of choosing this option, an indeed revolutionary metamorphosis of the economic world order might be expected, then, according to the aforementioned hypothesis, a catastrophical international conflict might be avoided.

This view is also rooted in some conclusions, already elaborated by the classics of economic and political theory and of international law. It is also reflected in blueprints of peace. Some experts who take into account classics and other authorities, are therefore of the opinion that any society needs a new "Encyclopedia," basic mutations and any government a kind of "revolution."[159] These propositions seem to be of relevance not only to national societies, but to the international community as well.

If possible accidental occurrences, with the unpredictable results of uncontrolled adventurism is excluded, the international community is characterized in its present stage of evolution by the predominant role of the superpowers in questions of human survival and by growing limitations imposed upon superpowers by the interaction of socio-economic, political national and other factors. All of them strengthen the prospects of a truly revolutionary change in the economic and possibly later in the political world system. However, these prospects depend upon its realization without the use of violent means or the provocation of global wars that presumably become unthinkable, irrational and probably also preventable. Whether this change also eliminates the non-economic conflicts, divisive conflict antithetical to survival or encourages the imposition of certain ideas, beliefs, or forms of government as well as culture and civilization remains problematical. History and theory do not give a clear answer to this question. Intraparty conflicts in the USSR or China and chronic Sino-Soviet antagonism rather point to the possibility of conflicts not only of non-economic, but also in principle of both ideological and of non-ideological character as well.

Notes

1. Adelman I., passim.
2. Heilbronner R.L., *The Great Assent* (Harper, New York 1963) p. 21.
3. Austrey J., *Le Scandale du Développement* (Paris: M. Riviere 1965) pp. 100 and 163.
4. Peroux, F., *Léconomie du XX siècle* (Paris: PUF 1961) p. 155.
5. Ibid., p. 28.
6. Balandier G., *La Mise en rapport des sociétés "différentes" et le problème du sou-développement* RTM (1962) p. 121.
7. Nutzinger H.G., *Vorläufiger Bericht über die Arbeitsgemeinschaft zwischen entwickelten und unentwickelten Ländern* (5. XI. 71 Symposium, Rheda Schloss) pp. 1, 2.
8. Renouvin-Duroselle, pp. 246-49.
9. Heilbronner, p. 109.
10. See the analysis of Cobden's and Mill's views in Q. Wright. A Study of War (II ed., Univ. of Chicago Press 1965) and in the same author's "War" in the *International Encyclopedia of Social Sciences* (Vol. 16 Macmillan and The Free Press) pp. 461-4.
11. Heilbronner, pp. 27 and 57.
12. *Ibid.*, pp. 70 and 83.
13. Adelman, p. 42.
14. I am indebted to Mr. Saul Zarhi, the economic editor of the Hebrew *Encyclopedia of Social Sciences* (ed. by D. Knaane and published by Sifriyat Hapo'alim beginning with 1962-1970) for allowing me to read his paper on some economic doctrines relating to "development and Conflict in the Age of Imperialism."
15. Winks, pp. 1-3.
16. Boulding K.E., "Twelve Friendly Quarrels with .Johan Galtung," *JPR*, (Vol. XIV, no. 1. 1977) pp. 75-86.
17. Heilbronner, pp. 53-54.
18. *Ibid.*, pp. 64-5.
19. See the excerpts from Hobson's study in Winks, pp. 11, 19, 23, 25.
20. Barnet, pp. 35, 210, 224, 227 and 332.
21. Beard Ch.A., *The Devil Theory of War* (Westport: Greenwood Press, 1977 3rd. ed.) pp. 15, 23, 29, 91-2.
22. Morgenthau H.J., *Politics among Nations* (New York: H.H. Knopf 1967, IV ed.) p. 45.
23. Barnet p. 210.
24. Luxemburg, R., Accumulation of Capital (New York: Monthly Review Press, 1964) quoted by Barnet *op. cit.*, pp. 163-4.
25. See excerpts from Lenin's study in Winks, pp. 26-30.
26. Morgenthau, p. 46.
27. I dealt with these issues in more detail in my study in Hebrew, *The Nuremberg Trial* (Jerusalem, Yad Vashem Publication, 1961).
28. Cf. Laqueur, *op. cit.*, pp. 202-3.
29. Morgenthau, pp. 46-50.

30. See f.i. the findings in J. Viner "Peace as an Economic Problem," *International Economics* (Glencoe, The Free Press, 1951).

31. Mushkat M., "Is Territory Changing its Role in World Politics?" *International Problems* (Vol. XVI, no. 3-4 (32), 1977) pp. 43-58.

32. Barnet, pp. 167, 227-8 and passim.

33. Important excerpts from his work, "Imperialism and Social Classes" (New York: World Publishing Co. 1968) are reproduced in Winks. We refer particularly to pp. 87-88 and 90-91.

34. Barnet, pp. 206, 209, 213-4 and 225 and see his references to H. Magdoff, *The Age of Imperialism*, (New York: Monthly review press 1964) p. 52 and V. Perlo, *Militarism and Industry* (New York: International Publishers Co. 1964) p. 124.

35. Cf. Laqueur, p. 135.

36. Merle M., Politique Intérieure et Politique Exterieure" *Seminaire D.E.A.* 1975-76 (Un. de Paris I) pp. 8-9 and see his book *Sociologie des Relations Internationales* (2 ed., Paris: Dalloz 1976) pp. 252-4.

37. Adelman, p. 108.

38. Emmanuel A., "Les Sociétés multinationales et le dévéloppement inégal" *Review International of Soc. Sc.* (Vol. XXVII, no. 4, 1976) pp. 824-44.

39. Lichtheim G., *Imperialism* (New York: Praeger 1971) pp. 824-44.

40. Barnet, pp. 137-8, 159, 210, 223-4, 229, 237, 334 and passim.

41. Scott R., (ed.) *The Politics of the New States* (Allen and Aberdeen Univers. Press, 1970), pp. 25-6.

42. The Eastern Bloc's debt to the West was at the end of 1976 estimated as 32 to 35 billion dollars. See P. Drouin's articles *Le Monde* (7.VI. 1977).

43. The total debt of the developing countries increased in the period from 1967 till 1973 from 51 to 119 billion dollars. See *Les Socialistes*, p. 58.

44. Merle M., Politique. *op. cit.*, p. 9.

45. See R. Jackson in A. Brian et P.M. Henry, Pour un autre dévéloppement (Presse Univer. de France, 1976) and J. Conchol in "Faim et Dévéloppement" quoted by P. Drouin, "Croissance et Contrainte," *Le Monde* (27-28.II.1977).

46. Green R.H. "Petroleum Prices and African Development," *International Journal* (vol. XXX, no. 3, 1975) p. 392.

47. Villermé R., Tableau de l'état physique et moral des ouvriers dans les fabriques de coton, de laine et de soie, 2 vols. 1840.

48. Heilbronner, *op. cit.*, p. 85.

49. Merle M., Sociologie *op. cit.*, p. 456 and Drouin P., *loc. cit.*

50. Bommensath, M., "La hantise de l'emploie," and Hadler W. "Une croisade contre la misère" quoted in *Le Monde* (27-8, II.1977) pp. 18 and 19.

51. Merle M., *Sociologie.* op. cit., pp. 238-9. For the prospects of further Western growth, incomparable with the lamentable accents in Brezhnev's report presented at the XXVI Party Congress in February 1981, see, i.a., *Die Zeit*, No. 46.XI.1980, p. 47.

52. Stein L., *Economic Realities in Poor Countries* (Sidney: Angus and Robertson, 1972) p. 40.

53. Green R.H., pp. 238-9.

54. Galtung J., "Poor Countries vs. Rich: Poor People vs. Rich, Whom will the NIEO benefit" *Chair in Conflict and Peace Research* (Univ. of Oslo, paper no. 63 (n.d.) pp. 6 and 9-10.

55. "Un colloque 'mondialiste' sur le nouvel ordre économique," *Le Monde* (27-28.II.77) p. 4 and cf. with the remarks on J. Tinbergen's "Reshaping the International Order," *Le Monde* (22.X.1976).

56. Epstein E.J. and Kahn H., "Refuting the Doomsday Prospects," *Current* (no. 187, Nov. 1976) pp. 13-8 and cf. "Die Zukunft hat wieder eine Zukunft," *Die Zeit* (no. 2/31.XII.1976) referring to W. Leontieff's *The Future of World Economy* and its stress on the supremacy of political, social and institutional factors upon the physical ones and therefore its opposition to the concept of the limits of growth. See also J. Stanovnik "Towards the NIEO," *RYIA* (Vol. XXIX, no. 669, 20.II.1978) pp. 8-10.

57. *Catastrophe or New Society?* A Latin American Model by A.O. Herrera, H.D. Scolnik, G. Chichilnisky, G.C. Galopin, J.E. Hardog, D. Moscovich, E. Oteira, G.L. de Romeo Brest, C.E. Suarez and L.T. Talavera, (IDRC) Ottawa, 1976) and on Prof. Deutsch's conclusions see "Change or Face Disaster, Economic Scientists Warning," *The German Tribune*, 12.VIII.79, No. 902, p. 6.

58. See W. Brandt, "Schluss mit Armut und Aufrüstung," *Die Zeit*, No. 8, 15.II.1980, p. 9 and the report of the 14 Conference on the UN in the Next Decade, "International Development Strategy," Porvoo, Finland, June 24-29, 1979. A serious fault of Brandt's report is a lack of any specific suggestion of just how the poor countries can repay their huge debts for former development assistance and the future one, and whether it will really become increased and more effective. By and large this is rather questionable, both because of the oil-producers' stinginess, the economic crisis in the West and the Soviet Union's indifference as well. This is one reason more why the recent stage of the North-South Dialogue during the 11th Special Session of the UN General Assembly on global economic negotiations, expected to last in New York from August 25 till September 15, ended 10 days later in bitterness and confusion. Although it succeeded in drafting, by consensus, the International Development Strategy, this actually was only a non-binding rhetoric. While the South wants the decisions made in a central body to be based on a one nation-one vote system, the North prefers to work for this matter, too, through the existing international agencies, like the International Monetary Fund, controlled by it. Needless to stress, the two concepts shall never meet and breathe a new life into the six-year old blueprint for a new International Economic Order. In the meantime the oil-producing countries are sitting on a $115 billion surplus (by mid-1980), as a result of their swinging price increases in the years which have played havoc with the economies of the richer nations and considerably set back the poor countries. Third World states face very lean times, indeed, their oil bill alone amounts to $40-50 billion. Neither the regular 1980 GA UN Session, nor other bodies succeeded in narrowing the gap between the North and the South, the gap which the Special Session and various later conferences have failed to close and which to a large extent is created by OPEC and Soviet policies with regard to the Third World. One of the consequences of this situation is the end of even the remnants of democratic rule in the Third World, its leaders' reliance on paramilitary and military instruments of power and the spread of the worst forms of authoritarianism. Cf. also G. Chichilnisky, R. Falk and J. Serra, "Authoritarianism and Development: A Global Perspective," *IFDA Dossier*, No. 19, Sept.-Oct., 1980.

59. M. Timmler, "Verlieren die Industriestaaten die Initiative? Beilage zur W.Z., *Das Parlament*, B 44/79, 3.XI.79, p. 20.

60. Theirry H., *Le Tiers Monde dans les relations internationales* (Institut d'Etudes Politiques de l'Universite de Paris, 1976-7) pp. 18-9.

61. Buchanan K., in *Developing the Underdeveloped Countries*, ed. A.B. Montjoy (London: Macmillan, 1976) p. 30.

62. *Ibid.*, pp. 46-7 and see the reference there to P. Worseley, *The Third World* (London: 1964) pp. 14-5.

63. Merle M., Sociologie. . . *op. cit*, pp. 456-8 and cf. Barnet *op. cit., p.214.*

64. *Bartelt M., "Forschungspolitik und Gesellschaftliche Entwicklung,"* *Aus Politik und Zeitgeschichte, Das Parlament* (B.27 1976) p. 34 and cfr. Merle, *op. cit.*, p. 216.

65. Labarde Ph., "Vers un phase offensive", *Le Monde* (1.III.1977) p. 17.

66.Adelman, pp. 133 and 147 and cfr. with J.K. Galbraith, published in *Die Zeit*, nr. 10 and 11 of March 1981.

67. Heilbronner, pp. 165-7.

68. Thierry, *op. cit.*, pp. 30-32.

69. Rostow W.W., *The Stages of Economic Growth: A non-Communist Manifesto* (Cambridge Univ. Press 1960) pp. 29-30.

70. Barnet, p. 75.

71. Staley E., *The Future of Underdevelopment Countries; Political Implications of Economic Development* (Praeger, New York, 1961).

72. Scott, *op. cit.*, pp. 17-21.

73. Montjoy, *op.cit.*, p. 33.

74. Scott, *op. cit.*, p. 19; Montjoy, *op. cit.*, pp. 13, 30, 45, 46-47.

75. Chubin Sh., Implication of the Military Buildup in Non-industrial States: the case of Iran (a manuscript), *The Pugwash Conference in Military Technologies and the Third World, Feldafing 1976*, p. 37.

76. Comp. the remarks on his considerations in the *International Peace Research Newsletter* (Vol. XIV, no. 3 1976) p. 10.

77. Bukharin N.I., *Imperialism and World Economy* (New York; International Publishers, 1929).

78. See f.i. the writings of Henry Grossman and particularly of Fritz Sternberg, *The Coming Crisis* (New York; The J. Day Co., 1946) and cf. with L. Basso's considerations in "Spheres of Influence in the Age of Imperialism." *The Russel Centenary Symposium* (Nottingham: Spokesman Books, 1972) pp. 111, 116, 123, 125 and ff.

79. Brown Barrat M., The Russel Symposium, *ibid.*, p. 66.

80. Mandel E., *ibid.*, p. 90.

81. For the details of the German program in its first version see Bahr E., "The Gyminich Theses: Development Policy of the FRG," *Aussenpolitik* (no. 3, 1975) p. 319. For its recent version see "Siebzehn Thesen sur Politik der Zusammenarbeit," "E+Z" 7.8.78, p. 4.

82. See the considerations presented in the editorial and in the article of J. Ripert and A. Bressand, *Politique Etrangère*, vol. 40, No. 2/1980, especially pp. 785, 293 and 305. Let us also add that the Brandt Commission has recommended a meeting of 25 world leaders to deal with the fundamental problems of the world economic order. Its important assumption is that development policy is not only a contribution to the evolution of just, democratic and viable societies and therefore to peace; and that it is not only a question of morality but of reason, too, and it has to do

with the national economies of the First and Second Worlds as well.

83. Published in "Jahresgutachten 1979/1980 des Sachverständigungsrates zur Begutachtung der Gesamtwirtschaftlicher Entwicklung," *Deutscher Bundestag*, 8 Wahlperiod, Drucksache 8/3420, 22.11.79.

84. Emmanuel, *op. cit.*, p. 841.

85. Basso, The Russel Symposium *op. cit.*, pp. 134-5.

86. Hoffman, S., "Notes on the Elusiveness of Modern Power," *International Journal* (Vol. XXX, no. 2, 1975) pp. 184-5 and Nye J.S. "Independence and Interdependence." *Foreign Policy* (no. 22, Spring 1976) p. 143.

87. Strange S., *Int. Journal, ibid.*, p. 210.

88. Hoffman, *op. cit.*, passim.

89. See the excerpts from Lenin in Winks, p. 28.

90. Heilbronner, p. 172.

91. Clark G. *A Place in the Sun* (New York: 1936) and Cairncross A.K., *Home and Foreign Investment 1870-1913* (Cambridge 1953).

92. Heilbronner, p. 172.

93. Jouve, pp. 239-41.

94. Morgenthau, *op. cit.*, pp. 55-60.

95. Fieldhouse, D.K., in Winks, pp. 35-50, the editor's introduction pp. 4-7 and see also Barnet, pp. 214-5.

96. Pinto R., *Le droit des relations internationales* (Paris: Payot 1972) pp. 57-8.

97. Tucker R.W., pp. 14 and 101; Lichtheim G., *Imperialism* (New York: Praeger 1971) p. 117; Moore B., *Reflections on the Cause of Human Misery* (Boston: Beacon Press 1972) pp. 53-4; Dahrendorf R., "International Power: A European Perspective" *Foreign Affairs* (October 1977) p. 78; Barnet *op. cit.*, pp. 17, 209 and 214-5.

98. Fieldhouse and Winks in Winks.

99. Barnet, p. 224.

100. *Le Monde* (26-27.VI.1977).

101. Arendt H., *On Violence* (New York: Harcourt, Brace and World, 1972).

102. Kumar M., pp. 42, 44, 46 and 158.

103. Tucker, p. 92.

104. Kumar, p. 100.

105. Barnet, p. 334.

106. Tucker, p. 83 and 94 and his reference to K. Knorr, *Power and Wealth; The Political Economy of International Power* (New York: Basic Books, 1973) p. 197.

107. Horowitz, D., *Hemispheres North and South* (Baltimore: John Hopkins Press, 1966) p. 94.

108. Tucker, pp. 25, 79 and 135 and Dahrendorf *op. cit.*, p. 76.

109. Winks, p. 2.

110. Blaug M., in Winks, pp. 31-4.

111. Emmanuel, *op. cit.*, p. 834.

112. See Pannikar K.M., in Winks, pp. 105-14.

113. Greene M., in Winks, pp. 92-7.

114. Strachey J., *The End of Europe* (London: v. Gollancz. 1959).

115. Marx K., and Engles F. On Colonialism *op. cit.*, pp. 103 and 358.

116. *Ibid.*, pp. 299 and 309.

117. Myrdal G., *Rich Lands and Poor: The Road to World Prosperity* (Harper and Brother, 1967), passim.

118. Senghaas D., "Multinational Corporations and the Third World," *JPR* (1975) p. 257.

119. *Ibid.*, p. 259; Elsenhans H., Overcoming Underdevelopment *JPR, op. cit.*, p. 294; Bosse H., Socio-cultural factors of underdevelopment *loc. cit.*, p. 315.

120. Marx K., and Engels, *op. cit.*, pp.40-41, 82 and 87 and see U. Melotti, Marx and the Third World, Macmillan, London, 1979. The Marxist assumptions on this role of capitalism are most frequently disregarded by some of his contemporary interpreters. See, f.i., a very interesting critical analysis of the classical and Marxian theories of accumulation, distribution and trade in J. Robinson's *Aspects of Underdevelopment*, Camb. Un. Press, 1979, which also stresses the inadequacy of theoretical analysis when applied to the Third World. It is also worthwhile to note in this context that Marx's idea of the Asiatic mode of production embodies both state ownership and communal (village) property. Hence, it is not surprising that the East German dissident, Prof. R. Bahro, used this concept in order to explain contemporary East European and Soviet societies, stressing their primitiveness and economic failure, frequently remedied thanks to Western help and its rôle. However, Bahro paid for this contention with prison. For quite an interesting approach to this problem, see.i.a. M. Sawer, *Marxism and the Question of Asiatic Mode of Production*, The Hague, M. Nijhoff, 1977.

121. Vayrynen R., and Herrero L., "Sub-Imperialism," *Instant Research in Peace and Violence* (no. 3/1975) pp. 164, 166, 171 and 175.

122. Takayangi S., "Violence in the Third World and its Implications on Contemporary Politics," *Peace Research in Japan*, the Japan Peace Research Group (Tokyo, 1973).

123. Carrere R., "Les Conflits Economiques," *Etudes Polemologiques* (no. 19, 1976) p. 42.

124. Brown S., "The New Legitimacy," *International Journal* (vol. XXX, no. 1, 1975-6) p. 19.

125. Morrison D. J., and Stevenson M. M. "Social Complexibility, Economic Development and Military Coup d'Etat, Convergence and Divergence of Empirical Tests of Theory in Latin America, Asia and Africa," *JPR* (no. 4, 1974) p. 345 and ff.

126. Hoselitz B., "Patterns of Economic Growth," *The Canadian Journal of Economics and Political Science* (no. 4, 1955) p. 416.

127. Marx K. and Engels F., *op. cit.*, p. 87.

128. Curley J., and Mellman S. in *Conversion from War to Peace*, edit., by W. Meyers, Gordon and Bread (New York, 1972) pp. 7 and 14.

129. See the polemics on this problem in M. Mushkat, "Peripheric Capitalism," and D. Senghaas "Periphery Capitalism without Quotation Mark," *Intereconomics* (Welt Archiv Hamburg, no. 5/1975) p. 143 and (no. 4/1975) p. 288.

130. Richardson L.F., *Statistics of Deadly Quarrels*, eds. Q. Wright, C.C. Lienau (Pittsburg: Boxwood 1960) and Q. Wright A *Study of War* (Univer. of Chicago Press, 1965).

131. Winks, p. 2.

132. Shiratory in "Peace Research in Japan" *op. cit.*, p. 71.

133. Clark R.P. Jr., *Development and Instability-Political Change in the Non-Western World* (The Dreyden Press, 1974) p. V.

134. Bouthol G., and Carrère R., *Le Défi de la Guerre 1740-1974* (Paris: Presses Universitaire de France, 1976) pp. 137-8; M. Mushkat "El Territorio y el Conflicto del Medio Oriente," *Revista de Politica Internacional* (no. 140, Julio-Augusto 1975) p. 51.

135. Eisenstadt S.N., *Modernization and Change* (Prentice Hall, 1966) p. 24.

136. Black C.E., *The Dynamics of Modernization* (Harper and Row, 1966) p. 26.

137. Huntington S., *Political Order in Changing Societies* (Yale Univer. Press, 1968) p. 43.

138. Clark, *op. cit.*, pp. 103-15 and 124-6.

139. Kende I., *Local Wars in Asia, Africa and Latin America 1945-69* (Budapest: Hungarian Academy of Science, 1972) p. 23.

140. Clark, *op. cit.*, p. 41 and ff.

141. Winks, p. 16.

142. Czempiel E.O. "Frieden und Konflikt in der Gesellschaftslehre" *DAS Parlament* (B.20/74, 18/V/1974) pp. 16 and 22.

143. See the definition of self-reliance given by Li Chiang who stressed that it does not mean "Self-seclusion" *BPP* (No. 1, 1975)p. 24 and see also assessments of the following publication *Die Aussenpolitik China's*, eds. E. von Groeding and M. L. Naeth (München: Verlag Oldenburg 1975).

144. See the reference to Myrdals Criticism of the slogans in the "New International Economic Order," in H. Hvem "The Politics of NIEO," *BPP* (no. 1, 1975) p. 34.

145. McNamara R. S., "Absolute Poverty," *BPP* (no. 1, 1975) p. 34.

146. Power J., "Third World Poverty: 2 Solutions," *Int. Herald Tribune* (4.III.1976).

147. "The Dag Hamarskold Report on Development and International Cooperation," *BPP* (no. 1, 1955) pp. 35-6.

148. Boulding K., *Conflict and Defense, A General Theory* (New York: 1962) p. 5.

149. Von Georg von Koppenfels "Die Bedeutung des Abkommens von Lomé," *EA* (no. 1, 1976) p. 10 and see the opposite view in Jutsamo K., The Lomé Convention—The Sun Never Sets, *Instant Research in Peace and Violence* (no. 3, 1975) p. 138 and see also "Les Socialistes et le Tiers Monde" *op. cit.*, p. 101. For the text of the Lomé II Convention of 31.X.73 see, i.a., K. Meyer, "Die Zweite Konvention von Lomé," *EA*, No. 1, 10.I.1980 and ff. (In addition to the EEC countries, the new Convention now comprises 58 TW states).

150. Brzezinski Z. "The Changing World System," *Int. Herald Tribune* (10.X.1975).

151. See f.i.the relevant conclusion in E. Kripendorf (Hg) *Friendensforschung* (Koln: 1972) p.22.

152. See the elaboration of this proposition i.a. in G. Ziebura (Hg) *Grundfragen der deutschen Aussenpolitik seit 1871* (Darmstadt: Wiss. Buchgesellschaft, 1975).

153. Mushkat M., "Figures du Socialisme Africain, *Mondes en Développement*, (no. 9, 1974) p. 59.

154. Weiller J., "Integration et Cooperation au stade de la Coexistence des Systèmes," *Economies et Sociétés* (vol. VIII, no. 8-9,1974) p. 1114.

155. For more details of this qualification already at the end of the fifties see i.a. P. Moussa, *Les Nations Prolétaires* (Paris: PUF, 1959).

156. Guittard O., "Bandoeng ou le reveil des peuples colonisés," *Collection: Que sais-je?* (Paris: PUF, 1961) p. 125.

157. See the observations on this question in "Global Political Assessment," *op. cit.*, pp. 1-2.

158. Fontaine A., "La Chine de Hua Kuo-feng," *Le Monde* (7.VII. 1977).

159. Weiller J. and Coussy J., *Economie Internationale, Automatismes et structures*, vol. 1 (The Hague: Mouton, 1975) p.1

Chapter 3
Underdevelopment, International Security and Peace Research

1. The Origins of Underdevelopment

The opinion that the Third World's inferiority is caused by racial factors may still be found even in some serious scientific studies.[1] Most experts, however, regard it as completely unfounded. We shall not, therefore, deal with this sort of argumentation, the more so since its adherents not infrequently identify themselves with the worst forms of colonialism and domination. They do not even hesitate to rely on sources which inspired Nazi "philosophy." Neither shall we analyze the views that regard maldevelopment as a product of inevitable historical and geographical circumstances. Those who hold these views stress the role of destiny or of the climate, the lack of natural riches and of the ensuing fatalistic approach, passive behavior and attachment to the obsolete forms of life. They view them as inevitably preventing or choking the initiative which is necessary for economic progress and social betterment. They ignore the fact that neither were many present day flourishing Western-European countries, nor Japan rich in resources, and that the hard climate of Canada and the northern parts of Scandinavia and the historical hardships of Hong Kong, Singapore, Australia and New Zealand, did not prevent their socio-economic advancement. Siberia and the Chinese deserts, and China's cold and hot regions, in their own way, too, are going through a finally beneficial process of transformation.

Today, students of the problem are more than ever inclined to believe that man is able to overcome even the most negative natural impediments and historical misfortunes. The belief in progress, science and technology, so strong in the political doctrine of the Enlightenment, held by Marx and by present-day eminent representatives of different disciplines and orientations, is not to be entirely dismissed. The perfection of arms, ecological waste, and scarcity of various raw materials do not justify the "doomsday" prophecies, in any case, no more than does the current deplorable situation of the Third

World. Some students even maintain that the most important task in its development is, therefore, not to disturb indigenous process and forms of evolution gradually leading to basic changes in the internal structures.[2] Others completely reject the view that mankind needs Hobbesian, Rousseauian, Stalinist or other totalitarian solution for its survival. They think that in the Third World, too, respect for democratic institutions, for individual freedom and liberties of all national, tribal and other groups is a condition for a beneficial social change.[3]

True enough, we must not dismiss entirely or even underestimate the sometimes great impact of physical, geographical and other objective factors. Focusing on them, however, means detaching the issue from its fundamental context and admitting that some societies move in a vicious circle.

This kind of approach seems to contribute very little to the understanding of the problem. Yet it helps those who frequently exploit the situation in Third World countries and aggravate their misery to run away from responsibility for their deeds.[4]

Below we shall limit ourselves to considering the two main concepts, the so-called liberal and radical trends in theories of development. We shall try to arrive at our own conclusions by a reexamination of their empirical findings and politico-philosophical foundations.

W. Röpke, L. Robbins, H. Ellis, J. Viner, M. Allais, E. Gudin and many other scholars in the USA and the Western European countries and in South-America, Asia and Africa, as well, are reckoned as representatives of the first school.[5] P.T. Bauer was among the most successful in presenting its fundamentals in a clear and quite persuasive way.[6] According to the followers of this school, underdevelopment is a temporary phenomenon, a historical phase on the nation's way to higher historical stages. That is why less developed countries must not be regarded as afflicted by backwardness or retrogression. They, like all other countries, are simply undergoing a natural development process. In the past their present situation was characteristic for all of the even most highly industrialized countries of today. They can even speed up their progress, benefiting from the experience and fundamental institutional changes realized by those already more developed.[7] The most effective means of combatting maldevelopment is therefore to acceterate the process of evolution, taking into account the lessons from the history of the socio-economically advanced countries.

This conviction was the starting point of the Pearson Report, of the Jackson Study and of all UN postulates. Recommendations worked out by other international, governmental and non-governmental organizations, by many public and scientific bodies and individual experts have usually adopted the same platform in their blueprints for the cure of the world economy, for closing the gap between the rich and poor nations and for the elaboration of development aid models. These recommendations, however, failed to propose other alternatives.[8]

True enough, militants of the New International Economic Order (NIEO) echo to some extent the above-mentioned opinion. Their adversaries, who maintain that the NIEO will probably aggravate, rather than improve the situation and actually tend to accept the same supposition. They are convinced that some nations, poor in the past and especially, oil-producers, will join the rich in the reconstruction program, while the poor will become even poorer.[9] The weakness of the liberal concept lies mainly in the fact that it passes over Europe's politics in the Third World during the last two hundred years. No doubt, Western Europe to a large extent could succeed in accelerating its industrialization with the help of Third World cheap raw materials, a fact which also made possible the establishment of the international division of labor and the formation of world consumption patterns according to European and, later, Euro-American interests. The Third World has become a supplier of raw materials and of cheap manpower to the present industrialized nations. The Third World has been forced to become the consumer of expensive goods and to receive investments from these nations.[10]

Nobody can question that, beginning with the early phase of capitalist development in the 16th century and with the successive formation of world trade, Asia's, Africa's and America's contribution to the speeding up of Europe's industrialization grew from year to year.[11] Only recently has it been diminished or even come to an end. And it is not necessary to agree with Marx[12] and his present-day followers rendering conspicuous the exploitation of the countries of the present Third World[13] in order to acknowledge the proper findings, which have also been established by many anti-Marxist writers.

By contrast with other continents, the causes of Europe's leap since the end of the Middle Ages have been many.[14] Political, constitutional and other changes in government and administration, developments in industry and commerce, demographic growth, the germ of a scientific, technological and cultural revolution are among the internal and most important factors of its impressive and rapid metamorphosis. Paul Baran is not the only present-day Marxist who notes the positive role of capitalism in human history, capitalism being a European creation. Yet this does not mean that external factors of the process may be minimized or ignored.[15]

F. Perroux was most probably one of the first in modern literature of the subject who emphasized so strongly that it would be deceitful to examine the economic problems of any state or even of any individual without considering the impact of the external world, of the international configuration.[16] Today most students of the problem have therefore concluded that backwardness is not determined by indigenous causes only, but is caused by external forces as well. Some also maintain that for the developed countries of today it was not always necessary to pass through a stage of underdevelopment in their evolution, that underdevelopment is not a self-evident and inevitable stage in the historical process of all societies.[17] Hence, there is the assumption that for a better understanding of underdevelopment it is not enough to study societies and the economies of particular states. It may be much more useful to pay attention not to micro-units, but to the problem in its totality. The solution requires global attention and world-wide action,[18] although the specific local issues may also be very important and to ignore them would lead to mistakes.

Research, which was used as a starting point of the liberal school, was sometimes inclined to believe that it would be sufficient to change the politics of world commerce[19] or even only of investment[20] to solve all social problems. Its adherents have hoped that in the long run this may create beneficial changes in the international division of labor. This assumption was critically reexamined by J. Tinbergen[21] and by a group of scholars sharing his approach to the matter.[22] Others, like G. Myrdal, pinpointed the primary necessity to better first of all the conditions of life in the Third World. According to Myrdal this is the only way of preventing a further enrichment of the rich and a greater impoverishment of the poor. Contrary to his critics from the radical school, Myrdal also postulates basic changes in the government of all less developed countries as a condition of their progress.[23]

Like Myrdal, the majority of modern liberals well understand the necessity of planning and governmental intervention which are needed in order to advance and modernize the economy and to take care of the wretched strata of society. None of them is rigidly devoted to pure free-marked concepts and generally they do not represent a group of scholars or practicians of uniform unambiguous class-oriented views as has sometimes happened with liberals in the past. This is another reason why prominent Third World leaders have frequently accepted their theoretical conclusions and many of the reforms proposed by First World politicians, especially by those politicians who are regarded in the West as partisans and builders of the welfare state. This is particularly clear if we consider that few of these politicians have rejected totally the program of the New International Economic Order. The majority advise the realization of its essential principles, speak about the inevitability even of nationalization which, true enough, has been practiced for years in the West and admit that a pure free-market system in its classical meaning is obsolete.[24]

It is true that there also were exceptional positions, like that held by P.T. Bauer and B.S. Yamey[25] and by a few other traditionally liberal economists. By and large, they have made the liberal school unpopular, and not only in the Third World. They actually help those who deny that it is possible to cure the world system by evolutionary reforms, constructive developmental aid and cooperation policies and call for overthrowing the existing world economic order, if necessary, by force. Bauer and Yamey deny any link between the alleged responsibility of the West for the poverty of the less developed world and the duty of the West to correct inequalities and redress injustice. They stress the existences of wider differences in incomes and rates of progress within the Third World countries than within the West. They say that attention should be paid to the fact that the rapid progress of large parts of the less developed world and the virtual stagnation of other parts is simply one aspect of the diversity of the Third World. In their opinion, the idea of a wide and widening gap between the developed nations and the Third World is similar to the notion that the poverty of the Third World has been caused by actions of the West, both past and present, the notion being full of loopholes. They recall that Western governments and Western enterprise brought rubber to Malaya and tea to India, which were not indigenous to these countries; that in the period of the free coffee market, in 1857-1906, Brazil's balance of trade improved at an average compound rate of about 4 percent a year; and that, on the other hand, the extreme backwardness of the aborigines, pygmies, nomads, or African tribesmen can hardly be blamed on exploitation in international transactions, since these groups have few or no contacts with the rest of the world. Bauer and Yamey point out that the UN list of least developed countries consists predominantly of countries which —like Burundi, Chad, Ethiopia, Lesoto, Rwanda, or the Maldives—do not spring to mind as countries even moderately involved in international trade, investment and the activities of multinational corporations; and that conversely, the economically most advanced Third World countries and groups are those with whom the West has developed the most extensive and varied economic contacts such as Malaysia, Singapore, Brazil, Venezuela, or Mexico.

Taken separately, all these facts are true, as it is true that the world is not divided into two sharply distinct homogeneous collectives with a widening gap between the two categories, a gap which supposedly reflects only the exploitation of one category by the other. No less true is the fact that in almost all cases, in the Third World as in the West, the principal determinants of economic achievement and performance have been human aptitudes, motivation, aspiration, mores, modes of thought, social institutions, and political arrangements.

However, all these notions must not be generalized and utilized in order to deny the frequently disastrous outcome of foreign rule and exploitation, in the past and in new forms, in present times. The latter are frequently a consequence of imposed institutions, political arrangements, social, cultural and racial discrimination, economic subjection, harmful terms of trade, and even of assistance,[26] while the recent jump of the oil prices has been an unprecedented blow to all, but especially, to the poorest nations.

True, it is not hard to present the prognosis of a world class struggle[27] as a fanciful idea. Not less fanciful, however, is the total denial of the negative role of all kinds of external penetration into large parts of the Third World. They frequently made impossible a positive evolution of indigenous forces. They turned many Third World countries into vessels of ignorance and misery, into suppliers of cheap services, products and raw materials. They became merely a place for making investments, building factories, business and sources of employment which mainly benefit the metropolises. It is an undeniable fact that the conquest of South America and both of Africa and great parts of Asia hastened the progress of European capitalism and the "development of underdevelopment" of the conquered territories. This notion, originally shaped by G.A. Frank, was in different forms adopted not only by his followers. It was also accepted by many liberals, because it described the growth of one part of mankind to a large extent at the expense of another part, a situation which has finally deepened social and national inequities in an unprecedented way.

As proven by Simon Kuznets and Suendra J. Patel, these inequities among and inside nations in our times are an absolutely new phenomenon. True enough, we are inclined to agree with the orthodox Marxist, F.H. Cardoso, that any identification of underdevelopment with dependence is certainly a simplification. But, on the other hand we tend to accept the assumption of R.M. Marini that—to paraphrase Marx—the proper method of studying the anatomy and prospects of underdeveloped peoples is the study of the anatomy of developed countries and of the history of their leap, as the study of the anatomy of monkeys helps in the understanding of the anatomy of man. We also accept S. Amin's affirmation that, if we look deeply, there is no essential difference between the Stalinist forms of oppression and present principles of Soviet rule which limit individual and collective liberties for the sake of industrialization and the English models of growth as embodied, inter alia, in the Enclosure Act and the Poor Laws.[28] However, these and other well-substantiated statements only set off Bauer's and Yamey's unjustified generalizations which are rooted in true findings but analyzed out of their context and frequently misinterpreted and discussed in disregard of other facts and conclusions. By and large, thus this kind of presentation has finally contributed to the corroboration of the wrong perception of underdevelopment, as merely a result of colonialism, oppression and aggression in complete disregard of impact of all indigenous factors.

Thus, A. Emmanuel,[29] S. Amin,[30] A.G. Frank,[31] Ch. Palloix[32] and many other representatives of the radical school regard any form of socio-economic backwardness mainly as a product of imperialist policies.

They base many of their theses on various old Marxist affirmations, to a large extent on R. Luxemburg's, R. Hilferding's, Lenin's, Stalin's or Varga's conclusions. Yet, not only do they not take into account Max Weber's or Schumpeter's interpretations of imperialism, but they also pass over the comments on its essence viewed against a background of nationalism (Langer); of power politics (Baumgart); of the specific new contradictions between highly industrialized and backward societies (Luethy) ; of political structures and constellations of interests (Winslow); of free trade mechanisms (Robinson, Gallagher) or of the consequences of social domination (Wehler); the impact of these factors being independent of the forms of government and of their definition as capitalist, imperialist or socialist.[33]

The findings on exploitation and domination of overseas territories by Europeans in the past and in changed forms in modern times are rarely denied by anybody. This, however, has not been enough to incline most of the Third World leaders to reject entirely the postulates of the liberal school and to refuse to adopt them in their programs, proposed in various international organizations and conferences, also for the sake of reforming and even of reconstructing the world economy. And this happened not only because many of these leaders have been anti-communist-oriented and nationalist, but above all because they are pragmatists. They try to draw benefits from the cooperation with the First World and are aware of the shortcomings of the Second World, which is able to supply arms, but is unqualified to act as a catalyst of modernization and to combat misery.

Most of the Third World leaders, however, share in various ways the Malayanese-Cargo theory. It says that nature *a priori* endowed all peoples equally with its riches. The highly developed nations of today violated this natural law and deprived the poor ones of their lot. The poor nations' demand for help is based on the right tied to the obligation of the rich nations to restore the natural law of equality.[34]

This concept contradicts not only the liberal view but also the Marxist perception of the human condition, to a large extent, as a product of man's activity. The West frequently conceives development aid as charity, as a moral issue and not as an obligation and even not as an enlightened self-interest. The Soviets maintain that only the bourgeois North is guilty of past exploitation and continuing discrimination, as if they themselves have never conducted or profited from colonialist policies. More and more, Third World rulers do not accept this differentiation and demand from the Soviets, too, disinterested assistance.[35] In spite of this divergency, for various reasons they act together with the Soviet Bloc or China. Important for them is the Soviet Bloc's or China's support given unreservedly to all programs of decolonization and elimination of racialism and they are also attracted by the Soviet industrial achievements. Mutual understanding is sometimes a result of analogical problems deriving from maldevelopment or inefficiency. Close ties are frequently determined by ideological outlooks, but first and foremost by the common belief that socio-economic progress cannot be achieved without dictatorial methods and physical coercion.[36] Needless to emphasize, a common front facilitates both partners' pressure on the West to get more profits from this source, while the Third World has no illusions as to the limitations and unwillingness of the Communists to assist it unselfishly and effectively in other than the military field and in other ways than in connection with the interbloc rivalry. Actually, the Third World tries to follow the Soviet search for commodities, technological knowhow and trade preferences in the Western World.

This trend, however, also plays a certain role in the impact and even popularity of the Western, in principle, liberal outlook in the Third World. This trend is reflected in different forms of blueprints for industrialization, beginning with their more precise presentation in 1975 at the Lima Conference[37] and ending with some recent interpretations of the NIEO. The latter defines its role more as an instrument for the elimination of the aberrations of the world economy and for its cure, and less for its reversal, a view which understandably deserves a strong criticism of the radicals, too.[38]

True enough, most of developmental programs are an outcome of pragmatic and nationalist approaches. These approaches, however, are also rooted in Western liberal traditions and very rarely Soviet-oriented. This is also the case of the proper resolutions adopted in pan-African, pan-Arabic, pan-Islamic and other regional, functional and supposedly ideological frameworks. This is no less characteristic of many recommendations of the so-called non-aligned, the "77," the "plebeian" and other Third World groupings. Actually, they were and remain loose compounds of entities with different levels of cultural and socio-economic development, with contradicting views and interests. Frequently they oppose each other to such a degree that the existence of the so-called North-South Conflict seems to be an invention,[39] whereas the South-South confrontations are a bitter reality. What unites them is primarily the hope not only to get more aid from the First World when acting collectively but also the optimistic conviction that if they repeat its experience they will overcome more easily at least the most painful stigmas of backwardness and become more viable and independent.

These expectations strengthen the morale of the LDC's, their acceptance of developmental aid and advice given by the West. This is the more evident since the West's previous or present undertakings have already borne fruit.[40] These undertakings do not deny at all the validity of Soviet experience and do not differ from Soviet commercial practice. This explains why even Soviet writers sometimes reject the assertions of the "radical school" that all forms of Third World stagnation are exclusively a result of terms of trade imposed by the West.[41] It is worthwhile to mention that the proper criticism has been voiced particularly strongly by Fidel Castro who did not hesitate to say that the Third World oil-producers are mainly responsible for the deterioration of the economies of the LDCs.[42] Many Third World researchers have long ago emphasized that the misery in their countries is caused less by colonial exploitation than by the internal socio-economic conditions and to a large extent is a consequence of little attention paid to agriculture and of the priorities given to industrialization, following Western or Soviet models. Hence, there is the call to give up these tendencies, to proceed with a political and economic decentralization which better corresponds with local mores and ways of life and culture. This decentralization might, therefore, favor the promotion of fruitful original initiatives and facilitate the efforts in the direction of self-reliance.[43]

This does not mean that all the claims of the "critical school" are groundless, that all of its conclusions are rejected by all First and Third World experts and that they have already accepted all premises and postulates of the "liberals" and empiricists.

As it has been recently so convincingly argued by J. Reuveny, it is paradoxical that the overly empirical orientation and the more or less unilinear theory of development and modernization of the Western social science community has opened the way to the "radical," old and neo-Marxist and neo-evolutionist approaches. According to him, this has also strengthened the tendencies to macro-theorizing associated with philosophical issues, reinforced by divergent cultural and scientific perspectives and filled the vacuum which resulted from the stress on facts and lack of generalizations.[44]

By and large, Reuveny does actually admit, in this way, the important contribution of the non-Marxist school to social science in general and to the theory of modernization in particular. But is he entirely right in setting off only its negative aspects with regard to the theoretical and practical aspects of the problem and viewing even the defeat of South Vietnam as a failure of Western developmental concepts? True enough, he does not confine himself to criticizing some confounding generalizations of Bauer and Yamey. He treats similarly the historically based assertions of W.W. Rostow, dealt with in another part of this study, those of Daniel Lerner,[45] and of other non-Marxist, anti-Marxist and neo-liberal authors.

By the way, Rostow's recent analysis has little to do with old-fashioned liberalism. It is, of course, not a communist, nor a non-communist, but rather a human manifesto, pleading for North-South co-operation based on principles of equality and justice and on the supposed obligation of the West, determined by common interests and possibilities, to ease the miserable condition of the Third World and to act for a proper satisfaction of its fundamental needs. True enough, Rostow has increasingly stressed recently the necessity of governmental involvement in family planning, agriculture, energy, raw materials, the environment, research and development and in the joint efforts to overcome stagnation. However, he emphasizes the right of any state to act independently and in its own way for the realization of partnership inevitable in our times.[46]

Reuveny ignores this neo-liberal, to some extent, social-democratic approach. In his opinion, all its representatives seem to overemphasize the unilinearity and economic determinism which is merely typological inductive and fails to resolve basic theoretical issues such as reconciling structure and dynamic or synchronic and diachronic perspectives. It is true, that Reuveny, following the complicated semantics of the radicals, mentions Karl Deutsch, one of the outspoken critics of dependency theories and his evidence as to the low emancipatory capability of most developing countries and of the irrelevance of the World Order as the key to social and economic development.[47] He does not, however, draw any conclusions, neither from this evidence—which has finally focused on indigenous factors— nor from other similar findings. The latter more or less deny the critical school's theses on peripheric capitalism and structural violence. These findings prove the critical school's inability to provide a central theoretical core to the subject of our discussion and to other relevant problems. Furthermore, Reuveny is also silent on the economic approach, which characterizes more almost all representatives of the critical school of peace and development theory than liberal classicists and, of course, the neo-liberals. It may be, therefore, worthwhile to emphasize again, but in a context different from the one previously presented, the erroneous consequences of building theories which are based on pure or predominant economism, especially in relation to conflict analysis. As we have mentioned above, these attempts were also rejected many times by Marx and Engels.

2. Confusion in Conflict Analysis Rooted in Economic Approach

Recently, more and more experts both in the West and the East tend to suggest that the economic approach has failed to provide adequate solutions to the ever aggravating problems of world markets. The even regional inadequate solutions that it proposed have been chiefly based on integrative or similar economic designs.[48]

Even the documents of the European Community dealing with the problems of its enlargement[49] and the relevant literature[50] underrate the difficulties of noneconomic character. At the same time, military experts of the community no longer hesitate to criticize the under-estimation of geographical, human and other factors little depending on the economic ones. This criticism is undertaken even more frequently not only with regard to political issues, but to strategic security issues as well, of the Mediterranean and other parts of the Atlantic region.[51]

The insufficiency of economism in the political field is blatant in the recent analysis of détente. Détente is today less and less conceived as a means to strengthen world peace and more as an instrument of serving temporary common interests of the superpowers and of reducing the danger of their collision,[52] an instrument far from being effective as it was demonstrated by the Soviet aggression against Afghanistan. However, this did not prevent a recrudescence of utopian approaches. The stress again is put on their importance and merit even as a method of inquiry, prevision and action both in the internal and international scenes. The opinion that it is preferable, especially as regards the human rights issue and the struggle for the reconstruction of the world economy with a greater consideration of the human factor, sharply contrasts with conclusions and interpretations based on *Realpolitik* or designs actually aiming at exploitation, different kinds of domination and power politics. These interpretations, both when presented as neo-Marxist or as hostile to any kind of revolutionary trends, are used inter alia, for the explanation of Soviet imperialism. They were largely applied in the aftermath of World War II. We also find them in the analysis of the "Cold War" and more recently in the analysis of the so-called West-East and North-South conflicts. Even some partisans of this kind of interpretation, particularly the one with regard to the post-colonial countries' peripheric situation in the world economy, are of the opinion that there are various possibilities to ease or seriously combat misery, economic and political dependency and exploitation, especially by noneconomic measures.[53]

However, economism has not ceased to be a dominant characteristic of modern research on the correlation between underdevelopment and international security and on economic and political imperialism. It disregards the failure of universal, regional and continental organizations to put an end to territorial and other noneconomic disputes and to eliminate their causes leading from time to time to bloodshed in order to achieve changes of borders, changes that do not bring any real profit.[54] Nobody will claim that profit was the moving force in the conflicts at the beginning of 1979 between China, Vietnam and Cambodia, all "socialist," ideologically "fraternal" countries, between Uganda and Tanzania, two non-aligned Third World nations. Profit was not the cause of tension between the praetorian governments of Chile and Argentina, which, thanks to the successful mediation of the Vatican, fortunately did not grow into a bloody conflict a few months earlier or of the continuing military encounter between the Islamic North and "Marxist" South Yemen.

The critical school in theory of development and conflict does not pay any serious attention to conflicts of the above-mentioned kind, which have nothing to do with economic interests and which—to use the language of the Nigerian leader General Obasanjo—"invite" foreign intervention,[55] and endanger peace in their region and in all the world.

The discourse on confusion in conflict and development theories based on economic approaches aims to emphasize the importance of other than economic factors in deepening backwardness and provoking collisions. These factors are chiefly of internal character and depend on social, administrative and other, obsolete, structures. They paralyse efforts towards peaceful co-operation, necessary in order to promote developmental schemes. They are frequently a result of tribal, racial, religious, ethnic or other irrational animosities and are mainly, if not always, responsible for the growth of tensions in the Third World, which tend to expand and may finally undermine international security.

For many years attention has been primarily paid to the menace to peace bred by the situation in South Africa and Rhodesia and, no doubt, without fundamental changes in these parts of the Black Continent, a bloody conflict seems to be inevitable there.[56] This region, however, particularly after the proclamation of Zimbabwe under a black government in March 1980 no longer is the only powder keg of Africa. The Black Continent has not yet succeeded in curing its festering wounds, such as Egypt, in result of its pan-Arabic, pan-Islamic and pan-African policies in the Nasserite era; Sudan, following the repression of the southern tribes; Nigeria after the Biafra uprising; and due to its Islamic background, Burundi, Tchad, Angola and other areas.

Today still continues the confrontation between Algeria and Polisario (the Liberation Movement of Western Sahara) fighting on one side and (once also Mauritania) Morocco on the other side; between Ethiopia and Somalia, (and not only because of the claims to a great Somalia and its role in Eritrea), whereas tensions and confrontations between Egypt and Libya, Tanzania and pre-Amin Uganda, Zaire and Angola still do not belong to the past, the more so since the Soviets act there by proxy with the help of Cubans and Eastern Germans and directly through military advice and arms supplies.

The rejectionist front against Sadat's peace initiative has actually become larger since the overthrow of the Shah's regime in Iran. It is a continual threat to the stability in the Near and Middle East, while the Vietnam's occupation of Cambodia, the war of China against Vietnam and the Soviet occupation of Afghanistan increased the menace to peace that has started to glimmer in Asia.

No clear economic reason can be given to explain these and other

South-South and Soviet-Third World conflicts. All efforts to explain the former by imperialist policies and the latter only by Soviet aggressive designs equally are doomed to fail. The "Zone of Storms," comprising the three *As*, Africa, (Latin) America and Asia,[57] is chiefly a region of socio-economic earthquakes of local origin. Even if they bear marks of outside involvement and take place because of foreign aid and in result of Soviet aggressiveness and inter-superpower rivalries, this does not hide the racial, tribal, religious, national and other irrational motivations.

3. Underdevelopment, Military Expenditure and Militarization of the Third World

The possible new world war will certainly not be the war between the South and the West, however there is no reason to disregard the dangers of the growing TW arsenals.

Their impact has been felt in all discussions relating also to arms control and arms reduction, including those of the 1978 and 1982 UNGA Special Disarmament Sessions. In different forms the impact had been felt even earlier also in the debates outside the UN including those of the Brandt commission.

The fact that military expenditures increased between 1959 and 1977 from 97 to 334 billion dollars,[58] that on the eve of the UNGA Disarmament Session they reached 400 billion dollars a year and that they are still increasing proves that even in times of détente the problem was far from solution. And although the Third World's share in the total arms expenditures has increased from about 4 percent in 1963 to about 15 percent in 1978, it will be naive to maintain that this spiral is determined by the North-South conflict, or that this "conflict" explains another fact, namely, that during the past 15 years the world's armed forces have increased by nearly 30 percent, to approximately 26 million persons.[59] This number is continuously growing and mutual suspicions and the consideration of the Soviet aggression against Afghanistan, breed difficulties for renewing the SALT and other arms control negotiations. It is therefore naive to claim that the North-South "conflict," even if some armaments reductions will be agreed upon by the East-West "conflict" partners, will create more means available for development purposes.

It is true that the Third World has lately become a serious market for arms supplies, particularly for Soviet arms, because Moscow regards arms supplies as an excellent means of political expansion. However, the role of the West, not only of the US, but of France, Britain, W. Germany and Italy should also not be belittled. After all the enriched oil-producers' arms imports for themselves and their protégés, including terrorist movements, come from these countries, eager to induce and fill orders for arms in exchange for oil deliveries.

Although there is no doubt that the possible new world war will not be the war between the South and the West[60] even if the Third World continues to enlarge its arsenals,[61] we should not disregard the ensuing dangers.[61] Most peace researchers have been unable to foresee and pinpoint these dangers, inter alia, because they have viewed the militarization and the Third World's arms race merely as a consequence of Western politics aimed at exploitation and maintaining the peripheric status of the Third World.[62] By and large, this conclusion contradicts certain findings of various UN organisations. In their relevant publications not only a necessity, but also a possibility of transition from war-orientations to peace-orientations and therefore, from arms race to arms control and disarmament, has been convincingly presented for years. However, this possibility is, to a large extent, dependent on the policies of the Third World.[63] A similar conclusion can also be drawn from already years-old studies of this subject,[64] which reject the illusion that deterrence and arms race can play any role in building regional or international security.[65]

It may be worthwhile to mention in this context some calculations worked out for the Middle East ten years ago and their conclusions which presumably have not remained without an impact on the peace initiatives beginning, to some extent, to materialize since Sadat's famous visit to Jerusalem in 1977.

The above project assumes that by the year 2000 the Arab-Israeli conflict has already been resolved, the Palestinian problem solved either within an existing Arab state or through a newly evolved Palestinian state.

The central assumption of the project is that by the year 2000 frontiers will lose in this region, like in Western Europe of today, their present-day importance, changing into functional frameworks of co-operation between all neighboring countries. Their peoples will live better and longer: In Israel the longest life expectancy will rise from 60 to 80 years and in Egypt from 35 to 65 (taking into account that by the year 2000 the population of Israel will reach 5 million people and of Egypt 50 million). The GNP will rise in Israel from \$3.5 billion in 1965 to \$15 billion, in Egypt from \$4 billion to \$16 and per capita from \$1,400 to \$3,000 and from \$200 to \$400,respectively. The percentage of young people completing secondary education will rise in Israel from 20 percent in 1950 to 99 percent, in Egypt from 7 percent to 99 percent. The relevant numbers for university graduates will rise from 50 per thousand of population in Israel to 100 and from 10 to 50 in Egypt. The computers in Israel will increase from 110 in 1969 to 5000, in Egypt from 15 to 3000. Similar developments will occur in all other ME countries and a common ME market will become a reality, establishing closer relations with Turkey, Cyprus, the Gulf states and Iran.

In the same period a new division of labor will be formed in the area. Egypt will become a center of engineering industries: steel, cars and motors, Israel of electronics, computers and medicine, Syria of food industries and textiles. Iraq and the Gulf will become the centers of petrochemical industries and reconstructed Lebanon of banking, trading, transport and communications services. The ME may also become the market garden of Europe, a center of tourism, all this on condition that the money currently spent on armaments is dedicated to development, research and scientific purposes.[66]

The majority of peace researchers, however, and especially those of the critical Scandinavian and West-German schools, continue to focus on the origins of conflict.[67] They have not paid any attention to the possibilities of a peace initiative neither in the Middle East nor in any other areas of confrontations. Predictions, like those mentioned above, are without any significance for them. They support on principle one party in the conflict, overlooking its methods and purposes of combat and disregarding the dynamics of the struggle for peace in our nuclear era.

They have generally misinterpreted the conclusions of experts which stress that military regimes in many Third World countries, succeeded in taking over the rule and in continuing their rule because of their efforts to put an end to corrupt regimes and to promote modernization. These researchers view the TW arms race and militarization merely as a product of Western imperialist conspiracy[68] and any military corps as performing a repressive function, all this in accordance with the obsolete conclusions of Marx shaped with regard to the role of the *ancien régime's* armed forces.[69]

There are many theories attempting to explain the causes of the arms race, particularly threatening in our times. Some of them are based on the Richardson scheme of action-reaction, others on the perception of real or fictitious dangers, on the wish to prevent any surprise attack by the hostile neighbors or rivals and to deter such an attack. They also focus on the impact of the military-industrial complex and of other bureaucracies and ruling elites.[70] In light of these and other theories, there seems to be no justification for reducing the problem of militarization and of its influence on maldevelopment to merely a question of foreign interests and outside pressures and for conceiving it solely in economic categories. A critic of capitalism has no need for this kind of approach and to ignore the role of the Soviet Bloc in this matter is far worse than reductionism and erring.[71]

True enough, military investments and training have frequently contributed to modernization and socio-economic progress in countries of every type of regime, in the capitalist countries, in the so-called socialist ones, the Third World countries and those with mixed economies like

Israel.[72] It is worthwhile to recall in this respect the gigantic leap of the US following its participation in WWI, WWII and in the Korean and Vietnamese wars, of France after de Gaulle's decision to make France militarily more independent, of Russia's technological aggrandizement following her military efforts and of other nations as well.[73]

This does not mean that we have to ignore the disastrous socio-economic aspects of different types of militarization, especially in TW countries.[74] We must not disregard the dangers of the arms race in general and in the underdeveloped parts of the world in particular. After all, although 80 percent of military expenditures is spent on conventional armaments and forces, the greatest single threat to mankind is that of nuclear war. While many TW countries, like Libya, Iraq and Pakistan, do all what is possible in order to follow India's example and also to become armed with nuclear weapons, the nuclear arsenals contained in 1963 approximately 4000 primitive warheads which was, however, enough to destroy our civilization. Today they contain tens of thousands of sophisticated nuclear weapons, with a total nuclear explosive power equivalent to that of about one million Hiroshima bombs. And the capability to produce nuclear weapons is spreading world-wide through peaceful nuclear programs, while militarization does not stop on dry land, but has already encompassed oceans and outer space, while the implementation of international disarmament agreements is entirely unsatisfactory[75]. This arms race only to a small extent is induced by the search for profits.[76] It has nothing or very little to do—at least directly—with the Third World miserable condition, with its peripheral role in the economy or with the thesis on structural violence. Nevertheless, the latter is strongly emphasized by the critical school of peace and development research as the main war-productive element of our times. This thesis actually, is a peculiar form of economism, already ridiculed a century ago by Marxists and non-Marxists alike.[77]

By and large, the appropriate terminology is far from being exact and indeed is ambiguous when aiming to describe different forms of exploitation.[78] Till our days some of its forms in all parts of the world remain predominantly determined by internal causes. And as regards the Third World local conflicts and inter-state wars, some TW countries strive to get nuclear weapons, nobody claims that all of them are a result of outside interference neither from the West nor from the Communist Bloc.[79] We have already mentioned the various causes of the arms race in general and in the Third World in particular. The theories about the "aggressive West," about its conspiracy to achieve and maintain a world capitalist economic system dominated by the US cannot stand any serious scrutiny, no more than the assumption that the Leninist theory of imperialism is still valid, as some peace researchers claim.

In the opinion of some serious TW experts, these theories, to a large extent, are detached from realities and correspond to cliche-presentations of biased researchers.[80] They cannot help us to understand the nature of the East-West antagonism, nor the East-West conflagrations, nor the so-called North-South Conflict or the South-South rivalries. Particularly deplorable, is the fact that these theories ignore that the latter have often led to the most atrocious forms of exploitation and bloodshed, sometimes of a genocidal kind.

The assumption that the Leninist theory of imperialism is still valid makes no sense in the nuclear era and not only because the world never was and certainly is not today, neatly divided into two classes of countries: one rich, aggressive, expansive and exploitative and another poor, peaceful-oriented, minding exclusively its own matters, reluctant to profit from others, but ready, because of the threat or dominance imposed on it, to attack its enemy.[81]

The above-mentioned assumption is also obsolete because of the features of the "new imperialism," and because of the military take-overs and the arms race in the Third World.[82]

Even the four ME wars and the continuing arms race in this region, as well as the rejectionists' stand, have their own "local" causes[83]; here too, as everywhere else, we are still far from the messianic era when violence and the need to oppose it are only a memory from the past.[84]

Unfortunately, there are no societies, be they called capitalist, socialist or otherwise, that are ideal in the sense that they do not need means of coercion to enforce respect for their laws and order. Even in the best organized society it is necessary to maintain police in order to combat various forms of crime and knavery.[85] If the call for struggle against structural violence was directed against regimes à la Hitler, Stalin or Idi Amin and Bokassa's that would make sense. But when it is directed against the West, accusing it of the sole responsibility for the backwardness and exploitation of the Third World, supposedly mainly caused by arms supplies (true enough, these supplies have been financed by Western treasuries and only recently also by oil-magnates), it means the approval of anarchy, adventurism, and finally, of terror directed mostly against innocent people. Needless to say, not only Marx and Engels, but to a large extent more or less openly Lenin, Mao and Castro condemned this kind of terrorism.[86] What is more interesting is the fact that at the end of his life, Kropotkin, regarded as a leading ideologist of anarchism and terrorist class methods, stopped to support this method of settling social matters.[87]

By attributing an exaggerated role to the West-European part in the present-day arms race,[88] leading representatives of the Critical School of peace research minimize only the imminent danger caused by the Soviet arms race, the ensuing superpower rivalry and by the moving forces of the arms race in the Third World. As regards the latter, we must stress that its share in the military expenditures has proportionally been growing even more than that of the rival Western and Eastern blocs. The Third World's arms expenditures have been rapidly increasing exclusively for irrational reasons and to the detriment of the national economies.

At present, world military expenditures surpass a billion and a quarter dollars per day, 100 times more than the international governmental organizations dealing with development aid spend yearly. Five to 6 percent of the world's total output of goods and services are diverted to military ends. More than sixty million people throughout the world, both military and civilians, are engaged in the public and private sectors in occupation related to military production.

According to the SIPRI 1976-1978 yearbooks, the authority source in this field, the world military expenditures have reached already in 1976 the sum of $334 billion, that is 5.4 billion more than in 1975 and about 30 times more than in 1900.

The relevant numbers relating to NATO and the WTO (The Warsaw Treaty Organization) show a certain reduction (to 78 percent in 1975 from 91 percent in 1955 and to 70 percent in 1976 from 85 percent in 1977). However, this is not the case with the Third World, where, (excluding China) the relevant figures are 15 percent in 1976 in comparison with 3.2 percent in 1955 and approx. 12 percent in 1975. This explains why the military expenditures of the Third World grew by 40 percent between 1973 and 1974 and by 70 percent between 1974 and 1975. More than half of the supplies went to the Middle East. In 1976 the military expenditures of this region reached 52 percent of the Third World total (excluding China).

In 1976 the number of countries which import heavy arms was 95, of which 75 were located in the Third World.

It is true that the greatest menace to peace lies in the perfection of nuclear arms which, for the time being, mainly are in the hands of the superpowers and of a few other countries. But the continual arms race in the Third World, particularly in the Middle East, even after the first turn towards a peaceful arrangement in this area, presents no less a threat to world security. It is a factor able to escalate the local conflict, the more so since the Middle East is the most armed region of the world.

Whereas American military expenditure in 1974 and in 1976 amounted, on the average, to 6 percent of the yearly GNP and the Soviet military expenditure amounted to 12 percent, that in Israel reached 35 percent, in Egypt—30, in Saudi Arabia—15, in Jordan—12 and it ceased only in Iran[89] following the fall of the monarchy in 1979.

The underlying motivation for this incontrollable arms race which has already lasted for more than three decades, is quite different from the seemingly logical theoretical thesis, that arms are produced and bought solely in order to protect national security and to deter the potential enemy.[90]

This is most evident not only in the nuclear arms race, promoted chiefly as a part of the so-called superpower deterrence strategy. But the superpowers can afford to play this dangerous game which is not so lethal for the Western economy (though it prevents more rapid development of Soviet Bloc civilian economy). Some Western countries have even succeeded, through their arms sales, in improving their balance of trade, hit by the hike of oil prices. But the underlying motivation for the Third World preoccupation with military games seems to be determined largely by internal causes and recently by its desire to establish a New International Military Order (NIMO) as an instrument in the struggle for a New International Economic Order (NIEO). However, this destructive activity obviously does not promote the NIEO, but instead only worsens from day to day the economic situation, not only of the countries most hit by the rise of oil prices, but even of the rich developing countries as well.

Ironically, the region where 3000 years ago the prophet Isaiah proclaimed high principles of brotherhood of men and of peace based on disarmament, today, because of the "rejectionists'" aggressive designs, is a powder keg which might explode the globe. The Middle East, in fact, is the most militarized region of the world.

The SIPRI Arms Trade Records show that approximately 4,100 jet aircraft for combat purposes, excluding trainer versions of combat types, were transferred to the Middle East in 1950-1975. Deliveries of heavy, medium and light tanks amounted to about 13,500. Operational jet aircraft for combat probably numbered about 2,300 in the Middle East at the end of 1975, while the number of tanks was approx. 10,500. By comparison, NATO forces in Europe in the same period numbered about 3,000 tactical aircraft and 12,250 main battle tanks.

As we have already mentioned above, the Middle East's growth of militarization has not stopped following the Israeli-Egyptian peace arrangement. It is important to stress that Middle East arms have been and continue to be, among the most up-to-date in the world, equal or even surpassing those of NATO and the WTO. The consequences of this constant flow of more and more sophisticated weapons into the region are grave and might prove fatal for the countries involved.

They include direct effect on the economies of these countries, the waste of natural resources, a social regression caused by these two factors, the growing indebtedness and dependence on foreign powers and the weakening of prospects of resolving the conflict comprehensively and of drawing other countries soon into the frame of the Israeli-Egyptian accord.

Hence, there exists an obvious need to stop the arms race in the Middle East, for the benefit of the peoples in this area, for their security and the security of the world. Needless to stress, any agreement in this respect, concerning a greater stability, a beginning of an arms control and disarmament arrangement and producing a real peace-building in the area, to a great extent depends on the agreement between the two superpowers. Both have political and economic stakes in the area, both seek to increase their influence there, but, because of their rivalry, they complicate if not hinder the reconciliation of the adversaries. This situation is likely to continue, unless the USSR will acquiesce in the loss of its leading role in Egypt and in the peace-making process following its break of relations with Israel and unless it stops its unilateral, almost unreserved support of the Arabs, even of the most fanatical of them, like the Kaddafi camp and the Iraqi communist hangmen. This situation will continue for as long as inter-superpower and, what is more important, local, arrangements are not made that would take into consideration not only the vital interests of the conflicting parties, but of the rival superpowers as well.

The first step in this direction will be the freezing of the arms build-up in the region. The import of sophisticated weapons to the Middle East must be stopped. This goal will be attained when a comprehensive settlement of the conflict in the area is achieved and a consensus of the arms suppliers is reached.

In view of the continuing turmoil in Lebanon, various encounters in other ME countries and the "rejectionists'" designs to act against Egypt and to prepare a new aggression against Israel, the necessity of working towards at least a minimal coordination of the superpower policies in the area becomes increasingly urgent. By and large, this seems to be true not only because of the imminent danger of provoking a new confrontation under present conditions of an uncontrolled arms race, but because of the disastrous economic and social situation in the Middle East, aggravated by the continuing militarization. After the first steps towards a peaceful Egyptian-Israeli cooperation, the militarization instead of diminishing has increased and not only because of the impact of the "rejectionist" front, but also because of the continuing mutual distrust of the "reconciled" parties.

Those who are alarmed by the negative economic consequences of the militarization point to the fact that military losses in the GNP following the Middle East wars in the years between 1949 and 1969 reached the sum of 55 billion dollars at 1960 prices. Actually, in 1969 alone, the sum was more than 8,9 billion dollars, which was more than the total income from oil revenues in the region that year. Other findings are not less instructive.

Egyptian losses in that year were ten times greater than its income from the Suez canal in 1966, and Israeli losses were three times greater than all capital inputs, governmental and private alike.[91]

The disastrous impact of the rise of military expenditures on the Middle East economies had already been evident in the period between 1953 and 1970, but became especially alarming after the 1973 war. The military expenditures in the five Arab confrontation states increased from $258 million in 1953 to $2,066 million in 1970, and in Israel from 64 million to $1,075 million. The respective changes in the proportion of the GNP were from 5.5 percent to 14.6 percent and from 6.1 percent to 19.5 percent. The military expenditures were rapidly gaining momentum. In the Arab countries they increased from $2,400 million in 1973 to $8,300 million in 1974 and to $16,500 million in 1975; in Israel they increased from $1,700 million in 1973 to $3,600 million in 1975.[92] While military imports in Egypt and Syria amounted to 9.9 percent of the total import in 1965, in 1974 they already amounted to 19.8 percent and the military import of machinery, transport and equipment amounted in 1965 to 42 percent of the general ME import; in 1974 it already reached nearly 100 percent of this import. The relevant numbers for Israel were 5.5 percent and 15 percent, 19.9 percent and 62 percent.[93]

The military expenditures of Egypt in 1976 were $4,080 billion (in constant prices), of Syria—$628 billion, of Jordan—$173 billion and of Israel—$3,076 billion.[94] Consequently, the economies of the ME countries, particularly of Egypt and Israel, have been severely strained and a continual deterioration in the balance of payments became habitual for them. In Egypt the deficit grew from $516 million in 1972 to $3,000 million in 1975, and in Israel from $1,100 million to $3,700 million.[95]

These debts limited the prospects of receiving further credits and promoting new investments and development designs.[96] This caused in its turn, increasing unemployment, soaring prices and growing inflation, as well as the failure of plans for improvements in agriculture and industry, in education and research. This more or less characterizes all the confrontation states, but particularly Egypt and Israel, where economic growth, which before 1973 was fluctuating between 8 and 12 percent, has recently become almost nil, whereas the rise of prices reached 20 percent in 1973 and 40 per cent in 1974 and is still growing.[97]

According to B. Hanson, the average annual rate of growth of the Egyptian economy was 4.5 percent between 1960-61 and 1973. Excluding the growth in services which occurred mainly in defence, the average annual growth of civilian Gross Domestic Product was only 3.8 percent (or only 3.5 percent if certain upward bias is taken into account). Most of this growth occurred during the first half of this period, which means in fact, that the growth rate since 1967 and up to 1973 approached zero.[98]

It is true that after the 1973 war the rate of growth increased, mainly due to extensive inflows of capital. However, the inflation at the rate of 25 percent was mostly caused, like in Israel (where it reached more than 100 percent in 1980 and similarly in Egypt) by the heavy burden of military expenditures, and it has prevented the reconstruction of the Israeli and Egyptian economies. The efforts to rebuild it in Egypt have also failed due to the decrease of Arab aid which dropped by 30 percent in 1976 from its 1975 level and is likely to diminish again after the peace arrangements beginning with 1979.

In all confrontation states, but also in Egypt and Israel, the wasteful process of continual arms race has been gaining momentum not only because the military hardware cannot be used for productive purposes and the ME countries have to pay for arms imports in products that could be otherwise used for satisfaction of the basic needs of the population. This process also changes the civilian technology, its large parts being put at the disposal of the military. This stops economic growth, causes maldevelopment and prevents social and cultural progress.

Nevertheless, some political factions in Israel and Egypt and the governments of Libya and Iraq still have not abandoned the tremendously expensive nuclear option, even after a peace arrangement had been signed by the former two countries.

Although there is no evidence whatsoever that the manufacture of nuclear devices has already taken place in Israel and Israeli governments have declared many times that Israel would not be the first to introduce nuclear weapons into the region, there is a growing consensus that Israel already has a number of atomic bombs at her disposal. It seems, that some Israeli politicians have used the nuclear argument as a refined weapon in a psychological warfare. This strategy is of some importance if we consider the "rejectionists'" feats against Israel and Egypt and especially the Libyan and Iranian efforts to obtain means enabling them to develop their own nuclear weapons.

The Israelis have been reluctant to sign the Non-Proliferation Treaty (NPT) because they realize that their refusal is an important instrument of psychological warfare. However, the Khadaffi camp seems to have another purpose. Some American politicians, on the other hand, took advantage of Israel's and the some-time Egyptian refusal to sign the NPT in order to oppose their efforts to get technical aid even for a peaceful use of nuclear energy. By and large, some Israeli, Egyptian and other Arab hawks dismiss the possibility that a nuclear option may lead to further political pressures and to economically disastrous results because of the financial burden which will be borne by other countries. There is no need to stress either, that while nuclear deterrence may have some validity in superpower relationship, it is devoid of any rationale in a limited area such as the Middle East, where no second strike possibility exists.

The statement of Dr. Sigward Eklund, Director of the International Atomic Energy Agency, made after his visit to Israel in April 1976, confirms that competent Israeli authorities are aware that their country will benefit more from joining the NPT than from a nuclear option. The promotion of peace in the region, however, might become possible only if Egypt and Israel's (and not only their) self-delusions about nuclear power are finally destroyed and the designs of the present Iraqi and Libyan governing elites, justifying proper defense measures, brought to an end.[99]

We know from the recent SIPRI's findings that during the 1970s the arms trade with the Third World has increased at an annual rate of 15 per cent and that between 1970 and 1977 four countries supplied 90 percent of the major weapons exported to this "world" (USA—38 percent, USSR—34 percent, UK and France—9 percent). The largest importing region was the ME, which received more than 50 percent of these exports in 1977, 70 percent in 1978 and even more in 1979-80s.

We cannot doubt any more that if the current rate of increase of military expenditure continues, it may be estimated that in the year 2000 the world will spend on arms about $1 million millions at today's dollar valuation. The current figure is about double the gross domestic product of the whole of Africa and about 10 times the total official development assistance given by the developed countries to the underdeveloped ones.[100]

The SIPRI evaluations stress that the Third World share in world military spending continues to increase. The major share is that of the Middle East whose expenditure, at constant prices, has quadrupled during the past seven years. The turn in the Egyptian-Israeli relations has not contained but even strengthened this tendency in the "rejectionists" camp. Hence, there is no room for doubt that a significant reduction in military expenditures could help the development of many ME and all TW countries. Moreover, the economic aid from the industrialized countries is unlikely to increase unless the military budgets of these countries are reduced.

However, the arms race in the Middle East as well as in the other parts of the Third World not only reflects the political decisions of the dominant factors in the present international system who are the principal producers and suppliers of weaponry. Nor is it determined only by the latter's desire to get petrodollars and improve the West's balance of payments, hit by the hike in oil prices. It would be wrong to claim that the arms race in the Third World is caused by world capitalism's tendency to maintain the peripheric status of the post-colonial countries.[101] The Third World arms race is certainly not so much a tool of foreign exploitation and enslavement, as a response to domestic quarrels and conflicts, although these are realized through means and methods that are not always of the Third World's own making.[102]

It might be worthwhile to point out here that the USA's alarm at the threat of strangulation supposedly facing this country and the West in general because of the OPEC's oil policy is entirely false. Milton Copoulos' findings published in his study prepared in the summer of 1980 for the Heritage Foundation refer not only to the 27.8 billion barrels of proven US reserves in themselves sufficient to put this country ahead of all other oil-rich nations. The study also indicates potential US reserves of between 276 and 444 billion barrels, enough to support current levels of consumption for the next 46-74 years without importing a single drop of oil. However, policies at the state, federal and private monopoly levels have sabotaged attempts to develop domestic reserves and actually helped to strengthen the OPEC dictates.

As a matter of fact, half a billion barrels of oil lie buried in Santa Cruz off the Coast of California. There are an estimated 76 billion barrels of recoverable oil in Alaska, perhaps as much as 113 billion. Today Alaskan production is only about 1.6 million barrels a day, about 13 percent of total US production.

Let us recall that nowadays the largest oil producers are the USSR (586 million ton), Saudi Arabia (510 million ton), the USA (479 million ton), Iraq (175 million ton), Iran (145 million ton, before the war between Iraq and Iran), Kuwait (130 million ton), Venezuela (125 million ton), Nigeria (114 million ton), China (108 million ton) and Libya (101 million ton). But in all of Alaska, with potential reserves greater than the proven reserves of Venezuela, Abu Dhabi, Mexico and the Soviet Union taken together, only seven oil rigs are currently operating, compared with 366 in Louisiana and 807 in Texas. The Georges Bank and Baltimore Canyon offshore fields (each of them is estimated to equal the North Sea discovery) are not exploited because of court charges and the restrictive leasing policies of the Department of Interior.

However, the government's and monopolies' policy has its stifling effect not only on the US production. Negotiations with Mexico, which possesses 40 billion barrels of proven reserves, enough to make her a rival of Saudi Arabia, have been torpedoed by the intransigence of US officials and the American oil lobby.

But even if we assume that one day the USA will run out of oil, its domestic supplies which are enough to serve here for 46 years, would give America and all the West the time to develop proper alternatives.[103]

This is another reason why many scholars are of the opinion that the intensified militarization of the underdeveloped countries can only to a small extent be explained by crisis situations in the capitalist world[104] and that it is wrong to assume that any transfer of military technology represents the transfer of social systems.[105] Such an assumption, as we have already pointed out, leads in the end to the minimization of Third World efforts to establish a New International Military Order as an instrument of its struggle for a New International Economic Order. This thesis also minimizes the significance of the internal roots of these efforts as well as their war-productive role on the world arena, which of course varies from country to country. The militarization of Libya, Iraq, Algeria, Pakistan, India and not so long ago of Iran, is—of course—different in size, causes and effects from other TW countries, but it is not entirely devoid of some common features, consequences and dangers.

There are also many ways to explain the dramatic turn in the Israeli-Egyptian relationship. One of the reasons and perhaps, not negligible one was no doubt, the socio-economic situation in these countries. Although economic causes are rarely at the root of international conflicts, they seem to play a very important role in producing efforts to end them and in making the negotiations ripe for this purpose. The recent turn in the Middle East proves this once more and even stronger than the events in the aftermath of the two world wars and on the eve of détente.

But to explain this kind of developments exclusively or chiefly by economic factors seems to be a gross simplification. In any case, this cannot help us to understand better the assumption that no efforts to build the NIMO as a means to achieve the NIEO can bear fruit, the more so since the discussions about the latter are full of ideological fervor and evangelism, instead of being based on rational argumentation. These discussions usually are a cry against foreign domination, but do not suggest any constructive program for curing the situation. Such an approach ignores the real moving forces of economic growth as well as the inevitability of the LDC's acceptance of a code of conduct that is mutually beneficial for them and the developed countries. It also fails to take notice of the very strong bargaining position of the industrialized countries. True enough, the underdeveloped countries demand from the developed ones to fulfil their moral (and perhaps, not only moral) obligation to help them to get rid of their misery. Moreover they, the LDCs, expect them to do so even should they show no inclination to co-operate with their benefactors.[106]

To assume that the West has a sole responsibility for the militarization of the Third World and that this is a part of its conspiracy towards reimperialization and recolonization of the Third World is a distortion of realities. It represents another dubious attempt to explain politics solely through economic argumentation. This results in confusion and is harmful to the attempts to explore objectively the dangerous process of militarization. One should take into account the fact that the above-mentioned SIPRI and other statistics emphasize the threat to human survival caused by the arms race. Some of them point out the prospects of curing the ills of Third World societies. But none of them point to the fact that the military expenditures of the Third World are not covered by the Third World countries themselves. They do not ruin their GNP and are actually financed by the superpowers and recently, to some extent, by some oil-producers too. By and large, it is possible to agree with Emile Benoit[107] and Gavin Kennedy[108] that militarization might be beneficial to certain economic undertakings. It results, for instance, in the construction of roads, harbors, airfields and in the diffusion of modern technological knowledge acquired by the army staff itself and by those working for its programs.

I am, however, inclined to accept the criticism of some of these conclusions because the quoted above SIPRI statistics, but not only them, prove that in the end most forms of militarization has a negative effect on the LDC's economies as well as on other aspects of life.

Usually, the transfer of military technology helps to reinforce the local tribal, patriarcho-feudal, authoritarian systems which are repressive and aggressive and stifle any opposition. Moreover, they direct the angry masses towards adventurism beyond the borders.

The armies and militarization are not a negligible cause of regional conflicts. Consequently, the regional conflicts produce the desire to enlarge the arsenals. This vicious circle is most cynically exploited by the Soviet bloc. The adherents of a NIEO take advantage of it in their pressure for the NIMO. They hope that the NIMO would finally lead to a NIEO.[109]

It would suffice to consider the 33 years-old Israeli-Arab conflict, the five years of the Algerian-Moroccan—and not long ago also—Mauritanian encounter, the three years of the Somali-Ethiopian war, the Angolan-Zaire and the recent North-South Yemen, Chinese-Vietnamese and Vietnamese-Cambodian collisions in order to conclude that the West and the Communist imperialism may aggravate these conflagrations, but they do not provoke them. They are largely produced by local, internal and regional factors. It is enough to see the list of arms buyers, which also includes the poor and even the poorest countries in the sub-Sahara region, in Asia and in South America, in order to conclude that the process is affected by events of indigenous character and by the desire to become militarily strong.[110] These poor countries want military strength in order to achieve some degree of equality with their neighbors, sometimes in order to get prestige or to oppress internal opposition. Frequently they want to get means, regarded as indispensable, to eliminate the remnants of colonialism and racialism. They want also to use the argument of military power to speed up the end of economic disparities not only between them and their rich "brothers," but also between them and the Western and Communist Blocs.

It may be instructive in this context to focus on some aspects of the situation in the Middle East. Although Arab states could make good use of the Palestinian manpower and intellectuals, they preferred to keep them in refugee camps in order to use them as a powder keg in their struggle against Israel. They did not try to get rid of the political, social and economic burden imposed on them by refugee camps and to assist the Palestinian Arabs in the creation of their own state in the territories that they had occupied or annexed. Instead, they aroused the Palestinian national aspirations, while persecuting the Palestininans in the Gaza Strip and the West Bank. Jordan even did not hesitate to suppress by bloodshed their revolt during the "Black September" of 1970.

And again, when Egypt decided to choose the path of peace and signed a treaty with Israel, nations that were far from the theatre of the confrontations, like Libya and Algeria, continued to remain in the camp of the most extremist rejectionists, stubbornly opposing the attempts to resolve the conflict peacefully.

This clearly demonstrates the irrational policy, completely lacking any economic motivations and aiming to use force to attain "ideological" goals.

We have already mentioned that many causes produce wars and that only rarely the economic factor is decisive. The examples are numerous. We can mention here the still lasting conflict between Somalia and Ethiopia, kindled by the Eritrean national liberation movement. Or the permanent friction between Egypt and Libya. Or Algerian support of Polisario in her fight against Morocco and till 1979 against Mauritania, until she decided to reconcile with the movement struggling for the independence of Western Sahara. All these conflicts, or that between Vietnam and Cambodia, have nothing or very little to do with economic motivations. These motivations have been also completely absent in the war between Yemen and Egypt, in the recent encounter between the two Yemenite states, in the disputes between Egypt and Syria, between Egypt and Iraq or other "rejectionist" states. Their role was minimal in the sum total of conditions that led to both World Wars, to the Korean or Vietnamese wars and to the Chinese-Vietnamese conflict, which China has formally justified by her desire to free Cambodia.

It may be worthwhile to point out here that the Egyptian peace initiative might not less be attributed to US pressure and Israel's willingness to pay a high price to Sadat for breaking the vicious war circle, than to Egyptian or Israeli immediate economic interests. On the contrary, Sadat had to consider the anti-Egyptian stand of Saudi Arabia that would inevitably follow under Palestinian pressure, the Israeli-Egyptian peace treaty and the ensuing loss of a very important source of the financial support. He expected this, but nevertheless came to the conclusion that Nasserism with its messianic, pan-

Arabic tendencies was at the root of his country's misery and that his people were tired of the constant sacrifices for the Palestinian cause. Israel, in spite of mystics-nationalists and power-politicians in her government, decided to give up oil fields, other natural riches and important military bases in Sinai and to commit herself to respect the legitimate rights of the Palestininans, all this in hope that this would finally ensure her acceptance by all nations of the region, strengthen, in the long run, her security and guarantee her survival in the area, whose nations till recently have all been hostile to her.

As we have already mentioned in other contexts, the thesis on the plurality of causes of conflicts, especially of international ones, is deeply rooted in past and present doctrines of Marxist, non-Marxist and anti-Marxist experts.

Almost daily it is proved by reality, namely, by various armed and non-armed conflicts in different parts of the world between countries of both identical and antagonistic political systems. This thesis also helps us to understand the weakness of the idea of collective economic security as a condition of political security. True, this notion ties, and rightly so, the designs for a better future for mankind to successful efforts to stop the arms race, to promote disarmament plans and in this way, too, to obtain more capital, manpower and talent to combat underdevelopment. However, it confuses causes with consequences and puts the carriage before the horse. Political security cannot be born of economic security: the contrary seems to be true. That is why the only way to reach international economic security is, in our opinion, by solving political controversies, by peacefully resolving conflicts. However, this is inevitable without the willingness to reach compromises acknowledging vital interests of all parties and promoting for this purpose negotiations and other means of preventing collisions and settling differences. That is why it is so important, if this aim is to be reached, to stop the arms race, to put an end to the policies of balance of power and of deterrence and to end the militarization of the Third World. A secure and just international economic order seems to be feasible only if it is built by progressive reduction of racial, national, tribal, class and other tensions and by curing other ills of humanity, especially in the less developed parts of the world.[111]

Later, we shall examine some aspects of the theories of collective economic security not yet discussed. However, let us stress already here, two things that seem important to us for a better understanding of both the relationship between underdevelopment and international security and of the so-called North-South Conflict.

It would suffice to follow the discussions in the United Nations Conference on Trade and Development and in other bodies dealing with the specific problems of the Third World in order to notice that the respresentatives of the Western nations have recently paid more and more attention, not only to problems of political détente, highly important in the nuclear era. They also considered the security aspects of demographic, ecological, purely developmental and the respective commercial, monetary and of course, raw material issues.[112]

In the estimated 1978 world earnings amounting to $8,800 billion the share of the West with its population of 693 million was 64 percent of the total, that of the Eastern bloc and China with their population of 1,304 million 19 percent and that of the developing countries with their population of 2,167 million was only 17 percent.[113] If one takes this into account we could easily (and mistakenly) conclude that the above-mentioned Western willingness to deal with the ever growing socio-economic problems can be simply explained by its desire to save vested interests and to guarantee further profits. A similar mistake can be made and not infrequently is made, by establishing figures of allegedly enormous profits from Western (but not from communist) arms trade. These profits are supposed to be a basic factor producing the underdevelopment of the TW[114] and are regarded as a condition of the industrial world's prosperity. Hence there is the additional argumentation in favor of the dependency theories. According to these theories, the economy of certain countries is conditioned by the development and expansion of another economy to which the former is subjected.[115] In this context dependency is analyzed as a reflection of the dominance of others, which is achieved also by promoting sales of weapons; and by the process of militarization, as if the military expenditures and their system foundations were detached from their local background and created predominantly, if not exclusively, by external forces.

Hence there is a thesis that the rich "underdevelop" the poor, as has been pointed out in A.G. Frank's well-known and frequently quoted saying.[116] According to this thesis there is a deepening gap between underdevelopment and growth of military expenditures in the less developed countries.[117] True enough, the military expenditures are mainly financed by the arms suppliers if not used by them to balance their deficits caused by the hike in oil prices.

As a matter of fact, the West pays increasing attention to various aspects of the underdevelopment issue, neither because of the dubious profits, nor because its possibilities of military intervention are rather limited today.[118] This growing attention is not even caused by the fear of the rich that they will be more than anybody else endangered by any global conflict, simply because they have more to risk and to lose. They also realize that empire is no longer a source of prestige or an enterprise bringing reasonable returns or any tangible benefits.[119] The growing tendency of the West to promote a peaceful settlement of conflicts and especially of the North-South Conflict, seems rather to be related to other arguments: that nowadays war does not help to acquire wealth; that developmental undertakings are an incentive to international profitable cooperation; and that peace-orientation is a by-product of modern states' being interested mainly in cultural values, scientific and technological achievements and communication. All this has produced abundance and the respective process of homogenization of men. This process gradually encompasses all parts of the world and sooner or later will remedy the bitter situation of the still underdeveloped countries.[120]

This conclusion does not necessarily reflect Rostow's doctrine which we have discussed above and which views development as a linear path along which all nations travel by passing its certain stages. In contradiction to this and similar approaches, peace is regarded by us as a factor promoting development and/or determined by it.

We have come to this conclusion, not only because of the peculiarities of the superpower relationship in the nuclear era and the inter-dependence of all nations. It was also shaped by the awareness of the imperative to speed up the above-mentioned process in order in this way, too, to eliminate the danger of provoking a suicidal East-West clash that might be caused by outbursts in the Third World. We cannot doubt any more that today the war-threat is "exported" from the South to the North and from the USSR to the South rather than from the Western industrialized to the underdeveloped countries.[121] But, of course, the deterrence strategy and the nuclear race of the superpowers engendered by Soviet aggressiveness is the basic permanent threat to the survival of our civilization.

Unfortunately, the communist world[122] is not sufficiently aware of this fact, or does not interpret it correctly, while OPEC who finances the arms supplies to some of its TW partners seems to be unaware of it at all. But the West is becoming increasingly aware, particularly after the Soviet conquest of Afghanistan, of the danger coming not only from the Soviets but from the South as well. This explains its efforts to combat backwardness, misery and the disrespect for the law and the rules of democracy in the Third World, strengthening its orientation towards alignment with the Soviet Bloc.

The development aid of the Western industrialized nations amounted to $14.8 billion in 1977, while OPEC offered $5.5 billion and the Communist Bloc only $0.6 billion.[123]

Yet the developing countries' requirements with regard to terms of trade and tariffs, to the elimination of all forms of protectionism, the creation of funds for price stabilization of all raw materials, more effective transfer of capital and technology, to other forms of constructive aid and preferences,[124] are continually growing. If we take as a yardstick the developing countries' expectations, the recent steps agreed upon by the West in various conferences, including the UNCTAD Manila Conference in May-June 1979, may indeed seem disappointing.[125] This is contrary to Tanzanian president J. Nyerere's concept that regards the struggle for a New International Economic Order as a long and complicated process that has all chances gradually to succeed mainly thanks to the Western contribution.[126] And the reason why the West gives it is not because it is a besieged fortress losing its power and close to destruction. We have already stressed in another context that there has never been ground for pessimistic generalizations and exaggerations with regard to the allegedly complete stalemate of the TW.[127] It is even less justified to see the West and with it all the world as approaching a grand apocalypse, even if we acknowledge signs of a temporary crisis at this juncture of the twentieth century.[128]

It seems that in order to overcome this crisis the West is willing not only to decrease its protectionist measures.[129] It is also inclined to give a new role to GATT in order to make of it both a milestone on the road to freer trade and a more effective instrument of aid first of all to the poorest, but also to other weak countries.[130] This includes the pro-Soviet oriented countries or even those belonging to the Communist Bloc as recently demonstrated by the efforts to save Communist Poland, shocked by the strikes of 1980-81. As it happened at the UNIDO Conference at the beginning of 1980 in New Delhi, the West only rejects the demands that are absolutely unacceptable to its basic politico-economic foundations[131] It does not seem to be guided by profits earned from less developed countries and military expenditures and by a desire to keep its privileged position. The West is aware that all nations are increasingly interdependent and that there is a growing interdependence of OECD and OPEC.[132] It realizes that there is no alternative to promoting economic decolonization, social progress, gradual elimination of the gap between the hungry and the well-to-do nations and the steps for a more certain international security.

The West believes that the Communist Bloc will not dare to provoke a global war for the fear of mutual and total annihilation. However, it is aware that the Communist Bloc is not yet ready to give up attempts of expansion even by military means, although it limits these actions to the Third World.[133] Instead, the West tries to make its governments more viable and to put an end to the deadly quarrels inside its ranks. The West also seems to be more and more interested in reducing military expenditures and in stopping the process of militarization, especially in the less developed countries. It is inclined to promote their and other countries' democratization and the Third World's peaceful, increasingly more equal incorporation in the framework of a more just and finally completely reconstructed (by eliminating one-sided privileges) international system.

That is why we reject the thesis that it is impossible to reform the present world system without using violence and that this system continues to be a product of defended dominance on the world market and of repressive mechanisms. Its continual positive change is a fact and this change is an ongoing process which takes place without self-breakdown or destruction of the system by its adversaries, contrary to the claims of some modern peace researchers.[134] The latter most frequently ignore the fact that only a framework of social institutions, capable of continuous evolution and relatively painless adjustments without the use of force, is an indispensable prerequisite for modernization, economic growth and justice as well. This is the case of the Western democracies, but also applies to changes not only within national borders.[135] It is valid with regard to the international system as well, the more so if we take into account the implications of the nuclear era. We also have to take into consideration that the present limits of combatting underdevelopment and promoting growth and stability in the Third World, so important for improving the international system, are predominantly indigenous, social and to a large extent independent of the world system.[136]

The belief that the poor will soon become powerful enough to provoke the confrontation with the rich and that the rich are interested in freezing their development is a piece of romantic nonsense. So is also the belief that the rich are rich only because they exploit the poor and that their wealth and destiny exclusively depend on such an exploitation. The opinion that OPEC has drastically changed equations of economic power and is on the way soon to reverse even those of military power and establish a world hegemony of the TW can be dismissed as a similar fantasy. It seems almost certain that industrialized capitalist and socialist states and their blocs, will remain for a still indefinite period of time, the principal holders of power in all fields. They may only cease to be able to remain the principal creators and guarantors of order necessary for human survival[137] if their rivalry continues in present forms. We should not, however, exclude the possibility that becoming increasingly aware of this evolution and eager to prevent any clash between themselves, the Soviet Union will give up operations à la Afghanistan and all industrialized nations, with time, will be inclined to act more constructively against underdevelopment and for arms control. However, this seems to be dependent, above all, on prospects of change in Soviet policies.

For the time being the arms race seems endless, although even the newest weapons are soon outmoded; arms strain limited budgets, drain scarce resources, are useless in many cases, ineffective or hurtful in others, almost never add to the security of the Soviet Bloc or stop the reaction of rivals and, finally, if used they may rather destroy all they are to protect. Hence the hope that the Soviets will not remain for ever locked in the arms race and also because of socio-economic difficulties may decide one day to bring it to an end, aware that it may result in a political and economic collapse of themselves and not only all other countries and even more increase the dangers to mankind's survival.

But let us check this assumption, also by considering some historical lessons of the relationship between underdevelopment and peace and by examining center-periphery theories, in order to reassess the role of peace research and of the idea of collective economic security based on these theories and conceived, as a means to remedy the wretchedness of the TW and its impact on the international security.

4. The Struggle for Economic Power and the Impact of Trade Profits on the Prospects of War-Prevention

Above we have already dealt with different causes of colonial expansion and imperialism at the end of the former century and with their new forms and the changes in Western policy in our days.

The problem continues to be the subject of intensive research not only by economists and historians, but by the representatives of other disciplines as well.[138] It is a starting point of various new economic[139] and political theories, based, inter alia, on center-periphery relationships and structural violence in the international system,[140] and of surveys of the ensuing tensions affecting international cooperation.[141] However, we are still far from a concept unanimously accepted either by various schools of Marxists, or by non-Marxists or anti-Marxists, in spite of the generations-old discussions on this subject.

Students of international law usually stress the role of debates on disarmament, especially in the years 1895-99, and point out the contribution of Levi, Decamps, Kamarovsky and of others to the formation of judicial and other peaceful means for the resolvement of conflicts detrimental to trade and efforts to strengthen international security. They also emphasize the international organizations' projects of promoting commerce and preserving peace. Historians recall that these students of international law had predecessors even in antiquity and in the Middle Ages. True enough, today they have supporters even among many financial leviathans.[142]

Actually, Norman Angels and Andrew Carnegie, the American millionaires who lived in the 19th century, or the Swedish magnate Andrew Nobel of the same period, were not the first to suggest that wars do not pay and to become promoters of pacifism. Nor was Montesquieu the only one who preceded modern pacifists by blaming wars not only because they are barbarious, but also because they are too expensive as a political method.

Richard Cobden in England and Michel Chevalier in France were among the scores who in the years of bourgeois growth, pointed out that peace was important to trade and vice versa, that war was harmful to business.

Even Roosevelt's call in 1937 for a free access to and a proper distribution of raw materials, in order to prevent tensions and wars, (in various forms this call is echoed in present-day discussions on the same subject) can be traced to old proposals on this matter.[143]

These and opposite views were to some extent surveyed—although in another context and for the purpose of a different argumentation—in the previous chapter. However, we have not yet dealt in more detail with the impact of military budgets on commercial activities and interests and with the two opposing views, according to which the military budgets might be harmful or beneficial for commerce.

Those who believe the first are sure that the continued growth of military budgets must at a certain moment lead to the use of arsenals and to the outbreak of wars. Their opponents, like Lambelet, do not see any interdependence between investments in arms production and conflicts.[144] They point out that the development of military industries has not always led to open hostilities. As a matter of fact, the latter were frequently not preceded by growing military budgets and sometimes broke out after a long period of balance of rivals' might, or even after arrangements to ease tensions and decrease the arms race. Lambelet mentions the war in Korea, which broke out after a serious reduction in military budgets. He also speaks about other wars that probably could have been prevented, if one of the parties had continued to enlarge its arsenals. We also know that the outbreak of WWII was preceded by comprehensive discussions on disarmament and in a situation of military weakness not only of the forthcoming anti-Nazi alliance. By and large it was compelled to arm itself after it was attacked and after the failure of the efforts to appease the enemy. It is not a secret any more that many leading German generals opposed even the invasion of Czechoslovakia because of the lack of military preparedness and followed the Führer when his blackmail proved successful.

From the research done by Singer and Small, Singer, Bremer and Stuckey[145] we learn about the changes that took place in the 20th century, by contrast with the 19th century, with regard to the influence of military power and alliances. In the past the latter had facilitated the outbreaks of hostilities. However, they have recently tended to strengthen stability, if only to consider the role of NATO and of the WTO in our times in Europe.

By and large, the nuclear option nullified the rationality of planning global wars. Doubtless, all immense investments in nuclear arsenals are merely made for purposes of deterrence. Unfortunately this strategy does not eliminate the threat to peace that ensues from the arms race.

We cannot therefore easily dismiss the pessimistic views, like those of the West-German philosopher and atomist C.F. von Weizseaker, who stresses that the continuous and rapid perfection of military technology, in spite of all control agreements, may lead to a nuclear global clash; an assumption which cannot be ignored just because appeals for promoting disarmament have been also gaining support among the governmental echelons.[146]

It may be worthwhile to emphasize that Luterbacher accepted the above-mentioned conclusions of Lambelet. However, he argues that there is no room any longer for generalizations on military power's impact on stability or non-stability in present-day international relations and of the efforts for its aggrandizement. It seems to him, that it is impossible to clarify this question today in a non-ambiguous way.[147] This argument corroborates the assumption about the plurality of causes leading to hostilities or contributing to their prevention. However, Ruloff and other students of this problem think that it is much easier to prevent an escalation when pressures can be used and when they are supported by military might.[148] Their opponents maintain, however, that only by decreasing the arms race and the respective investments, it has been possible to prevent the majority of conflicts after WWII, including some of those viewed as unavoidable in the Middle East and in this way to contribute to their solution through diplomatic efforts.[149] This strategy can also put an end to those politics, especially in the Third World, including the Middle East, which is also a result of the fact that governments regard the arms race as the means of gaining authority and prestige. Frequently, for this reason only, they promote their military industry or increase their arms imports[150] (which in the latter case actually favors the creation of military industries and the realization of other programs of militarization). We have already mentioned that the industrialized nations have relatively reduced their military budgets during the last years, while the less developed nations have increased them, and most probably—if to rely on the Western sources—the USSR have done the same.[151]

Some students see in this tendency a new aspect of imperialism,[152] because the role of the Western nations as arms suppliers is continually growing, particularly after the energy crisis and due to their search for petrodollars, necessary to improve their balance of payments.[153] The analogical or even more dynamic role of the USSR in this field prompts others, and not only the Chinese, to accuse it of social-imperialism, while a parallel tendency also characterizes some oil-producers. This strategy, however, also seems to be an excellent means of enlarging influence and exploitation of the less developed countries, which with the help of their rich "brothers" spend more and more money for military purposes, most frequently at the expense of really vital developmental needs.

As a matter of fact, arms sales have recently amounted to more than 30 percent of French exports and their total doubled in 1974, in comparison with 1973 arms sales. Since then it has been steadily growing. The same happens with the British arms exports which amounted in 1973, to the sum of 405 million pounds sterling and since then has been continually increasing. The German arms exports and those of other industrialized countries to the TW have been growing as well, both Western and Communist. Yet, the dominant role in this matter is still played by the USA and the USSR. However, Soviet arms exports are included in different budgetary paragraphs of general commerce and their exact evaluation is very complicated.[154]

Carter's declaration of 28 July 1977 that he, in cooperation with France, other European exporters and even the USSR would press for limitation of arms exports to the Third World, raised doubts. Unfortunately they proved to be justified. Almost simultaneously with the first declaration, the USA decided to make important arms sales to Egypt, Sudan, Somalia and Chad. The total of American arms sales in this period reached the unprecedented sum of $30 billion. Other suppliers to the Third World, particularly the Soviets, have also continued to sell arms. As regards the Latin-American countries, most of them have succeeded in placing 70 percent of their arms orders in Europe after the USA had introduced the "human-rights clause," while the Soviet arms sales to Ethiopia, South Yemen and other less developed countries have in a very short time doubled if not tripled.[155] Since the above-mentioned American declaration and similar Soviet announcements, there has not been any sign of an effort to stop the dangerous flow. The arms imports to the Third World and its militarization continue on a dangerous scale.[156]

These facts prove the conclusions of several above-mentioned theories at least with regard to the present situation in the Third World. According to their findings, the Third World is neither a nonaligned part of the globe whose main aim is peace nor it is completely dependent on the industrialized nations who supposedly sell arms to it just in order to keep it in a condition of underdevelopment and misery. In the light of the same facts, no less unfounded are the concepts ascribing all Third World conflicts and the ensuing arms race to the process of modernization, to the pains of development. Groundless also are the views that state that the Third World countries are victims of warrior societies with their colonial and imperialist conquests which are a result of their transition to ever higher stages of might and expansion, as demonstrated by the Rostowian models and by their followers.[157] Not less groundless, however, in consideration of the above-mentioned facts, are the alternative approaches, formed in response to the former. They are based on satellite models, focusing on productivity and effectivity and on the search for markets, raw materials and other riches. All this, according to the authors of these models, gave birth both to the two world wars and to various wars of liberation from colonial dependence, as well as to many civil wars that broke out earlier and later to fight ills produced by foreign domination and exploitation.

However, considering the above-mentioned and other facts, one might also come to the conclusion that the tensions produced by dynamic economic development or by maldevelopment are not the most dangerous. The most lethal tensions are those generated by inter-tribal frictions when they are supported by military aid of industrialized nations which offer it because of their ideological and political rivalry and in order to improve their monetary and oil-supply difficulties. These kind of frictions are the major cause of local wars that might easily escalate because of the South's rich ability to force industrial countries to sell their arms in exchange for oil. Hence there is a growing menace of the mounting military budgets of the Third World countries that are produced by South-South collisions. These budgets arrest the dynamics of economic development and social amelioration, but they also increase the troubles in the world monetary system. The Third World countries spent something like $70 billion in 1979 on direct military outlays, of which probably $10.6 billion (over 15.5percent) was spent on imports (compared with about 2.5percent for the whole world). They amounted to almost a quarter of world military expenditure and to four-fifths of world imports. Between 1978-79 the situation worsened.[158]

Some argue that tea and other products that India sells to Russia in exchange for missiles or anti-subversion training, or the oil that the USA, France, West Germany and Britain get from the Persian Gulf, or other countries in exchange for Phantoms, Mirages or other arms is used for the production, which is consumed by Russian, American, French, British and West German (and to the less extent by East-German, Polish or Czecho-Slovak) workers. One can claim that this trade is therefore productive, at least for this reason. However, the tea and coffee equivalent received by India, Brazil, Saudi Arabia or the Gulf in the form of weapons or military instruction is not consumed by their peoples and never can be. This sort of trade enriches narrow stratas of society, the civilian and military bureaucracies, and is harmful to democracy and individual freedom. It helps to strengthen the repressive regimes.[159]

Similar tendencies are not unknown in some industrialized countries. The above-mentioned yardstick of consumption can be almost equally applied to less developed and Soviet dominated countries. In all cases military development of the Third World produces bloodshed in the Third World itself as well as the possibility of negative economic redirection and conflagration elsewhere.

Hard work, individual efficiency, economic policies allowing to benefit from foreign trade, were used in the past, as the best explanation of success of small industrial countries, like Belgium, Switzerland or Austria. A high degree of industrial and agricultural modernization, internal political stability, a well functioning framework of social institutions, high quality of labor, research and enterprising energy that facilitated the expansion of exports were considered as the best way to cope with smallness and absence of natural resources.[160]

Today, even countries like Switzerland and Sweden, put a stress on their military industries (sometimes at the expense of other industries) not only because of defence needs, but because the Third World demands arms and is willing to trade them for oil and other important raw materials.

Some experts continue to explain the process of TW militarization, to a certain extent, following M. Weber by the role of armies in national integration, by incompetence and demoralization of the civilians, by the inacceptance of their traditionally fruitless authority and policies.[161] Unfortunately, these experts disregard the role of South-South conflicts and of the search for prestige through militarization which is facilitated by the East-West rivalry for influence and oil consumers' wish to exploit the situation by reducing their deficits through arms supplies.

Charles Levinson in his pamphlet "Vodka-Cola" ridiculed the West for depriving its workers of bread by delivering complete factories to the USSR that could produce goods competing with its own products.[162] He ignored a more dangerous aspect of the dilemma resulting from the present type of the East-West trade leading also to the military strengthening of the East and the enlargement of its arms supplies to the Third World. The East's supplies to the Third World not only are an instrument of winning competition with the West, but—as proved by the Afghan case—are also a war-productive factor on local and quite possibly on a global scale as well.

R. Triffin is reckoned among those eminent economists who pointed out many years ago the disastrous effect of military expenditures on the international monetary system and on the terms of world trade and, consequently, on developmental prospects of the countries concerned. He proposed to reduce military expenditures in a drastic way, also in order to arrest inflation, the deterioration of payment balances and to stimulate the process of economic growth and social development.[163]

True enough, we shall understand much better the real causes of the growing inflation, various signs of the economic crisis in all parts of the world and especially the causes of the stagnation in the Third World and the resulting from all this tensions if we take into account that the world military expenditures during the years 1948-80 grew from approximately $50 billion to $500 billion; but only in the Third World their growth in the years 1950-72 was from $4 to $15 billion and is still continuing.

This deepens the gap between the different parts of the world and undermines its political stability.[164]

This is the reason why some experts are of the opinion that military expenditures not only threaten peace, but also result in immense losses in the national economies. If the proper means were invested in other than military industries, more capital could have been available for productive purposes, for the growth of the national product and for the industrial potential of the different nations. According to them, military expenditures lead to reducing economic development and not only at the time when they are made, but in the forthcoming years as well because they prevent the employment of the existing means for productive investments that years later could enlarge the national output.

Let us also add that there are interesting findings on the positive influence of trade and various forms of economic and other forms of co-operation between the East and the West on decreasing tensions in their mutual relations. This leads to strengthening détente and increasing efforts to achieve more stability and progress in the Third World. It is worthwhile to quote for this purpose Lodggaar's conclusions. He speaks about the years immediately after the October Revolution and about the initial period of détente.

The share of machinery imports from the West in the total of Soviet investments in chemistry reached 25.7 percent as early as in 1969, in wood industry—14.3 percent, and in other light industries—26.6 percent.

These facts were used to explain the USSR's growing interest in détente,[165] and its efforts to save it and not to decide immediately on a military intervention in Poland, which may end with stopping any trade between the West and the Soviet Bloc. However, what happened in Afghanistan shows that the Soviets prefer making use of the Western weakness, disunity and indecisiveness to profit politically from any local tension. They wish in such a situation to enlarge their influence and are prepared to risk military adventures for this end.

Needless to stress, trade between the USSR and the West and interbloc commerce in general have grown appreciably in the recent years. Their impact on the human rights issues, in spite of all difficulties and still strong repressions of the dissidents and Jews who wish to emigrate to Israel or join their families in other countries, has also become recently evident.

It is worthwhile to stress that the annulment of the 1972 Soviet-American trade agreement which was formally tied to the Jackson Amendment and to American pressure for emigration and human rights[166] was actually a consequence of modest credits and tough conditions of the deal.

One could assume therefore, especially after the Belgrade Conference of 1977 convened to examine Helsinki decisions and to further them, that the Soviet Communist Party 1976 Congress' resolution to continue the assistance to all national liberation, anticolonial and anti-imperialist movements fighting "reactionary regimes" will not entirely stop Western efforts to save under new conditions détente and that even some future progress can be expected at the subsequent follow-up conferences after the failure of the Madrid negotiations in 1981 because of the Soviet vital interest to avoid a return to the Cold War. This then challenges Brezhnev's report at the XXVI Party Congress in 1981, a period of further economic deterioration in Russia and in other parts of the Soviet Bloc, which was particularly painful in Poland. Already at the end of 1979 it became clear, however, that the USSR has continued to exploit such opportunities, as it had in Angola, Ethiopia and elsewhere, and that while trying to come to an agreement about reducing the different items in the arms race, it continued its efforts to achieve military superiority.[167] However, it is also a pure simplification to view the obligations taken by the USSR in August 1975 in Helsinki and reaffirmed in Belgrade in 1977 and to some extent in Madrid in 1981 as absolutely senseless, although the Soviets gave them a rigid and selected interpretation[168] from the beginning. The opposite seems to be true. The above-mentioned Lodgaard's findings on the strong correlation between commercial ties, stability and tranquility in national relations and indirectly on the prospects of decreasing the East-West tensions (his findings were also confirmed by K. Goldman and other students)[169] appear not entirely void if we consider the Soviet efforts to soften the strong American reaction to the aggression against Afghanistan and all Western warnings on the steps to be taken by them in the event of an aggression against Poland.

On the other hand, we know the good results already produced by the change and enlargement of the Lomé Convention on 31 October 1979 and by various new bilateral and multilateral North-South arrangements and negotiations to bring the North-South Dialogue and other constructive proposals to a successful end. All of them and especially the Brandt Commission[170] seem to confirm the correlation between the decrease of tensions and the options for better co-operation in conditions of more stability in the relations between the industrialized and the less developed nations. This assumption, however, will remain valid on the condition that the East-West rivalry does not become worse and the solution of the Afghanistan problem is achieved. This is necessary in order to prevent similar acts of aggression, to strengthen common efforts to cure the socio-economic ills of the Third World and to discontinue the flow of arms that kindles the South-South conflicts. However, it is worthwhile to stress again in this context, too, that any success in the struggle against underdevelopment will depend not only on this, or another level of the West-East historical conflict, but—and may be not to a less extent—on the internal situation in the Third World: on changing its outdated structures, on their democratization, on essential reforms in the administration and education, in the systems of training and in the health institutions. All this means the enlargement of the proper budgets and the reduction of military expenditures and in this way hindering foreign intervention and subordination to arms-suppliers.

The views pinpointing the dependence of backwardness on the growth of military budgets, by regarding them as factors of failure and self-destruction, are therefore very persuasive. It is very difficult indeed to deny that these factors do not strengthen negative, actually ruinous, developments in national economies and in the Third World societies. They facilitate bloody encounters, tribal and other tensions, cause losses in goods and lives, deepen retrogression and weakness and retard any progress. True enough, quite a few experts question this conclusion. Some of them argue that military expenditures and armaments in general do not play any important role in containing development and in making decision to go to war. Others are even sure that marshalling of important skilled labor and capital resources of the less developed countries for military purposes actually has a substantially positive effect on the development process as well as on strengthening international security. The basic conclusion of a number of surveys of the problem is that there is no major correlation between the military, diplomatic, administrative and other variables coded, and whether war did or did not occur between the opposed powers during the time selected.

Naroll's and Bullogh's findings confirm the opinion shared by many politico-military specialists that governments' attention to military and related resources does not as a general law either guarantee peace or promptly lead to war.

Both "peace through deterrence" and "peace through unilateral disarmament" concepts are regarded by them as simplistic and naive and historically unsupportable.[171]

On the other hand, Barbera points out that war stimulates production, including outputs normally associated with development. But at the same time war destroys men, minds, materials and money. His conclusion is that war has neither hindered nor stimulated world economy and culture. According to him, war does not create inpenetrable barriers between nations, neither does it improve global communication. It has neither led to irreparable breakdowns of, nor to differential increments to, the key social process of centralization, consociation and co-operation that determine economic growth and human development. According to this approach, war does not significantly affect the differential application of mechanisms of the quality of nations, but confirms its irrelevance to development.[172]

We have already mentioned above in another context the view on the Third World military and militarism as in some sense good for progress; its followers assert that in a certain way they facilitate development through planning and creating war industries, training people in technology and replacing the civilians incapable of ruling society. This view encouraged theories that associate development with high military expenditures, and by deviation, with high military imports. This is also an "economic history" view persuasively propounded for Western European countries before World War I by Werner Sombart.[173] In different ways it has been repeated by students of Japanese or post-revolutionary Russian economic history. They have claimed that in these countries only the military have succeeded in providing stable, large-scale institutions, capable of containing the social effects of modernization; that only they could stimulate the supply of modern social, economic and educational infrastructures; that they most perfectly provide a large and stable outlet for modern large-scale industry; generate a technology capable of wide application; act as a focus for national aspiration and national effort, including the mobilization of resources, in a fragmented social setting; and that they endow tradition-oriented societies with a high degree of rationality; or do all this together and a lot more besides.[174]

The functional, sociological view is parallel to the one abovementioned.[175] It argues that in industrially advanced countries the military's appetite for technology facilitates innovations and in this way promotes research and progress. In less developed countries the process is different: the military's appetite for arms, results in reliance on imports of weapons and finally in containment of their own industries. However, it also produces high level of training, increase of discipline and technological knowledge. This leads to social modernization.

Sombart was of the opinion that war is not an outcome of capitalism, as the Marxists had claimed, but that capitalism was the outcome of war, because businessmen were forced to work for war and in this way promoted development and progress. He regards war not as an offshoot of economic structures, but as their projection.[176]

However, as Nef pointed out, Sombart merely examined the economic consequences of the production which worked for the war as if this could be kept separate from the economic consequences of its use.[177] Actually the situation in Germany was more similar to that in England and in other countries in the past and recent times. By and large it was England's avoidance of wars in the years 1540-1640 to which much of her economic progress in these years must be ascribed. And her militaristic behavior in the following century was one of the causes of British economic regression in the period between the "early industrial revolution" and the 18th century.[178]

T.S. Ashton made clear the position about those who confuse causes and consequences of wars, economics and technology, a position rarely questioned today because wars sometimes lead to inventions and those who make wars are reckoned among the pioneers of technological progress and sometimes of economic boom, but rarely of economic and social development.[179] There is a growing literature on the effects of war on social stratification.

Wars not only lead to the enrichment of the "death" traders and the impoverishment of the rest of the people, but also produce other negative effects of social differentiation.[180] Discussing warfare in the Mediterranean world in the 16th and 17th centuries, the renowned historian Ferdinand Brandel concluded that we are still ignorant about the nature of war.[181] However, he said, we already know a lot about their origins and consequences both in the past and in the present and not only about the said stratification and other socio-economic results and reactions of different classes in many countries.

We know, for example, about the criticism provoked by the effects of war taxation of private fortunes in the 13th and 14th century England;[182] of the direct taxes in the early Tudor England;[183] about the catastrophic blow to a previously booming German economy following the Thirty Years War;1|☙★ the crippled economy and the disastrous decrease of population in South Netherlands and the stagnation in the North during the Dutch war of liberation (1568-1648); the almost total ruin of the prosperous provinces of Flanders and Brabant;[185] the complete devastation of the Netherlands in result of the Spanish War, while Spain succeeded in getting only political and religious gains. Only the neutrals got real economic profit from the Spanish War.[186]

No wonder, therefore, that the preamble to the Peace of Muenster reads almost like the preamble to the United Nations Charter, elaborated in consideration of WWII: "Let all persons know that, after a long succession of bloody wars which for many years have opposed the peoples, subjects, kingdoms and lands which are under the obedience of the Lords, King of Spain and States-General of the United Netherlands, the aforesaid Lords moved by the Christian piety, desire to end the general misery and prevent the dreadful consequences, calamity, harm and danger which the further continuation of the aforesaid wars in the Low Countries would bring in their train. They invite and call upon other princes and potentates, to allow themselves to be moved by the same piety and to avert mishaps, destruction and disorders which the heavy plague of war has made men suffer for so long and heavily."[187]

It is true that not only hospital practise and preventive medicine have been among the important areas where militarism has then led to innovations and improvements on national scale.[188] True enough, war can be either incentive or detriment in other fields of scientific, technological and economic or sometimes even social development. Many fields of science with known military applications were rapidly stimulated during different wars, like pharmacology, bacteriology, psychology, psychiatry, surgery, chemistry, physics, industrial sociology and, of course, different fields of technology.[189] As a matter of fact, war expenditures have been frequently regarded as rivals to expenditures on social welfare. However, in some cases they have led to bettering the life conditions of the workers and produced other changes in their favor. The reason for this was that it was necessary to prevent social and political conflicts and to increase national solidarity. Not only the famous British Beveridge Report aimed at the abolition of poverty and made in the wake of WWII is a case in point.

Hence, it is worthwhile to stress that it is wrong to generalize about the impact of wars on socio-economic progress of nations and on their trade. As a matter of fact, this impact depends on the special circumstances of particular wars, on the general situation of the countries concerned and on the international constellation as well. That is why there were cases in the past of substantive gains and growth during wars here and there and that they were not only of political, but of economic and social importance as well.

To the extent that war involves: 1) killing of people and destruction of real capital; 2) diversion of scarce labor, capital and raw materials from productive to unproductive use; and 3) an increase in the risks and uncertainties of mercantile or manufacturing enterprise, there is no doubt that war must have a negative effect on economic growth and social development.[190]

On the other hand it is true that to the extent that war requirements 1) draw into productive use till now under-employed factors; 2) stimulate output of industries whose expansion reduces costs or creates opportunities in favor of innovating enterprise—its effects are more likely to be growth-promoting than growth-retarding.

What is more, for the countries concerned, success or failure in war may further affect industrialization by enlarging or diminishing either their national markets for domestic produce or their access to crucial raw materials or to other resources.[191]

This may be said, of course, only with regard to past wars, some present local wars and all other wars conducted with the use of conventional weapons and to some extent only if they are not too much sophisticated.

As regards lessons from the past we have already mentioned the Thirty Years War's destructive results for Germany as well as the Dutch War of Liberation' destructive results for South Netherlands. It may be interesting to add that it was calculated that the war for the Spanish succession could have been no less disastrous for the Netherlands;[192] that most of the 18th and 19th centuries wars had a similar effect; that WWI was a catastrophic breakdown not only for industrial progress and political stabilization,[193] and that the same happened to all European countries in result of WWII, where its consequences with great difficulties and massive American aid could be overcome only after many years and are still felt.

However, for Britain in the period 1700-63 the evidence suggests a positively beneficial impact of war on industrial development, whereas the outcome of the later wars of 1776-83 was obviously bad.[194] Similarly, the results of the American participation in recent wars have been different, sometimes positive and sometimes negative. But the US growth and not only in industry, after WWII is an unquestionable fact.

These conclusions, in the opinion of many experts, can hardly be applied to the Third World where in all circumstances the wars and military expenditures seem to aggravate backwardness and misery. However, many students of the problem, as we have already mentioned, are of the opinion that the most efficient agency for transferring technology and exposing large numbers of the population to it, are the armed forces. This thinking is rooted in the belief that training in military technology finally results in mastering civilian technology as well and that military build-up in many cases involves basic infrastructural additions, like airfields, harbors and other installations. The latter have significant visible benefits for the civilian sector of the economy, in addition to the less quantitative technology transfer spin-off of technical training programs and the like.[195]

Pierre Benoit, quoted above, argues that there are significant indications that the TW defence programs might, on balance, have benefited its civilian economies. He concedes that these indications suggest that less emphasis on maximizing traditional investments, and more emphasis on improved training, motivation and productivity in the non-industrial sector (including the repatterning of certain defence programs) might substantially contribute to maximum development; it may finally reduce defence burdens, and later on facilitate TW arms-control agreements.

According to Benoit, military programs will yield, to the extent consistent with military security, maximum development benefits if they: 1) train large numbers of civilians in skills partly utilizable in civilian roles and maintain them in reserves rather than in a large standing army; 2) build dual-use transport and communication infrastructure (partly utilizable by civilians); 3) minimize the domestic production or commercial import of advanced and heavy industry and rely mainly on labor-intensive intermediate technology, supplemented by aid-financed advanced weapons with primary defensive capabilities and low maintainance costs, such as anti-tank and anti-plane missiles; and 4) maximize civic action programs to reduce the overhead costs of forces and equipment required for deterrence but rarely for combat.

Benoits' study covered the growth rates, investment rates, foreign aid receipts and certain other variables of 44 less developed countries between 1950-65. This material was analyzed primarily by means of correlation analysis. The 44 country sample covered about three-quarters of the population, GNP and defense expenditures of the Third World, excluding mainland China. The sample analysis was supplemented by case studies of India, South Korea, Mexico, Israel, Egypt and Argentina.

In order to establish if there was no bias in the data, a regressive analysis was undertaken as well. It ommitted three countries, namely, Jordan, Burma and South Vietnam. Some of them had military governments and all not being ruled democratically, with heavy defense burdens, exaggerated their growth rates.

However, the repeated analysis did not show different results. The investigators came to the conclusion that in principle military governments did not have greater military expenditures than civilian governments.

That is why it is wrong to ignore these and other similar findings and to reject completely the possibility of positive impact of the said expenditures on economic growth and sometimes even on social development. But do these findings suffice to make generalizations and can they apply without any reservations to the situation after 1965?

The latter is characterized by the advent of strategic parity between the superpowers, the uncertainty as to the extent of the relaxation between them, given their continual competition and the search for marginal advantage in contested "gray" areas. This, on the one hand, favors political multipolarity that diminishes dominant tensions, decreases rigid alignment and enhances prospects of manoeuvers for different TW states. On the other hand, however, this facilitates the waging of South-South conflicts, an interrupted increase of militarization and totalitarization of many less developed countries. This also leads to the abandonment of developmental aims by "pretorian governments," primarily interested in giving privileges to the ruling elites.

True enough, this sometimes leads to an improved training, but only of selected units more specialized in repression of the opposition than in civic action programs and not infrequently used for military adventurism, aimed to prevent the organization of groups calling for socio-economic change. In these circumstances military training cannot be diverted to skills utilizable by civilians and the recruited force usually becomes a basis of standing internal security armies and police. Because of their nature, domestic production or commercial import of all kinds of weaponry starts to grow and funds, if available, are utilized for purposes blocking developmental efforts.

On the other hand, the growth of arms export following the rise of oil prices was practically imposed on the industrial countries and each of the superpowers has taken advantage of the situation and used this increase of arms export as an instrument of reducing or even terminating the influence of her rivals. This, for example, happened in the summer of 1977 with American arms deliveries to Somalia, Sudan and even Chad in response to the flow of Soviet arms to Ethiopia and South Vietnam. The American arms supplies to Egypt are also a case in point.

The call "no more Vietnams" was answered by the appeal "no more

Angolas," but whereas the American involvement in South-East Asia has truly come to an end, Soviet intrusion in Africa and the Indian Ocean provoked American and other Western mobilization. This mobilization has led to new forms of imperialism, sub- and mini-imperialism, to use this ambiguous term which today more fits to describe Soviet politics, both military and economic, than American or Western politics.

What is more, some of the TW countries, namely, the Arab oil producers, multiply their arms imports in order to dictate their will to the poor "brothers." This, too, we need to have in mind when we use the term "mini-imperialism." This form of imperialism is still supported by various TW countries which believe that the united Third World should become equal to the industrialized world also in terms of warfare capacities, because they think, without this there is no possibility to solve their painful problems and to put an end to their inequality in all other fields.

Hence, the Third World countries, and especially the Middle East countries, are reluctant to accept the thesis that the best way to promote development is to end conflicts by negotiations, compromises and arrangements guaranteeing their security and furthering their peaceful cooperation. That is why the Third World countries prefer to accept the theory that "the weakness of states is always the greatest threat to peace and the clearest invitation to attack."

This statement of one of the Iranian prime ministers in the times of the Shah's rule could have been made by any of the Middle East leaders. Some of them endorse this statement also in consideration of recent local wars. True enough, most of them have been fast, lasted a few days or weeks, have been launched by surprise and rapidly created *faits accomplis*. This has happened because of a high level of preparedness and stocks of weaponry and other materials enabling to conduct these wars at least for some time independently of outside importers.[196]

This is one reason more why the belief is so strong, especially in the Middle East, that a build-up of large inventories of weapons and spares, stocked in depots or warehouses, might enable a country to take responsibility for her own defense, resist foreign pressures and finally achieve greater stability.

This belief is frequently strengthened by the limited power of the United Nations, the unreliability of allies, the fear of indirect aggression, like, for example, the terrorist attacks and guerrilla operations. The undefendable from the geographic point of view, often very long borders, the rapid attrition rates of most of the recent local wars that not only are very short, but very intensive as well, the dubious prospects of getting arms supplies in time because the suppliers are very distant and because of the possible pressures upon them, all this makes the Middle East countries to believe that it is much safer to stock arms. They realize the imperative of self-reliance.

However, this need for self-reliance has reduced the positive aspects of many factors in existence in the years 1950-65, which have been discussed by Emil Benoit in his above-mentioned study. This decrease is also produced by the fact that détente was never applied universally, that it may sometimes seen by different states as a potential threat to security in regions where the inter-bloc competition does not affect directly the inter-superpower relationship, but where the civil war, quasi-internal conflicts and open foreign intervention are a part of life.

We have already mentioned the cases of Egypt and Israel as an illustration of disastrous results of such situations. Egypt pushed into the vicious circle of wars and arms race by Nasser's pan-Arabic, messianic policies suffered more than any other country in the Middle East. Saudi Arabia's "generous" aid could not prevent her nearing a socio-economic bankruptcy, nor more than the "generous" Soviet support and arms deliveries. As a result, the present shift in her policy will demand a lot of time for a radical remedy.

However, Egypt's present efforts to solve the painful problems by shifting the stress from military to development issues, may fail if the Soviets are replaced by the French, British and Americans as arms suppliers and the conditions for prospects of investments and socio-economic growth are not completely changed.

The catastrophic results of the Egyptian model, remind the outcome of military adventurism of Indonesia and India years ago. They suffer from the consequences of their policies even today. This case has been frequently used and misused as an illustration of the outcome of a choice of "development" through military aggrandizement. This choice is characteristic for areas with large and small local wars. They apply "satellite" models chosen by governments relying on foreign support, even if the result is dependence on one of the superpowers or on alliance with national, religious or ideological "friends" and "brothers" who never neglect their own interests.

It is true, that the priority given in Israel to an authentic economic growth, social development and scientific and technological progress gave the country not only military victories during a generation. Because of this Israel's GNP has increased as well as standards of life, which reached in 1972 the sum of $2300 per capita. Iraq, Syria and Jordan had only a GNP of $250 to $350 in the same period.[197]

However, because Israel was not recognized by her neighbors and suffered from repeated wars, her dynamic development has stopped. Multiplying difficulties arose from both conjectural and structural economic crisis, from failure to attract and absorb new immigrants because of the necessity to give up the development in favor of the military model of growth. Consequently, the political and military dependence increased. Today it is based only on the United States, while the debts in the 1975 budget of approx. $8 billion reached $10.5 billion and the defense expenditure was 30 percent of GNP and 40 percent of the national budget. Imports were 3.9 percent higher than exports and reserves of foreign currency declined in the from $800 to $300 million and today approach the "red line."

Investments fell from $151.2 million in 1973 to $45 in 1974; the standard of life decreases continually, inflation increases, which simultaneously aggravates all internal conflicts, economic, ideological and political. The strikes sometimes almost completely paralyze even vital fields of the national economy and the normal operation of the state administration.[198] All this has produced in 1977 the fall of the labor government that ruled the country since the day its independence was proclaimed. This, of course, was a result not only of ideological and political miscalculations but also of a false economic policy and of the consequences of wars imposed on the country.

The case of Israel proves how external factors are able to stop the constructive development of a country, while the example of Egypt shows how the same can happen mainly due to internal politics, although also directed towards war. Needless to stress, both super-powers but, first and foremost the Soviets, have contributed to the aggravation of the ME situation. Their policy has turned the area of a conflict between two nationalisms, each with its legitimate claims but unable to find the way to peaceful coexistence when pushed into the arena of superpower rivalry. The latter grew with the USSR's failure to keep its influence in Egypt, the increasing importance of the oil issue and the hike of oil prices. The relevant incomes, as we have already pointed out, have been used for the time being, merely to finance the arms race in the region.

It is true that some of the oil exporters, namely, Iran in the times of the Shah and Saudi Arabia quite early decided to spend money on important developmental undertakings and their relevant plans include both industry and agriculture.[199] However, till now a great part of their income has been devoted to "military" rather than civilian development, to the accumulation of funds in banks abroad and investments in the United States, Britain and other Western countries, while the aid to the poor "brothers" has been very limited.[200] The aid to Egypt and some other countries stopped, for political reasons.

Moreover, military expenditures of the oil-producers help the growth of sub- and mini-imperialism; they generate local conflicts produced by old and new tensions, mainly of internal character and while the investments in foreign banks reinforce political dependence, the still insufficiently enlarged infrastructure diminishes the effectivity of developmental processes where they already take place.

In order to understand better what is going on in the Middle East, we have also to consider the efforts of the industrialized countries to diminish their dependence on oil. Explorations in Alaska, in the North Sea and in the Mexican Gulf are slowly becoming profitable and efforts are made to develop nuclear, solar and other energy sources. We might therefore assume that, in spite of the indecisive steps taken by the West during the Tokyo summit in July 1979, the unique chance of the Middle East nations will be lost because their wealth is used mainly to buy arms and this naturally cannot help to solve their political and socio-economic problems.

It is true that for the time being the role of the Third World is still strong in the UN and other international organizations, but disunity in its ranks (and not only because of the gap between the rich and poor "brothers") will probably diminish it sooner than expected.[201]

The Third World also lacks unity with regard to its essential political problems, including the Israeli-Arab conflict whose continuation results in an uninterrupted growth of military expenditures that are ruinous for all parties.

It is true that military expenditure, as we have already mentioned above, to a certain extent sometimes contributes to the enlargement even of the heavy industry, more rapidly promote technological progress and scientific research and of course, create profits from the exports of weapons. In this way they limit their negative impact on the national economy.[202] However, at the last count, in the Middle East as in all TW countries, they do prevent the use of available funds for constructive and really productive purposes. In conditions of peace or even a decline of tensions these funds could be directed towards welfare ends, towards improving standards of living and assisting in planning a better future.

The present deterioration of the standards of living and the curtailing of educational and scientific budgets make the above prospects and calculations appear unrealistic. Moreover, the growth of military expenditures reduces capital investment in lasting goods.

It may be worthwhile to stress here that even regional and "ideological" frameworks have been prevented from easing the situation. Thus, the Arab Common Market could not better the conditions of its poor members. Its activities remained quite limited and its internal turnover did not amount in 1972 to more than 6.3 percent in exports and 10 percent of imports of the total of the respective member-countries, a situation which did not change in the years 1974-79. This fact indicates too, that the causes of stagnation, crisis and regression are rooted in tensions and conflicts, rather than in lack of funds and organizational instruments for their operation.

It seems, therefore, that it will be impossible to approach a solution of the economic troubles of the area without containing or, better still, terminating the military "developmental" tendencies, without bringing all parties by direct and indirect means to an understanding through compromise and normalization of relations. This consequently will lead to a betterment of a situation in other parts of the Third World.

Considering the Middle East situation we are not too eager to adopt the above-mentioned conclusions of Lambelet. In principle he might be right, like all other followers of similar theories, conceding that it is impossible to prove the existence of a direct and an immediate relationship between war, misery and backwardness or between peace and development in all cases. It is true that there were many wars absolutely independent of the dynamics of military investments and preparedness and of the arms races of one or more potential belligerents. There were also other wars that could have been prevented or limited or more rapidly finished, would deterrent forces and military capacities exist.

However, what happens today in the Middle East and in various large parts of the Third World, where plenty of South-South conflicts take place stimulated or not by outside influence, seems rather to confirm another conclusion. It is not trade and profits that are at the root of these conflicts. Lives and goods could, of course, be saved, prospects of development strengthened, if it were possible to put to an end to or at least seriously limit military expenditures and to replace war budgets by peace budgets. However, the core of the problem is how to eliminate the use of force and how to put an end to the attempts to solve disputes by violent means. Such a strategy is extremely complicated because most of all conflicts are determined not by economic, but by other, in principal, irrational motivations.

5. The Center-Periphery, Dependency and some Peace Research Approaches to Underdevelopment and International Security

While analyzing the interrelationship between underdevelopment and international security, some critical peace researchers tend to concentrate rather abstractly on a structural theory of imperialism. They speak about the latter's product, namely, a center-periphery and dependency world model and about its violent methods of exploitation and domination. They perceive imperialism as a "sophisticated" type of dominance relation that cuts across nations, basing itself on a bridgehead which the Center Nation establishes in the center of the Periphery Nation, for the benefit of both.[203] Despite declarations of an intention not to adopt wholesale the Leninist theory which bases imperialism exclusively on private capitalist economic relationship, many critical peace researchers have been reluctant to analyze the nature of Soviet imperialism generated by state capitalism. They actually continue this escapism in spite of scientifically well-grounded findings not only of liberal, social-democrat or Eurocommunist researchers and politicians, but of orthodox pro-Soviet communists inside and outside the Eastern Bloc.[204] Moreover, they have made no comprehensive analysis of the functions of imperialism in different historical periods and social situations; neither have they taken into account the fact that Western imperialism which is frequently rooted in nationalist outlooks and search for profits (nowadays belonging to the past) is basically different from ideologically justified Soviet imperialism. Some stages of the Western imperialism's economic, technological, managerial and scientific development produce anti-war tendencies. However, Soviet policy cannot, by its nature, free itself from a strategy of expansion, although sometimes it has to limit this expansion for technical reasons and out of fear for a nuclear clash suicidal in our times.

Furthermore, many of the writings classified as critical peace research not only ignore the above-mentioned facts; they have not yet been concerned with various aggressive and imperialist tendencies in some oil-producing Arab and Moslem countries. The latter, like Soviet tendencies, are also rooted in specific ideological motivations.

With almost the only exception of Egbert Jahn's writings on Soviet militarism,[205] most of the critical peace researchers regard this subject as a taboo. They choose to disregard the fact that their concepts of imperialism, center-periphery and dependency, are based exclusively on an economic approach. The latter, as we have already mentioned, was often critisized even by Marx and Engels. Today more than ever it is simplistic in its dichotomic outlook. It is rejected even by those radicals who call for taking also into account demographic, climatic, psychological and of course, ethnic, national and other political and social dimensions of the underdevelopment issue.[206]

The center-periphery outlook in modern peace research has influenced the analysis of other aspects of Third World problems particularly its perception of social progress, in terms of a true world-wide socialist revolution, that is expected to be a panacea for all ills. This perception seems to be determined by a disbelief in reforms and in the possibility of gradual changes in national and international systems; it emphasizes the ability of science to create lethal weapons, but denies its potential to find ways for mankind to live in better conditions and in more security in a not too distant future.

However, the concept of the Third World as a periphery of metropolitan capitalism is still highly controversial not only because it is not supported by findings of important experts, including those of the Third World; it is risky, above all, because it can be counter-productive to efforts to increase self-reliance and promote co-operation which is determined by different forms of present-day interdependence of all nations, military and political as well.

According to the Latin-American school of dependency or to the school of Biaroch (who follows Baran and Sweezy and is followed by Amin, Galtung and Senghaas)[207] the interrelation between the centers and peripheries explains how aggressive capitalism has caused and maintained backwardness in colonial territories and in the new states. All these authors underrate (or simply pass over in silence) the internal causes of underdevelopment. Nor do, they consider the fact that various forms of colonialism and imperialism existed in Africa, Asia and America long before their conquest by the Europeans. They picture colonialism as the outcome of exclusively external, essentially European forces. Such a presentation of the problem is, to say the least, one-sided.

Actually, colonialism and underdevelopment do not necessarily have a causal connection; and political independence from Western economies is not always identical wich a choice of the best way to development. When Ghana and several other colonial territories became independent states, they were more highly developed than other states, like Afghanistan, Ethiopia or Liberia, which have never been colonies. On the other hand, quite a few countries fell a victim to colonialism just because they were underdeveloped. Portugal and Turkey are among the poorest countries in the world today, although once they were great powers. If per-capita gross national product is used as a criterion, an undeveloped country and ex-colonial territory like Libya stands equal with Italy because of the former's large oil exports. Kuwait, another still undeveloped country, but rich in oil, has overtaken Great Britain and the United States in per-capita GNP. Countries like Gabon, Turkey, Chile and Nicaragua have almost the same GNP—although the first gained its independence about ten years ago, the second, a former empire, has never been a colony, and the other two have been enjoying political independence for more than one hundred and fifty years. All of them have been encompassed by the so-called center-periphery relationship only during the last two decades. These examples demonstrate that a state is not secure from under-development and its consequences simply because it never had to surrender its independence, or if it shook off its colonialist yoke many years ago.[208]

All Third World countries, including the Communist-oriented, want to co-operate with the industrialized capitalist nations. They realize that only in this way they can get rid of their backwardness. The Soviet Bloc—itself looking for credits, knowhow and preferential treatment that it hopes to get from the West—makes only a very small contribution to socio-economic progress in the post-colonial world. It is true that links with the Western center are sometimes disadvantageous (both politicaly and economically); but they, paradoxically, offer the only hope for rescue from a desperate situation and for progress beyond the "peripheric" status.

However, some peace researchers tend to disregard not only this fact; they also very frequently ignore internal factors of backwardness and the endemic conditions of the Third World. This position seems to be influenced by a simplification of some conclusions of André Gunder Frank, C. Furtado and other researchers of development and underdevelopment who studied these problems merely in regard to Latin America. It is also influenced by A. Emmanuel's "unequal exchange" and similar theses which in different ways have been exploited by the French "Tiers Monde" study group, by some Scandinavian, West-German and African scholars, like J. Galtung, D. Senghaas and particularly by Samir Amin.[209] Not infrequently this position is misleading because, not only to a large extent, it is detached from the realities of the Third World (i.a. as it has been convincingly pointed out, among others, by G. Myrdal)[210] and from the internal causes of underdevelopment. It also ignores the present role of the USSR in the Third World and does not say anything about important features of the current international system which are affected by OPEC's oil policy and by the growth of the West's tendency to act both in order to ameliorate the condition of the LDC's and to strengthen international security.

Samir Amin, who is usually silent about the Soviet socio-economic experiments and contribution to development efforts and the struggle for peace, hints that only a socialist experiment might provide an escape from backwardness and misery. However he does not say what kind of socialism is needed for this purpose. As a matter of fact, he thinks that no solution is possible during this generation and asserts that the problem can be solved only in a society that would emerge from a world-wide radical revolution.[211] He admits that his study merely promises utopia for the TW countries of today. Such unwarranted pessimism characterizes not only some students of underdevelopment, but peace researchers as well.[212] It may be worthwhile to stress that this view has little to do with Marxism because Marxism was proud to have turned utopian socialism into a scientific discipline and a tool for gradually changing the nature of man by preventing wars and speeding up the progress of states, ripe due to evolution and/or revolution for social metamorphosis. However, some of the pessimistic school's protagonists may claim credit for having used Marxist terminology for only a very black prognosis. This, too, prevented them from predicting the emergence of a rich part of the Third World. In contradiction to Lenin's assumption of the whole of colonial possessions as a factor of revolutionary might, it is to a large extent a center of dictatorship, reaction, arms race and of a fanatic warfare. This fact and the policies the Third World's richer segment make increasingly difficult the liberation of entire continents from misery and bloodshed. The abovementioned prognosis has also led many of its adherents to the conclusion that any arrangement for improving the existing international order, for changing the present terms of trade and for any progress towards arms control would actually result in a more effective oppression of the Third World.[213] They interpret the South-South conflicts exclusively as an outcome of imperialist plots, disregarding even the impact of traditional warrior orientations.[214] That is why the picture of the Third World given by the dependency-theorists is not only incomplete but is also static in its concepts as well.[215] Hence, it is so important to reappraise the dependency approach in the light of its partisans' pseudo-Marxist and empirical argumentation.

G. Reid and E.J. Yanerella are among those critical scholars who have recently stressed the need to see social realities in their totality, as a dynamic and historical whole. According to them, from G. Lucas and A. Gramsci to T. Adorno, H. Marcuse and other representatives of the Frankfurt and recently not only of the neo-Marxist schools, the category of totality is the basic revolutionary concept for critical social inquiry.[216]

However, the dependency theory is almost completely silent about the role of the Soviet Union in the struggle for influence in the Third World and especially in the Middle East.[217] To a large extent it ignores the indigenous causes of intra-Third World frictions. It actually conceives the international system mainly as a reflection of the North-South contradiction. Reid and his colleagues criticize "establishment figures," like Boulding for their scientism, the French structuralists, followers of Levi-Strauss, the orthodox Marxists L. Althuser and H. Schmid for attributing—to use B. Ollman's wording—an identity to the whole independent of its parts and for asserting the absolute predominance of this whole over its parts. Actually, as we have pointed out above, this, too, applies to methodology of certain peace researchers and dependency theorists. And as regards their static approach objections, I.W. Zartman seems to be right in pointing out that they ignore even the findings of the studies on decolonization accounting for the successive stages of changing North-South relations in favor of the South; this occurs even in the field of educational systems and, of course, in the fields of monetary, trade, administrative and other undertakings, particularly with regard to TW's frequently independent posture in international conferences and organizations.[218] Some critical peace researchers and dependency theorists—also in result of their static picture of the Third World, usually based on passed moments in its history—reject the notion of "development without growth;" they also deny the supposedly totally illusionary trickle-down processes, and the prediction of betterment based on a rise in gross national product. However, they also negate the importance of the critical social notion of development. By and large it is aimed at improving the most disinherited, wretched strata,[219] at terminating the demographic explosion and at learning from the experience of those peripheries which have succeeded in liberating themselves from subjection and backwardness.[220] This facilitates the exaggerated but not completely unwarranted conclusion of the critics that some peace and development students are interested in neither bringing to light the real causes of conflict and backwardness, nor in elaborating means for overcoming these ills. Rather, they prefer to use them for abstract naive calls for justice. According to the critics, such calls are frequently counter-productive to the efforts to establish the specifics and necessity of peace research as an independent discipline. True enough, they lack any scientific foundation or political importance[221] Instead, they are oriented to strengthen radical political attitudes unacceptable even to socialist and pacifist students and activists.[222]

The growing objections to approaches of many peace and development students are raised because they use ambiguous terminology and employ such terms as "structural violence" instead of "class" or "party elite" dominance.

True enough, there are no—at least for the time being—ideal social structures that do not require coercive measures to combat crime. Structural violence which uses such means to uphold law and order is therefore a necessity. In some cases it is necessary to oppose "structural violence" when it represents the despotic regimes like those of Hitler, Stalin or Idi Amin. To struggle against them by any means is not only moral but even legitimate. However, some peace and development researchers and among the latter especially the partisans of a new International Military Order, prefer to speak against the use of force no matter for what purpose.[223] This leads to negation of the use of force even to protect justice and democracy and of the right of nations to defend themselves against threats of subjugation and annihilation and contradicts even the views of renowned leaders of the Communist Movement.[224]

To condemn all use of force means to abandon finally the right of self-defense and the right to act against aggression. Not only does this terminate *ius ad bellum* recognized in these cases, but this also destroys principles of *ius in bello*. Specifically, it means the acceptance of the criticism of the Nuremberg principles of punishment of criminals guilty of Nazi war and other crimes and the rejection of the premise that force is sometimes indispensable and justified for the defense of the community against those who are bent on destroying it.[225] This also results in the glorification of terrorism and anarchy.[226]

Boulding most probably had this in mind when he criticized Galtung's disregard of all hierarchies. He was inclined to identify armed forces and the use of force in general with methods and means of oppression on the one hand and with the same means applied without any restraint in the struggle against injustice,[227] on the other hand.

Some peace and development researchers completely ignore this fact and support changes of humanitarian law which contradict the needs of the law of war-avoidance and conflict-resolution.[228] They even ridicule the assumption that in the nuclear era and on the threshold of their post-colonial development the industrialized countries have become peace-oriented.[229]

Hence, they dismiss A. Lewis' thesis and A. Gallaher's similar conclusions deriving from his interpretation of underdevelopment based on the concept of "traditionalism." They also totally reject the previously mentioned Rostowian model and all other developmental models, including those underlining the role of individual motivation and the need for achievement.[230] That is why they concentrate on underdevelopment as an exclusive product of exploitation and militarism . They speak about the Third World subjection to the European imperialists throughout all the ages of modern history and they have come to the conclusion that there is a positive interrelationship only between socialism and development.[231] However, this conclusion has only very little to do—not only with the reality of the Socialist Bloc—but with the policies of the TW leaders as well. The latter, like the Eastern-Europeans, are eager to obtain both technology and bread in the West, while the USSR, looks for opportunities to continue its expansion.

It might therefore be paradoxical to point out that J. Galtung, who is reckoned among the most brilliant popularizers of the dependency and similar theories, recently has not hesitated to recall that the most important and pioneering contribution to peace-thinking and to organizational undertakings for the sake of human security has been made by Western civilization.[232] It also seems right to ascribe to the West the comparatively low impact of the action-reaction criterion on its policies even in cases of high international tension,[233] as it has been evidently demonstrated following the seizure of the American Embassy in Teheran. It is cardinally opposed to that of bureaucratic momentum, ideological dogmatism and aggressiveness which are extremely strong in the communist decision-making. It is also very contrary to the politics of the Third World, divided by deadly quarrels and characterized by impulsive actions and ultimative postulates.

We know very little about the Soviet hawks in the Politburo, the army and military technocracy. However, by comparison even with our very limited knowledge of their activities, quite radical writers like Reid[234] have serious doubts about the correctness of Pilisiuk and Hayden's description of the American society as a military-industrial complex, encompassing all strata of the population and therefore, in this respect, surpassing their "socialist" partners.

The weakness of the dependency theorists lies not only in the above-mentioned simplification. They offer no explanation as to why some neo-colonial countries are more liberal than the others, some more authoritarian, some civilian, some military, some peacefully oriented, some aggressive. According to them, they all are underdogs dominated by core forces in the international economy.[235] One of the recent exponents of such views,

I. Wallerstein, argues that the development of capitalism beginning in the fifteenth century entailed, by its nature, the formation of a core, semi-periphery and periphery, which resulted in the present international division of labor responsible for the weakness, backwardness and exploitation of the Third World.[236] This heavy stress on international constraints does not take into account the internal forces and natural resources in explaining regime and economy types of different Third World countries. After all some of them have currently become topical factors in the economic life of the world and in the political situation of various regions.

By and large, national systems are not merely offshoots of the world order (and the latter is not merely an expression of domestic structures), but they are a cause of forces interacting in both of them. True enough, the dependency theorists are not the only ones exploring the impact of the international system—of course, not always a negative one—upon domestic politics, upon types of regime and economy, institutions, coalitions, their ends and means. By the way, only some of them stress the role of international economy, others merely pay attention to the political-military rivalry or to war-preparedness and armed conflicts of both national and international character.

Among the former, together with dependency theorists, are some representatives of the Gerschenkronian school with their arguments, to some extent similar to the Leninist assumption, about the late industrialization as a factor pushing towards expansion and dominance by use of force.[237] The latter, too, pay little attention to the role of internal factors. They have pinpointed the fate of Germany after two world wars, of the Republican Spain or the Soviet Revolution and the fate of Italy after 1943 and of Austro-Hungary in 1918, produced, according to them, above all by the external causes.

Needless to stress, the fate of the People's Democracies after WWII and the Prussian reforms and military growth in the former century, the Zinoviev letter and British elections of 1924 and the US declaration of war after Pearl Harbor only strengthen their argumentation. However, all these events illustrate how international politics and domestic structures affect each other.[238]

Thus, considering this fact, many liberal economists and students of international economic relations frequently stress the role of interdependence.[239] Some neo-mercantilists, state-oriented Marxists[240] and partisans of the primacy of world order issues do the same. But this also characterizes various critics of the doctrines on the exclusivity or fundamental importance of domestic structures in the formation of foreign policy[241] or on the role of leadership.[242]

By and large, those who stress the primacy of all kinds of external factors in the shape of the world system suffer no less from reductionism than the dependency theorists and than other partisans of the superiority of exogenous forces who underrate or negate completely the impact of internal forces.

Peter Gourevitch succeeded better than anybody else in showing through a critical review of all relevant modern theories the growing interaction of domestic and external factors in the shape and role of politics on national and international levels. This interaction is a result of the increasing interdependence of all nations which exists in spite of the state's ability somehow to limit or control various transnational actors.

The fact is that multinational and transnational enterprises and other agents of "group interests" acting beyond the state borders may actually have greater economic power and control of resources and frequently of decision-making than the majority of individual members of the community of nations. Actually these agents of "group interests" are non-governmental only in a constitutional sense. All this does not contradict the former assumptions on the power of multinationals and on the intertwining of all kinds of internal and external factors also in issues of peace and war.[243]

That is why Gourevitch seems to be entirely right to me in concluding that the international system is not merely a consequence of domestic politics and structures. It also produces these structures and this remains relevant with regard to the governmental and non-governmental levels and to their impact on world security and the role of the TW in this matter. This is one reason more why any analysis of international relations and internal politics can be relevant and useful if they are viewed simultaneously and treated as wholes.[244]

It goes without saying that there have always been many component parts of growth and backwardness and of their impact on peace and policies of war. Hence, it has been an illusion to suppose that the balance sheet can be either brief or straight.[245] Actually, it is impossible to understand them in isolation and it is erroneous to maintain that the interrelationship of underdevelopment and world security is simple.

It is well known that today the dominant forms of nationalism and frequently not only in the most developed countries do not place the highest priority on increasing the state's power or wealth through exploitation of other nations.[246] In the First World and to a much lesser extent in the Second World, too, the stress is put on scientific, technological, managerial and administrative progress.[247] However, some parts of the Third World do not yet share this tendency and prefer to believe in self-reliance because they have been disappointed by the meager results of the transfers. Yet the growing need for a renewed analysis of power as competence and not only as dominance[248] is far from being accidental. This happens in various parts of the globe, including the important segments of the TW. Many experts connect this phenomenon with the approach of the post-industrial phase of the world's development and with the TW's attempts to use all means to improve its miserable situation. Hence, there is also an increasing interest in obtaining strength through appropriate politics and in information about politics. This, in its turn, requires some knowledge of the politics of information. Its shape and role in any society and especially its impact on regional and world security cannot be understood in isolation from that society's economic and political system.[249] This has been blatantly illustrated by the events in the Middle East on the eve of the October War and not to a lesser extent by the case of the Soviet occupation of Afghanistan.

These facts, too, but first and foremost the method of simultaneous analysis of internal and external politics viewed in their interrelationship, as a whole, can shed more light on the interaction between (under)development and world security. It can also facilitate a better understanding of advantages and realities of the the idea of a collective economic security system as a factor of war-prevention and peace-building. Masao Kunihiro called this method intermestic which is a cross between international and domestic.[250] In our days of disappearing distance and increasing mutual dependency, whatever is happening outside national boundaries is bound to affect our situation at home, directly or indirectly, with various degrees of intensity and within varying periods of time. Similarly, developments on our domestic front are bound to affect world affairs, no matter how small or great our country is. Some countries are affected more fundamentally and immediately than others, but none seems to be free from its impact.

The intermestic approach is therefore also required for a proper analysis of the subject matter of this study and for drawing the proper conclusions.

6. The Idea of Economic Collective Security

Some of the above-quoted doctrines and findings may still seem not sufficient enough to accept or reject entirely various hypotheses and to justify various conclusions of this study.

It may still be necessary to make a further assessment, first and foremost, of data proving that low military burdens are always associated with markedly superior social development performance, or that such high burdens or rates can never be associated with such development.

Most of the relevant investigations, however (those already quoted above and others[251]—with the exception and that only to some extent, of the above-mentioned writings of E. Benoit and Gavin Kennedy) prove beyond any doubt that social welfare expenditures decrease following the growth of defense budgets. They also do not leave much room for doubt as to the dangers of the continuing arms race and arms transfers, nuclear and conventional,[252] in different regions[253] and on global scale as well.[254] These dangers are particularly great in the Middle East.[255] However, the arms race has nefarious economic, political and military implications elsewhere, too. Unfortunately, it is very difficult to halt it or even merely to control it and to prevent the continual perfection and proliferation of arms.[256]

Hence, the continuing effort to use the relative calm in different areas for the sake of a systematic change which will promote more development. Efforts are also made to use multifarious old and new means and strategies to further the cause of peace.[257]

The Indian S. Dasgupta, the Egyptian B. Boutros-Ghali and the German E.O. Czempiel, as well as other eminent peace researchers from different countries, have often pointed out that wars and actually any armed conflicts, produce the greatest injustice; they make the mighty richer and stronger while reducing the bulk of the Third World to penury; therefore these ugly events must be avoided at all costs.[258]

No wonder, therefore, that not only scholars, moralists, philosophers, religious leaders and other public figures, but also renowned statesmen of various political orientations devoted a lot of thought to policies of disarmament and to humanitarian principles which they regarded as factors of greatest importance to war-avoidance.

Finally, the crop of international legal documents concerned with different aspects of this issue, beginning with the Geneva Convention of 1864, the Hague Conventions of 1899 and 1907 and ending with the Covenant of the League of Nations, the Briand-Kellog Pact of 1928, the UN Charter and the recent relevant enactments and resolutions, is far from being poor.[259]

Among the most important agreements reached in the last thirty years are: the Antarctic Treaty, the Treaty Banning Nuclear Weapons in the Atmosphere, in Outer Space and Under Water, the Treaty on Principles Governing the Activities of States in the Exploration and Use of Outer Space Including the Moon and Other Celestial Bodies, the Treaty for the Prohibition of Nuclear Weapons in Latin America, the Treaty on the Non-Proliferation of Nuclear Weapons, the Treaty on the Prohibition of the Emplacement of Nuclear Weapons and other Weapons of Mass Destruction in the Seabed and the Ocean Floor and the subsoil. Thereof, the Convention on the Prohibition of the Development, Production and Stockpiling of Bacteriological (Biological) and Toxin Weapons and on Their Destruction, and the Convention on the Prohibition of Military or Any Other Hostile Use of Environmental Modifications.

To this list we must add the conventions concerned with humanitarian law, with the punishment of war criminals as well as many bilaterial arrangements, like the two Soviet-American agreements on the limitation of strategic arms and on the limitation of underground nuclear tests (i.a., SALT I) the agreements on the prevention of nuclear wars concluded by the USSR with the US, France and Great Britain and the Israeli-Egyptian Peace Treaty of 1978.

All these documents, as well as the Helsinki-Belgrade-Madrid documents and recommendations and numerous resolutions of the UN and other international organizations and conferences, governmental and non-governmental alike, not only have helped to improve the international climate and to create the atmosphere of détente. They also have diminished the risk of an armed conflict between the superpowers and of other forms of East-West confrontations. However, they have not put an end to the East-West rivalry, particularly strong in the periphery, which is liable to trigger a global catastrophic clash. This clash is quite possible, the more so since the political détente has not been accompanied by effective measures of military disengagement and at least gradual disarmament and has not stopped arms transfers. The UN 1978 Special Disarmament Session also has not changed the situation. The further developments in nuclear and conventional weapons technology have daily increased the threat to the survival of the human race, while the negative impact of the Soviet intervention in Afghanistan on détente and especially on prospects to better the TW's condition at the expense of military budgets cannot be denied any longer.

There are two main doctrines trying to explain this deplorable situation. One, viewed as a rationalist or classical, argues that the goal of security is the defense of the state against actual or potential enemies; and in the present international system of ideological and political controversies this leads to permanent weapons development and weapons acquisition. The other one asserts that weapons development dictates a strategic model of the "military-industrial complex" which only serves to justify concurrent or subsequent acquisition.[260] The two approaches are the starting point of the deterrence doctrine, which currently prevails both in the West and East and produces the vicious circle preventing the superpowers and their allies from leaving the path of war and starting peace-building. It goes without saying that this doctrine strengthens the dangers rooted in the indigenous conflict-productive forces of the Third World. However, since the Third World permanently suffers from the consequences of backwardness, malnutrition and starvation and its shape and artificial unity are a result of the search for remedies for its ills, no wonder that many of its leaders continue to make a reasonable assumption that disarmament may release funds necessary for reducing the socio-economic penury of the LDCs—a central issue in present-day world politics.

Needless to stress once more, for many poor countries the program of a New International Economic Order is more political than economic. This is true at least in the sense that bloc-voting in the UN and other international organizations and conferences and ostentatious declarations by groups of poor countries are almost the only means they have of pressing visibly for favorable—for them—decision-making in the West and not infrequently—although still in a very limited form—in the East as well.

By and large, all functional international economic rules are only a complementary set to the underlying political and military security relations and it is wrong to maintain the contrary. Economists, too, often tend to ignore the fact that the favored by them functional management of economic relations among nations is related to the consequences of power or other kind of politics. Actually, the search for international economic security is strongly linked to and even based on, considerations of military security and international political relations and not vice versa.[261]

However, this assumption has been frequently blurred, not less than another thesis, namely, that there is no basic contradiction between traditionality and modernization, and that the latter must not entirely erase the former or always lead to a contest between them.[262]

The UN General Assembly pointed out already in 1971 (Resolution No. 2880(XXVI) of 21 December 1971) that there is a close link between the efforts to strengthen international security, disarmament and development; and that it is also necessary to build a system of collective economic security that would actually be an essential part of the struggle for peace.

True enough, the decisions of international organizations and conferences establishing the said link, as well as considerations on the interrelationship between peace and humanity's well-being are already generations old; they can be traced to the Holy Scriptures of all religions and to the utopian writings since antiquity till the present time, as we have already pointed out in another context in the introductory remarks to this study.

We have mentioned there that in different forms they continue to be an important topic of discussions in the UN. They are frequently raised on every opportunity of negotiating conventional and nuclear arms control, arms limitations and disarmament. They are topical in the debates on issues directly relating to the basic contemporary socio-economic anomalities and pains, particularly acute in various parts of the Third World that have the lowest income per capita. They are blatantly reflected in the Brandt Report, in documents of the 1980 Special Session of the UN General Assembly convened to deal with the global problems of economic cooperation in the documents prepared for the UN Conference on the Situation in the LDCs scheduled for September 1, 1981, and for the Paris summit meetings on this subject foreseen on August 27 and 28 1981, and in constitutions of many international organizations.

The UNESCO Constitution states that wars are made in the minds of men. It is frequently stressed that in one sense, of course, this statement is indisputable. If the hatred of war, the reluctance to use power to solve disputes between individuals and nations, the wish to abandon any form of violence in human relations were absolute and universal, there would be no wars. True enough, human nature and, above all, human instinctive behavior frequently make war possible, but they are not its cause. It goes without saying that the view that militarism and all ensuing conflicts are biologically determined cannot stand serious scrutiny; in principle they are a product of human condition, a social phenomenon, an outcome of the shape and evolution of various human relationships; and as regards foreign policy and its instrument—wars—they are, first and foremost, an expression of the relevant societies.Of course, war is frequently caused by outside factors and decided upon as a programmed response to what other nations do or are expected to do in contradiction to our interests and goals.[263]

Recently we can notice a tendency in the study of peace (as pinpointed by D. Senghaas[264]) to give priority to the individual's aggressive behavior in explaining social and political conflagrations. This tendency is a result of frustration but, indeed, it is very alarming. After all, it reminds the biological approach of K. Lorenz,[265] which was ruthlessly exploited by the Nazis. To some extent it also follows the thinking of Machiavelli, Luther, Malthus and, especially, Hobbes; but today more than ever before it is devoid of any scientific basis,[266] despite various tragic events in days of war and terror that make us see men as bloodthirsty wolves.

But none of the past and present atrocities can blur the facts showing the growth of humanitarian and cooperative, friendly and even fraternal relationship on the individual and some collective (including national) levels. This is one reason more for justifying the rejection of the misleading assumption, still voiced here and there, on the biological roots of poverty or on the priority to be given to the struggle against misery as a means of international security.

Poverty is, of course, frequently a cause of injustice, suffering and misery, but it is also a cause of weakness and therefore, in spite of all denying this fact theories, can never be a threat to world peace.[267] However, these outlooks, too, are reflected in numerous international and, especially, UN documents, and clearly only because of the impact of poor nations' growing majority on the bodies requested to elaborate them.

The above-quoted UN resolution is only one of many other declarations pinpointing the problem. Needless to stress, only when the process of political decolonization has started, the misery of the majority of post-colonial states was "discovered" and the gap between them and the industrial nations (unfortunately, in many cases still continually growing) was made public knowledge. As for development assistance it has been sometimes unveiled as an instrument of new forms of exploitation benefiting the donors. The issue then was introduced to various international fora and, finally, there was a cry for remedy coined as "collective economic security." However, this terminology conceals the fact that the attainment of the latter actually and only depends on the building of collective political and military security.

The UN Secretary-General's note of 19 March 1973 (Doc. E/S 263), the Preamble to the "Strategy for Development," the papers on "Disarmament and Development," the UN Secretary-General's report of 21 June 1973 presented at the fifty fourth session of the Economic and Social Council and other documents quoted in the Introduction to this study, rightly stress that security cannot be achieved when the bulk of world capital, human talent and manpower is used for destruction—not construction.

Actually, this has already been said, although in diverse forms, in the Preamble to the Peace of Westphalia of 1648 and more specifically in the Covenant of the League of Nations, in its different resolutions and particularly in the Preamble to the UN Charter and in its different dispositions.

The idea of collective economic security doubtless can be even traced directly to the formulation of the Charter's principles and purposes. Unlike this document, however, some fairly well-balanced, recent UN and other international organizations' resolutions—like some scientific enquiries and press comments[268]—emphasize the link between the proposals on economic collective security and the demand to reconstruct radically and forcibly the present world system—with the aim to establish a New International Economic Order. These resolutions reverse the priorities and avoid saying the essential, namely, that progress in solving socio-economic problems is only possible in a peaceful world where hatred and bloodshed no longer exist or are reduced to a minimum. Unfortunately, peace and harmony will hardly be achieved without bringing to an end strategies labelled in Soviet literature as "international class struggle," strategies which breed fear and endless action-reaction policies, an incessant arms race, tensions and tendencies that turn the Third World into an arena of turmoil and conflicts.

As we have already mentioned in another context, the concept of collective economic security seems to us rather dubious as an instrument of advancing solutions to painful socio-economic problems of the really wretched parts of our globe. Being purely economic in its essence, it may at best assist in focusing on the humanitarian aspects of the struggle against poverty or it may have a bargaining value in negotiations for more development aid from the West. It can also save the East and the TW "nouveaux riches" from trouble.

Still the concept seems rather dubious to us if its purpose is to go down to the real socio-economic roots of the problem and not merely to focus on its humanitarian aspects and bargaining value in negotiations for more development assistance.

However, consider only the failures of economism in both Western and Eastern integration efforts,[269] the non-economic factors of overcoming stalemate and regression situation in some Third World countries,[270] non-economic motivations of détente[271]; and then it would not be too complicated to point out the persuasive force of conclusions opposite to those relating to the postulates of collective economic security; and the rationale of all those claiming that the latter can only be a function and result of building a system of political security. Hence, there is a call to base political economy on politics instead of economics and to move from non-politics to politics.[272] This seems to be fairly justified, the more so since it seems quite reasonable to admit that different and sometimes dangerous conflicts may break out even when the goals and program of economic collective security are achieved. The reason why this might happen is that the majority of international conflicts have not been rooted in economics at all.[273]

However, the idea of economic collective security is far from being an expression of parochial approaches, like some dependency or structural violence theories.[274] It is based on many true findings and reasonable hypotheses and conclusions. Its weakness, therefore, mainly lies in the reversal of priorities. It is also tied to the fact that many researchers find it difficult to admit that any progress towards more security and hence welfare, too, depends on political and not on economic decisions no matter how immense and frequently almost decisive their impact on politics is.

It, therefore, seems fair to say that whether peace or war would pay does not depend on economic gains, a secondary factor in comparison with those of political, national or military character.[275] Hence, the importance of stressing once more that the belief that the NIEO can be achieved through building a NIMO is purely an abstract and misleading simplification.

Certainly we cannot doubt the multiplicity of motivations for the arms race. They are or were different for Saudi Arabia, Iraq, the pastmonarchist Iran, Libya of today or Egypt and Israel in the pre and past and present on the one hand, and for the Philippines, Thailand, Ethiopia, Somalia, Sudan, Mozambique, Angola, or for various mini-states, on the other. There are also, of course, many different methods and ways of explaining the dramatical turn towards peace in Egyptian politics. However, in all of these and other TW conflictual cases we could detect at least some of the grass-roots of the wrong concept of collective economic security.

It is also worthwhile to point out in this context that economic causes are rare as regards the origins of international conflicts; but they are very important in any process nearing their end. It is quite easy to illustrate this hypothesis i.a. by the recent metamorphosis of the Egyptian politics.

However, the efforts directed towards the creation of a New International Military Order as an instrument of the NIEO have nothing to do with any kind of steps able to facilitate the end of conflicts. On the contrary, like the efforts exclusively based on the concepts of structural violence, dependency, and the call "all or nothing" which often means nothing if not worse than nothing,[276] the work for the establishment of the NIMO seems to us to be detrimental both to the struggle against underdevelopment and to the world security.

This hypothesis, also, requires a more detailed elaboration; but it cardinally differs from those trends in development and peace research that merely represent an attempt to use scientific methodology to support pacifism and socio-economic progress in the Third World.[277] This attempt is based on the right conviction that from any point of view misery, backwardness and war are intolerable, a conviction which neither helps to understand the bitter facts, nor to eliminate them.

It will be unreasonable to deny that there even is a close relation between the misuse of wealth and economic inequalities on the one hand and the spirit which, with the progress in education, leads to social conflicts and sometimes to war, on the other hand. By and large, in various national and international circumstances the greed for wealth can ultimately end in strife and war.[278] This does not mean, however, that the poverty-stricken nations are most likely to initiate wars. True enough, only power, sometimes only economic power, knowledge and different other kinds of wealth and other qualities enable nations to fight. If the poor, tempted by the spectacle of luxury, sometimes might be prepared to embrace a warrior ideology, they do it rather in order to improve their bargaining position than to attack the mighty. They also do it because they believe that in ending underdevelopment, effective "development of development" is an indispensable condition of peace, trade and other forms of mutually beneficial co-operation that in our nuclear era are not less necessary for the rich and strong than for the poor and weak.

The bulk of literature on political development considers it in terms of bringing to an end foreign intervention, real or imaginary and old-fashioned but actually dying out models of western imperialism. However, its essence, in terms of social mobility, cultural values, real socio-economic progress and pluralist democracy, seems to lie, above all, in the institutionalization and strengthening of the latter[279]; it also might depend on preventing the "new egalitarianism" from developing into a form which would closely resemble the old, purely formal, nation-state equality. It seems that in order to achieve this, the socio-economic development must not simply attack disparities in wealth and power *per se*. Rather, it has to be directed against the particular form of disparity which deepens the misery and humiliation of the masses in some countries while at the same time enriching other nations, be they partners of the Western, Communist or the so-called non-aligned blocs or simply groupings of the "underdeveloped" oil-magnates.[280]

If we take into account the implications created by the nuclear threat and the proclamations by the rich and powerful about their adherence to the principle of equal sharing and, more significantly, that they regard it to be in their own national interest – not only the time seems to be ripe, but circumstances are favourable to build a truly international new egalitarrianism.[281] The latter must be based not on altruism, philanthropy and other veiled forms of exploitation, but on need, on legitimate expectations, the respect for human rights and on inevitable national and international remedies necessary for assuring our survival.[282] Before concluding our observations on the blueprints of collective economic security, it may be useful–in addition to the latter argumentation–to corroborate some problems we discussed previously. There are usually five accepted explanations of conflict and arms race. They point out: 1) imperial and national rivalries, power politics and expansionist schemes; 2) security dilemmas caused by aggressive and rapacious policies of neighbours and other parties; 3) the system of competition and ideological or religious enmity; 4) profit or vested interest and 5) the technological momentum.[283]

According to renowned experts, the Southern solidarity will probably not withstand the centrifugal forces within the coming years.[284] The 1980s quarrels within individual countries or between many African and other TW states are likely to erupt into violent conflicts. This can frequently occur as a result of communal–tribal and subnational–antagonism and in the form of civil or inter-state wars with or without involvement of foreign political or transborder military intervention; but all of them show tendencies towards escalation.[285]

It is enough to consider all this in order to understand how multifarious are the causes of conflicts, how various are their faces and forces driving the arms waves into the Third World, nowadays the major arena of armed collisions.

It is true, the superpowers and their allies have different economic and strategic interests at stake in the Third World. The West tries to prevent the USSR there from establishing itself as a dominant military actor and to ensure that it is not deprived there of access to important resources; the Soviets look for military facilities in order to counteract the West's and China's influence. They act directly or indirectly with the help of Cuba, East Germany and other "allies", including various remnants of anticolonial, national-liberation and revolutionary movements.

However, any effort to build also a collective economic security system seems to be deemed to fail at least for the time being and this not less in consequence of the East-West rivalry than of the South-South conflicts and quarrels. Hence, there is the need not to limit ourselves in any inquiry on security problems to the analysis of the generally established motivations of encounters and of arms hikes. Not less important is the need to see that there is no necessary connection between disarmament proposals (for instance, the Soviet ones)[286] and the goal of disarmament and development aid as tools of foreign policy.

Some experts even maintain that it is enough to read Dedring's book on the recent advances in peace research[287] to be convinced that the relevant studies have discovered no evidence, neither from history or economy, nor from the individual or group psychology, of any connection between violence (and especially international wars) and power or wealth.

It is possible to say the same about the frequent lack of connection between foreign trade and exploitation and dominance, even in colonial form, after reading the books of Eberlein and Reichel,[288] Calvez[289] or Albertini.[290] This can also be said on the belief that with the attainment of economic security, justice and disarmament all conflicts will be resolved, as it derives from the conclusions of the "Western" student Hinsaw and the "Southern" one, Kumar.[291]

One might paraphrase B. Moore's statement and say—in contradiction first and foremost to the Communist belief in the importance of trade to strengthening peace-oriented policies—that any form of exchange of goods and services is a kind of exploitation and a degree of coercion.[292] If this is so, then Senghaas' postulate that the only way to save the LDCs from dependence is their disassociation from other parts of the world, may seem be right.[293] This view, however, not only contradicts the tendencies of all TW leaders to strengthen their commercial and other ties with the industrialized countries, to increase and make more effective the latters' development aid; it also contradicts their efforts to get from them various preferences and to break their protectionist policies that restrict the access of TW products to their markets. This position is also entirely opposed to the growing willingness of the West to meet the essential requirements of the Third World,[294] also because it is apprehensive of its dependence on the South, which for the time being, at least in some matters, is greater than the South's dependence on the North.[295]

It may also be worthwhile to stress in this context that many East-European students find it necessary to point out the importance of trade in the struggle for a New International Economic Order. They regard it as one of the proper amelioration methods to be realized in a complicated, gradual and rather long-term process.[296] This view contradicts the conclusions of some of their Western colleagues who regard the NIEO as the only proper instrument for a rapid solution of the LDC's painful problems and for helping them to become equal partners in the world system.[297] Thus, these Western scholars ignore the fact that any equality of treatment in a society of radical inequalities both national and international can only lead to discrimination in favor of the stronger. They also disregard the fact that the commitment to development does not always lead to a greater measure of justice and equality[298]; and they tend to ignore the fact that multinational corporations, if pressed to act against their own interests, are capable of giving up all their investments in the Third World and of compensating themselves through inner investments. Such a development may, no doubt, be a catastrophe for the Third World. By and large, these corporations do not necessarily counteract various trends favorable to the NIEO. Not infrequently they operate as an instrument of rationalisation of the world economy, not passing over any of its parts.[299] We have already quoted the opinion of the Marxist scholar Emmanuel about the role of the transnationals in promoting the process of modernization of the Third World. Even some of their strongest critics do not deny that their activities have to be also considered as a stage in the historical process of internationalization of capital and labor. They have already started to tighten their co-operation with Communist countries.[300] They are rarely concerned with arms manufacture—in principle owned or controlled by the states. What is more, they sometimes even manifest their interest in the reduction of armaments. In this way they increase development undertakings, making them more practical, possible and of course, profitable.[301]

It will be difficult if not impossible to advance the proposals for a collective economic security system if their adherents in politics and scholarly studies continue to disrespect the above-mentioned facts. We agree that they seem paradoxical, but nevertheless they are undeniable.

True enough most students of peace and development differ fundamentally from strategic analysts. While the latters' goal is to assert the hegemony or victory of one party over the other, the former perceive the problem in terms of socio-economic and human values and needs. But this approach does not mean consensus on all matters. The minimalists first and foremost try to contribute to the elimination of violence and to prevention of international wars. In their opinion, the realization of even only this task may open the road not only to a stronger economic collective security, but to a political security as well. In considering the present animosities on the world scale, they do not reject even the deterrence strategy. According to these empirists, it may facilitate a gradual arms and troops control, a gradual and finally complete disarmament and reduction of armed forces, whose numbers today surpass the number of teachers in the world. This, they believe, will lead to the reduction of gigantic military expenditures which today are equivalent to a yearly national income of the poorer half of mankind and the money will be spent instead on combatting hunger and backwardness.

The goal of other students of peace research, is not only to establish the methods of war-prevention, but also to elaborate the methods of preventing any kind of violence. They conceive the deterrence strategy as being entirely mistaken. Not only do they doubt its possible contribution to war-avoidance, but they view it as an instrument of militarization which facilitates coercion and restriction of individual and national freedom. And, in considering the continual progress of military technologies as the root-cause of the present arms race, they focus on the growing threat to peace produced by it.

Hence, they are predominantly interested in studying the best ways to a continual reduction and final elimination of all aspects of militarization.

By and large, their perception of militarism is frequently very simplistic. They regard militarism as merely an instrument of the giant nuclear powers' struggle for world dominance and neo-colonial presence. They regard it as superpowers' expression of reliance on force, authoritarian regimes and economic subjection. They view militarism as entirely detached from its causes in the Third World, both in its poor and its rich, oil-producing parts.[302]

However, although the world today is politically polarized, their findings may little by little not only influence non-governmental organizations, but some governmental elites, too. Still, we cannot doubt the difficulties of strengthening peace in this way or building a collective economic security.[303]

Another group of peace researchers admits that real peace is unattainable without basic structural change, with the use of force, in both national and international systems. That is why they give preference to revolutionary activities over scientific enquiry, although they define their work not only as consciousness-raising but as truth-finding as well.[304] This approach actually means the renunciation of both the pure scholarly and applied approaches to the problem and the choice of the utopian,[305] if not the scholastic dogmatic road.[306] This approach was strongly criticized by many Marxists, too. They said it favored the use of a terminology based on "empty boxes."[307] In practice, it often meant giving up any specific effort in favor of propaganda.[308] This can lead neither to the construction of a politically and militarly reasonable world order, nor to the creation of a collective economic security system. It is actually opposed to the desirable and feasible goals of the gradualists. The latter have already been more than enough disappointed by the Soviet-like experiments. They are very much frustrated and even shocked by the uncertainties of the age of nuclear progress, economic crisis and authoritarian tendencies. They therefore prefer a realistic, at least in the short run, activity for progress towards both development and peace, a progress step by step.

Notes

1. R. Higgins, *Economic Development*, II ed., N.Y., 1968, pp. 209-266, and see the criticism of R.J. Barnet of this approach, in his *Roots of War*, Penguin Books, Baltimore, 1973, p. 5.

2. Cf. with Kwesi Botchwey's remarks in the *International Peace Research Newsletter*, No. 1/1978, p. 28 and J.K. Nyerere's concept of self-reliance in his *Freedom and Socialism*, New York, 1970.

3. See A. Rappaport's conclusions in *American Thinking About Peace and War*, edit. by K. Booth and M. Wright, The Harvester Press, Sussex, 1978, and also see S. Marks, "Development and Human Rights," *BPP*, No. 3/977, p. 245-6.

4. For more details on this hypothesis see I. Sachs, Patterns of Public Sector in Underdevelopment Economies, Bombay, 1964.

5. G. Caire, "Ideologies du Dévéloppement," *RTM*, No. 57/974, p. 24.

6. P. T Bauer, *Economic Analysis and Policy of Underdeveloped Countries, Cambridge Univ. Press, 1957.*

7. Cf. with the conclusions of I. Illich in M. Bohnet, Das Nord-Sued Problem, Müchen, Piper, 1971, p. 197 and ff.

8. H. Singer and J. Ansari, *Rich and Poor Nations*, G. Allen and Unwin, London, 1977, pp. 141-2.

9. For a more detailed analysis of this problem and the relevant documents see, i.a., K.P. Sauvant and H. Hasenpflug, (ed.), *The New International Economic Order*, op. cit passim.

10. G. Desanne de Bernis, "Sous-Dévéloppement. Analyses et Representations," *RTM*, No. 57/1974, p. 111.

11. *Soziales Fortschritt durch Entwicklungshilfe?* herausg. von F. Buettner, Cladius Verlag, München, 1972, p. 40. R.W. Tucker, p. 7 and see R. M. Marini in *Peripherer Kapitalismus*, herausg. O.D. Senghaas, Suhrkampf, Frankfurt, 1974, p. 102.

12. K. Marx, *Das Kapital*, Vol. II, Berlin, 1978, p. 779.

13. E. Mandel, *Folgen einer Theorie. Essays ueber das Kapital von Karl Marx*, Frankfurt, 1967, p. 47.

14. Cf. with F.H. Cardoso's remarks on the simplistic approach to imperialism in Senghaas, *op. cit.*, note 11, p. 227.

15. See the remarks of G. Arrighi, idem, p. 227 and the references of R. Nurkse on the Marxist theories and especially on Barans' approach in Bohnet, *op. cit.*, note 7, p. 65.

16. F. Perroux, "La Methode de l'Economie Générale," in *L,Economie du Sie-'cle*, Presses Un. de France, 1961, p. 511.

17. C. Furtado, *Développement et Sous-Développment*, Presses Univ. de France, 1966, p. 126.

18. Destanne de Bernis, *op. cit.*, p. 108.

19. H. Singer, "The Distribution of Gains between Investing and Borrowing Countries," *American Economic Review*, May 1950, p. 259.

20. R. Prebisch, "Commercial Policy in the Underdeveloped Countries," *American Economic Review*, May 1958, p. 259.

21. B. Herman and J. Tinbergen, *The International Division of Labor. A Quantitative Illustration*, Rotterdam, 1969 and J. Tinbergen and al. *Reshaping the International Order. A Report to the Club of Rome*, New York, 1976.

22. T. Colpaert, "Les Pays en voie de développement et l'opinion traditionelle sur la division du Travail," *Studia Diplomatica*, No. 1/1975, p. 113.

23. G. Myrdal, *Asian Drama: An Inquiry into the Poverty of Nations*, Pantheon Books, 1968.

24. See Naini in *Die Neue Weltwirtschaftsordnung*, herausg. von D. Kebschull, W. Michalski and H.E. Scharrer, Verlag HWWA, Hamburg, 1977, p. 51 and 55 and Kuehne, idem, p. 98.

25. P.T. Bauer and B.S. Yamey, "Against the New Economic Order," *63 Commentary*, No. 4, April 1977, pp. 25ff.

26. P. Bairoch, *The Economic Development of the Third World Since 1900*, Methuen, London, 1975, p. 209, Singer and Ansari, *op. cit.*, p. 26 and also see Jaegeler in Kebschull and all, *op. cit.*, note 24, p. 129.

27. See. f.i., Yochimsen's conclusions in Bohnet, *op. cit.*, note 7, p. 33.

28. See the quotations from Kuznets and Patel in Senghaas, *op. cit.*, note 7, p. 65 and Cardozo, idem, p. 218 and also Stevenhagen, there, pp. 280-290 and Amin, idem, pp. 84-5.

29. A. Emmanuel, *Unequal Change, loc cit.*, and see its critical reappraisal by M. Massarrat, "Die Theorie des Umgleichen Tausches in der Sackgasse," *Die Dritte Welt*, No. 1/1978, p. 41.

30. See, f.i., S. Amin, *L'Afrique de l'Ouest est bloquée*, Paris 1971 and his *L'Accumulation à l'Echelle Mondiale*, Paris, 1972.

31. A.G. Frank, *Lumpenbourgeoisie and Underdevelopment, Dependency, Class and Politics in Latin America*, Monthly Review Press, New York, 1972.

32. Ch. Palloix, *L'Economie Mondiale Capitaliste*, Paris, 1971, Vol. II, p. 55 and ff.

33. See, f.i., S. Amin's remarks on the development path of the USSR in Senghaas, *op. cit.*, note 11, pp. 83-85.

34. For the reexamination of this thesis see i.a., J. Harth in J. Tinbergen, Hersg. *Der Dialog Nord-Sued*, Europ. Verlaganstalt, Koeln-Frankfurt, 1977, p. 30.

35. W. Hoffmann, "Der Baer an der Hintertuer," *Die Zeit*, No. 23, 28 May 1976, pp. 25-26 and cf. with U. Kollatz's remarks on the "Soviet Bloc as Alibi" in his "Entwicklungszusammenarbeit aus Politik und Zeitgeschichte," *Das Parlament, B. 50*, 16 December 78, pp. 17-18.

36. See E. Shils, *Political Development in the New States*, Hague, 1962, p. 75 and cf. M. Mushkat, *Africa: The Transition to Independence* (Hebrew) Bronfman Publishers, Tel Aviv, 1971, pp. 130-131; also see R.C. Horn and J. Hopkins, *The USSR and the Third World*, Chicago Univ. Press, 1974.

37. *UN Monthly Chronicle*, NO. 5/1975, p. 39.

38. T. dos Santos, f.i., is of the opinion that there is no room for hope of promoting scientific development without a basic replacement of private by collective property. See his "Transfer Technologique et dépendence économique," *XIX RTM*, No. 74/1978, p. 398; Kebschull pinpoints the TW states' lack of unity of perceptions and views even as regards the UNCTAD postulates. See Kebschull and al. *op. cit.*, note 24, p. 268.

39. D. Hansen, "The Political Economy of North-South Relations—How Much Change?" *International Organization*, No. 29, 1975, pp. 921-947 and cf. with I. Sachs, "Développement, Utopie, Projet de Société," *XIX RTM*, No. 75/1978, p. 648.

40. A. Broches, "Le Financement du Développement Economique," *Chronique de Politique Etrangère*, No. 4/1967, p. 403 and S. Ringen, "Fruits of the United Nations," *JPR*, No. 2/1974, pp. 55-6.

41. B.G. Gafurov, *Vostok i Sovremennost*, Moscow, 1974, pp. 278 and 284-5.

42. F. Castro, "Oil, Money and Development," *BPP*, No. 1/1975, p. 31.

43. J. Omo-Fudaka, "Development Strategy," *BPP*, No. 2/1974, pp. 147-48 and see also *BPP*, No. 1/1975, p. 31.

44. J. Reuveny, "Development Theory: Marxist Challenge and Non-Marxist Response," *International Problems*, No. 1-2(35), 1979. For a critical reappraisal of different theories of development see I. Roxborough, "Theories of Underdevelopment," Macmillan, London, 1979.

45. D. Lerner, "Modernization—Social Aspects," in *The International Encyclopedia of the Social Sciences*, 1968, pp. 386-95.

46. See, f.i., some of his reconsiderations in W.W. Rostow, *The Diffusion of Power: An Essay in Present History*, Macmillan, New York, 1972 and cf. with Barnet's observations on the Rostowian theories, Barnet, p. 75 and also see J. Coussy, "Les métamorphoses récentes du Discours utopique sur les relations Nord-Sud," *RTM*, No. 75/1978, p. 611.

47. K. Deutsch in S. Rosen's and J.R. Kurth's (ed.), *Testing Theories of Economic Imperialism*, D.C. Heath, Lexington, 1974, pp. 24-30.

48. A. Schueller, "The Failure of Economism in Western and Eastern Integration Policy," *Inter-Economics*, No. 9-10/1978, pp. 227-235.

49. See f.i., *The Fresco on Enlargement*, the document prepared for the European Council of Ministers on 20.IV.1978.

50. Ch. Heimpel, "Enlargement as a Factor Accelerating the Transformation of the European Community," *Lo Spettatore Internazionale*, No. 2/1978, pp. 119-122.

51. G. Buis, "Forces, Armaments et Securite en Méditerrannée," *Politique etrangère*, No. 4/1978, p. 396.

52. C. Bell, *The Diplomacy of Détente*, M. Robertson, London, 1977, particularly the first 5 chapters.

53. Coussy, *op. cit.*, note 46, pp. 601 and ff.

54. D. Kappeler, "Territorialkonflikte in Afrika und die Grundsaetze der Organization der Afrikanischen Einheit," *EA*, No. 17, 10 Sept. 1978, pp. 561-570.

55. *Survival*, vol. XX. No. 6, Nov.-Dec. 1978, pp. 268-9.

56. R.W. Johnson, *How Long will South Africa Survive?* Macmillan, London, 1977.

57. E. Jouve, p. 17.

58. Cf. with W. Bruns' remarks about U. Albrecht's "Ruestungskonversionsforschung," *Das Parlament*, No. 41, 13.X.79, p. 11.

59. See the *SIPRI World Armaments and Disarmament Yearbooks* for 1976-78.

60. For the proper statistics see i.a., *The Military Balances of the Institute for Strategic Studies*, London, 1970-78 and cf. with U. Albrecht, P. Lock and H. Wulf, *Arbeitsplaetze durch Ruestung?* Rohwolt, Hamburg, 1978, p. 8.

61. R. Dahrendorf, "International Power," *Foreign Affairs*, Oct. 1977, p. 76.

62. A. Eessing Cahn, J.J. Kruzel, P.M. Dawkins and J. Huntzinger, *Controlling Future Arms Trade*, McGraw Hill Book Company, New York, 1977, p. 39 and also see "The Declaration of Principles on Disarmament," *BPP*, No. 2/1978, p. 99 and Huisken's observations on the growth of TW hostilities in the "Canberra Seminar," *Neue Zuericher Zeitung*, No. 63, 17 March 1978.

63. D. Senghaas, "Militarism Dynamics in the Contemporary Context of Periphery Capitalism," *BPP*, No. 2/1977, p. 2.

64. *Economic and Social Consequences of the Arms Race*, UN New York, 1972 and *Social Consequences of the Arms Race and its extremely Harmful Effects on World Peace and Security*, Report of the UN Secretary-General, Doc. A/32/88 of 12 August 1977. In addition to *The UN Treaty Series and Proposals Collection*, SIPRI's publications, too, are an excellent source for the proper documents. For a scientific perusal of the problem see i.a., B.v.A. Roeling, "International Law and the Maintenance of Peace," *Netherlands' Yearbook of International Law*, vol. IV, 1973, particularly p. 18 and ff. Also see *The Disarmament and Development Report of the Group of Experts on the Economic and Social Consequences of Disarmament*, UN New York, 1972 and M. Janowitz, *The Military in the Political Development of New Nations*, Chicago, 1964. See also the conclusions of the editors of *The World Military Order*, ed. by M. Kaldor and E. Eide, Macmillan, London, 1979.

65. See, i.a., M. Mushkat, *Theory and Realities of International Relations*, (Hebrew), II ed. Am Oved Publishers, Tel Aviv, 1968, pp. 91, 100, 110 and 126 and see I. Meyers, *Conversion from War to Peace*, Gordon and Breach, New York, 1972 and E.O. Czempiel, *Schwerpunkte und Rolle der Friedensforschung*, Kaiserverlag, 1972, p. 105.

66. *The Middle East in the Year 2000, A Project*, The Association for Peace, Tel Aviv, 1970.

67. P. Lock and H. Wulf, "Ruestung und Unterentwicklung, Aus Politik und Zeitgeschichte," B 18, 5.V.1979 pp. 6-7 and cf. with S.F. Finer, The Man on the Horseback, London 1962 and M. Janowitz, *The Military in the Political Development of New Nations*, Chicago, 1964.

68. For the dogmatic, old-fashioned sovereign-oriented view also on this matter see i.a., the contributions of G. Haraszti, G. Tunkin or A. Kaliadin and A. Gromyko in Doernberg, Galtung, Gromyko, Senghaas (Hrsg.), *Probleme des Friedens, der Sicherheit und der Zusammenarbeit*, Pahl-Rugenstein Verlag, Koeln 1975. For a criticism of the deterrence policies see, i.a., Bartell in R. Beitz and T. Herman, ed. *The Illusion of Security*, Freeman, San Francisco, 1973, p. 275.

69. D. Wolpin, "Militarism, Socialism and Civilian Rule in the Third World," *Instant Research on Peace and Violence*, No. 3-4, 1977, pp. 105-133 and see Steven Wright's observations in the *International Peace Research Newsletter*, No. 1/1978, p. 9.

70. U. Albrecht, D. Enrst, P. Lock and H. Wulf, *BPP*, No. 2, 1971, p. 173.

71. Y.B. Pinatel, "Politique et Securité extérieure en Développement," *Politique Etrangère*, No. 4-5, 1974, p. 444.

72. For new perceptions of Western and Communist imperialism see, i.a. the contributions of quite radical authors, like E. Mandel, L. Basso and others in *Spheres of Influence in the Age of Imperialism*, Spokesman Books, Nottingham, 1972.

73. M. Mushkat, Jr., "The US Defense Purchases," and the same author's

"Defense Spending in the US," *International Problems*, No. 27 and No. 28, 1975, pp. 65 and 68 and his "Defense and Structural Transformation of Industry in Israel," *Co-Existence*, No. 2/1978, pp. 207-18.

74. See the analysis of the arms race following the Korean War in G. Mai, "Westliche Sicherheitspolitik im *Kalten Krieg*", Bospard Verlag, Bospard, 1977 and D.C. Gampert's and A.R. Vershlow's introduction to *Controlling Future Arms Trade* and in its authors observations in G. Cahn and al. *op. cit.*, note 62, pp. 3, 44, 120.

75. See, f.i., the predictions of Alan Newcombe and Frank F. Klassen about the nations being likely to be involved in atrocious wars in the coming years, *International Peace Research Newsletter*, No. 1/1978, p. 10 and K. Jettmar's reappraisal of the South-South conflicts in Buettner, *op. cit.*, note 11, pp. 80..

76. See the SIPRI publication *The Implementation of International Disarmament Agreements*, Stockholm, 1973.

77. See the contradictory conclusions of G. Thayer in his *War Business*, Simon and Shuster, New York 1969 and cf. with Barnet's findings, *op. cit.*, note 1, p. 45 and calculations of V. Perlo, *Militarism and Industry*, Int. Publ. Co., New York, 1963, p. 124), pointing out that only some corporations living from defense budgets profit from the war business.

78. Marx and Engels, *Selected Correspondence*, Foreign Languages Publ. House, Moscow, 1953, pp. 489-500; For details on the few so-called economic wars see, i.a. Renouvin et Duroselle, pp. 86, 153, 157 and also 168.

79. R. Shiratori, *Development and Peace, Peace Research in Japan*, Tokyo, 1973, p. 71 and cf. J. D. Singer, "The Peace Researcher and his Audience," *BPP*, No. 1/1975, p. 68.

80. M. Merle, "Le Système Mondial: Réalité et Crise," *Politique Etrangère*, No. 5/1978, p. 497.

81. H.C.F. Mansilla, "Der Neue Absolutismus. Industrialisierung ohne Demokratie in der Dritten Welt," *Die Dritte Welt*, Vol. 7, No. 4, 1979, p. 523.

82. Barnet, p. 121, see also *International Peace Research Newsletter*, No. 1, 1978, p. 28, Singer and Ansari, op.cit., note 8, p. 46 and Bohnet, Arme und Reiche in Bohnet, *op. cit.*, note 7, pp. 211-12, 246 and ff.

83. S. Decalo, "Military Take-Overs in Africa," *International Problems*, No. 26/1974, p. 80.

84. See M. Mushkat, "The Diffusion of Economic and Military Power and its Impact on the ME Conflict," in D. Carlton and C. Schaerf (ed.), *Arms Control and Technological Innovation*, Croom Helm, London, 1977, pp. 247-254.

85. Ch. Boasson, "International Law, Conflict and Peace Research," *Israel Law Review*, No. 2/1975, p. 178.

86. A. Rothstein, "A Marxist View on Terrorism," *Labour Monthly*, September 1973.

87. Th. Weiss, "The Tradition of Philosophical Anarchism," *JPR*, No. 1/1975, p. 13.

88. J. Galtung and D. Senghaas (ed.), *Kann Europa Abruesten?* Muenchen, 1974.

89. Cf. the figures quoted by the Soviet diplomat V. Issraelyan in *Unitar News*, vol. X, 1978, pp. 12-13 and see *SIPRI*, 1976, 1977 and 1978.

90. *Die Zeit*, No. 42, 2 October 1977, p. 33.

91. See a more detailed analysis of this problem in M. Mushkat, "The Socio-Economic Malaise of Developing Countries as a Function of Military Expenditures: The Case of Egypt and Israel," *Co-Existence*, vol. 15, No. 4/1979, pp. 135-45.

92. H. Askari and V. Corfo, "Economic Implications of Military Expenditures in the Middle East," *JPR*, 1974, p. 341.

93. See *The Military Balance 1970-71*, Institute for Strategic Studies, London, 1970, and *The Military Balance 1975-76*, Institute for Strategic Studies, London, 1975.

94. P. Lock and H. Wulf, "Consequences of Transfer and Military Technology in
the Development Process," *BPP*, No. 2/1977, p. 129.

95. *SIPRI*, 1977, p. 229.

96. *The Economist*, June 28, 1975; *Newsweek*, October 13, 1975; and *The Israeli Statistical Yearbook, 1975*, p. 177. See also P. Rivlin, "The Burden of Israel's Defence," *Survival*, vol. XX, No. 4/July-August 1978, pp. 146-154.

97. *The Israeli Statistical Yearbook, 1975*, pp. 151 and 237. For the analysis of various aspects of the burden of security in the ME see the relevant chapter in Z. Y. Herschlag's *The Economic Structure of the Middle East*, (Brill, Leiden, 1975), in his *The Economic Implications of Peace in the Middle East*, (Horowitz Institute, Tel Aviv, 1973) and his "The Middle East Economy in Transition from War to Peace," in A. Arian (ed.) *Israel—A Developing Economy*, Van Gorcum, Holland, 1979.

98. B. Hansen, "Arab Socialism in Egypt," *World Development*, Vol. 3, No. 4/April 1975, pp. 204-211; see also the same author, "Middle East Development Prospects—What They Look Like in 1973,"in S. S. Alexander (ed.), *The Economies and Politics of the ME*, 1974, p. 4. See Y. Menzly, "The Economic Factor in Egypt's Peace Policy," *International Problems*, vol. XVII, No. 1 (33), Spring 1978, pp. XIX-XXVIII and V. Cygielman in *New Outlook*, Vol. 20, No. 9/1978, pp. 50-52 and 54.

99. S.J. Baker, "The International Political Economy of Proliferation," in D. Carlton and C. Schaerf (eds.), *Arms Control and Technological Innovation*, Croom Helm, London, 1977, pp. 70-101 and D. Dowty, "Nuclear Proliferation— The Israeli Case," *International Studies Quarterly*, March 1978, pp. 17-18. Y. Nimrod, "Atomic Weapons for Israel?" *New Outlook*, No. 5 (184), Sept. 1978, pp. 32-34. Egypt has recently signed the NPT and Israel is reconsidering too its position.

100. *World Armaments and Disarmament, SIPRI Yearbook 1978*, passim.

101. As pointed out by D. Senghaas in his "Militarism Dynamics in the Contemporary Context of Peripheric Capitalism," *BPP*, No. 2/1977, p. 103 and also see similar views in U. Albrecht, *Technology and Militarization of the Third World*, there, p. 125.

102. A. Eide, "Arms Transfer and Third World Militarization," *BPP*, *op. cit.*, p. 104.

103. See W. Raspberry, "Our Own Energy Enemy," *Washington Post*, 20 July 1980 and *Die Zeit*, No. 22, 23 May 1980.

104. P. Lock and H. Wulf, "Consequences of Military Technology on the Development Process," idem, p. 127.

105. M. H. Kaldor, "The Significance of Military Technology," p. 122.

106. G. C. Abbot, "From Rhetoric to Reality," *International Journal*, vol. XXXIV, No. 1. Winter 1978-9, pp. 2, 6, 9 and 13-14.

107. For details see, inter alia, his book *Defence and Economic Growth in Developing Countries*, Lexington Books, Mass. 1973.

108. As presented by him in his publication *The Military in the Third World*, Duckworth and Company, London, 1974.

109. J. Oberg, "The New International Economic and Military Orders as Problems of Peace Research," *BPP*, No. 99, p. 23, passim and there, the same subject as treated by J.Berg, p. 142ff., and see J. Oberg "The International Military Order—The Real Threat to Human Security, An Essay on Global Armament, Structural Militarism and Alternative Security," *Chair on Conflict and Peace Research*, University of Oslo, Paper No. 65 1979.

110. See note 93 and compare with the conclusions of M. D. Wolpin, "Militarism, Socialism and Civilian Rule in the Third World: A Comparison of Development Costs and Benefits," *Instant Research on Peace and Violence*, vol. VII, No. 3-4/1977, pp. 105-134.

111. For another version of this thesis also see M. Mushkat, "Le Tiers-Monde et la Sécurité Internationale," *Etudes Internationales*, vol. IX, No. 4, Dec. 1978, pp. 539-562 and his article "Rueckstaendigkeit, Entwicklungshilfe und Friedensforschung," *Zeitschrift fuer Politik*, vol. XXV, No. 2, June 1978, pp. 194-216.

112. For a new interesting viewpoint on ways to combat poverty see Dr. Albert Tevoedjve's study ("Poverty: Wealth of Mankind," 1980) introduced by Y. Tinbergen and Don Helder-Camara.

113. These figures are quoted from the *GT*, No. 894, 17 June 1979, p. 7.

114. P. Lock and H. Wulf, "Ruestung und Unterentwicklung, Beilage zur Wochenzeitung", *Das Parlament*, B. 18/79, 5 May 1979, passim, note pp. 25-6.

115. Th. dos Santos, "The Structure of Dependence," *American Economic Review*, Papers and Proceedings, vol. 60, May 1970, p. 231.

116. For a more detailed presentation of these views see the collection "Peace, Development and the New International Economic Order," *Proceedings of the 7th IPRA General Conference*, Tampere, 1979, especially part one: "Militarism."

117. See, e.g., P. Streeten's, "Changing Perceptions of Development," *Finance and Development*, vol. 14, September 1977, No. 3, p. 15, and cf. C. Shuhler, R. T. Berendt and P. Baran in M. Bohnet, *Das Nord-Sud Problem, Konflikte zwischen Industrie und Entwicklungslaender*, K. Pipper Verlag, Muenchen 1971, pp. 77, 78 and 89.

118. For a persuasive analysis of this problem see E. P. Stern, (ed.), *The Limits of Military Intervention*, Beverly Hills, London Large Publications, 1977.

119. R. W. Tucker, pp. 39 and 86.

120. Comp. D. W. Orr, "Modernization and Conflict," *International Studies Quarterly*, vol. 21, No. 4, December 1977, p. 594.

121. Cf. H. Ki-Zebro's statement in *Le Monde*, 28 May 1977.

122. For a too glaring but not completely unsubstantiated analysis of this thesis see, inter alia, H. Graf Huyn, *Der Angriff, Der Verstoss Moskaus zu Weltwirtschaft*, Fritz Molden, Wien, 1978.

123. K. Seidl, "Western Nations Reminded of Foreign Aid Commitments," *The German Tribune*, No. 885, 15 April, 1979.

124. For a brief recapitulation of these requirements see, inter alia, *Die Zeit*, No. 17, 20 April 1979.

125. E. Wisdorf, Trade and Aid, *GT*, No. 894, 17 June, 1979, p. 7.

126. See his statement at the Arusha Meeting of the "Group of 77", *D+C*, No. 2/1979, p. 3.

127. See M. Mushkat, "Le Pessimisme dans l'etude des problèmes africains est-il justifié?" *Civilisations*, vol. 22, pp. 285-196, and cf. the conclusions of B. H. Kay, "Kein Grund fuer Entwicklungspessimismus," *E+Z*, No. 12/1978, p. 6.

128. G. Eckstein, "Heading for Apocalypse?" *Dialogue*, vol. 11, 1978, No. 2, pp. 21-26.

129. See the "North-South Dialogue, *GT*, No. 886, 22 June, 1979, p. 2; W. Hofmann, "Die Dritte Welt wird ausgepurt," *Die Zeit*, No. 22, 25 May, 1979 and *Le Monde*, No. 10657, 6 May, 1979.

130. W. van den Wyenbergh, "New GATT Treaty," *GT*, No. 887, 29 April, 1979, p. 6.

131. H. Heck, "New Delhi Conference Leaves Doubts about Bases of Cooperation," *GT*, No. 9241 24 February, 1980, p. 6.

132. F. Nong, *Oil Politics in the 1980s*, McGraw Hill, N.Y. 1978, p. 130.

133. Ch. Bertram, "Moskaus Drang in die Dritte Welt," *Die Zeit*, No. 19, 4 May 1979, p. 3.

134. G. Simonis, *Aussenpolitik und Abschreckung*, Frankfurt, Campus Verlag, 1972, pp. 3, 5 and 186.

135. See S. Kuznets in *The Economic Consequences of the Size of Nations*, edit. by A. Robinson, Macmillan, London, 1960, p.12.

136. For a detailed analysis of many aspects of this assumption see F. Hirsch, *The Social Limits of Growth*, Harvard Univ. Press, 1976.

137. Tucker, pp. 49, 93, 139.

138. In addition to writings examined in Chapter II focusing on the economic causes of wars consult also, inter alia, L. Robbins, *The Economic Causes of War*, London, 1939, the same author's *The Economic Problem in Peace and War: Some Reflections on Objectives and Mechanisms*, 1948 and E.M. Winslow, *The Pattern of Imperialism*, New York, 1948.

139. See, e.g., E. Silberner, *La Guerre et la Paix dans l'histoire des doctrines économiques*, Sirey, 1957, and the polemological literature of the subject focused on economic-demographic approach in the works of G. Bouthoul and R. Carrère (*Le Défi de la Guerre*, 1740-1970, Presses Un. de France, 1976) and their criticism but also some approval by the communist writers, like V. Secares, *Polemologia si Problemele Pacis*, Editura Politica, Bururasti, 1976, particularly pp. 25-30.

140. For a critical reappraisal of a student of these concepts, J. Galtung, see inter alia, H. Holm, "On a Major Event in the Social Sciences," *Cooperation and Conflict*, No. 1. 1978 (reviewing Galtung's *Essays on Peace and Research*, Vol. I-II, Ch. Ejlers, Copenhagen, 1975 and 1977) and M. Mushkat, "Peace Research Reassessed," *International Problems*, vol. XVII, No. 1-2 (35), pp. 11-46.

141. See, e.g., *Tensions Affecting International Understanding*, A Survey by O. Klineberg, Soc. Science Res. Council, 1950.

142. For details see, inter alia, M. Mushkat, *Theory and Practice of International Relations*, (Hebrew), Am Oved Publishers, Tel Aviv, 1967, pp. 92, 99, 100, 110, 125, 130, 145 and N. Newcombe, "Alternative Approaches to World Government," *Peace Research Reviews*, vol. I., Feb. 1967.

143. Renouvin and Duroselle, *op. cit.*, pp. 86, 246-249 and 272, passim.

144. See f.i. J.Lambellet, "Do Arms Lead to War?" *JPR*, No. 2/1975, p. 123.

145. J. D. Singer and M. Small, "Alliance Aggregation and the Quest of War,

1815-1965 in J. D. Singer (ed.), *Quantative International Politics*, The Free Press, New York, 1968 also *The Wages of War, A Statistical Handbook*, New York, 1972. and see J. D. Singer, S. Bremer and J. Stuckey, "Capability Distribution, Uncertainty and Major War, 1820-1965" in B. Russett (ed.), *Peace, War and Numbers*, Sage, London, 1972.

146. F. Barnaby, "Peace Research: The Whys and the Wherefore," *Nature*, vol. 265, 24 February 1977.

147. U. Luterbacher, "Bipolarity and Generative Factors in Major Power Military Activity, 1900-1965", *JPR*, No. 2/1975, p. 129.

148. D. Ruloff, "Dynamics of Conflict and Cooperation between Nations," *JPR*, No. 2/1975, p. 109.

149. G. Thayer, *The War Business. The International Trade in Armaments*, Palladin, London, 1969, pp. 279 and 301.

150. J. Stanley and M. Pearson, *The International Trade in Arms*, Chatto, London, 1972, p. 7.

151. See, inter alia, J. le Theule in *Le Monde*, 29 July, 1971 and SIPRI statistics.

152. J. Oberg, "Arms Trade with the TW as an Aspect of Imperialism," *JPR*, No. 3/1975, p. 215.

153. W. Albrecht, D. Ernst, P. Lock and H. Wulf, "Militarization, Arms Transfer and Arms Production in Peripheric Countries," *JPR*, No. 3/1975, pp. 200 and 207-8.

154. For details see *Arms Trade Register, The Arms Trade with the Third World*, SIPRI, MIT Press, 1975. On the methods of measurement see SIPRI, *The Meaning and Measurement of Military Expenditure* and Oberg, op. cit, note 148, p. 224.

155. *Le Monde*, 30 July, 1977.

156. J. Ki-Zebro, *Le Monde*, 28 May, 1977.

157. See the analysis of the Rostowian model in the previous chapter.

158. See n. 150, *SIPRI 1976*, pp. 127-8 and 140-1 and SIPRI, *The Arms Trade*, pp. 83-4 and the proper figures in SIPRI 1977, 1978, 1979 and 1980.

159. D. Childs and M. Kidron, "India, the USSR and the MIG Project," *Economic and Political Weekly*, vol. VIII, No. 38, 22 September 1973 and "Waste: US 1970 and Black Reformism: The Theory of Unequal Exchange," in M. Kidron, *Capitalism and Theory*, Pluto Press, London, 1974.

160. See the conclusions of S. Kuznets, W. A. Joer, F. Kneschnurek, J. Jewkess and others in *The Economic Consequences of the Size of Nations*, edit. by A. Robinson, Macmillan, London, 1960, pp. XVI, 32, 15, 113 and passim.

161. R. Scott (ed.), *The Politics of the New States, Allen and Unwin*, Aberdeen Univ. Press, 1970, p. 2

162. See criticism of this view in *Le Monde*, 22 August, 1977.

163. Cf. the survey of his proposals based on an article in the *New York Times* and condensed in the Israeli Daily *Ha'aretz* of 27 March, 1973.

164. SIPRI 1974, pp. 126 and 130 and see note 153, and see K. Waldheim, "World Economically Divided Could not be Politically Stable," *UN Monthly Chronicle*, No. 71/1975, p. 66.

165. S. Lodgaard, "On the Relationship between the East-West Economic Cooperation and Political Change in Eastern Europe," *JPR*, No. 4/1974, p. 325.

166. R. Efron, "The Jackson Amendment and the Fight for Soviet Jewry's Right to Emigration," *International Problems*, vol. XV. No. 29, 1976, p. 62; cf. W. Standard, "A Congressional Miscalculation," *N.Y. State Bar Journal*, Nov. 1975, p. 545.

167. W. Wagner, "Power and Diplomacy—Two strings of Détente's Bow," *GT*, No. 726, 14.III.1976.

168. E. Guz and H.Y. Wesselohn, *Der Kongress von Helsinki*, Verlag Bonn Aktuelle, Stuttgart, 1975, p. 8.

169. K. Goldmann, "East-West Tensions in Europe 1946-1970; A Conceptual and Quantative Description", *World Politics*, No. 1/1973, p. 106ff.

170. F. Fischer, "Die Unabhaengige Komission fuer internationale Entwicklungsfragen (Brandt-Komission), Gruendung, Arbeitsweise und Zielsetzung," *Europa Archiv*, vol. 33, 10 November 1978, No. 21, pp. 703-710.

171. R. Naroll, V. L. Bulogh, F. Naroll, *Military Deterrence in History — A Pilot Cross-Historical Survey*, State University of New York Press, 1974.

172. H. Barbera, *Rich Nations and Poor in Peace and War: Continuity and Change in the Development Hierarchy of Seventy Nations from 1913 through 1952*, Lexington Books, 1973, pp. 3, 134, passim.

173. W. Sombartg, *Studien zur Entwicklungsgeschichte des modernen Weltkapitalismus, II, Krieg und Kapitalismus*, Duncker und Humblot, Muenchen und Leipzig, 1913.

174. Kidron, op.cit., passim.

175. See, e.g., S. P. Huntington, *Changing Patterns of Politics*, The Free Press of Glencoe, New York, 1962, Chapter 1.

176. Sombart, op.cit., pp. 3-5 and vol. III, passim.

177. J. U. Nef, *War and Economic Progress*, Cambridge University Press, Mass, 1950, p. 65.

178. *War and Economic Development, Essays in Memory of David Joslin*, edit. by J. M. Winter, Cambridge (Mass.) University Press, 1975, p. 5.

179. Idem.

180. See, e.g., P. A. Sorokin, *Mass and Society in Calamity*, New York, 1942 and S. Andreski, *Military Organization and Society*, London, 1954.

181. Cf. Brandel, *The Mediterranean and the Mediterranean World in the Age of Philip II*, Translated by S. Reynolds, 2 vols., London, 1972-3, vol. II, p. 836.

182. See Miller in Winter, note 178, p. 11.

183. See G.R. Elton's paper, ibid.

184. See G.Parker's paper, ibid.

185. Idem, pp. 49-50.

186. Idem, pp. 54 and 65.

187. Idem, p. 66.

188. P. Mathias, idem, p. 80.

189. R. MacLeod and K. MacLeod, idem, p. 112.

190. J. Harris, idem, p. 239.

191. Ph. Dean, idem, p. 91.

192. S. Shama, idem, p. 103.

193. C. Trebilcok, idem, p. 139.

194. Ph. Deane, idem, p. 92.

195. Cf. conclusions of Shahram Chubin, loc. cit. (The 1975 Pugwash Conference at Starnberg, Germany).

196. *Kayhan International*, 4 February, 1976 and see Chubin, loc. cit.

197. *UN Statistical Yearbook* 1973, New York, 1974, pp. 596-7.

198. The critical situation both in Egypt and Israel was already pinpointed in the end of 1975 and the beginning of 1976 by economists, political scientists and journalists, including foreign correspondents that were in principle pro-Israeli. See, J. Thornwald's considerations in *Die Zeit* of March 1976. Also cf. J. Brujonsky's conclusions (inter alia, in *International Problems*, vol. XV, No. 3-4, 1976, p. 71). He stresses the growth of Israel's dependence on the US, which amounted to more than 2 billion dollars in 1973 and since then has been steadily growing. The Israeli military expenditures increased from 9% of the national product to 45% in 1973 and were much higher in 1979, the year of concluding the Israeli-Egyptian peace treaty.

199. *The Economist*, 17 May, 1979, Survey, p. 75.

200. *The Economist*, 20 September, 1975, p. 84.

201. We have already pointed out the frustration of the "Fourth World" countries because of the small aid received from the oil-producers. In 1974 the oil revenues were approximately $60 billion, in 1975 $43 billion and the oil-producers pledged "assistance" in the amount of $21 billion but actually gave no more than $4.4 billion. This sum has already included the payment for Arab countries' arms, while the Africans actually received $650 million in 1974 and in the first half of 1975—$300 million. In the years 1976-79 the assistance given to the Africans did not grow essentially. See the conclusions of J. Friedmann, "Der Wolf ist gezaehnt," *Die Zeit*, No. 52, 19 December 1975. Till now, that is also after the immense increase of oil prices, the basic aid to the poorest is given by the West and the continuing rise in oil prices is worsening first and foremost the situation of the most affected countries and deepening their misery.

202. See note 192, pp. 558-67.

203. J. Galtung, "A Structural Theory of Imperialism," *JPR*, No. 2/1971, p. 81ff.

204. For a summary of discussions pinpointing the dangers of Soviet imperialism, with the participation of S. Carillo, J. Ellenstein, J. Radice, L. Colleti, R. Lombardi, L. Magri, G. Pajetta, J. Pelikan and F. Coen see, inter alia, *Aneks* (the journal of the Polish left in exile), no. 16-17, 1977.

205. See, e.g., E. Jahn, "Kommunism—und was denn?" *Rowohlt*, 1974 and *BPP*, No. 1/1979, pp. 91-121.

206. M. Bohnet, op. cit., p. 49. For a succinct description of dependency theories see K. W. Deutsch, "Theories of Imperialism and Neo-Imperialism," in St. J. Rosen and J. R. Kurth (eds.), op. cit., pp. 24-30.

207. For the presentation of these theories, in addition to the previously quoted publications of Galtung and Senghaas, see, inter alia, P. Bairoch, *Le Tiers Monde dans l'Impasse*, Paris, 1971; S. Amin, *L'Afrique de l'Ouest Bloquée*, Paris, 1971 and R. Bonnain-Moerdijk, "La Colonization—Force Externe, Revue du Tiers Monde", *RTM*, vol. XIII, No. 5/1972, p. 409.

208. G. A. Cosgrove, "Colonial Legacies and Development Prospects in the Third World," *International Relations*, vol. IV, No. 11/1972, pp. 63 and 56.

209. See, inter alia, essays of M. Ikonikoff, C. Furtado, Y. Coussault, P. Goulène and S. Amin in *RTM* , vol. XIII, No. 52/1972 and Amin's study *L'Accumulation à l'Echelle Mondiale*, Paris, 1972.

210. See, e.g., G. Myrdal, *Le Défi du Monde Pauvre: Un Programme de Lutte sur le Plan Mondial*, Paris, 1972.

211. For a reappraisal of these views, M. Mushkat, "Genèse et Avenir du sous-dévéloppement," *EP* No. 11/1974, p. 30ff.

212. S. Amin, "L'Afrique de l'Ouest Bloquée," *Africa-Asia*, No. 42/1972, passim.

213. For a critic of this work see i.a. M. Mushkat, "Peace Research Reassessed," *International Problems*, vol. XVIII, No. 1-2, 1979, p. 30.

214. A. A. Mazrui, "The Ressurection of the Warrior Tradition in African Political Culture," *Journal of Modern African Studies*, vol. 13, 1975, p. 79.

215. M. Yamamoto, "Reflections on Japanese Attitudes Towards the North-South Problem," *Peace Research in Japan*, 1973, p. 69.

216. H. G. Reid and E. J. Yanarella, "Towards a Critical Theory of Peace Research in the United States: The Search for an Intelligible Core," *JPR*, No. 4/1976, pp. 320, 322, 327, 330-2 and 310, and also see B. Ollman, "Marxism and Political Science," *Politics and Society*, vol. III, Summer 1973, pp. 496 and 505.

217. B. Koenitz, "Sowietische Militaer und Entwicklungshilfe als Instrument ihres politischen Einflusses im nahen Osten," *Oesterreichische Zeitschrift für Aussenpolitik*, vol. 18, No. 4/1978, pp. 275-286.

218. I. W. Zartman, "Europe and Africa: Decolonization or Dependency?" *Foreign Affairs*, vol. 54, No. 2/1976, pp. 326-7. About the role of the indigenously determined local TW confrontations also see M. Merle, "Le Système mondial: Réalité et Crise," *Politique Etrangère*, No. 5/1978, p. 497.

219. D. Senghaas, "Zur Diskussion von Entwicklungsbegriff," *EZ*, No. 1/1975, p. 12.

220. N. Becker, *Entwicklungshilfe: Das Ziel ist klar, doch wer kenne den Weg?* idem, p. 14.

221. G. Kuhnlein, *Die Entwicklung der kritischen Friedensforschung in der Bundesrepublik Deutschland*, Frankfurt, Haag and Herchen, 1978, pp. 46, 118, 177 and cf. with H. Groten's conclusions (in his *Friedensforschung — Anspruch und Praxis*, Baden-Baden, Nomos Verlag, 1977), with N. G. Onuf's conclusions ("Peace Research Parochialism," *JPR*, No. 1/1975, p. 71) and with the conclusions of Prof. R. Vucadinovic ("The Values and Scope of Peace Research") *YRIA*, No. 628, 8 June 76, pp. 10-12.

222. For the tendency of peace and development researchers to mix problems of security with those of justice see K. E. Boulding, "A Program for Justice Research," *BPP*, No. 1/1974 and the same author "The Learning of Peace," *International Studies Notes*, vol. 1, no. 2, summer 1974, p. 7, his "A Letter to the Editor," *BPP*, No. 2/1974, p. 191 and "Twelve Friendly Quarrels with Johan Galtung," *JPR*, No. 1/1977, p. 78.

223. See e.g., E. Krippendorf, "Chile, Violence and Peace Research," *JPR*, No. 11/1974, p. 95.

224. See R. Jenkins, "Who are these Marchers?" *JPR*, No. 1/1965, pp. 46, 51 and 57; H. Savon, "Recherches sur la Paix," *EP*, No. 15/1975, p. 56; D. Rivera, "Let us Face Chile, Yes, But: Which Chile?," *JPR*, No. 11/1974, p. 105 and the statement of the Secretary General of the Chilean Communist Party, *Le Nouvel Observateur*, No. 640/1977, p. 75.

225. Ch. Boasson, "International Law, Conflict Resolution and Peace Research," *10 Israel Law Review*, 1975, pp. 178-191.

226. I. Nardin, "Philosophy and International Violence," *The American Political Science Review*, vol. LXX, No. 3, p. 955.

227. K. E. Boulding, "Twelve Friendly Quarrels. . ." p. 78.

228. See, e.g., G. Abi-Saab, "Wars of National Liberation and the Laws of War," *Annales d'Etudes Internationales*, vol. 3, 1972, pp. 93-117.

229. B. Berberoglu, "The Meaning of Underdevelopment," *International Studies*, 17, No. 1/1978, passim.

230. W. A. Lewis, *The Theory of Economic Growth*, Homewood, Ill., 1955, p. 371, A. Callaher, Jr. (ed.), *Perspectives of Developmental Change*, Lexington, NY, 1968, p. 3.

231. Berberoglu, op. cit., p. 73; cf. E. Obminskij, *The Mechanism of Exploiting Developing Countries*, Hungarian Academy of Science, Budapest, 1976, passim.

232. J. Galtung, *Trends in Western Civilization Program—(No. 16), Social Cosmology and the Concept of Peace, Chair in Conflict and Peace Research*, University of Oslo, 1978, p. 19.

233. Cf. H. Rattinger, "Armament, Détente and Bureaucracy, The Case of the Arms Race in Europe," *Journal of Conflict Resolution*, XIX, No. 4/Dec. 1975, pp. 571-545.

234. Reid and Yanarella, op. cit., p. 320 and M. Pilisiuk and T. Hayden, "Is there a Military-Industrial Complex which Prevents Peace?" *The Journal of Social Issues*, XXI, July 1965, p. 67.

235. P. Gourevitch, "The Second Image Revised: The International Sources of Domestic Politics," *International Organization*, No. 4, 1978, pp. 888-891.

236. I. Wallerstein, *The Modern World System*, The Academic Press, New York, 1974.

237. D. Gerschenkron, *Economic Backwardness in Historical Perspective*, Cambridge, Harvard Univ. Press, 1963.

238. Gourevitch, op. cit., pp. 882-3.

239. R. Keohane and J. Nye (eds.), *Transnational Relations and World Politics*, Cambridge, Harvard Univ. Press, 1971.

240. R. Gilpin, *US Power and Multinational Corporations*, New York Basic Books, 1975 or the earlier quoted Magdoff, Baran, Swezy and particularly H. G. Nutzinger who called Galtung's and other critical peace researchers' terminology "empty boxes" (see his."Konflikte zwischen entwickelten und unterentwickelten Laendern," *Rheda-Schloss Symposium*, 35 October 1971, pp. 1-2.

241. As, e.g., in S. Hoffmann's *Primacy of World Order; American Policy since the Cold War*, McGraw Hill, New York, 1978.

242. E.g., K. Kaiser, *German Policy in Transition*, OUP, London, 1968.

243. As, e.g., in M. Brecher's *Decisions in Israel's Policy*, Yale Univ. Press, New Haven, 1972.

244. Gourevitch, op. cit., pp. 907-11.

245. J. Fawatt, *International Economic Conflicts, Prevention and Resolution*, Europa Publications, London, 1977, p. 5.

246. P. Bairoch, *The Economic Development of the Third World since 1900*, Methuen, London, 1975, p. 194.

247. R.. Gordon and J.. Pelkmans, *Challenges to Independent Economies*, McGraw-Hill, New York, 1974, p. 5.

248. B. A. Carrol, "Peace Research," *BPP*, No. 4/1973, p. 340 and see Weizsacker's considerations in his essay in S. H. Mendlowitz (ed.), *On the Creation of a Just World Order*, The Free Press, New York, 1975, pp. 111-150.

249. A. Craig, "Information and Politics: Towards Greater Government Intervention?" *International Journal*, vol. XXXIV, No. 2, Spring 1979, p. 209.

250. M. Kunihiro, "The Intermestic Age," *PHP*, Tokyo, No. 6, June 10, 1979, p. 6ff.

251. See, e.g., B. M. Russell's investigation of the US, Canada, Great Britain and France in his book *What Price Vigilance? The Burden of National Defense*, New Haven, 1970; F. Pryor's observations in his *Public Expenditures in Communist and Capitalist Nations*, Homewood, 1968; J. McCormick, *Defense and Social Welfare Trade-Offs: A Test with Latin American Data*, Dept. of Political Science, Iowa State Univer., 1976; M. D. Wolpin, "Militarism, Socialism and Civilian Rule in the Third World: A Comparison of Development Costs and Benefits," *Current Research on Peace and Violence*, vol. VII, No. 3-4/1977; or F. Gottheil, "An American Assessment of the Military Burden in the ME," *Journal of Conflict Resolution*, September 1974.

252. For details, in addition to SIPRI publications, see *The Pugwash Kyoto Symposium: A New Design for Nuclear Disarmament*, W. Epstein and T. Toyoda (edits.), Spokesman, London, 1977; H. Haffendorn, "Der internationale Ruestungstransfer, Motive, Folgen und Kontrollmoeglichkeiten," *33 EA*, No. 11, 10 June 1978, p. 331.

253. M. Thee, "European Security and the Arms Race," *BPP*, No. 1/1979, p. 3; and see: *Force Reductions in Europe*, a SIPRI Monograph, Stockholm, 1974.

254. K. D. Voight, "Gefahren des Ruestungswettlaufs und Aufgaben der Ruestungskontrolle, Aus Politik und Zeitgeschichte," *Das Parlament, B 11*, 17 March 1979, pp. 23-29.

255. U. Bialer, "Thinking the Unthinkable: The Possibilities and Implications of Strategic Bombing Against Israel in the Next War," *Journal of the Royal United Services Institute for Defense Studies (RUSI)*, December 1977, pp. 65-71; Y. Evron, "The Role of the Arms Control in the ME," *Adelphi Papers*, No. 138, London, 1977; J. C. Hurewitz, *Weapons Limitations in the ME, The Stanley 17th Strategy for Peace Conference Report*, Oct. 7-10, 1976, Warrenton, Vir., pp. 49-58; also see D. R. Tahtinen, "Implications of the Arab-Israeli Arms Race" and V. Yorke, "Palestinian Self-Determination and Israel's Security," *VIII Journal of Palestinian Studies*, issue 31, 1979, pp. 3 and 46; also see R. Owen, "The Role of the Army in Middle East Politics," *Review of Middle East Studies*, No. 3/1978, pp. 63-8.

256. H. Rickert, "Neue Waffentechnologien, Waffenarten und Kampfmittel," n. 254, pp. 3-22.

257. E. O. Czempiel, "Peace as a Strategy for Systematic Change," *BPP*, No. 1/1979, pp. 79-90.

258. E. O. Czempiel, "Frieden und Konflikt in der Gesellschaftslehre," *Das Parlament*, Beilage B 20, 18 May 1974, p. 9; S. Dasgupta, "Peacelesness and Maldevelopment," *BPP*, No. 4/1975, p. 346 and the quotation of Boutros-Ghali in *Polemologie*, Recherche sur la Paix, Irénologie," 1, *Les Cahiers du CRESUP*, 1977, Louvain-La-Neuve, p. 6.

259. The different documents are listed and analyzed in my book *International Cooperation and International Organizations*, (Hebrew), II ed., Bronfman Publishers, Tel Aviv, 1968, pp. 337-86 and 417-72 and briefly in my article "The United Nations and Disarmament," in *YRIA*, No. 392/1966.

260. W. Harriet Critchley, "Does Doctrine Precede Weaponry?" *XXXIII Inter-*

national Journal, No. 3/Summer 1978, pp. 524-6.

261. Cf. R. Gordon and J. Pelmans, op. cit., pp. 85 and 134.

262. Cf. R. Hettlage, "Modernitaet als Post-Traditionalitaet," 7, *Die Dritte Welt*, No. 1/1979, p. 38ff.

263. Cf. Barnett, pp. 5-6.

264. D. Sengaas, "Peace Research and the Causes of Social Violence," *BPP*, No. 1/1976, p. 66.

265. K. Lorenz, *On Aggression*, Bantam Books, 1967.

266. S.S. Kim, "The Lorenzian Theory of Aggression and Peace Research: A Critique," *XIII, JPR*, p. 253 and ff.

267. For the opposite view see, inter alia, K. F. Schade, "Entwicklungspolitik und Friedenspolitik," *Zukunfts und Friedensforschung Information*, No. 1/1969, W. D. Vevey, *Economic Development and International Law*, Assen, 1972 or Jean-Luc Vellut, "Smaller States and the Problems of War and Peace," *JPR*, No. 3/1976.

268. See, e.g., M. Salem "Vers un nouvel ordre économique international," *Journal du Droit International*, No. 4/1975, p. 753 and ff., R. Seitz, *Die Internationale Rohstoff Politik* and O. Matzke, "Entwicklungspolitik als Gesamtgesellschaftliche Aufgabe," *Aus Politik und Zeitgeschichte*, B/17.79, 28.April, 1979, pp. 3 and 16 and P. Droin, "Quelle Sécurité économique mondiale?" *Le Monde*, 6 and 7 May 1977.

269. A. Schneller, "The Failure of Economism in Western and Eastern Integration Policy," *Inter-Economics*, No. 9-10, Sept.-Oct. 1978, pp. 227-235 and also see L. Gordon, *Growth Policies and the International Order*, McGraw Hill, N.Y., 1980, p. 64.

270. H. Elsenhans, "Der Algerische Weg der Ueberwindung von Unterentwicklung," *Die Dritte Welt*, Sonderheft, 1975, pp. 196-232.

271. C. Bell, *The Diplomacy of Détente*, Robertson, London, 1977, particularly the first five chapters and cf. J. Coussy, "Les metamorphoses récentes du discours utopique sur les relations Nord-Sud, *XIX, RTM*, No. 5, July-September, 1978.

272. W. Ophuls, *Ecology and Politics of Scarcity*, San Francisco, Freeman, 1977, pp. 180, 226 and ff.

273. Barnet, passim.

274. N.G. Onuf, "Peace Research Parochialism," *JPR*, No. 1/1975, p. 71.

275. Y. Z. Herschlag, *Hakedaut hakalkalit shel Hashalom*, Hauniversita, 1979, p. 5.

276. K. Boulding, "A Letter to the Editor," *BPP*, No. 4/1974, p. 5.

277. I. Bellany, "Peace Research; Means and Ends," *International Affairs*, No. 1, 1976, p. 13 and cf. the conclusions of W. D. Eberlein and R. Reichel, *Friedens und Konfliktforschung*, Muenchen, Piper, 1976, passim.

278. Cf. L. Gordon, op. cit., p. 1 and S. Kuznets, *Economic Growth of Nations*, Harvard University Press, Cambridge, Mass., 1971, pp. 346-8.

279. M. Kumar, pp. 160 and 168.

280. Cf. D. L. Johnson, *Dependence and Underdevelopment, Latin America's Political Economy*, Doubleday Anchor Books, 1972, p. 414.

281. R. W. Tucker, pp. 58, 62 and cf. A. Pellet, *Le Droit International du développement. Collection "Que sais-je?"* No. 1731, Paris, 1978,pp. 87 and cf with G. Meuloz in his "La C.N.U.C.E.D.—Droit International et Dévelopment, Bruxelles, 1981.

282. D. Schachter, *Sharing the World's Resources*, Columbia University Press, New York, 1977, pp. VIII, 8 and 9.

283. See M. Thee "The Arms Race, Armaments Dynamics, Military Research and Development, and Disarmament," *BPP*, No. 2/1978, p. 105.

284. R. D. Hansen, "The Political Economy of North-South Relations. How Much Change?" 29 *International Organization*, 1975, p. 921 and ff.

285. C. Legum, I. W. Zartman, S. Langdon and L. K. Mytelka, *Africa in the 1980s, A Continent in Crisis*, An Introduction by C. Gwin, McGraw-Hill, New York, 1979, pp. 23, 32, 39, 45ff. About the specific causes of violence in the Third World and the role of underdevelopment in its outbreaks produced by indigenous causes during the different stages of the process of overcoming its consequences and during the attempts to build a "New Military World Order" see also S. Takashi and K. Nakamura, "Peace Research in Postwar Japan," *Peace Research in Japan 1978-79*, Tokyo, University Press, 1979, pp. 25 and 27. About the dangers of the new problem arising from the metamorphosis in the diffusion of power from the North to the South and caused by the uneven diffusion of power through the arms trade with the South see Hessing Cahn, op. cit., p. 11, and also G. Myrdal, *The World Poverty*, p. 34, where he speaks about the motivations for the rebellious mood and violence in the Third World.

286. *International Détente and Disarmament*, A Collection of Articles by Finnish and Soviet scholars, Tamperere Peace Research Institute and the Finnish Peace Association, Helsinki, 1979, p. 75.

287. *Recent Advances in Peace and Conflict Research, A Critical Survey* by J. Dedring, Beverley Hill, Sage Books, London 1978.

288. W. D. Eberlein and P. Reichel, *Friedens und Konfliktforschung*, Piper Verlag, Muenchen, 1976.

289. J. Y. Calvez, *Aspects politiques et sociaux des Pays en Voie de Dévéloppement*, Dalloz, Paris, 1971, pp. 203-4.

290. R. von Albertini, *Europaeische Kolonialherrschaft 1880-1940*, Atlantis Verlag, Zurich, 1976.

291. C. E. Hinsaw, *Toward Political Responsibility*, Wellingport, Pa., 1954, p. 22 and M. Kumar, p. 181.

292. B. Moore, *Reflections on the Cause of Human Misery*, Beacon Press, 1972, p. 53.

293. D. Senghaas, "Gibt es eine entwicklungspolitische Alternative fuer die Dritte Welt?" Aus Politik und Zeitgeschichte, *Das Parlament*, B 7, 18 February, 1978, pp. 9-10 and see his article "Dissociation as a Development Strategy," *BPP*, No. 2/1979, p. 192. For the unpracticality of this proposition see, inter alia, Gordon, op. cit., p. 63.

294. Schachter, op. cit., p. 8. The motivation of the Lomé II Convention of 31.10.79 reflects this in an unambiguous way. See K. Meyer, in Zweite Konvention van Lomé, *EA*, No. 1, 10.I.80 (in addition to the EEC countries, the new convention comprises now 58 TW states).

295. S. Takashi and K. Nakamura, op. cit., p. 26.

296. See, e.g., I. Voicu, "La liquidation du sous-dévéloppement et le nouvel ordre économique international," *Révue Roumaine d'études internationales*, No. 1(43), 1974, p. 81ff, or J. Stanownik, "Towards the New International Economic Order," *YRIA*, No. 683, 20 September 1978, pp. 1-6.

297. Cf. H. Elsenhans, UNCTAD IV, *Zeitschrift der Oesterreichischen Forschungsstiftung fuer Entwicklungshilfe*, Wien, 1976, vol. II, p. 13.

298. Tucker, pp. 58, 62 and 103.

299. Barnet, pp. 215 and 229.

300. D. Sengaas and H. Menzel, (Hrsg.), *Multinationale Konzerne und die Dritte Welt*, Westdeutscher Verlag, Opladen, 1976, pp. 47 and 198-9.

301. S. Rosen op. cit., p. 272 and Senghaas and Menzel, op. cit., p. 242.

302. Cf. W. Leontieff in "Disarmament, Foreign Aid and Economic Growth," *Peace Research Society (Int.) Papers*, vol. 11, 1965, pp. 155-164 and cf. O. Y. Palme, "Disarmament and Development," *YRIA*, No. 683, 20 September 1978, pp. 13 and ff.

303. M. Thee, "Militarism and Militarization in Contemporary International Relations," *BPP*, No. 4/1977, pp. 297 and 299.

304. See *Transition*, vol. 2, No. 4/1975 and for details of this position consult R. Falk, A *Study of Future Worlds*, North Holland Publ. Company, Amsterdam, 1975.

305. H. End, "Utopische Elemente in der Friedensforschung," *Zeitschrift fuer Politik*, No. 2/1973, p. 109.

306. H. Savon, "Recherches sur la Paix," *Etudes Polémologiques*, No. 15, 1975, p. 56.

307. H.G. Nutzinger, op. cit., pp. 1-2.

308. See, e.g., Krippendorf "Chile, Violence and Peace Research, *JPR*, No. 11/1974, p. 95.

Some Conclusions and Observations

An attempt has been made above to define the Third World, to discern the significance of its main characteristic, underdevelopment, to explore its roots, and, finally, to analyze the impact of underdevelopment on international security. An exhaustive review of numerous theories in this regard has led to the conclusion that no theory is sufficiently comprehensive and convincing; nevertheless, many of them provide important insights for the understanding of various aspects of the problem and, therefore, cannot be ignored entirely in any attempt to reach valid conclusions and to make useful recommendations.

Research on the present subject of inquiry indicated that it seemed erroneous to conceive peace as a static situation of no war or merely a state of formal non-belligerency. It was felt necessary to view peace in positive terms as an ever-continuing process aimed not only at the prevention of armed conflict, but also at the pacification of incipient or raging conflicts. Also, true peace must denote conditions of striving for socio-economic betterment, making more certain reciprocal, useful and just the relationship between communities and individuals.

This concept of peace equated with international security also was observed to be linked with any developmental activities and the necessity for their promotion.

Some economists claim that development depends merely on growth.[1] Actually, development is more likely to be determined by internal and external structural changes that respond to the needs of wide strata of the population and its multifarious ethnic, tribal, and other groups; hence the growing interacting roles of national and international institutions to speed up changes.

Many serious observers, particularly those analyzing the political role in connection with the development reinforcement and peace-keeping task, concentrate on the inadequacy of the state, the advantages of furthering the idea of a World Government and the menace of superpowers' reliance on military power as the principal means of deterrence.

Others stress efforts to strengthen international security by promoting trade and other mutually beneficial relations among nations, by reinforcing democracy, human rights, or by establishing a socialist society, and by containing man's aggressive instincts.[2]

Statesmen and thinkers since the age of feudalism and absolutism, particularly those who dealt with the causes and outcomes of the two world wars, occasionally have stressed the importance of trade and human rights. Their views were opposed by many mercantilists and their latter-day disciples. Modern mercantilists (or, neo-mercantilists) underscored the capitalists' allegedly insatiable need for new markets and raw material sources, for cheap manpower, and the use of force to secure it; thus capitalist "exploitation," imperialism and colonialism have been described by socialist thinkers. They characterized economic growth as self-serving enrichment induced by desperately felt needs to protect investment by conquest and exploitation of foreign peoples. The so-called imperialist-capitalist exploiters were luridly pictured as ruthless warmongers and conspirators of economic blight to the extent that it served their interests. Such theories are grossly without historical foundation or at best widely exaggerated. Such were the pseudo-scientific theories of imperialistic politics, based on sentiments concerning misery of wars. The latter was pictured as resulting from bourgeois government only; but such were also some of Weber's assumptions of the rationality of the capitalist system.[3] The historical record suggests that the difference between socialist and capitalist exploitation and imperialism is a distinction without foundation. It was easy and glib, if grossly untrue, to maintain that beginning with the revolts and wars of antiquity until the present era of military conflict, one of the main factors of social and national encounters has been, on the one hand, the wish to put an end to subjection and exploitation and, on the other hand, the wish to rule and become rich. These two tendencies have sometimes been represented as the "fundamental laws of history" in general and of development in particular.[4] Already in the 19th century, however, when armed confrontations of all kinds became unprecedently larger and more persistent, eminent social scientists and economists became increasingly reluctant to accept the thesis of the interdependence between war and peace and the process of development; rather, they pinpointed the role of other factors, such as culture, national life-styles, traditions, religion, and the complicated forms of international relations.[5]

Today some still believe with not much justification that war and military expenditures favor development. The majority consider war and militarism mainly to be destructive to prospects of justice, economic progress and development in all fields of life.[6] Some, of course, doubt whether it is possible to precisely forecast the socio-economic results of militarization and warfare while others are of the opinion that wars are irrelevant to fundamental issues of human progress and economic development.

The recent world wars and subsequent conflicts, especially in the Third World, produced a further polarization of views. Even schools using entirely different variables frequently arrived at similar conclusions that success in power and development results in internal and external conflicts and that stagnation and backwardness also sow the seeds of animosity and conflict. Some analysts believe that the lack of economic growth as well as the level of development or underdevelopment, are influenced by so many factors that the role of wars is slight, if not non-existent. According to them, internal development represents a vast complex of cultural elements, relationships with the external world, the form and trends of the national structure and its integration and various features, facts and occurrences; consequently war cannot be but one relatively unimportant event that exerts influence on the process of development.[7]

One is reluctant to accept the view that war has no impact at all on development. The contrary conclusion seems more acceptable, even if limited to consideration of the impact of World War II on the US, Western Europe and the USSR—and the Korean and Vietnam wars on the Third World and less developed countries recently. In the former case, increased development rates were manifested; in the Soviet case positive growth and development was confined to the military with economic stagnation and retrogression and declines in living standards widely evident.

True enough, South Korea and, previously, Taiwan succeeded after two decades in achieving an economic leap. They and, above all, Japan deserve a special notice. These countries were not followed by any other non-European nation; these when involved in conflicts wallowed in misery. The detrimental impact of the Third World's militarization on its economies and societies has already been mentioned. During the 25 years between 1950 and 1975, the Third World was a theater of approximately 168 armed conflicts, civil and international wars, which means seven wars each year on the average.[8] This mainly seems to account for its present impoverishment and for the growing gap between the underdeveloped Third World's countries and the industrial nations. This seems especially evident if we consider its military expenditures during the recent years[9] which have been fifteen times greater than all development aid received, and almost equal to the total national incomes of the Third World. The military expenditures seem to be one of the chief causes of impoverishment, socio-economic stagnation and all other negative features of underdevelopment. Since the main Third World arms suppliers are the United States and the Soviet Union and, to a far lesser extent, such countries as France, Britain, West Germany, Czechoslovakia, Poland, and East Germany, it appears justified to see militarization as a major cause of maldevelopment that is fuelled by the inter-block rivalry and, nowadays, by the thirst for petrodollars as well.

Even if the problem is perceived in this way, there is no excuse for ignoring indigenous motives of Third World munitions dealers and militarists to eagerly instigate arms races.

Such Third World elements claim to rely on military power for defending national interests against real or imaginary threats of tribal and regional opponents. They also often envision a New International Military Order as the only appropriate instrument to promote a New International Economic and Technological Order. Rather than helping to realize such aims, the arms race tends to bring about the deterioration and ruin of the economies of their societies. This in turn makes the revival of imperialism and colonialism tempting and compelling. Now as in the past, imperialist and colonialist ambitions, but this time under socialist paroles, thrive on dependence on the arms suppliers and competition for arms they provoke. Easy access to arms, of course, also increases the danger of escalation of local conflicts.

The radical school of peace research should be given credit for drawing the attention of many statesmen, clergymen, cultural leaders and scholars, and a growing segment of the general public, to the disastrous results of the arms race for the Third World. It should, however, also be blamed for its reluctance to disclose intra-Third World sources of the disaster, which are unrelated to exploitation of the "South" by the "North." Indigenous factors also must be blamed for the entirely erroneous calculation of the rôle of military might in combatting underdevelopment.

The Scandinavian and West German schools of peace research succeeded in revealing many of the causes of the still continuing asymmetry in the North-South relationships, the negative results of economic dependence of the post-colonial states on their former metropolises, the destructive outcome of the Third World militarization, and the sorrowful rôle of the multinationals in this and other fields. However, they confined themselves to stressing above all these exogenous factors of socio-economic maldevelopment and almost entirely ignored the function of Soviet politics, and even more, the basic indigenous grass-roots of the problem. Hence, the tendency towards reductionism and onesidedness, which are progressively eroding though not dismissing the entire scholarly crop,[10] the latter being of growing importance in the analysis of the Third World militarization.[11] If at all valid, generalizations on structural violence and on the peripheric framework in the capitalist world economy are less significant. Also, because of reductionism and generalizations, the above-mentioned schools of peace research have been unable to perceive properly the changing image of the Third World—an image determined not only by the enrichment of its oil-producing segment, but by the new composition of international agencies and conferences. This actually made the First World increasingly dependent on the majority of LDC's in all kinds of international forums. The LDC's have to be more than ever interested, no less than in détente, in economic de-colonization, which, in blunt contradiction to past Western imperialistic traditions frequently continues patently in worldwide Soviet agression and expansionism. All this has resulted in the new forms of the previously interrupted North-South dialogue.[12] It has also precluded changes favoring developing countries in the World Bank and International Monetary Fund,[13] in GATT and, above all, in the willingness to accept the most important postulates of the NIEO and to promote radical reform in the bilateral North-South agreements, and in the activities of the European Economic Community and the OECD.[14]

By consideration of these steps, many well-known radical sociologists seem to accept an awkward thesis for them to the effect that capitalism can be non-expansionist, that its new tendencies towards stability may become even institutionalized, and that aggressiveness ceases to be its necessary consequence.[15] On the other hand, important representatives of the Third World who take these developments into account open more hopeful prospects in the struggle for solving painful Third World problems.[16] In this context, the growing rôle of international law in speeding up favorable changes in the international arena is also frequently pin-pointed, first and foremost in reflecting an expanding consensus between the parties and norms committing the industrialized nations to truly effective aid to the LDCs.[17]

Some radical analysts do not pay sufficient attention, if any, to these facts and only rarely take into account the diversities of the Third World. As already stressed in another context, the Third World is divided by differences of location, culture, religion, resources, conflicts of interest and political and ideological orientations. Actually, it only constitutes a pressure group on developmental issues. This amalgam has therefore no objective foundation for partnership composed of congruent or reasonably similar parts, for the rich countries of the Third World are not only the most influential but the most selfish as well.[18] This prevents the formation of military or political solidarity or a socio-economic polity with the capabilities of an effective make-weight and initiator of decisions of war and peace on the world scene.

Some peace researchers seem as oblivious to this reality as they are to aspects determined by the growing ineluctable interdependence of all nations regardless of whether such trends are recorded in the formal declarations of the First, Second and Third Worlds. However, global interdependence alters the practical meaning of a present-day sovereignty despite the growing forces of chauvinism, nationalism and aggressivness, as was blatantly illustrated by the Soviet conquest of Afghanistan and Soviet threats to Poland. This interdependence, too, persists in dissipating (at least to some extent) the likelihood of a global collision. There have already been practical results of this evolution which have been confirmed by various arrangements. This evolution finds its doctrinal expression, inter alia, in J. Rosenaus' consideration of interaction and interpretation of the national and international systems. They form the basis of the so-called "Linkage Theory" that purportedly measures the world system's inputs and outputs into various national communities and vice versa. National interactions seem to have shrunk the world since the beginning of nuclear era. True enough, they limit,[19] although do not yet exclude, the possibilities of using (mainly local) wars as an instrument of policy regardless of the parties' (mainly in the TW) military power and their economic development. Moreover, the mentioned interaction is unable, at least in the near future, to end or seriously limit all the negative and purely indigenous factors causing international and local conflicts which frequently tend to escalate into larger confrontations. It also is unable to contain the "ideologically" overloaded Soviet expansionism, strengthened by the great powers' tendencies and their fears of being surpassed or surprised or of losing opportunities.

The above-mentioned indigenous factors also seem to be at the root of socio-economic backwardness in the TW. Consequently, various basic elements of the North-South encounter cannot be properly explored without considering conditions in the South that sometimes have little to do with the economy and foreign involvemet in it; rather, these conditions have more to do with traditions and history, and, recently, with the impact of the rich segment of the Third World on the international arena and with Soviet intervention in the affairs of post-colonial countries.

Communist students pass over these facts in silence. They consider the North-South confrontation to be a product of capitalists' greed for profits, of their interest in amortizing overseas investments, of their search for preferential import and export conditions, and their imperialist and colonialist inclinations.[20] Western analysts inclined to adopt Marxist or economic determinist assumptions also believe that underdevelopment of the Third World is solely determined by exploitation of the industrialized nations for whom it is a matter of survival.[21]

Conservative and radical followers of this and similar determinist approaches therefore stress the urgent necessity of an effective, prompt reorganization of the international economy to solve the malaise of the Third World.[22] They aim to promote basic reform in world trade and in the international monetary systems. First and foremost, they seek to regulate the prices of raw materials and to overcome the difficulties created by the lack of credits for developmental purposes. Also, they propose in the near future to lead and direct the exploration and operation of new energy sources vital not only for the poor nations, but for the industrialized countries as well. Some experts conceive the New International Economic Order as one of the most important means to achieve these aims.

Others challenge the foregoing an deny the possibility of ameliorating the situation of the LDCs through the NIEO.[23] These critics predict that the proposed reforms will reinforce rather than reduce standards of living and levels of satisfaction with regard to basic needs; moreover, they assert that the NIEO proposal will not open new employment opportunities to the multitudes of the Third World poor and destitute. In the end, they foresee the proposed reforms consolidating old patterns of domination. Many believe that the NIEO will only lead to the even stronger restoration of the old international system.[24]

More moderate analysts, however, who realize that the LDCs constitute a bloc representing prevailing elite interest, try to discover obstacles to development rooted in the Third World itself,[25] moreover, they search for solutions and practical ways for the NIEO to function effectively in international economic relations.

Even within the limits of the old market economy, they envisage contributions to the promotion of favorable change in the growth and progress of the LDCs.[26]

Some students are aware that the Third World's underdevelopment is equally the result of its specific history and internal structure, as well as colonialism and economic discrimination, all of these factors having inevitably led to social insecurity, maldevelopment, and the generation of conflicts within and among the underdog countries that today exacerbate international conflicts.[27] Those who are acutely aware of the twofold origins of the increasingly intolerable situation are convinced that, without the effort to suppress indigenous causes, no pressure or action on earth directed to the outside world contingent on external inputs and outputs can produce anything worthwhile.

This is yet another reason why at least some NIEO elements are regarded as important and why preference is given to political and even moral factors over economic ones. It is difficult to see why they should not be accepted by the industrialized countries and soon fruitfully put into operation.[28] Hence some courageously voiced opinions (even in the Communist countries) in support of possible, constructive solution of painful Third World problems have been forthcoming. They include arms expenditure reductions, and proper financing of developmental undertakings by substantial aid hikes not only of the First and Second Worlds, but especially by the oil-enriched Third World oil producing countries.[29]

The increase of cooperative and to some extent integrative and convergent tendencies in the Communist Bloc is a relatively recent, uneven and uncertain phenomenon. It was formally demonstrated only at the 1975 Helsinki Conference, but still remains fragile in light of the 1977-1978 Belgrade Conference and of the Operation in Afghanistan. However, it seems almost certain that detente and intrabloc economic and even humanitarian cooperation will continue and that probably a further step in the arms control negotiations and the SALT agreements is imminent. Hence, the possibility of multiplying developmental aid and making it more constructive and effective to relax Third World tensions. It should not be excluded if only the changing world situation would result in partial reduction of armament budgets.

However, this will not suffice to realize a radical change in the LDCs so long as the indigenous causes of underdevelopment are not eliminated. These indigenous causes strangle democratic reform, enhance militarization and resort to violence. Reminiscent of the Soviet experience, violence as an instrument of modernization was not undertaken in the Third World because of its political sympathies or ideological ties with the Second World,[30] but rather as a result of internal dissent.

The West does not believe this to be true and regards it as evidence of a pro-Communist posture. Consequently, Third World anti-colonial movements, as well as economic and social reform in post-colonial states, are suspected as machinations of Soviet intervention if such programs deviate from established European patterns. Such Western attitudes have produced not a few mistakes, misunderstandings, and gross failures of perception; consequently Western intelligence has produced a distorted image of domestic and international LDCs activities.[31] Western suspicions on the other hand, also have reinforced the determination of Western Europeans and Americans to maintain their privileges and to defend the status quo in countries recently liberated from colonial dependence. Such foreign interests established in postcolonial Third World countries, even if contrary to the local interests, patently are obstacles to development and general social reform.

If the definition of modernization is accepted as an inevitable and continuous process of changes in all "traditional" societies, which result in new forms of production, distribution, and ways of life determined by progress in industrialization, science, and technology, the outcome need not always result in violent internal and external conflicts. It can and usually may find its expression in efforts and adjustment of tendencies to uphold the old to those pushing towards renewal and change.[32] Such efforts and adjustments have been proper for all kinds of human relations since antiquity. They characterize the interactions of individuals and all sorts of groups and communities in their mutual contacts; consequently, they help to shape various forms of socio-political stratification and their accomodation.

Some claim that nowadays the aforementioned efforts and adjustments result in the basic contradictions of international dimensions: between communism and capitalism (East-West conflict); highly industrialized and underdeveloped countries (the North-South conflict); white and colored peoples (the racial complex); and, the rich and poor (the class outlook). Others see them at the root of the present antagonism dividing the allegedly privileged cities and the wretched countryside.[33]

There seems to be some truth in all of these hypotheses, although all suffer from the well-known deficiences of generalizations. Yet their lack of theoretical and practical value results not from inadequate concretization and differentiation, but rather from neglect of recent changes that seem to strengthen prospects of settling conflicts to maintain peace and to deal more effectively with the problems breeding antagonisms that divide all countries and peoples. The possibility of terminating these conflicts to a large extent may be increasing due to the unavoidably growing interdependence of all nations in an age of technological and industrial sophistication of unprecedented proliferation.

These emergent realities prove that persistent adherence to dogmas is an absurdity that nullified the value of many analyses of social issues. The affirmation of the possible escalation of all kinds of wars in the nuclear era that ultimately may annihilate mankind will not be considered here again. However, it seems worthwhile to stress that even some Communist writers usually hostile to "cosmopolitanism-universalism" do not anymore deny that the present level of interdependence of all countries is so high, that even with the existing power balance in a world of various persistent contradictions, a new world community is already in the making. The emergent community envisaged by them seems to them to evolve more or less by force of social necessity, which in turn derives from the "objective" needs of all peoples and classes. They claim this to be evident today within individual states and through them in the international arena.[34] Some of these writers no longer hesitate to describe the new phenomenon in terms similar to that of Western writers.[35]

There are Communist writers who no longer doubt that the growing interdependence of nations make the solution of critical developmental issues feasible; it depends, in their opinion, however, on the good will and the potential of the West and is not therefore only a matter of the latter's responsibility for the colonial past. Yet, these writers are silent on the heavy tribute the Soviet Bloc exacts for any form of assistance, and sometimes even for political support.[36] They merely stress the role of unjust distribution of world riches,[37] and the West's refusal to enjoin their redistribution. According to them, this leads to tensions and threatens warlike complications.[38] Similarly, they shrink from properly illuminating not only the negative impact of Soviet reluctance to participate in aid programs and of Soviet political and military involvement and clearly aggressive acts in the Third World, but they also neglect the rôle of their own domestic contradictions, of the anti-democratic regimes, and the abuse of aid received from abroad. This tragic reality is highlighted strongly even in J. Tinberg's report to the Club of Rome, and Tinberg indeed is very cautious not to find fault with the LDCs or the communist countries.[39]

Various Soviet writers also pass over in silence the fact that economic growth may be due to mastering technology, to expansion of human knowledge, to education of the labor force,[40] and to basic social and institutional reforms. Perhaps because of the peculiarities of the Soviet model, some of these writers even prefer to ignore the fact that the strategy of satisfying the basic needs of the poor is a cheaper and much more effective means to promote developmental ends than continuing a policy of economic growth at any price.[41] They also disregard another fact that hundreds of millions of desperately poor people have been hurt rather than helped by economic growth; for this not infrequently helped to deepen injustice[42] as was shown by the experience of the USSR. Most of these writers are equally deaf to the argument that the most common cause of violence at all levels since World War II has been internal and often based on ethnic grounds,[43] or "ideological" as regards the Soviet expansionism. It is clear that disregard of these and other facts reinforces dogmatism, which is present, as already pointed out elsewhere, in many theories adopted by Western scientists too.

Dogmatism mainly characterizes authors who claim that all painful Third World problems are nothing more than an outcome of imperialist exploitation.[44] By and large, it consists of huge doses of provincialism and reverse chauvinism,[45] as reflected in various forms of vulgar anti-Americanism that even blames the United States for the backwardness of Papua. It also is characterized by flight from deeper insights into ongoing changing realities; therefore, also by utopian approaches revealing tendencies of extreme pessimism, which on the one hand, produces reliance on the myth of LDCs self-sufficiency, and on the other, creates still another myth of their non-existent solidarity and its ensuing power to challenge the First World.[46] This concept also leads to the belief that only human conscience may really become a moving force behind social change. This has become an emphatic article of faith in the World Order Model and similar future-oriented projects; hence the author's deep scepticism about their benefits, particularly if they are based upon an almost Stalinist assumption that the worse it is now the better it will be later. Equally doubtful is their assertion that moderation of any conflict-producing behavior tends to produce toleration of misery, repression and environmental decay, and acquiescence in extreme forms of inequality.[47] This commendation of conflict is a result of the commitment to the explanation of poverty in the South only as a consequence of its dependence on the North and of the affirmation that the LDCs malaise cannot be abolished or contained within the framework confines of the present International Economic Order and through its gradual reform. According to some of the authors of the above-mentioned models, this goal is unattainable until the capitalist system is overthrown. Consequently, they shrink from the admission that moderate statecraft can at least facilitate some reduction in defense expenditures and create increments able to alleviate misery,[48] so as to diminish suffering which totalitarian regimes have inflicted on the masses.

It is needless to stress that improved relationships must seek change in both domestic and international policies, since neglect in one realm can engender failures in the other. What is more, no changes in the international system, be they violent or gradual, and however justifiable, are likely to mean much to most of the poor nations, if they themselves do not make a diligent effort to solve their own problems. External change, by itself might even be pernicious if they only succeed in distracting attention from the fundamental internal issues or if they help the corrupt authoritarian elites to buy time to stave off badly needed domestic reform. To concentrate, therefore, only on the struggle relating to the external aspects of the Third World's condition might not only be fruitless, but also very expensive in terms of human suffering occasioned by the sacrifice of human life in any violent outburst aimed to reach a radical change. On the other hand, improvement of the present level of existence seems to be quite feasible through reciprocally useful arrangements. As regards the growing tendency in the West to choose this way to relieve the deplorable situation in the South, it seems to neither result from guilt about the satisfaction of crying needs nor fear of attack by the Third World; rather this tendency is due to perception of a simple moral obligation to help those most hurt by want, irrespective of why they are in need, and to a practical obligation in the West's own interests to seek to eliminate the seeds of distrust, bitterness and indigency in the international system.

One does not have to be guilty of creating poverty to feel the moral imperative to reduce its consequences. Nor has one to be in danger or weak to seek tranquility and pay the really small price to avoid subversive behavior caused by social pathologies and benefiting to the competing superpower. This is all the more so because stability is an important factor in painless acceptance of unavoidable changes, as well as promoting the benefactor's own vigor and well-being.[49] As regards the Third World's ability to challenge the West, one is inclined to agree—even after the mild American reaction to the seizure of the US Embassy in Teheran—with those Communist authors who maintain that it has neither the military nor the economic power to match the industrialized countries.[50]

Its main weapon, OPEC, may be expected to decline in force before 1985; moreover OECD figures show that Western aid allocations have not been determined on the basis of increased petroleum imports: nearly 60 percent of the flow was to Egypt (and once to Syria), whereas oil producers are themselves looking for investment opportunities and financial security in the First World. Price increases for Third World raw materials made and enforced by them are passed back reciprocally because of the inflationary spiral provoked by such price hikes; thus, any cartel action can be a two-way street on which the arbitrary economic thrust of one side more or less automatically provokes the reprisal of the other in self-adjusting capitalist balance of payments. The economic power of the South consisting of raw materials, trade, and dispossession of investments, thus cannot be used with impunity against the First World; on the contrary, such Third World tactics as debt repudiation, expropriations and commodity centralization are more likely to boomerang to the LDCs disadvantage than to paralyze the entire world economy. This encourages Western sceptics and opponents of Third World development to threaten to forget their "self-imposed humanitarian obligations" in the interest of maintaining their self-respect" if the South persists in bickering with and annoying its "benefactors." The NIEO militants in this case will be abandoned not only by the First but by the Second World as well.[51] The latter will even more gladly drop them when the Second World sees that its "aid" to LDCs does not operate in favor of the USSR and its global strategic plans even within the framework of détente,[52] when it is reconstructed after the still possible solution of the Afghan case.

As for the debt argument, it should be stressed that the majority of the Third World countries, especially the poorest, have very little to do with this burden or privilege, mainly because they have no credit balances in international trade. As a matter of fact, nine countries account for more than 80 percent of such debts—among them, Brazil, Mexico, South Korea and Israel—and they are progressing quite well in economic development compared with the rest of the LDCs.[53]

The political instability of the Third World and the threat of escalation of domestic civil war have less to do with the debt problem than other socio-economic difficulties, which are especially acute in the poorest countries that are more frequently than the others involved in war. Their disruptive behavior, terrible grinding poverty, and impact of their numbers in various international bodies, have brought about more radical politization of the world economy. This is reflected in the growth of governmental and non-governmental administrative intervention, especially by the superpowers, for the sake of easing the difficulties and achieving more (the Western position!) or less (the Soviet position!) stability and power.

The Third World has built grandiose visions of these corrective interventions as a promising opportunity to match political independence with economic sovereignty and to forge a new economic order to allow them to wipe out the afflictions of poverty and sociocultural backwardness themselves independently of the North. This tendency has grown especially strong after disillusionment with measures attributable to economic liberalism, the increasing gap between the industrialized and underdeveloped countries, and the continuous deterioration of their standards of living (the latter is blamed only on the allegedly unjust Western terms of trade and aid). First and foremost, this tendency is an outcome of growing South solidarity, which has been exercised on an unprecedented scale on the international level as most recently manifested in various OPEC decisions and UN resolutions as well.[54]

Real and illusory changes in the power configuration of the North-South relationship, dating back to the beginning of the decolonization, are due to the growing importance of oil and other non-renewable natural resources located in the South. They are also attributable to the fact that power in most developing countries in the absence of a genuine bourgeoisie and local working class was taken over by civil and military bureaucrats[55] who were inclined to extreme chauvinism and violent military adventurism.

Truly, concepts of national rights, needs, interests, power, security, and all the means for their realization are objectively undefinable, concretely unidentifiable, empirically untestable, and scientifically unmeasurable.[56] What matters, however, is not so much the true meaning of these terms, but the manner and purpose of using them by governing elites and, even more, the results actually achieved.

The Western vulnerability to the Third World's sources of supply of raw materials is claimed by some not to be so great and that it will diminish in time because the Third World has neither means or capability to meet the overwhelming economic and military power of the industrialized countries. Any attempt to hit them economically could easily boomerang, because of technological and commercial dominance alone.

On the other hand, the selfishness of the oil enriched countries has menaced Third World solidarity and its potential as a pressure group. The outcome of the struggle for the NIEO has been for the time being a redirection in the ranks of the world economic leaders; not only some of the important oil-producing countries, but Canada, Australia and shortly Brazil and Mexico will most probably join them.

It must be admitted here that the new grouping will not disregard the needs of other formations; that it will rather continue the peace-oriented policies of its West European and American founders; that also it will try to strengthen détente and seek a proper solution to the sorrows of the world's poor. Fear of the global clash will likely compel the industrialized powers to act with restraint and strictly on grounds of self-interest in order to promote a more fair distribution of the world's wealth. The Western reaction to the Soviet aggression against Afghanistan and the American patience with regard to the seizure of the US Embassy in Teheran are a case in point. Only a gradual peaceful change and proper devotion to human needs and justice, if they are also based on an enlightened self-interest, efficiency and profitability, are likely to cure the World economic and political malaise.[57]

Scientific and technological progress, consequences of the nuclear era and the growing interdependence, make this goal attainable without violence for the first time in history, despite contrary Soviet tendencies. True enough, prospects of this kind of metamorphosis are still remote and nebulous since they are overshadowed by the arms race and by unsatisfactory progress with regard to all three baskets of the 1975 Helsinki Declaration. These prospects are concerned not only with security and economic cooperation, but with human rights as well. Above all, they are hindered by the Soviet aggression against Afghanistan, Soviet intervention in other parts of Asia and Africa and Soviet threats to Poland and other "allies." In their totality they are rightly considered as conditioning peace in Europe and in the rest of the World. In the light of the Belgrade, Madrid and Helsinki Conferences and the Soviet expansionism their analysis proves, too, that the North-South and chiefly the East-West conflicts, as well as the South-South ones, stand in the way of world peace and wellbeing. Resolution of these chronic conflicts is fundamental to world security and wellbeing. It is necessary in order to combat effectively hunger and maldevelopment and to divert valuable resources and energy from armaments to developmental purposes.

On the eve of the de-colonization era, F. Fanon wrote that the wellbeing and progress of the West had been built with the sweat and corpses of Negroes, Arabs, Indians and Orientals and this could no longer be overlooked.[58] The schools of dependence, of peripheric capitalism and of structural violence, and similar theories are all based to varying extents on Fanon's hypothesis. They concentrate on the impact of capitalist expansion, on the precapitalist modes of production prevailing in the Third World before the Europeans' arrival; they also focus on European subjugation mechanisms claimed to result in the stagnation of some nations to the benefit of others' development, i.e., the enrichment of colonial masters or, to use A. G. Frank or Samir Amin's terminology, in the "development of underdevelopment."

Historical and empirical inquiry do not confirm such generalizations adopted as axiomatic starting points of the mentioned theories. Their postulates of course, raise serious questions about the veracity of all concepts which conceive conflict solely as a function of under or overdevelopment and as an outcome of foreign exploitation and enslavement. Detailed surveys prove the existence of a number of causes leading to deadly quarrels. Mostly, these are indigenous and non-economic in character and reflect the plurality of factors producing human misery, growth rate differentials and inequality in the well-being of nations.

Lenin's assertion that politics is just a condensed expression of economics is less convincing on the basis of comprehensive research than the dictum based on Clausewitz's definition of war as a continuation of politics by other means. Politics very frequently has nothing to do with either economics or rational motivation. Even many of Fanon's enthusiastic partisans—and not only those from academia—raised amidst the Third World masses and reckoned among its avowed advocates and militants are aware that it is much more important for them not to overlook the domestic origins of backwardness, obsolete social institutions, the evil role of corrupt leadership, than to emphasize their people's contribution to the might and wealth of the industrialized countries. The latter was never too great or essential and presently is very doubtful. Unprecedented burgeoning Western production forces nowadays are more and more attributable to intellectual perfection, technological innovation, administrative effectiveness, continuing revolutionary progress in science and communications, and unprecedented market efficiency.

As regards the failures of many Third World governing elites, they result rather as a consequence of their corruption than of foreign intervention. Their weaknesses were compounded and reinforced by ignorance and fear of any change (even in family life and mores). Developmental aims and plans recommended by well-meaning foreign donors and experts were subverted because of incompetence in the use of modern technology, indifference, and disregard for the need of training. Psychological handicaps incurred by the transition from a primitive agricultural society towards industrialization, and of the population explosion, practically negated all progress.

The ensuing tensions and conflicts that resulted from the process of modernization and external intervention were sometimes unavoidable if change towards progress was to begin without any preparation. Obstinate obsolescence of life styles and modes of production as well as the leader's unshakable belief in automatic, prompt reconstruction of society and governments, were no less responsible for resultant conflicts and extremism.[59]

The thesis on the fundamental contradiction between the cities and the countryside has already been mentioned as a main feature of modern socio-economic history. It is easy to claim that to some extent this thesis corroborates Lin Piao's theory of the partition of the world into urban versus rural and conflict between exploiting industrialized nations versus the undeveloped exploited rebelling ones, divisions begetting inevitable collisions.[60] Different versions of this monolithic concept overlook not only internal differentiation within nations and international coalitions but feebleness and immutable stagnation of the Third World and its inability to challenge the First and the Second Worlds. The call to emulate the great October Revolution and to lean upon a courageous small elite revolutionary vanguard ignores that the Bolsheviks only succeeded in overthrowing capitalism in Russia in a peculiar historic situation and at the close of World War II. "Socialism" was imposed on Eastern European countries by Soviet conquest. On the other hand the LDC's tendency to cooperate with the relatively strong economically and militarily unified West, which is prepared to respond to their essential claims also because of the consequences of the nuclear age, makes poor prospects indeed for some Third World plans to challenge the industrialized countries.

By and large, China itself never adopted in practice Lin Piao's principles during his lifetime and certainly not after his mysterious death, nor during the Mao and post-Mao periods. On the contrary, the present situation of the People's Republic of China pushed its leaders— as we have already mentioned—towards closer cooperation with the USA and Western Europe in the face of the Soviet danger and growing tendencies to speed up economic development. World security could perhaps benefit from this development.

Two decades ago Fanon laid down the foundations for concepts a la Lin Piao and others, which continue to inspire the perception of underdevelopment as exclusive result of colonialist aggression.[61] This led to the belief that it was only possible to wipe out colonialism by violence since colonialism was conceived as the basis for establishing and maintaining industrialized countries' wealth. Fanon could foresee neither the possibility of pacific decolonization nor even the absence of opposition by the colonialist powers to grant to their colonies political independence. He did not conceive that the former metropolies might one day become interested also in assisting their past dependencies in economic decolonization, albeit for self-serving reasons and to eliminate worldwide threats of thermonuclear incineration. By and large, concern over self-preservation and survival induced many former colonialists to initiate modernization in foreign territories while still under colonial rule: moreover, the same applied to endeavors in human rights and education of the natives at the time when various non-economic motives obstructed the full liberalization of dependencies earlier and when income yielded by colonies was already greatly surpassed by the cost of governing them.

A number of points already have been made to show, on the one hand, the growing competition of rival blocs' militarization in the Third World, the competing blocs' means of effectively ameliorating existing social and economic problems with developmental aid on the other. The latter seems essential to the preclusion of disruptive behavior and its escalation, sometimes for the sake of realizing humanitarian principles, and to meet demands of morality and justice. Since the 1975 UN General Assembly debates, there has developed a growing consensus to follow this path, although the other still holds its attraction; the voice of the pessimists thus should not be disregarded since full reliance on the optimists' prognosis is not warranted. If mankind succeeds to evade catastrophe, progress will most probably be quite slow and achieved through a struggle between the two mutually disruptive tendencies, which may occasionally cause armed clashes and exacerbate existing ones. Fear of global war and growing interdependence on the other hand, most likely would tend to preclude or assuage tension and conflict.[62] This does not mean that Soviet and, as a reaction, Western neo-imperialist or new sub-imperialist tendencies of some autocratic oil producers and other commodity-rich Third World countries will automatically end.

The proper conclusions still require further theoretical and empirical explanation. Until recent times very little consideration has been given to various new aspects of the interrelationship between underdevelopment and international security. Even less attention was payed to proving the thesis that the acuteness of the North-South conflict and the difficulties in reducing it are to a large extent at present a result of the East-West controversy. Moreover, the assertion that common interests of all peoples will grow stronger with time, will narrow their disagreements, and make solution of critical Third World problems easier, has yet to be sufficiently substantiated and proven.

The definition of interests is still subjective, particularly when it does not consider the outlooks, beliefs, expectations, and behavior of all parties. If views are entirely at variance, goodwill or objective basis for compromise are non-existent and violent collisions are often unavoidable. Generalizations neither help to understand the roots of conflict nor how to end them. On the other hand, precise detailed examination and understanding of the peculiarities of each extant conflict and ways to bridge opposing attitudes and postures may be very helpful. In fact, scrupulous consideration of the real interests of adversaries, in an impartial even-handed manner can make the role of a mediator or arbitrator really effective in various circumstances.[63]

The North-South confrontation, which has in fact been weakening, though not in rhetoric, for the last few years, proves that arrangements are at hand, based on notions of real interests, outlined above. It is no longer true that the West is still devoted only to preserving the status quo of the existing world order.[64] Neither is it true that the West considers Third World development exclusively in terms of its own, economic, political and cultural values and institutions[65] or strives to uphold the structure of dependency; thus the LDC's economies are no longer conditioned by the West's expansion and subjected to its dominant position.[66] On the other hand, the South is becoming aware that ultimative demands are fruitless, if not self-defeating. Perseverance in such demands amounts in practice to no more than a bargaining pressure tactic meant to secure equitable solutions acceptable to all sides.

It might be hoped that the Brandt Commission and other governmental and non-governmental, explorative and operative forums will at last effect constructive proposals and initiate their realization. They might not lead to dramatic turns precisely because they require neither unreasonable sacrifices from the rich nor drastic socio-economic achievements of the poor; but the beginning of an ongoing curative process may be expected to ease tensions. Many Third World leaders and experts consider the possibility of gradual change as realistic, desirable and, today, more feasible than ever.[67]

In another context, liberal views on development and peace have already been mentioned. In their present form, they are to some extent characterized by an optimistic socially progressive outlook. It already has been noted that this approach considers backwardness as a relative and traditional phase of societies advancing to higher levels of development. It considers retrograde pecularities, stagnation, and obstinacy in preserving traditional forms as exceptions to the universal process of modernization that sooner or later will be eliminated[68]; hence it elaborates a multitude of means and solutions for each nation taken separately with its particular circumstances, traditions, issues and history. It is clear, however, that these solutions to any Third World country's problems must also take into account mostly recent experience of other peoples both in the First and Second Worlds.[69] This is all the more necessary because various undertakings are both influenced and initiated by these peoples, because all of them are more than ever disposed to give preference to cooperation rather than confrontation[70] and because the West is evermore interested in placating the LDCs as well as in improving their situations. Doing so, the West adopted the notion of development also refering to structural changes directed towards reducing the former dependency of the South by reconstruction of the world economy.[71]

This, too, contributes to the growing tendency of the Third World to cooperate in Western policies which do not fail to have a certain impact also on the East because this tendency takes into account common needs, universal responsibility, and moral duties. This tendency has already ceased to be merely a matter of wishful thinking or brilliant tempting proposals. Despite all controversies, it already reflects the growing direction and dynamics of new realities and their objective and subjective causes. Truly, this does not yet find an accurate expression in the normally noisy accusatory adversary debates by international bodies alleging sinister imperialistic and exploitive conspiracies. It is also true that violent conflagrations and Soviet interventions often seem to refute the new tendency. Yet, its flow and probably only temporary ebbs can be discerned and measured. This sort of movement strengthens cautious optimism if not only growth of national income per capita, quantities of resources assigned to development functions, expenditure increase for armaments and military purposes, but the gradual social metamorphosis is taken into account as well. The positive results of industrial and agricultural modernization and of institutional growth in the fields of health, education, culture and even research by and large leads to the significant improvement of living standards.

Some students maintain that such progress and advancement be they even very modest, strengthen peace by themselves because of the functional connection of peace with prosperity.[72] A similar correlation is supposed to exist between power and international security.

Many writers argue that an improved level of existence even of a small but influential stratum might induce decisions giving preference to economic over military undertakings. Others stress that underdevelopment or the concentration on overcoming its hard consequences in some countries evoke fear of war, particularly if they are weak nations. This compels them to think that they may become embroiled in conflicts likely to reduce their achievements to a state of total collapse. Because of such fear, they may be inclined to give up even the idea of building the NIMO as an instrument of NIEO.

Both contentions raise serious reservations. The majority of bloody conflicts in recent decades occurred in the Third World, although nearly 79 percent of all international conflicts, including those of the very weak belligerents, were started as a result of reliance on military superiority or the assumption that the antagonist is weaker and unprepared. On the other hand, there is sufficient evidence showing that economic and/or military power and high levels of development also do not automatically lead from tension and hostility or any desire for expansion to war even in authoritarian countries. Truly no models based on military and economic strength, on power alliances and ideological affinities, or on proximity to foci of conflagrations unambiguously explain the causes of avoiding or entering wars.[73]

It seems that the problem is too complex for reliance on only a few factors to explain the origins of armed violence under all circumstances.

If this and various theories already mentioned in another context are considered, the conclusion seems justified that: a) development and power do not always tend to exert pressures for expansion and dominance by any means including war and, conversely, in certain circumstances may even intensify interests in peace; b) that underdevelopment is not always a factor of passivity, tension or acquiescence to given situations and misery, nor necessarily of rebelling since it can breed desires for gradual peaceful change and reliance on mutual understanding, cooperation, and on strengthening rational behavior. The latter is particularly likely if belligerents become aware of their military and technological weakness and without regard to their wealth of natural resources and financial power or their rule by militant elites.

Truly, in certain circumstances it is possible to secure political power, particularly in international organizations, by closing ranks and playing the card of natural resources without previously building a solid infrastructure; but this does not suffice to challenge the highly industrialized states not to mention the superpowers. It therefore seems worthwhile to corroborate the assumption of many eminent past and present experts of politics and economics who have dialectically envisaged correlations between peace and economic growth or war and development. These were sometimes entirely understandable in particular historical situations, but non-existent in other circumstances.

Most of them considered determination of peace as attributable to a variety of causes: economic factors, forms of government, conditions of freedom, tolerance, the rational and fair operation of trade and so on. Peace meant to them the respect for principles of democracy and justice in international economic relations, and this was considered a condition of their normality with mutual advantages for all parties. Needless to say this goal is still far from the realization both politically and economically in the present situation, which is pregnant with danger. Change would require immense efforts on the part of the developing countries themselves and their industrialized partners alike.

This is the reason why also some extremist students of peace who in the past disregarded or even completely ignored the indigenous factors have recently become more and more aware of the conflict producing role of the lack of Third World democracy. Development and international security rest according to them on prospects of the fall of authoritarian regimes and thereafter promotion of fundamental liberties and human rights in the developing countries.[74] Former rigid attachment to theories disregarding the essential role of this fact finally resulted in confusion. It would be therefore not in the least surprising if some frustrated representatives of the critical peace research have suddenly decided to give priority to the concept of aggressiveness in human nature[75] in their studies. In fact, this approach, as we have already mentioned, was reflected in the assumptions of K. Lorenz, employed by German National Socialism.[76] This neo-Hobbesian approach, as we have stressed in another context, was refuted again and again even by biologists who previously were disciples of racist theories,[77] as well as by many political scientists and peace researchers. The latter have not hesitated to stress that Lorenzian theory is not only misleading but even dangerous.[78] Eminent analysts of various aspects of social violence in general and of war in particular entirely ignore the Lorenzian and similar theories. They vehemently criticize any attempt to analyze national and international political confrontations in terms of individual aggressiveness and human instincts or by various Freudian psychoanalytical hypotheses.[79]

Most of the students dealing with the causes of violent group behavior outlined the dominant role of socio-economic change in the rise of group frustration: the impact of dictatorial rule, the lack of balance in the living conditions of various classes, the difficulties of national integration, the cruel behavior of governing elites, forceful repression of political or ethnic dissidents, and rigid attachment to obsolete socio-economic structures. All of these have tended to foster and intensify feelings of bitterness and injustice. Clearly, some rulers exploit tensions in order to push the embittered and rebellious masses towards military adventurism. Idealistic stands of radical militants struggling for change may also lead to violence and individual terrorism.[80]

The presentation of "structural violence" chiefly as an outcome of coordination between the rulers of the centers and those in peripheries or as merely a product of foreign intervention is therefore misleading. It is uprooted from the real background of violence and does not reveal its domestic motivation; on the other hand, it fails to provide sufficient evidence, proving the dominant or even exclusive role of outside factors in the realization of "structural violence." It may therefore be worthwhile in this context to return to some aspects of studies on peace and development insufficiently outlined above. They tend to prove that the contention that "structural violence" produces more victims than wars is completely unsubstantiated.

In the 366 armed mainly international conflicts between 1940 and 1974, the number of killed, including the 38 millions killed in World War II, amounted to 85 million. Tens of millions more perished from wounds, diseases, and malnutrition not directly attributable to combat, whereas the rest of the 13 billions of humans in the same period died from non-war related causes. The number of dead killed by economic exploitation or political repressions paled into insignificance.[81]

While the number of war victims between 1950 and 1959 was 3.2 million, between 1960 and 1969 3.8 million, and between 1970 and 1974 1.6 million,[82] it would be absurd to claim that in this period of rapid improvement of the working class situation in the West and the liberation of dependent peoples from colonial rule, the number of victims of "structural violence" could be higher, save for those killed in the Third World by their own "brothers" during civil strife, murder and repressions in the Idi Amin style.

It was ascertained by the Heilbronner inquiry that took into account, inter alia, B. Moore's calculation that the total number of victims of terror during the French revolution was approximately 40 thousand. Heilbronner doubted that such a number would have been murdered by the previous regime; but even if it had killed more, it would have failed in the attempt to prolong its rule by terror as the former political system was no longer able to function because of new economic foundations already taking shape within its structure. This, too, proves the uselessness of "structural violence" as a means of upholding political and economic privileges.

Besides, history teaches that feudalism and absolutism were not always abolished by force—by destroying Bastilles and instigating terror—nor necessarily by revolutionary means. War and rebellions à la Spartacus may have contributed to the replacement of slavery with feudalism; but in modern times, slavery has progressively diminished largely by pacific means almost to the point of nonexistence. Modern times have also witnessed the leap from patriarchal and feudal societies to capitalist or socialist structures more frequently than not without any violence or bloodshed. To be sure, improvement in living standards and other advances of the working class in the West after two World Wars were nowhere the result of an outburst like the October Revolution in Russia. The number of the "October Revolution" and of the Stalin regime victims attributable to "structural violence" goes well beyond tens of millions, quite probably surpassing the casualties of the holocaust of the Third Reich, and of all later Third World wars. In spite of all this, Soviet citizens still do not enjoy the standards of living and freedoms that masses in the West take for granted.

This explains to a large extent why former concepts of the class struggle and national liberation wars recently have lost their meaning and appeal for both the proletariat and communist parties in the West, for the remaining colonial peoples and for the majority of post-colonial countries. They no longer exhort bloody revolutionary violence as the one and only prescription for attaining social goals; for they have come to appreciate and dread the material and social destructive implications of any, and not only thermonuclear, war. This is the bottom line not only of Euro-Communism and Third World pragmatism, but of present Chinese and some Soviet interpretations of Marxist dialectical and historical materialism.

Some radical peace and development researchers however, simply pass over such ideological developments in silence. The fact is that extreme revolutionary zeal is confined to a steadily diminishing but noisy minority of actually counter-revolutionary elements, calling themselves "freedom fighters" but paving the way through reliance on all forms of violence for anarchy. Despite indisputable evidence of increasingly peaceful orientations of industrialized countries of all types of government enforced by the dread of nuclear war and obvious protective self-interest, these various terrorist groups exhort to violent action. It goes without saying that they do not pay any attention to the complex of direct and indirect interconnections between modernization processes and wars; moreover, they also deny all prospects of reducing antisocial individual behavior that leads to tension and the role of essentially noneconomic, nationalistic, ethnic, ideological and other motivations generating and escalating conflicts.

On the other hand, much energy and zeal by authentic scholars of peace and development are increasingly devoted to exhaustive inquiry into these motivations and other elements of national and international tensions that imperil not only Third World development, wellbeing, and even survival.

Frustrating as it may be, they dig and probe relentlessly also to discover undertakings necessary to counteract social and psychopolitical obstacles to Third World development and security. Some of these obstacles doubtlessly will be tainted by personal biases but this need not detract much from the diligent search for relevant factuality about evolving grass-root conditions of the Third World distress; nor from detailed investigation of the impacts of ongoing superpower rivalry and arms races on the situation in the LDCs.

Social science research once centered merely on consequences of imperialism and foreign exploitation, but currently treats such theses with greater caution, both when it is based on historical and statistical analysis or on qualitative and behavioral approaches as well.[83]

The psychopathology of individuals hitherto has not been given, and it seems rightly, much consideration as an important factor in serious research on social conflict and war. This is attributable to the characteristically collective group nature of such tensions and confrontations. Yet, in the present world ripe with dictatorship at all levels the attention of research may well be profitably directed to exploration and evaluation of the psychopathology of elite leaders, following the tragic consequences of the "cult of personality." Undoubtedly, the "charismatic" character of such Third World dictators as the former Ugandan "President-for-Life" Idi Amin goes far to explain domestic and international policies of their respective régimes. Such research should be however undertaken in conjunction with and not in place of existing modes of peace and developmental research. Acts of state, like ordinary crime or sex, for instance, are always the willful acts of fallible human individuals interacting with particular social and physical environments. To speak about "acts" of state or the "will" of the movement at best denotes figures of speech and at worst dangerous, errant, totalitarian activities which do not at least always, enjoy the support of the West or the East and are frequently contradicting political ends of the superpowers. To make the latter responsible for them too, is sheer nonsense.

Neglect of this hard truth and other bitter realities often has the same or similar effects on the meager crop of various peace researchers, not less negative than the dogmatic Soviet writings on peace and development. The latter routinely attribute all causes of underdevelopment and the threats to peace entirely to obsolete concepts of imperialism. They stubbornly remain loyal to Lenin's corroboration of Hobson's thesis, mechanically applying conclusions from fin de siècle realities to revolutionary changing conditions of our nuclear age.[84] Inflexible attachment to anachronisms shattered the hopes of those who believed capitalism to be in its final agony of mutual annihilation wars after which a socialist system would arise phoenixlike on the ruins of the old order and bring forth freedom, social progress, and eternal peace while it actually resulted in violent, repressive and exploitative "state-capitalism."

An increasing number of Soviet writers including those who believe war may still be useful to finish off the remnants of imperialism, consider armed revolt by the revolutionary vanguard inadvisable in today's world—not only when the same goal could be achieved more cheaply by peaceful means. They also are beginning to realize that total cost of war dwarfs the desired result and that nuclear war may cure the ills of society by annihilating the human species.

By and large, armed forces nowadays are rapidly becoming in the East and West a menace rather than a path to security.[85] This is certainly true of relations between the superpowers and between highly industrialized countries. Yet war remains feasible and in some cases even rational in the neo-Clausewitzian sense of a continuation of politics by other means in the Third World. Unfortunately, it is true as far as South-South and to some extent West-South and East-South relations are concerned.[86]

Since the stand of some peace and development researchers is actually similar to that of the Soviet dogmatists, they persistently view the solution of the Third World and international security dilemmas as entirely dependent on world revolution. Their contribution to the study of war, revolution and peace and exploration of their roots and means of prevention can only be of very little value. The starting point of their theories emphasize external conflict factors while neglecting basic indigenous causes and the negative impact of Soviet politics. Such limitations preclude their successful construction of an unambiguous, rational, relevant model that can provide valid insight into interconnections between underdevelopment and peace. The prospects of gaining more vital knowledge of these problems no less depend on giving up dogmas according to which states, nations, peoples, ethnics, classes and other groups and organizations are neatly and arbitrarily divided into aggressive, exploitative, incorrigible, imperialistic centers, and assorted victims.

Reality concedes that there are just and unjust, violent and pacific elements in opposing camps and that the so-called "socialist" Soviet world frequently continues to use the methods of classical imperialism. On the other hand, it also teaches that there are objective causes inviting diligent search—especially in the nuclear era—for ways to compromise and cooperate in order to gradually free humanity from the anxieties of present-day life. There are also subjective causes operating to the same end.

One of the fallacies of the current research on underdevelopment and war noted above is that it conceived societal phenomena exclusively in terms of things, systems and structures rather than in terms of human and humanly determined social interaction. This prevented the conclusion that all societies are maldeveloped only in different ways, that human capacities and limitations are more or less the same all over the world; and that the time has come to transcend the old outdated dogmas as guidelines to progress. Today it is more and more dependent on compromise and peaceful arrangement,[87] and less than ever on random decisions, emotional reactions and irrational considerations.

Notes

1. Clark, R. P. Jr., Development and Instability (The Dreyden Press 1974) p. 4.
2. Fetscher, I., *Modelle der Friedenssicherung*, 2nd ed., (Frankfurt: Piper 1973), passim.
3. Elster, J., *Leibnitz and the Development of Economic Rationality*, (University of Oslo: Paper n. 21, n.d.) pp. 4, 5 and 16.
4. Bielka-Kaltreu E., "Poverty and Wealth in International Politics" *YRIA* (n. 617, 20 December 1975) p. 3-4.
5. Adelman I., *Theories of Economic Growth and Development, Smith, Ricardo, Marx, Schumpeter and a New-Keynesian Model* (Stanford University Press, 1961) p. 108.
6. Czempiel E.O., *Schwerpunkte und Ziele der Friedensforschung* (Muenchen: Kaiser Verlag 1972), Chapter III.
7. Barbera H., *Rich Nations and Poor in Peace and War* (New York: Lexington Books, 1973), passim.
8. Davinic P., "The Developing Countries and Military Expenditures," *YRIA* (n. 613, 20 October 1975) p. 21.
9. SIPRI, p. 100.
10. Tenbruck von F., "Friede durch Friedensforschung?" *Frankfurter Allgemeine Zeitung* (n. 298, 22 December 1973).
11. *Peace Research Newsletter* (n. 61, 1975) p. 11-13.
12. Hofmann G., "Brandt Commission aims to break Deadlock," *GT* (n. 820, 1 January 1978) p. 6.
13. Mayer O. G., "From Confrontation toward Negotiation," *Intereconomics* (n. 9, Hamburg: 1975) p. 264.
14. "Neue Prioritaeten in der Entwicklungspolitik," *Neue Zuricher Zeitung* (n. 209, 10 September 1975) p. 11 and see R. Herte, "Agreement in Washington Monetary Conference is encouraging," *GT* (n. 9, 25 January 1976) pp. 1-3 and see also Krugman-Randolf I., "Das Ringen um neue Weltwirtschaftsordnung," E. und Z. (n. 9, 1975) p. 3.
15. Galtung H. and Wikers A., "Human Needs, Human Rights," and "The Theory of Development" *Chair in Conflict and Peace Research* (Paper n. 37, Oslo: 1976) p. 75.
16. Vrhunec M., "In the Struggle for a New Economic Order," *YRIA* (n. 623, 20 March 1976) p. 9.
17. Leitthof A., "International Law and the New World Economic System" *YRIA* (n. 616, 5.XII.1975), p. 23.
18. Lyon P., "Co-operation and Conflict within the Third World, Millenium, *Journal of International Studies* (n. 2, 1974) p. 138.
19. Rosenau J. N. (ed.), *Linkage Politics: Essays in the Converging between National and International Systems* (New York: The Free Press 1966), passim.
20. Napieralla J., "Transfer Techniki organizacji promiedzy centrami przemyslowymi swiata kapitalistycnego, *Przeglad Zachodni* (Vol. XXXII, Poznan: no. 4,

1976) p. 166.

21. Dumas M., "Qu'est-ce que le Nouvel Ordre Economique International?" *RTM* (Vol. VII, n. 66 April-June 1976) p. 286.

22. Carrère B., "Les Conflits Economiques," *EP* (n. 19, 1976) p. 27.

23. Galtung J., "Poor Countries vs. Rich; Poor People vs. Rich; Whom will the new International Order Benefit?" *Vienna Institute for Development* (Occasional Paper 4, 1977) p. 7 and p. 28.

24. Smith R., "The North-South Dialogue and the Economic Order," *Aussenpolitik* (English edition) (Vol. 28, n. 3, 1977) p. 274.

25. Mandi P., "The New Order of World Economy and the Process of Development," *Vienna Institute for Development* (Occasional paper 5, 1975) pp. 1 and 4.

26. *Pugwash Newsletter* (Vol. 15, n. 1-2 London: July-October 1977) pp. 44-5 and 47.

27. Henry P. M., "Aspects Economiques et Politiques d'un Nouvel Ordre Economique International," *Vienna Institute for Development,* (Occasional paper 6, 1975) p. 1.

28. Hughes H., "The External Debt of Developing Countries," *Finance and Development* (Vol. 4, Wash. December 1977) p. 22.

29. Banerjee J., "The Non-Capitalist Path and the Third World," *The Indian Institute for Defence Studies and Analyses Journal* (no. 3, 1974) p. 369.

30. Rutkowski J., Wspolczesne Problemy Pomocy dla Krajow Slabo rozwinietych, Przeglad Zachnodni (vo. XXXII, No. 4, 1975). pp. 215 and 235.

31. Heilbronner R.L., "Must America be Counterrevolutionary?" *The Developing Nations* (ed. F. Tachau, New York: Dodd, Mead and Co. 1972) pp. 226-8.

32. Tachau, loc. cit., p. 2-3, Black E. E. in Tachau *op.cit.*, p. 23, p. 232 and 237.

33. For details on this concept see Lipton M., *Why Poor People Remain Poor; Urban Bias in World Development* (Cambridge, Mass: Harvard University Press, 1977) p. 328.

34. Sahovic M., "The Creation of a World Community," *YRIA* (Vol. XXIX, No. 666 5 January 1978) p. 12.

35. Cf., Hirsch F., Doyle M. W. and Morse E. L., *Alternatives to Monetary Disorder* (New York: McGraw-Hill Book Co., 1977) pp. 84 and 101.

36. Greig I., *The Communist Challenge to Africa* (London: The Foreign Affairs Publ. Co., 1977) p. 81.

37. Mitran M., "Solidarnost i Sotrudnicestvo Razvivajusnchychsya stran," *Revue Roumaine d'Etudes Internationales* (vol. XI, no. 33, 71 1977) pp. 353 and 362 and Rutkowski J., *op.cit.*, p. 215.

38. Secares V., *Polemologia si Problemele Paâci* (Bucuresti: Editura Politica, 1976) pp. 240-244.

39. Compare with W. Schicking's review of the German edition of J. Tinbergen's report "Wir haben nur eine Zukunft," (Westdeutscher Verlag, Opladen 1977) in *Das Parlament* (No. 50, 17.XII.1977) p. 13.

40. Denison E., *Why Growth Rates Differ* (Washington D.C.: The Brookings Institution, September 1967) p. 299.

41. Demas W. G., "Die Teure Ungerechtigkeit," *E and Z* (2, 1978).

42. Adelman I. and Taft Morris C. *Economic Growth and Social Equity* (Stanford Univ. Press, 1973) pp. 178 and 192.

43. Said A. A. and Simmons L. R. (eds.) *Ethnicity in an International Context* (New Brunswick, New Jersey: Transaction Press 1976) p. 16.

44. Cf. Petras J. F., "Sociologie du Developpement ou Sociologie de l'Exploitation?" *RTM* (Vol. XIII, 67, 1967) pp. 610-11 and comp. P. M. G. Levy, "Polemologie, Reccherche de la Paix, Irenologie *Les Cahiers du CRESUP* (Nr. 1, Louvain-la-Neuve, 1977) p. 53.

45. Barrington Moore Jr., Reflections on the Causes of Human Misery and upon Certain Proposals to Eliminate them (New York: Beacon 1970) p. 114.

46. Rothstein R. J., "Inequality, Exploitation and Justice in the International System," *International Studies Quarterly* (Vol. 21 no. 2 June 1977) pp. 329, 339 and 347.

47. See Falk R. in Mendlowitz S. N. (ed.) *On the Creation of a Just World Order; Preferred Worlds for the 1990's* (New York: The Free Press, 1975) p. 220.

48. See Farer T.J., Preliminary appraisal of the *World Order Models Project* (WOMP) "The Greening of the Globe, International Organization," (Vol. 31, no. 1, winter 1977) pp. 146-7.

49. Rothstein R.L. *op. cit.*, pp. 320-13, 243, 37 and 357.

50. Stanovnik J., "Towards the NIEO," *YRIA* (666, vol. XXIX, 5 January 1978) p. 6.

51. Smith T., "Changing Configurations of Power in North-South Relations since 1945," *International Organization* (Vol. 31, no. 1, winter 1977) pp. 8, 9, 11, 15 and 18.

52. Greig I., *op. cit.*, p. 269.

53. Beim D. O., "Rescuing the LDCs" *Foreign Affairs* (Vol. 55, no. 4 July 1977) pp. 718-9.

54. Hirsch, Doyle and Morse, *op. cit.*, pp. 11, 43, 46, 49 and 50.

55. Furtado C., "Le Nouvel Ordre Economique Mondial," *RTM* (Vol. XVII, 675, 1976) pp. 574-5.

56. For an interesting attempt to justify this assertion see, inter alia, the conclusions of Naidu M. V., *Alliances and Balance of Power, A Search for Conceptual Clarity* (London: McMillan 1975).

57. Hirsch, Doyle and Morse, *op. cit.*, pp. 57, 133 and 138.

58. Fanon F., *The Wretched of the Earth* (Grove Press, 1966) p. 76.

59. Tachau, *op. cit.*, p. 3 and Gill R. T. in Tachau, *op. cit.*, pp. 15, 17, and 18.

60. See Lin Pau in Tachau, *op. cit.*, pp. 182 and 185.

61. Fanon F., in Tachau, *op. cit.*, pp. 192 and 194.

62. McAlister A. M., "International Interdependence and the National State," *Millenium Journal of International Studies* (no. 2, 1974) p. 17, passim.

63. Compare Bergstrom L., "What is a conflict of interest," *JPR* (no. 3 1970) pp. 197, 201, 207, 213 and 214.

64. Entessar N., "Dependence and Third World Development; a critical view," *Iranian Review of International Relations* (no. 9, .1977) p. 128 and his reference to Fossum L. E., "Political Development and Strategies for Change," *JPR* (no. 1, 1970) p. 18.

65. *Ibid.*, and his reference to Johnson D. L., "The Concept of Political Development," in Cockcroft J. D., Frank A. G. and Johnson D. L., *Dependence and Underdevelopment: Latin America's Political Economy* (Garden City, New York: Doubleday Anchor Books, 1972) p. 414.

66. *Ibid.*, p. 129 and his reference to dos Santos Th., "The Structure of Dependence," *American Economic Review, Papers and Proceedings* (Vol. 60 May 1970) p. 231.

67. Compare Ul Haq M., "The Rich and Poor Nations," *Current* (no. 176, October 1975) p. 45.

68. Black C. E., in Tachau *op. cit.*, p. 23 and Gill R. T., also in Tachau *op. cit.*, p. 12; for an interesting attempt to explore the convergence between new-liberalism and democratic socialism, see inter alia Kopp B., *Liberalismus und Sozialismus auf dem Weg zur Synthese* (III ed. Verlag A. Hain, Meisenheim) Gilan, 1977).

69. Horowitz I. L., in Tachau *op. cit., p. 58.*

70. Czempiel op. cit., p. 20 and passim.

71. Entessar N., *op. cit.*, pp. 28-29.

72. Horowitz D., *Hemispheres North and South, Economic Disparity Among Nations* (Baltimore : John Hopkins Paperbacks, 1966) p. 11.

73. Welde E., "Conflict Behavior of Nation-States," *JPR* (no. 3 1970) pp. 230 and 233-4.

74. Thee M., "On Priorities in Peace Research," *BPP* (no. 1, 1976) p. 69.

75. Senghaas D., "Peace Research and the Causes of Social Violence," *BPP* (no. 1, 1976) p. 66.

76. Lorenz K., *On Aggression* (New York: Harcourt Brace and World Inc., 1966), passim.

77. Eibl-Eibesfeldt I., *Love and Hate* (New York: Holt, Rinehart, Winston 1972) and see Droescher B. V., "Aggression Theories Amplified," *GT* (no. 718, 18.I.1976) p. 12 and Hellauer D., "Konrad Lorenz Theories taken to Task," *Sueddeutsche Zeitung* (7 November 1975).

78. Kim S. S., "The Lorenzian Theory of Aggression and Peace Research; A Critique," *JPR (no. 4, 1976, vol. XIII) p. 254.*

79. Fetscher, op. cit., p. 73.

80. For details on this approach see Hibbs D. Jr., *Mass Political Violence, A Crossnational Analysis3 (New York: Wiley 1973) and Sancho do Gramont in Tachau op. cit.*, p. 197 and ff.

81. Bouthoul G. and Carrère R., "Populations et Pertes (1970-1974) *EP* (no. 19, 1976) p. 67 (this is an extract of the introduction to their book *Le Defi de la Guerre 1940-1974*, Presses Universitaires de France, Paris 1976).

82. Savon H., "Une Recherche sur les Conflits Armés de 1970 à 1974," *EP* (no. 19, 1976) p. 53.

83. Heilbroner in Tachau *op. cit.*, 222. For details on the change of the proper tendencies see, inter alia Midlarsky M. I., *On War. Political Violence in the International System* (New York: The Free Press, 1975), passim.

84. See inter alia the considerations in N. Wolkow, "Die Entwicklungslaender und die internationalen Wirtschaftsbeziehungen," *Information, Zukunft und Friedenforschung* (no. III, 1976) pp. 122-129 and "Problems of War and Peace: A Critical Analysis of Bourgeois Theories" (Moscow: Progress Publishers, 1972) passim, and see also the critics of Tunkin G., Moca G. and Haraszti G. on the very moderate opinion of Neuhold H. relating to the negative impact of sovereign-orientated tendencies in Europe in Doernberg, Galtung, Gromyko, Senghaas (Hrsg.) *Probleme des Friedens, der Sicherheit und der Zusammenarbeit* (Koeln, Pahl-Regenstein Verlag 1975) and Ratschik Awakow, "Spezifik der Entwicklung der Drit-

ten Welt," Gesellschafts-Wissenschaften (Moscow: Vol. 3, no. 10 1977) pp. 143-154.

85. Lider J., "War and Politics: Clausewitz Today. Cooperation and Conflict" (Oslo: no. 3, 1977) pp. 195-6.

86. Apunen O., "Non-Use of Force: A Strategy for Peace in the Nuclear Age," Cooperation and Conflict (Ibid) pp. 171-2.

87. Cf. Glatung J. and Wirak A., "Human Needs, Human Rights and the Theory of Development, World Indicators Program," *Chair in Conflict and Peace Research* (Univ. of Oslo, 1976) pp. 2 and 56.